Writing beyond the Ending

EVERYWOMAN
Studies in History, Literature, and Culture

General Editors
SUSAN GUBAR AND JOAN HOFF-WILSON

Writing beyond the Ending

■

Narrative Strategies of Twentieth-Century Women Writers

Rachel Blau DuPlessis

INDIANA UNIVERSITY PRESS

BLOOMINGTON

Library of Congress Cataloging in Publication Data

DuPlessis, R. Blau.
  Writing beyond the ending.

  (Everywoman : studies in history, literature, and
culture)
  Bibliography: p.
  Includes index.
  1. American literature—Woman authors—History and
criticism.   2. Women in literature.   3. American
literature—20th century—History and criticism.
  4. English fiction—Women authors—History and criticism.
  5. English fiction—20th century—History and criticism.
  6. Narration (Rhetoric)   7. Feminism and literature.
  PS228.W65B55   1985   810'.9'9287   83-49512
  ISBN 0-253-36705-0
  ISBN 0-253-20345-7 (pbk.)

1 2 3 4 5 89 88 87 86 85

To my families,
but especially to my parents,
Eleanor Weslock Blau
Joseph Leon Blau

Contents

PREFACE

As is usual with projects that take ten years and a day to complete, along with the requisite mixture of meditation, bafflement, and longing, this work is written according to one conception, thus willy-nilly deemphasizing others. This study treats twentieth-century women writers exclusively, offering one reading of their major project; it selects for particular emphasis those writers who, I was convinced, would have to be understood to make a meaningful statement: Olive Schreiner, Virginia Woolf, Dorothy Richardson, H.D., Doris Lessing, Adrienne Rich. (Naturally, in that process, other people's central authors are unmentioned, notably Mansfield, Glasgow, Cather, Stein, Plath.) But consideration of women writers in relation to one another and to certain cultural conventions is hardly the only task of feminist literary criticism. Studies in the relation of male to female authors, gender-based readings of male figures and traditions, nuanced connections between history, culture, social identity, and gender are other necessary projects, only alluded to here. Further, an expository, "semi-objective" voice is hardly the only mode of feminist critical discourse. I am equally willing to defend—indeed to use—a voice and manner in criticism that depends on a poetics of interested meditation and offers situational, dialogic, and lyrical statements. However, I did not choose to do so here. It should also be emphasized that this reading and arrangement of meanings claims no privilege, finality, or neutrality. It is one—but one culturally necessary—production of possible meanings.

Some peculiarities and choices of arrangement need to be signaled to the reader. This book is arranged topically, not chronologically, a method of proceeding that is hardest on the one author, Virginia Woolf, discussed in the greatest number of chapters.

Writing beyond the Ending interprets the project of twentieth-century women writers as the examination and delegitimation of cultural conventions about male and female, romance and quest, hero and heroine, public and private, individual and collective, but especially conventions of romance as a trope for the sex-gender system.

Narrative in the most general terms is a version of, or a special expression of, ideology: representations by which we construct and accept values and institutions. Any fiction expresses ideology; for example, romance plots of various kinds and the fate of female characters express attitudes at least toward family, sexuality, and gender. The attempt to call into question political and legal forms related to women and gender, characteristic of women's emancipation in the late nineteenth and twentieth centuries, is accompanied by this attempt by women writers to call narrative forms into question. The invention of strategies that sever the narrative from formerly conventional structures of fiction and consciousness about women is what I call "writing beyond the ending."

The writers studied here all make a critique of androcentric culture in *non*-fictional texts—essays, memoirs, polemic, social studies of various kinds. So the literary practice of the authors selected for this book turns in general on their critical approach to the production and maintenance of gender categories. What then joins these writers is their desire to scrutinize the ideological character of the romance plot (and related conventions in narrative), and to change fiction so that it makes alternative statements about gender and its institutions.

My reading of nineteenth-century fiction is constructed to examine those cultural conventions to which twentieth-century women respond. In nineteenth-century fiction dealing with women, successful quest and romance could not coexist and be integrated for the female protagonist at the resolution. So chapter 1, "Endings and Contradictions," treats a number of nineteenth-century narratives with female heroes—both quest and romance plots—to show the choices that structure their resolutions.

The poetics of critique distances a reader from prime assumptions that have commanded universal or natural status, like the heterosexual couple, gender polarization, and the separate spheres of women and men. The second and third chapters show the consistency of positions taken by women writers through the century, from Olive Schreiner in the 1880s to three contemporary writers, all of whom place the critique of narrative at the center of their fiction in order to delegitimate certain plots and conventions.

Woolf's discussion of *"Life's Adventure,"* an imaginary book by "Mary Carmichael," an imagined contemporary novelist, proposes two critical acts for modern women writers: breaking the sentence and breaking the sequence. Both are ruptures with conventional literary practice. Breaking the sentence severs dominant authority and ideology. Breaking the sequence is a critique of narrative, restructuring its orders and priorities precisely by attention to specific issues of female identity and its characteristic oscillations.

Chapters 4, 5, and 6 touch on the revisions of the plot of romance through a discussion of early and middle Woolf, H.D., and the *Künstlerroman* by women. This group of chapters emphasizes the criticism of romance by bisexual and lesbian strategies, new paths through oedipalization, and other narrative versions of the psychosexual oscillation of female identity. Chapters 7 and 8, on the use of mythic narrative by women poets, renew the discussion of "story" as a symbol of ideology. The final chapters discuss a critique of romance and the interplay between dominant and muted in the social arena. The emphasis falls on moving away first from the couple (chapter 9), then from the family (chapter 10), and finally out of society as we construe it (chapter 11).

So there is an array of narrative strategies invented or deployed by female writers of the twentieth century explicitly to delegitimate romance plots and related narratives. These strategies involve reparenting in invented families, fraternal-sororal ties temporarily reducing romance, and emotional attachment to women in bisexual love plots, female bonding, and lesbianism. (Perhaps I should underscore here that heterosexuality is not a natural law, for it must be produced in individuals; nor is it exclusively a personal, private, or sexual choice, but a cultural and narrative ideology.) As well, the writers undertake a reassessment of the mechanisms of social insertion of women through the family house, the private sphere, and patriarchal hierarchies, inventing narratives that offer, in the multiple individual and the collective protagonist, an alternative to individual quests and couple formation. The exploration of all these strategies is the major task of the book.

One cannot claim complete exclusivity, as if no male novelist or poet had ever invented anything like the postromantic strategies I have outlined. Yet in modern novels about adultery, unfulfilled sexuality, impotence—much less those about romanticized sexuality—and in modern poems that pose the woman as muse, blessed lady, or fertile goddess, it seems that even debased, ironized, and fetishistic couple-based romance remains at the center and is the privileged resolution of more significant narratives by men than by women. The point does not have to be exclusive to be studied: For reasons that can be linked to their gender position, women writers formulate a critique of heterosexual romance.

I want to acknowledge the committed enthusiasm and perspicacity of the students in whose presence many of these ideas were first wound up and let loose: at Douglass College in 1973–74, and, from 1974 on, at Temple University, in numerous undergraduate English and Women's Studies courses. Aside from offering such dedicated students, Temple University also considerably aided and abetted this

heterosexuality
= cultural +
narrative
ideology

book with two summer fellowships, a grant-in-aid of research and a study leave in 1981–82. I am quite grateful for these and other sympathetic manifestations of departmental and collegial support that allowed this feminist project the space and time to come to completion.

For this book could not have been written without feminism, by which I mean a movement for profound social, psychic, and ideological change, and the specific context of effervescence in criticism and creative work, with its bold collective tasks of reassessing cultural production, dissemination, and reception. There are many whose work, example, presence, and dedication have created the intellectual climate and emotional tenacity to which I feel indebted. Robert Saint-Cyr DuPlessis and his feminism made contributions both prime and deep over the years. Nina Auerbach, the late Annette Kar Baxter, Sandra M. Gilbert, and my postgraduate mentor, Carolyn G. Heilbrun, undertook the writing of support letters for the grants for which I chronically applied. I hope all who can will gain some satisfaction for their time and effort by the appearance of this book.

In all discussions of H.D., here and elsewhere, I have been helped profoundly by the sisterly and scholarly support of Susan Stanford Friedman and her exemplary work on this poet. I would also like to express my thanks to H.D.'s daughter, Perdita Schaffner, for her generous interest in the ideas and approaches to which my work contributes.

In the case of the very intransigent chapter 6, I would like to thank a number of patient readers for their assistance and insight: Carolyn Heilbrun, Myra Jehlen, Judith Lowder Newton, Louise Yelin, Catharine Stimpson and readers from *Signs,* Sandra Gilbert and Alex Zwerdling for *PMLA,* and the Columbia University Seminar on Women and Society, whose participants donated their combined attention one memorable evening in 1978. Tillie Olsen and Margaret Laurence also responded with warmth and enthusiasm to the ideas about their works set forth in this chapter.

I am reluctant to implicate any scholar of the nineteenth century, in which I am an amateur; in mentioning Nina Auerbach, Myra Jehlen, Judith Newton, and Louise Yelin, I hope that my remarks do not disgrace their generosity.

The work on mythopoesis in poetry, which draws on my own practice as a poet, also draws on a special group of poets: Kathleen Fraser, Frances Jaffer, Mary Oppen, as well as Sandra Gilbert and Alicia Ostriker, poet-critics who, with me, participated in a Modern Language Association panel in 1980, and Ann Snitow and Myra Jehlen, helpful readers of the paper presented. Adrienne Rich knows how much her statement on the revisionary has galvanized and inspired these approaches.

There are others to whom I feel more generally indebted for context and contributions to this project: Carol Ascher, Carolyn Burke, Robert Duncan, Lee Edwards, Susan Gubar, Annette Kolodny, Estella Lauter, Nancy Miller, Kate Millett, Elaine Showalter, Hortense Spillers, and the late Barbara Cross, who taught the novel at Barnard College.

I would like to express my thanks to Temple University Library, particularly Wayne Maxson, former head of Interlibrary Loan, to the Beinecke Rare Book and Manuscript Library at Yale University and its former curator, Donald Gallup, and to Swarthmore College Library, particularly Lois Peterson of Interlibrary Loan, for their support of my projects.

None of these people are responsible for the deficiencies and *bêtises* of this work; I hope it makes some return to the cultural context that has sustained it.

ACKNOWLEDGMENTS

Acknowledgment is gratefully made to the journals, anthologies, and little magazines where parts of these chapters appeared in earlier forms: for chapter 8, to *Feminist Studies* III (1975) under Ann Calderwood, and to *Shakespeare's Sisters,* ed. Sandra M. Gilbert and Susan Gubar (Bloomington: Indiana University Press, 1979); for H. D. materials in chapter 5, to *Contemporary Literature* XX, 2 (1979), and to *Montemora* 8 (1981); for materials in chapter 11, to *Frontiers: A Journal of Women Studies* IV, 1 (1979); for the first glimmers of chapter 3 to *The Future of Difference,* ed. Hester Eisenstein and Alice Jardine *ch 3* (Boston: G. K. Hall & Co., 1980).

The author gratefully acknowledges permission to reprint passages from the following works:

"A Bronzeville Mother Loiters in Mississippi. Meanwhile, a Mississippi Mother Burns Bacon" and "The Last Quatrain of the Ballad of Emmett Till" in *The World of Gwendolyn Brooks* by Gwendolyn Brooks. Copyright © 1960 by Gwendolyn Brooks Blakely. Reprinted by permission of Harper & Row, Publishers, Inc.

"Cinderella" from *Transformations* by Anne Sexton. Copyright © 1971 by Anne Sexton. Reprinted by permission of Houghton Mifflin Company and The Sterling Lord Agency, Inc.

Collected Poems: 1912–1944 by H.D. Copyright © 1981 by the Estate of Hilda Doolittle. Reprinted by permission of New Directions Publishing Corporation and Carcanet Press, Manchester, England.

The Dream of a Common Language, Poems 1974–77 by Adrienne Rich. Copyright © 1978 by W. W. Norton & Company. Reprinted by permission of author and W. W. Norton & Company, Inc.

Helen in Egypt by H.D. Copyright © 1961 by Norman Holmes Pearson. Reprinted by permission of New Directions Publishing Corporation and Carcanet Press, Manchester, England.

HERmione by H.D. Copyright © 1981 by the Estate of Hilda Doolittle. Reprinted by permission of New Directions Publishing Corporation.

Writing beyond the Ending

■ *self-creation →*
    active struggle for
    new consciousness
    through new relationships

Endings and

Contradictions

Creative practice is thus of many kinds. It is already, and actively, our practical consciousness. When it becomes struggle—the active struggle for new consciousness through new relationships that is the ineradicable emphasis of the Marxist sense of self-creation—it can take many forms. It can be the long and difficult remaking of an inherited (determined) practical consciousness: a process often described as development but in practice a struggle at the roots of the mind—not casting off an ideology, or learning phrases about it, but confronting a hegemony in the fibres of the self and in the hard practical substance of effective and continuing relationships. It can be more evident practice: the reproduction and illustration of hitherto excluded and subordinated models; the embodiment and performance of known but excluded and subordinated experiences and relationships; the articulation and formation of latent, momentary, and newly possible consciousness.

RAYMOND WILLIAMS
Marxism and Literature (1977) *p212*

Once upon a time, the end, the rightful end, of women in novels was social—successful courtship, marriage—or judgmental of her sexual and social failure—death. These are both resolutions of romance. Sometimes the ends of novels were inspirational, sublimating the desire for achievement into a future generation, an end for female quest that was not fully limited to marriage or death. These endings were dominant, related to real practices of sexuality, gender relations, kin and family, and work for middle-class women. The cultural conventions of narrative and depiction by which these relations were, in Raymond William's terms, "performed," were dominant also.[1] No matter what notion of the sex-gender system one uses to explore the relation of women and men, and of women to society, the reproduction of these relations in consciousness, in social practice, and in ideology turns especially on the organization of family, kinship, and marriage, of sexuality, and of the division of all sorts of labor by gender. The point at which these basic formations cross, where family meets gender, where the division of labor meets sexuality, is the heterosexual couple. The "reproduction of the conventions of sex and gender" as well as the maintenance and production of new members

romance:
marriage
or
death

/ middle-class
women

1

of the social order centers on that couple. And depictions of that
couple are socially maintained.[2]

Romance plots of various kinds, the iconography of love, the postures of yearning, pleasing, choosing, slipping, falling, and failing are,
evidently, some of the deep, shared structures of our culture. These
scripts of heterosexual romance, romantic thralldom, and a telos in
marriage are also social forms expressed at once in individual desires
and in a collective code of action including law: in sequences of action
psychically imprinted and in behaviors socially upheld. Romance as a
mode may be historically activated: when middle-class women lose
economic power in the transition from precapitalist economies and
are dispossessed of certain functions, the romance script may be a
compensatory social and narrative practice.[3]

Any social convention is like a "script," which suggests sequences of
action and response, the meaning we give these, and ways of organizing experience by choices, emphases, priorities. The term offers to
social analysis what "ideology" offers to cultural analysis: "a generic
term for the processes by which meaning is produced, challenged,
reproduced, transformed."[4] Indeed, sociologists and other students
of social practices use terms like "scripts" to explain the existence of
strongly mandated patterns of learned behavior that are culturally
and historically specific, and that offer a rationale for unselfconscious
acts. Scripts are also integrated; a whole "social script" is an interlocking group of cognitive and emotional structures.[5]

Simon and Gagnon's analysis, cited here, is particularly valuable
because it argues that even so-called instinctual and physical acts like
sex are not ever transparent, but are created in and by social life. "It is
only because they are imbedded in social scripts that the physical acts
themselves become possible."[6] This kind of analysis illustrates that all
features of human life, even the most apparently impulsive—and love
has sometimes been viewed this way—are organized.

So too literature as a human institution is, baldly, organized by
many ideological scripts. Any literary convention—plots, narrative
sequences, characters in bit parts—as an instrument that claims to
depict experience, also interprets it. No convention is neutral, purely
mimetic, or purely aesthetic.[7]

All this is dramatically illustrated by an ironic letter by Virginia
Woolf and E. M. Forster on the banning and prosecution of an "unex-
ceptionable" melodramatic novel treating lesbians: Radclyffe Hall's
The Well of Loneliness (1928). They comment pointedly that social
values and, even more, legal apparatus decree that the subject of
homosexuality in novels is actionable while "murder and adultery"
remain "officially acceptable."

May they mention it incidentally? Although it is forbidden as a main theme, may it be alluded to, or ascribed to subsidiary characters? Perhaps the Home Secretary will issue further orders on this point. And is it the only taboo, or are there others? What of the other subjects known to be more or less unpopular in Whitehall, such as birth-control, suicide, and pacifism? May we mention these? We await our instructions![8]

This study rests on the proposition that narrative structures and *hypothesis* subjects are like working apparatuses of ideology, factories for the "natural" and "fantastic" meanings by which we live. Here are produced and disseminated the assumptions, the conflicts, the patterns that create fictional boundaries for experience. Indeed, narrative may function on a small scale the way that ideology functions on a large scale—as a "system of representations by which we imagine the world as it is."[9] To compose a work is to negotiate with these questions: What stories can be told? How can plots be resolved? What is felt to be narratable by both literary and social conventions? Indeed, these are issues very acute to certain feminist critics and women writers, with their senses of the untold story, the other side of a well-known tale, the elements of women's existence that have never been revealed.

One of the great moments of ideological negotiation in any work occurs in the choice of a resolution for the various services it provides. Narrative outcome is one place where transindividual assumptions and values are most clearly visible, and where the word "convention" is found resonating between its literary and its social meanings. Any *drawing on Macherey* artistic resolution (especially of a linear form that must unroll in time) *(also Eagleton,* can, with greater or lesser success, attempt an ideological solution to *I think)* the fundamental contradictions that animate the work. Any resolution can have traces of the conflicting materials that have been processed within it. It is where subtexts and repressed discourses can throw up one last flare of meaning; it is where the author may sidestep and displace attention from the materials that a work has made available.[10]

In nineteenth-century fiction dealing with women, authors went to a good deal of trouble and even some awkwardness to see to it that *Bildung* and romance could not coexist and be integrated for the heroine at the resolution, although works combining these two discourses in their main part (the narrative middle) are among the most important fictions of our tradition. This contradiction between love and quest in plots dealing with women as a narrated group, acutely visible in nineteenth-century fiction, has, in my view, one main mode of resolution: an ending in which one part of that contradiction, usually quest or *Bildung*, is set aside or repressed, whether by mar-

riage or by death.[11] It is the project of twentieth-century women
writers to solve the contradiction between love and quest and to replace the alternate endings in marriage and death that are their cultural legacy from nineteenth-century life and letters by offering a
different set of choices. They invent a complex of narrative acts with
psychosocial meanings, which will be studied here as "writing beyond
the ending."[12]

Why are these endings in marriage and death both part of a cultural practice of romance? Marriage celebrates the ability to negotiate
with sexuality and kinship; death is caused by inabilities or impro-
prieties in this negotiation, a way of deflecting attention from man-
made social norms to cosmic sanctions. This is a practice prominent in
the novel from its inception on. For the eighteenth-century novel,
Nancy Miller explores exactly these poles governing the heroine's
ascent and integration into society and her descent into death. The
"euphoric" pole, with its ending in marriage, is a successful integration with society, in which the gain is both financial and romantic
success in the "heterosexual contract"; the "dysphoric" pole, with an
ending in death, is a betrayal by male authority and aggression. Miller
sees little definitive narrative change in nineteenth-century texts:
"The ideological underpinnings of the old plot have not been
threatened seriously: experience for women characters is still primarily tied to the erotic and the familial; . . . female *Bildung* tends to get
stuck in the bedroom."[13] Even with the growing resistance from subtexts, traced, for example, in *The Madwoman in the Attic* by Sandra
Gilbert and Susan Gubar, the "heroine's text" still persists until the
ideological and material bases of that narrative choice are sharply
modified, not just on an individual, but on a cultural level. This is my
subject here. When women as a social group question, and have the
economic, political, and legal power to sustain and return to questions
of marriage law, divorce, the "couverte" status, and their access to
vocation, then the relation of narrative middles to resolutions will
destabilize culturally, and novelists will begin to "write beyond" the
romantic ending.[14]

In brief, this book argues that there is a consistent project that
unites some twentieth-century women writers across the century,
writers who examine how social practices surrounding gender have
entered narrative, and who consequently use narrative to make critical statements about the psychosexual and sociocultural construction
of women. For all the writers selected, the romance plot, as a major
expression of these social practices, is a major site for their intrepid

scrutiny, critique, and transformation of narrative. Anne Sexton's

"Cinderella" will do as well as any statement to indicate some of the feelings with which the romance plot and its resolution are regarded:

> Cinderella and the prince
> lived, they say, happily ever after
> like two dolls in a museum case
> . . . .
> their darling smiles pasted on for eternity.
> Regular Bobbsey Twins.
> That story.[15]

This concern enters their art works, not only in overt content and critical remarks but more drastically in the place where ideology is coiled: in narrative structure. As a narrative pattern, the romance plot muffles the main female character, represses quest, valorizes heterosexual as opposed to homosexual ties, incorporates individuals within couples as a sign of their personal and narrative success. The romance plot separates love and quest, values sexual asymmetry, including the division of labor by gender, is based on extremes of sexual difference, and evokes an aura around the couple itself. In short, the romance plot, broadly speaking, is a trope for the sex-gender system as a whole. Writing beyond the ending means the transgressive invention of narrative strategies, strategies that express critical dissent from dominant narrative. These tactics, among them reparenting, woman-to-woman and brother-to-sister bonds, and forms of the communal protagonist, take issue with the mainstays of the social and ideological organization of gender, as these appear in fiction. Writing beyond the ending, "not repeating your words and following your methods but . . . finding new words and creating new methods,"[16] produces a narrative that denies or reconstructs seductive patterns of feeling that are culturally mandated, internally policed, hegemonically poised.

Virginia Woolf once proposed that "there are only two ways of coming to a conclusion upon Victorian literature—one is to write it out in sixty volumes octavo, the other is to squeeze it into six lines of the length of this one."[17] Choosing approximately the latter course, I propose a brief survey of one main ideological dilemma of nineteenth-century fiction seen by the "Mary Carmichael" who will, in the rest of these pages, be responding to it.[18] The fact that "love was the only possible interpreter" of most of the women in literature, rather than, say, "knowledge, adventure, art," led, Mary Carmichael felt, to a rigidity and inflexibility of social and expressive possibility, to a world that rebuffed women as she knew them, that, indeed, rebuffed herself.[19]

> From somewhere would come an adoring man who believed in heaven
> and eternal life. One would grow very good; and after the excitement
> and interest had worn off one would go on, with firm happy lips being
> good and going to church and making happy matches for other girls or
> quietly disapproving of everybody who did not believe just in the same
> way and think about good girls and happy marriages and heaven; keep-
> ing such people outside. . . . If Rosa Nouchette Carey [the author sum-
> marized] knew me, she'd make me one of the bad characters who are
> turned out of the happy homes. I'm some sort of bad unsimple woman.
> Oh damn, damn, she sighed. I don't know.[20]

Writing beyond the ending begins when authors, or their close surro-
gates, discover that they are in fact outside the terms of this novel's
script, marginal to it. For the conventional outcomes of love, of quest,
were strongly identified with certain roles for women. Thus Mary
Carmichael will act to rescript the novel, so that one kind of narrative
love is no longer the only interpreter of the lives she depicts.

The picture of the nineteenth-century novel proposed here has
bracketed consideration of alternative circles of characters, such as
Nina Auerbach's "communities of women," prefigurations of open
form and the ethical and structural loosening of closure, analysis of
the plots in which male characters are heroes, and possible distinctions between male and female authors' versions of the plot of romance.[21] It is proposed here that Mary Carmichael was so intent on
identifying that with which she disagreed and that by which she felt
excluded as a potential character and as a writer that she saw no
particular alternatives. We can even sense, without regarding her picture as being damagingly distorted, that she may have exaggerated
slightly.

In nineteenth-century narrative, where women heroes were concerned, quest and love plots were intertwined, simultaneous discourses, but at the resolution of the work, the energies of the *Bildung*
were incompatible with the closure in successful courtship or marriage. Quest for women was thus finite; we learn that any plot of self-
realization was at the service of the marriage plot and was subordinate
to, or covered within, the magnetic power of that ending.[22] Look, for
example, at how even Elizabeth Barrett Browning, in a work celebrating female vocation, handles the dominating fact of female achievement in *Aurora Leigh:* she makes her hero's work facilitate the romance to be achieved. The famous "book" written by Aurora Leigh is
mentioned at two key junctures: once when she talks of her enormous
private loneliness, and once when her long-deferred suitor, Romney,
talks of how his love for her has been awakened in reading it.

However, the resolution subordinating quest to love reveals much tension. For one, quest is often vital within a narrative, and the nature of the resolution, obeying, as it does, social and economic limits for middle-class women as a group, is in conflict with the trajectory of the book as a whole. So there is often a disjunction between narrative discourses and resolutions, which may be felt as the "patness" of a resolution, or as the ironic comment of an author at closure. There may also be a sense of contradiction between the plot and the character, where the female hero/heroine seems always to exceed the bounds that the plot delineates. Thus the tragic power of certain nineteenth-century female protagonists, the tension between selfless love and self-assertion. An ending in which one part of a structuring dialectic is repressed is a way of reproducing in a text the sense of juridical or social limits for females of one class, when that class ideology encourages striving behavior for males. Yet when that closure is investigated, the repressed element is present in shadowy form. The struggles between middle and ending, quest and love plots, female as hero and female as heroine, class and gender that animate many central novels of the nineteenth century can be posed as the starting point, the motivating inception for the project of twentieth-century women writers.

In *Emma* (1816), by Jane Austen, the problem and charm of the main character lie in the same traits: her resolute and aggressive assurance, making matches as if she were a thoroughly disinterested party, misreading the marital hopes of those she considers her entourage, and interfering with the rational self-interest of many people, but especially of the man in search of a wife. The engagement of Emma's strong will and desire to dominate occurs each time Austen proffers an eligible person; the author graduates the interest of each man and of Emma's involvement until, with Mr. Knightley's apparent attentions to Harriet Smith, Emma is shocked that her impetuous scheming may have hurt her own best interests. At the point when she is sincerely repentant for her assumed powers, she is marriageable, and is therefore proposed to. Her proper negotiation with class and gender makes the heroine from an improper hero.[23]

In wedlock plots like *Pride and Prejudice,* because of the concentration on the heroine's force and her growing capacity for insight, her potential as a hero develops throughout the narrative; this paradoxically contributes to the force of the ending in marriage, by valorizing that social institution because it is the repository of so much personal energy. It is by the mediation of proper gender role that these passages occur. Gender proprieties are clearly implicated in Emma's acceptance ("What did she say?—Just what she ought, of course. A lady always does."), where the lack of dialogue produces discretion and reserve from what had been a babbling girl hero.[24]

Gender proprieties enter, too, into the allusions that the Elton and the Churchill engagements make to other kinds of romance plots— the feverish marriage-market tales of social advantage and the passionate stories of secret engagements. The parvenu economic vulgarity of Mrs. Elton's love of show is more than matched by the possessive romantic vulgarity of Frank Churchill's praise of his "angelic" fiancée, Jane Fairfax, to Emma: "Observe the turn of her throat. Observe her eyes . . ." (E, 331). The types of romance plots in these flanking relationships are not as promising for future happiness as is Emma's.[25]

The fact that the men married by these powerful female heroes are older, mature, temperate, and not indelicately passionate makes them trustworthy. The frequency with which such female heroes marry men so much "better" than they—in character sometimes, in wealth and class usually—is a way of using and occupying otherwise superfluous female energy. Rising up the imaginary ladder of maturity or class is a substitution for independent quest. In other cases, a male character is converted by the female, so that improvement of the man she will marry becomes the female's occupation. Often, there is an exchange of educative influence for class ascent. Soon after she accepts the man in the love plot, the female hero becomes a heroine, and the story ends.

But despite the dissolving of heroics and the assimilation into community, the tempering of wanton female invention is preserved from dullness by the spritely, deft, and insistent wit of Austen's style. That style buys back into the texture of our experience what we are asked to exclude morally, and in this everlasting exchange between tone and judgment, an antimarriage of author and female hero opposes the marriage of patrician hero and newly invested heroine.[26]

But the tension of achieving the resolution is palpable. The repressed term of the dialectic between love and quest may be readmitted in disguised form to the moment of resolution, because the energy and drive that once motivated the female hero are still powerful enough to be negatively acknowledged and displaced away from the (now) heroine. The last paragraph of *Emma* places that female energy in the jealous and disruptive chatter of Mrs. Elton, who has served the book throughout as an exaggerated and vulgarized picture of Emma's pretensions. Although she is out of keeping with a stability that need not call attention to itself, still she is evoked. So the energies of self-aggrandizement, displaced, can appear at the closure of the narrative, set in a character or a force that opposes the heroine precisely because it is the heroine's own trait factored out. St. John Rivers in *Jane Eyre*, the violent storm in *Villette*, and the flood in *The Mill on the Floss* also serve this crucial narrative and ideological function.

The problem of the resolution in *Jane Eyre* (1847) parallels that of its sister texts: a female character whose *Bildung* Charlotte Brontë made so dramatic and intense that it threatens the resolution in marriage, the "Reader, I married him," in which both *Bildung* and female hero are contained. Both quest and marriage plots form the basis of this work, which is structured as a novel of education and concerns the absorption of a marginalized character into kinship networks.[27] Access to a fulfillment that reiterates the status quo is always facilitated by having a character begin so marginalized, so removed from common sources of satisfaction (family, friends, social situation), that if a plot simply provides such a character with access to what must usually be taken for granted, the atmosphere of gratitude will finally impede any criticism from occurring. The critique of social conditions that orphans symbolize (poverty, vulnerability, exclusion) will be muted by the achievement of the blessed state of normalcy, so thrillingly different from deprivation. Through the mechanism of orphans, novels can present standard family, kinship, and gender relations as if these were a utopian ideal.

The courtship of Jane by Rochester proceeds through a landmine of cunningly intertextual false marriages.[28] There is a hidden wed*lock* with Bertha into which Rochester has been tricked and manipulated because of his former, now smoldering, lust, envy, and pride; that same entrapment he proposes to repeat in a far more subtle form on Jane. Rochester also has a charade "wife," Blanche Ingram, from a masquerade wedding tableau. We are present at a dramatically arrested false marriage ceremony, with Jane as fearful, decorated, enraptured bride. In this array of mid-book "marriages," Brontë has created a critical context in which the normal activities of courtship (and the normal narratives as well) take on a lurid and foreboding quality. Jane's bridal veil is rent by the mysterious Bertha herself.[29] But the falsest marriage of all those presented is Jane's complicit temptation to romantic thralldom with Rochester, which she purges through solitary suffering and the amazing discovery of a family cohort.

Jane Eyre may, in an individual or particularist tactic, change the material basis of marriage; when Jane becomes financially independent, the couple is socially interdependent. But Brontë does not change the emotional basis in romantic love. Jane still gives her life to serve Rochester in his humbled and mutilated state. The loss of his eye and his hand is a biblical retribution for adultery, and as such

brings cosmic authority to the tempering of the overweening erotic
male into a marked adult, more like a battered father than a potent
lover. The mutilation also creates the path for Brontë to have Jane
accede to a version of norms about wifehood, where husband and
household are to receive all her care. When a man is totally confined
to the private sphere (for all we are told by the narrative), then female
confinement to the same sphere does not seem so narrow. Because he
needs her, as the "one help meet for him," her booklong identity of
intelligent, loving service, most keen when it is service for a family, is
elaborated as her whole future identity. This despite the governessing
and self-improvement skills of the female hero.

*mutilation
of Rochester
enables Jane
to accede to
wifely norms
of caring*

Her blasphemous energies are also contained because the spiritual
blessing of the marriage is affirmed with God as a witness. Toward the
end of the novel, as the resolution takes shape, there is a growing
emphasis on coincidence, in preference to other more natural patterns of motivation. Brontë insists on providence, in the shape of a
god-uncle's legacy, in the intuition for "home" that brings the wandering Jane to her very own cousins, and in the voices that transfix both
Jane and Rochester.[30] That Jane is the site at which supernatural
forces collect enhances her heroic—even mythic—stature, but it also
provides the only tempering structure short of ironic piercing of
heroism. For the use of Providence in the latter third of the novel
prepares for a resolution that will wean Jane from the cosmic—from
St. John's self-idolatry—into the modest and tender feminine
usefulness as "prop and guide." Providence, in short, is the only force
compelling enough to displace Jane as quester from the heroic center
of the novel, as it is the only force patriarchal enough to temper
Rochester's earlier blasphemous claims that his Maker sanctioned his
sexual schemes.

The second suitor and first cousin of Jane, St. John Rivers, is rejected because of his idolatry, his instrumentality, his pride and delu-
sions of grandeur at the service of British and Christian imperial
claims. His manipulative drive and legalistic turns attempting to entrap Jane are severely rejected. Yet the novel ends with an unironic
peroration to St. John and his ambition. In the final paragraph, the
very last words of the novel even allude to the very last words of the
New Testament (Rev. [of St. John] 22:17 and 22:20). The apocalyptic
union of the yearning spirit with Christ himself, and the matching
cries "I come quickly" and "Even so come, Lord Jesus," mark the
displaced reassertion of ambition, quest, and spiritual striving, which
no longer reside in the character Jane Eyre. St. John represents the
ecstatic trace of all the energies of pilgrimage, mastery, and aggression that have been so central, the social and vocational dynamism

rejected for the female hero as she assumes the mantle of heroine-wife.

Here as elsewhere, the female character is embarked on heroic endeavors of resistance, mastery, self-realization, and even personal independence in one of the very few available professions. Yet by the end of the story, the plot has created a heroine, a character whose importance in the society of the book lies in her status as an object of choice and as an educative influence. Her integration into kinship and family bonds is signaled by the production of the infant of the next generation, which ends the story in this one.

Lucy Snowe in Brontë's *Villette* (1853), an English teacher at a repressive boarding school in a foreign land, is launched into vocation by a series of desperate propulsive choices where standing still would have meant annihilation. Yet vocation as such is viewed with great suspicion, always seen as second best. Lucy's outsider's, even voyeur's, views of domestic warmth make her yearn for traditional feminine destinies of protection and Home, even as she abjures the deceitful images that teach proper female behavior in the museum scene and is aroused by female power in the Vashti scene. Yet work and independence are depicted as a "denial and Privation" in a passage in the latter part of the book: to be the headmistress of a pleasant school that she has created is still to have "no true home," and she questions why she will have "Nothing [i.e., husband or children] at whose feet I can willingly lay down the whole burden of human egotism, and gloriously take up the nobler charge of labouring and living for others."[31]

Romantic love is severely judged, as pandering, as hypocrisy, as exclusionary, and it is as severely desired. The heroes and heroines are not Lucy's to touch; in Tantalus fashion they recede, both the upper middle-class stable domesticity of Polly and Graham and the sexual scandal of Ginevra and de Hamel. Lucy tries to break into that circle of heroines, but she is incompletely formed for either saccharine darlingness or salty flirtation. Suffering her increasingly jealous marginalization from these "normal" narratives, she realizes that the plots of the romances that flank her (a sentimental and a Gothic novel respectively, for the choice of plots is somewhat like *Emma*) are resistant to the depressive spoiler that she represents.

Thus Brontë has reserved the most complete vocation for her most neurotic character, and that equating of vocation and deprivation makes a textual undertow to the pilgrim's progress. This repressing of love is represented by the apparition of the nun, finally unmasked as a youth who enters the girls' school to seduce a willing student. The nun is the place where sexuality and repression meet, for the figure appears whenever Lucy must force down her already disguised passion. The nun is not used for any associations with spiritual calling, that is, as George Eliot will use St. Theresa, but rather to explore desire and entrapment.

But Lucy's negotiation with love does pose a richly textured alternative to the Gothic and the sentimental, the domestic and the scandalous romances. This alternative intertwines a quest for mastery and love, with Lucy the neophyte and M. Paul the guide, goad, and taskmaster. The relationship seems allusively erotic, with its games of dominance and submission, and full of the allusions to trial and torment, the tests of fortitude and purpose that one often has in quest. With this eroticized quest (and with the little school M. Paul sets up for Lucy as he proposed to her), the possibility for marriage linked with vocation has taken shape and has been sustained for the latter third of the book.

The deprivation and denial that follow express the ideology about narrative women that we are investigating. Even within the last paragraphs of the novel, the couple's forthcoming marriage is expected. But a dire change occurs suddenly. Lucy Snowe is denied the unprecedented resolution of marriage and vocation by a *coup d'auteur*: M. Paul drowns at sea. Readers of "sunny imaginations" who want the happy ending can be left, in the absence of the actual words announcing his death, "to conceive the delight of joy" (*V,* 451). The unprecedented utopian hope of marriage and vocation for the female hero is castigated as reader banality, the reductive yearning for a happy ending. Here too independence and quest have been punished with deprivation of love. The either/or choice between romance and vocation has been as forcefully maintained in this novel as it was in *Jane Eyre.*[32]

The task of *Middlemarch* (1872) claims to be precisely illustrative of the proposition of its Prelude: that some people, women in particular, are born with aspirations and energy, desiring passionate service to an ideal, and yet social circumstances harness them in a narrower yoke. George Eliot speaks to the contradiction between vocation and role in its largest sense: the middling, threatened community of intricate webbings meets the inchoate drive of individual difference. The failure to transcend is stated at the beginning, for the book claims to depict a character or two who could have achieved greatness, but who will end "dispersed among hindrances."

With waste, compromised vocations, failures of marriages, life lived in modest normalcy, the novel's apparent lesson is that life is a necessarily flawed combination of sublime yearning with turgid institutions of all varieties—financial, romantic, social. It is Eliot's triumph in the Garth plot and its educative confrontations to make conventional middle-march wisdom sound both accurate and savory. The Dorothea and Lydgate plots overturn good sense by outrageous desire in varieties of tragicomic wedlock. The same impetuous drives that make for their high ambitions override the sounder processes of temperate choice. Both Lydgate and Dorothea leap into marriage, the one "marrying care not help," the other marrying misogynistic pettiness, not large-souled breadth.[33] Eliot does not flinch as she works out the closure of possibility in the face of those marriages to Causaubon and Rosamond, the losses of desire and efflorescence in shame and bitterness, and then, with baleful tact, arranges the testing of the characters at that precise nadir.

Because of the misery of her first marriage, the narrative channels Dorothea's ambitions and desires for important action into her passionate declaration to Will Ladislaw, in defiance of Causaubon's last will and testament. The book asks us to applaud this shift from the desire for a grand autonomous life to a reasonable choice of life's companion. Indeed, in this second marriage, Dorothea even achieves fulfillment of part of her original dream "to help someone who did great works" (M, 251). So, for the most persuasive of reasons, female quest is rejected and the female helpmeet is again established at the resolution.

But at the end of the book, the narrator asks us to see Dorothea's life as a "sacrifice" and evokes, strangely, "many who knew her" for their opinions that her powers were not well used, or not fully engaged by being "absorbed into the life of another" (M, 576). These choral voices are curious, since community opinion and narrator sentiment had been running against the thought offered at the resolution: that Dorothea's strengths should have had a more glorious outlet. The fact that Dorothea herself half believes this is part of her yearning selfhood: "feeling that there was always something better which she might have done, if she had only been better and known better" (M, 575–76). That the narrator wants us to believe it seems to express an uncharacteristic reluctance to assent to the novel's tempering conditions. After having used her whole book to suggest with what we must be decently contented in the mellow "home epic" of middle range, Eliot reinserts discontent; the "epic life" suggested in the Prelude remains a permanent and sublime thorn in the side (M, 573, xii).

Thus Eliot is making contradictory statements, leaving the novel poised between the female hero's sublime scope, in the Dorothea/St. Theresa analogy, and her generally tragicomic moments, in the Dodo/Dorothea analogy. The contradiction we have identified appears again in the discrepancy between a narrator's opinion and an author's text, which shows that trace of female "ardour" exceeding "the common yearning of womankind" that will contain it (*M*, xiii).

Yet the quest part of the plots at the center of these books propounds something that the marriage plot with difficulty revokes: that the female characters are human subjects at loose in the world, ready for decision, growth, self-definition, community, insight. In the novels that end in marriage, and even some that end in death, there is a contradiction between two middle-class ideas—gendered feminine, the sanctified home, and gendered human, the liberal bourgeois ideology of the self-interested choice of the individual agent. This contradiction is most acutely visible in the voluntary and self-aware acceding of the protagonist to the received notion of "womanhood": "to live for others . . . to have no life but in the affections."[34] The highest expression of the female protagonist's moral and intellectual nobility and aspiration lies in her chosen understanding of her complex position—her influence, but her limits—as a woman. As a gendered subject in the nineteenth century, she has barely any realistic options in work or vocation, so her heroism lies in self-mastery, defining herself as a free agent, freely choosing the romance that nonetheless, in one form or another, is her fate. The female hero turns herself into a heroine; this is her last act as an individual agent.

A contemporary commentator in 1869 argues that there are two ideas about female character: woman is seen as an adjective, in service to man, or as a noun, "created for some end proper to herself."[35] Yet even as a modifier, she makes a statement. For although female narrative life will be structured by marriage, female power is, for a while, expressed in courtship.[36] In the plots involving Jane Eyre, Aurora Leigh, Dorothea Brooks, and Elizabeth Bennet, the clear moment of desire and the female outspokenness that provokes the endgame incorporate back into romance some of the boldness and aggression of quest, making romance temporarily the repository of female will.

Further, as Igor Webb has argued, women have a social power in courtship, given the massive and irreversible social changes of industrial capitalism, changing parental authority, and family ties. The "maintenance of status, system and family has to be negotiated by means of courtship." As well, by the end of the eighteenth century, a middle-class home is neither a workplace nor a place of manufacturing; hence middle-class women have been "stripped of economic functions." Courtship choice then gets portrayed and valued as women's work.[37] Yet by the same token, the deepening division between work and home, and the use of love "with its implicit enfranchisement of women" were difficult to reconcile "with the evident exclusion of [middle-class] women from productive life."[38] Judith Newton's argument interlocks with Webb's: through the mid-nineteenth century, the confrontation of female powerlessness with male power grows more acute; male power is more overt at the same time it is seen as less "natural" and more imposed by community and social relations. Novels register the antonyms of female power in courtship, powerlessness in community, functional action in the love script, un- or underemployment in productive life.[39]

The plot of courtship as social and gender reconciliation begins to break by the latter half of the nineteenth century. The contradiction between love and vocation in plots centering on women is accentuated, and romance (whether marriage or courtship) is less able to be depicted as satisfying the urgencies of, *inter alia,* self-development, desire for useful work, ambition, and public striving.

If possession of a hero/husband in the romance story stands for possession of a world, the distortions that might lead to the death of the main female character are clearly related. In some cases, the non-possession of a hero, the nonaccess to marriage will imply the loss of the world (in death); in other cases, possession by a nonhero—the erotic fall—will lead to death.

Flaubert knowingly puts Emma Bovary in her wedding gown at her funeral and then records how that once nubile beauty rots until it has presented itself as an unfillable, gaping hole—his trope for femaleness throughout. Death for the female protagonist in many nineteenth-century texts is the negative print of marriage—all the tones opposite, but the picture unmistakable. The relation of the rules of heterosexual romance to death is clear in a variety of texts.

Death comes for a female character when she has a jumbled, distorted, inappropriate relation to the "social script" or plot designed to contain her legally, economically, and sexually. Death is the result when energies of selfhood, often represented by sexuality, at once their most enticing and most damaging expression, are expended outside the "couvert" of marriage or valid romance: through adultery (Mme. Bovary, Edna Pontellier), loss of virginity or even suspected "impurity" (Tess of the d'Urbervilles, Lily Bart), or generalized female passion (Maggie Tulliver, Monica Widdowson). When a character is undernourished and underemployed by the social rules defining her place, she may protest, but even a feeble protest may lead to her doom. Sometimes death comes to a female character who cannot properly negotiate an entrance into teleological love relations, ones with appropriate ends, a character whose marginalization grows concentrically as the novel moves to the end. Death in general is a more than economic arrangement, for the punishment of one desire is the end of all.

When social, familial, and internalized restraints lose their force, when the character, for sometimes the most subtle reasons, has been marginalized or herself chooses experimentally to step aside from her roles, death enforces the restrictions on female behavior. In narrative, then, death is the second line of defense for the containment of female revolt, revulsion, or risk. Death is the price exacted for female critique, whether explicit *(The Awakening)* or implicit *(The Mill on the Floss)*. Death occurs as the price for the character's sometimes bemused destabilizing of the limited equilibrium of respectable female behavior—in her acceptance of a wrong man, a nonhero, or in her nonacceptance of a right one. And death occurs because a female hero has no alternative community where the stain of energy (whether sexual or, in more general terms, passionate) will go unnoticed or even be welcomed. This is why, in the twentieth-century critiques, community and social connectedness are the end of the female quest, not death. But in the nineteenth-century texts, death occurs as a "cosmic" or essentialist ending when a woman tests the social and historical rules governing the tolerable limits of her aspirations.

Yet her punishment is often treated as her triumph. Death itself becomes a symbolic protest against the production of a respectable female and the connivances of a respectable community.[40] So in texts ending with death, there is often a moment of protest—social energy or a desiring life—just as in the marriage ending, the protest is autonomy or vocation. When the character wants more and more, certainly more than she is allowed, yet can get less and less, the flare of energy or desire surrounding death is the trope of "more": the buzzing bees and flowers in Kate Chopin, the imaginary baby's nestling head in Edith Wharton, Tom's cry "Magsie" in George Eliot.

Lily Bart in Edith Wharton's *The House of Mirth* (1905) is an elegant marriageable woman, who is marginalized from a promising, dull marriage into greater depreciation and desperation. Never fully acquiescent, a little reluctant to settle, to obey the particular codes, although she is not ignorant of them, she always tries to gain a more favorable conjuncture and to keep every option open. She lacks an unquestioned complicity with the economic and social circumstances of the speculative marriage and divorce market, which she plays like a gambler. She is too daring for stolidness, yet too scrupulous for some of the more sordid exchanges of money and love in which she is, nonetheless, partially implicated.

[margin annotations: death = price for female critique; death because no alternative community for passionate energy; The House of Mirth]

Lily Bart is, in more ways than one, open to speculation. If gambling is one root metaphor, prostitution is another. Lily will never marry because she can't decide among the forms of prostitution and their various grades, from respectable to sordid, yet she cannot renounce the life altogether. She is an ornamental object to be purchased; she takes money for her charms. Yet she tries to gain without giving, a fact vulgarly, dangerously presented to her by Gus Tranor in his attempted rape. If never seduced, she is more and more compromised.

Lily's ambiguous suicide, occurring as a gambled side effect ("one chance in a hundred") of delivering herself from the temporary insanity of insomnia, is not willed; thus it is like all of Lily's decisions when she does not see that one option may genuinely foreclose another. In its coming, death is sensual, a seduction into the drug climaxing in her illusion of maternal bliss. Lily has been compromised by money, time, sexuality: all the high-risk components of female life. And yet she has arranged herself as a beautiful object so that her bier resonates with both narcissism and the failed community of the earlier tableaux scene.

The analogies with *The Awakening* are clear. The rules invented by a newly awakened but socially powerless individual cannot survive the impact of real power. When, at the end of Kate Chopin's *The Awakening* (1899), Edna Pontellier swims out to sea to commit suicide, she returns thereby to the scene of her double awakening into sexuality and autonomy. The death of Edna is her response to several kinds of possession—by husband, by lovers, by children: "They need not have thought that they could possess her, body and soul." She thereby expresses her opinion that she is her own to dispose of. Yet all avenues of apparent freedom—including adultery and the artist's life, which is itself half an expression of sexual freedom—had led to the dead end of oppressive ties. Feminine revolt comes up against the greater flexibility of society; her husband has face-saving strategies to declare that she has never really revolted. These being the rules of the world, her suicide is a protest of transcendent and a-contextual—that is, impossible—autonomy. She has claimed for herself the script of death usually punitively accorded female characters in her position.

The laws governing marriage, sexuality, and dependence are so insistent in the nineteenth-century texts because the practices of gendering make them so, given the relative absence of historical possibility for women's public life. In *The Mill on the Floss* (1860), we begin at the beginning of women's narrative death: in childhood. Maggie Tulliver, like most female characters, is born into a code that calls for asymmetrical damage. She is warm, passionate, forceful, and even

forms of prostitution (incl. marriage)

The Awakening (1899)

The Mill on the Floss (1860)

talented; she can do nothing with this but learn imperfectly to transfer her "wide hopeless yearning" for purpose and action into an almost depressive longing for dependency and love.[41]

As a sign of this limit to her energy, although Maggie would like to "read no more books where the blond-haired women carry away all the happiness," it isn't the love plot as a whole that she questions, just the convention that the dark-haired girl is always "the rejected lover" (*MotF*, 290–91). Maggie's hopeful substitution of dark for fair is just one more proof of the convention; she can rescript nothing. Her half-intended half-elopement with her cousin's fiancé is rejected too late for her to avoid suspicious taint.

Maggie has always been disruptive and intrusive while wanting never to be so. Repressing her power, she yearns for male approval, and during the scandals she creates by her need for love, she is torn between familial/fraternal and sexual love in ways she can barely negotiate, unequipped to choose between options for which her needs are all so intense. As a narrative idea, Maggie is Eliot's decisive measure of the degree to which only narrow norms of female behavior can be socially tolerated. The various situations in which she is caught are like the test for the witch on which Maggie is catechized early in the novel. If she drowns, she is proven innocent. At the end, Maggie will be so tried, proven innocent, but found dead.

But innocent of what? The simultaneous death of her brother, Tom, is a clue. Insofar as this novel concerns the double *Bildung* of the little brother and sister, it makes pointed comments about the values and rewards offered to the polarized sexes. The novel shows how gender is created in children, the differentials of behavior and values. Tom is without feeling and emotional depth, even cruel; Maggie is vulnerable to the point of masochism. Like other successful men, Tom has goals, skills of hard work, sublimation; he shares the dutiful, rigid, self-righteous character of male success. Women's talents are qualified out of existence; if Maggie is "quick" she must necessarily be "shallow" (*MotF*, 134). The flood, proof that quick water may also be very deep, is thus affiliated with the frustration of the female character.

The flood that carries the brother and sister to their deaths indicates all the capacities that they have repressed in order successfully to become male and female. The death is also Maggie's passion unrecognized, repressed, roiling up to bear them down; this is her dammed-up selfhood and her passionate desire for life, which cannot be repressed. A complex mixture of nature and culture combines to form the killing force. Tom and Maggie could almost navigate the flood with its currents, but the stuff made by people—the machinery—borne on that instinctual flood drags them under. For a brief moment

cf Patricia Boumelha

the flood is the breaker of boundaries, the temporary end of gender scripts, creating the "undivided" embrace of two "daisy-field" children, with allusions to a *liebestod* almost incestuous. The flood also breaks the family mill, which ground them all exceedingly fine. In short, the flood briefly destroys the oedipal nexus of gender. But when the waters recede, the landscape has not changed all that much.

What we have discovered in the marriage/death closure in the romance plot is a "place" where ideology meets narrative and produces a meaning-laden figure of some sort.[42] What we will study in the twentieth-century texts is the desire to produce several different figures at that place where text meets values.

CHAPTER TWO

■

The Rupture of Story and *The Story of an African Farm*

"Reader, I married him."
CHARLOTTE BRONTË
Jane Eyre (1848)

"Reader, it was not to have ended here."
TILLIE OLSEN,
Yonnondio (1932/1972)

But what will happen if, in process of solidifying the entire body of his story, the novelist finds himself out of facts or flagging in his invention? Must he then go on? Yes, for the story has to be finished: the intrigue discovered, the guilty punished, the lovers married in the end. . . . Better would it be, we feel, to leave a blank or even to outrage our sense of probability than to stuff the crevices with this makeshift substance: the wrong side of truth is a worn, dull fabric, unsteeped in the waters of imagination and scorched. But the novel has issued her orders; I consist, she says, of two and thirty chapters; and who am I, we seem to hear the sagacious and humble Trollope ask, with his usual good sense, that I should go disobeying the novel? And he manfully provides us with makeshifts.
VIRGINIA WOOLF
"Phases of Fiction" (1929)

Granite + Rainbow

To change story signals a dissent from social norms as well as narrative forms. This is because people are relatively more comfortable with stories whose elements are "renewed, recreated, defended and modified"; they are naturally drawn to those events, emotions, and endings which are recognizable, apparently corresponding to "experience."[1] The poetics of critique of the women authors here, that questioning of the construction of gender in narrative form, is cast in very literary terms ("disobeying the novel") precisely because it must distance the reader from codes of expected narrative and from patterns of response that had seemed to command universal or natural status. The novel as Woolf characterized it in "Phases of Fiction" is a dictatorial mother or muse, another manipulative Angel who not only marches with her regiment but leads it. If a novelist's maleness is expressed "manfully" in receiving the commands of the dominant

novel = dictatorial mother or muse

This chapter is dedicated to the memory of Ruth First, killed by a South African letter bomb in the Mozambique Embassy.

20

marriage plot
quest plot - punishment for female aspiration

form without flinching, a novelist's femaleness might, at very least,
consist in "leaving a blank or outraging our sense of probability"; at
most, it might lead to a rejection of dominant narrative.[2]

In the work of twentieth-century women, the marriage plot, with
its high status in novels, and the quest plot of punishment for female
aspiration were displaced, eroded, or removed from the center of the
novel. This project I have called writing beyond the ending, taking
ending as a metaphor for conventional narrative, for a regimen of
resolutions, and for the social, sexual, and ideological affirmations
these make.   *Eagleton*

The twentieth-century position is signaled for this study by a work
that exposes the critical collapse of several related narrative
paradigms, and by a writer who, inventing the "Shakespeare's sister"   *Schreiner -*
trope for muted women writers, well understood silencing, cultural   *invented*
marginality, and gender.[3] *The Story of an African Farm* (1883) by the   *Shakespeare's*
South African writer Olive Schreiner is a critique of three dominant   *sister" trope*
narratives, a critique deliberately articulated, intellectually principled,
and emotionally coherent.[4] The Christian story and the teleological   *critique of*
melodrama on which it depends features a battle between good and   *3 dominant*
evil, which conventionally ends with the triumph, or at least the mar-   *narratives:*
tyred justification, of right. This story about the revealed ruling pur-   *1) Christian*
pose of the cosmos is run aground in the first part of *African Farm*.   *2) quest*
The second story, a *Bildungs* plot, centers in *African Farm* on Waldo   *3) romance*
Farber, who searches vainly for purpose, but stops and simply dies.
The third story, centering here on Lyndall, combines various romantic thralldom and marriage plots in which fictional heroes and
heroines have traditionally acted. Taken as a whole, the book marks
the "end" of the consoling stories of the Christian, quest, and romance varieties.

Schreiner's narrative is set in the last half of the nineteenth century
on a lonely South African sheep and ostrich farm owned by self-
important Tant' Sannie. On the farm live her sweet stepdaughter, Em,
and Em's restless orphan cousin, Lyndall. Otto, the farm manager
and Waldo, his son, complete this uncoordinated "family." With Em as   *Em - Boer*
Boer, Lyndall as British, and Waldo as "African," the children also   *Lyndall - British*
symbolize the political problematic of South Africa.[5] The children are   *Waldo - "African"*
not exactly homeless, but they have only the thinnest ties of kinship
and are as marginal to the family system as Schreiner herself was, a
preternaturally young freethinker in a conservative colonial and religious outpost.

Into this group comes Bonaparte, a quintessential confidence man
of the type found most commonly in American (another colonial)
literature, or perhaps a cruel version of the African cultural motif of

the "signifying monkey."[6] By virtue of his outrageous lies, he is soon ensconced on the farm. And just as soon, he has so gulled, tormented, and deceived Otto that the good man is hounded to death. Bonaparte's false claims will concern his aristocratic relations; his apparent mission in coming to Africa was capitalist investment. His exploitation thus ricochets between a deformation of the aristocratic system (a lord who does not protect, but only exploits) and a parody of a capitalistic one, for he appropriates the labor of others by the investment of glibness. His melodramatic sadism ruins the already precarious human relations on the farm. His allusive ties to an economic system as well as to a spiritual one may explain why all the characters are powerless against him.

Otto's response to Bonaparte conforms to the Beatitudes, yet through them Bonaparte, the parasite, achieves an ever firmer grip on his host. "I was a Stranger, and Ye Took Me In" is one rather shameless chapter title, along with "Blessed is He that Believeth." In fact, the one who believeth is duped and the one who lies is rewarded in Schreiner's grim, earnest, and painstaking transvaluation.

Bonaparte's devilishness is expressed by his ability to confuse the world around him so that no adult can tell that he is lying; he effectively substitutes his fictions for their immobile sense of truth. When the child Lyndall wonders aloud about Bonaparte's veracity, Otto stoutly defends him. "If we begin to question everything—proof, proof, proof, what will we have to believe left? How do you know the angel opened the prison door for Peter, except that Peter said so?" (*SAF*, 48).

By exploiting the literal perversity of such extreme faith, Schreiner has made a narrative in which demonic lies take the place of truth. The problem of evil in the world is unseen by an utterly innocent patriarch, who is thus powerless to combat it. All in all, this part of Schreiner's story propounds the blasphemous notion that to live uncritically according to the literal Christian story is to put the devil in power.

Similarly, the child Waldo attempts to impose the patterns of biblical stories on his experience. But when he sacrifices a little lamb chop, replaying the Cain and Abel story, God does not break His silence to raise a fire on the child's altar. The implications of his moment of doubt terrify Waldo. Instead of considering that the whole story might be a fiction, Waldo is stricken with guilt and intensifies his grip on the same story to explain his new plight: "I am like Cain—I am not His. . . . God hates me" (*SAF*, 27). Waldo struggles, trying to make his experience conform to the one True Tale. But that story is shattered.

Waldo's spiritual crises recur and are never resolved, even in death.

As Otto is "God," Waldo is Schreiner's impoverished "Christ"—the reviled seeker, the one who suffers the world's burdens; yet he is a Christ whose father can never help him. This Christ has neither the full sanction of an entrenched belief system nor the satisfaction of an emergent one. Schreiner shows that when the Christian world view is no longer dominant, the Christian narrative melodrama of salvation is aborted.

In Part II of the novel, when Lyndall returns from boarding school, she and Waldo have ecstatic discussions (mainly monologues by Lyndall) about faith and women's rights. A hired man, Gregory Rose, conceives a pattern-book love for Em, and the two seem destined to live happily, if pallidly, ever after. However, Gregory has also fallen passionately in love with Lyndall. Although she is contemptuous, calling him a "tin duck," she suddenly offers to marry him, because she is pregnant (*SAF*, 218). But this marriage does not occur.

Two new characters, designated simply as Waldo's and Lyndall's strangers, come from the outside world with spiritual and carnal knowledge and a certain aura of promise for the plot, which is repeatedly undermined. The part of the novel devoted to Waldo alone strongly suggests a classic *Bildung,* and reader expectation is whetted for this convention. The provincial youth, alienated from his surroundings, has fathers who fail him: Otto by not recognizing his religious despair and Bonaparte by sadistically destroying the boy's invention, a symbol of self-improvement and human progress. Their paternal legacy, in typical *Bildungs* movement, creates an estrangement that provokes the hero to make a pilgrimage.[7]

One of the steps in this process is the crucial story of Waldo's stranger, the quest allegory that, read in isolation, typifies Schreiner's message for many readers. A man quests after truth, a "vast white bird" (*SAF*, 146). At his dying moment, he imagines that those coming after him use his hand-hewn trail to mount higher in their search. A single feather from the bird of Truth floats down, to signal that small portion of knowledge which the hunter has gained. He dies having done his part to bring about the progress of humanity. This martyrdom to meliorism is characteristic of Schreiner's position—and it constituted her own justification.

This story seems to offer a mirror of Waldo's life. He begins his travels "Anywhere," to "See—see everything" (*SAF*, 184). Yet on this quest, he finds both the social world and the world of work unspeakably repulsive. The plot of a young man from the provinces making a fortune, rising in status, is immediately denied its potential for organizing the action. Nor does he make any ironic negotiation with the world, exchanging innocence for enhanced knowledge. A degradation or naturalistic downfall plot, in which Waldo is ground down by brutalizing labor and hard liquor, is briefly essayed, but the character escapes it as well.

A promissory note in Waldo's quest plot had been given when the stranger said, "Well, I trust we shall meet again some day, sooner or later" (*SAF,* 159). Given the erasure of either success or downfall as organizing tools, the reader is on the watch for the fulfillment of this promise, in some recognition, some long- or short-term relationship, some link connecting the elements of Waldo's education with the man who had, in whatever unreliable way, given him a parable of his life's meaning. Schreiner has thus outlined at least three variations of a quest plot of education and has disposed of all with unseemly haste. The first two times may appear accidental, but when she gets to the reappearance of the stranger, one can conclude that she is deliberately bringing her readers to the end of narrative coherence in order to show the insufficiency of these conventional scripts for action. For Schreiner does produce a second meeting with the stranger, but, like her repeated epigraph, it comes to nothing. In an urban park, Waldo, looking boorish and wild, is asked, like the black servant he resembles, to retrieve something dropped by the Stranger's lady. He is rewarded with a sixpence thrown to the ground. The man does not recognize Waldo; Waldo recognizes him but cannot pursue his claim. Without a mutual recognition scene, without any connection to the allegory, without any pondering by Waldo, this scene retains only the shock value of systematically undermined possibilities for narrative design.

Waldo's quest ends with his belated discovery of a telos: love of Lyndall and of her work. "I am very helpless, I shall never do anything; but you will work, and I will take your work for mine. Sometimes such a sudden gladness seizes me when I remember that somewhere in the world you are living and working. You are my very own; nothing else is my own so" (*SAF,* 250). But this declaration is doubly doomed. For in fact Lyndall has no work; she has declared that after "A little bitterness, a little longing when we are young, a little futile searching for work, a little passionate striving for room for the exercise of our powers . . . then we go with the drove. A woman must march with her regiment. In the end she must be trodden down or go with it; and if she is wise she goes" (*SAF,* 176).[8] For despite her several potential vocations (playwright, actress, public speaker, orator-agitator), Lyndall is not the South African Aurora Leigh or Rhoda Nunn. Instead, she chooses love alone, and, as one of Schreiner's allegories states, life deserts her.[9]

Further, Waldo declares his love only in a letter, written when Lyndall is already dead. So these two characters never have a scene of recognition, despite Waldo's "nothing else is my own so," which recalls the passionate outcries in both Charlotte and Emily Brontë. Their connection will lie shattered, turning the acceleration of a potentially hierogamic union into a dead stall.

The relation between Lyndall and Waldo has many characteristics of hierogamy.[10] The two are polar opposites, although the typical male/female opposition of sky and earth is reversed. Lyndall is allied with the stars and sky because of her intellectual powers and desire for transcendence; Waldo is like the earth, a creative and nurturant force on which he draws and to which, at the end, he returns, dying among the chickens. Lyndall is elegant, educated, and articulate; Waldo is uncouth, self-taught, and silent. Their potential for fusing in a new cosmos is represented by her mid-book declaration at the pink moment of dawn. "'Waldo . . . I like you so much, I love you.' She rested her cheek softly against his shoulder. 'When I am with you I never know that I am a woman and you are a man; I only know that we are both things that think. Other men when I am with them, whether I love them or not, they are mere bodies to me; but you are a spirit . . .'" (SAF, 197).

The possibility of a hierogamic union between these characters and its impediments are expressed through Waldo's staff and Lyndall's box. The box, with its delicate leaves and cone projections, represents the fertility and transcendence that both fail her. And Waldo's rejection of quest is shown by the fate of his staff, carved to place on his father's grave. With no intimation of its meaning, Waldo's stranger had attempted to buy it, viewing it as an example of "primitive" art. After hearing the Allegory of the Hunter, Waldo simply gives it to him. Thus, ironically, does Waldo's pilgrim staff pass from his hands.

That Waldo and Lyndall should be so related is not surprising, given their biographical import. Both are projections, Waldo represents Schreiner's childhood, with its precocious debate between Christian sublimity and freethinking, the experience of her minister father's professional incompetence, and her being essentially orphaned from her still-living parents at age twelve. The character can be a boy because this powerlessness is not dependent on gender. Lyndall's is; her sense of self, her sexual torments, her fascination with sexuality, and even her seduction are drawn from Schreiner's post-adolescent life.[11]

Schreiner's versions of romance plots are, as we have already seen with hierogamy, more promissory notes that are never honored by the author, in her aim to discredit the narratives and those ideologies on which they draw.[12] In Lyndall, Schreiner has portrayed the contradiction between radical intellectual conviction and conservative psycho-

feminist
convictions
+
romantic
thralldom

logical mandates for female behavior. She shows a female hero torn
between feminist convictions and romantic thralldom. Lyndall desires
independence but still feels attraction to those conventions of sexuality—dominance, submission, hunter and hunted—which end with her
dependence and abasement. For Lyndall's stranger was her seducer.

Her stranger sees Lyndall as sexually enticing. The more she refuses him, the more "hunting instincts" are provoked. When she tries
to explain herself, he responds condescendingly: "I like you when you
grow metaphysical and analytical" (*SAF*, 224). Though sexually
aroused, she recognizes the transience of this passion, his bullying
character, and her masochism.

> "If you do love me," [the stranger] asked her, "why will you not marry
> me?"
>   "Because, if I had been married to you for a year, I should have come
> to my senses, and seen that your hands and your voice are like the hands
> and the voice of any other man. I cannot quite see that now. But it is all
> madness. You call into activity one part of my nature; there is a higher
> part that you know nothing of, that you never touch." (*SAF*, 224)

Robin Morgan
"The Politics of
Sado-Masochistic
Fantasies"

In Lyndall's fear of the stranger may be seen her fear of her own
boundless and unfocused power.[13]

Lyndall rejects marriage but travels with the stranger in free companionship. On this unnarrated journey, they quarrel and part. Her
decision not to marry, separating passion from her core identity, is a
radical choice not to sell herself into the system that she, along with
other turn-of-the-century thinkers, sees as a glorified version of prostitution. (Indeed, Schreiner's unfinished novel *From Man to Man* pursues this analogy of marriage and prostitution in two sisters who each
choose one of these paths.) In her feminist sermons to Waldo, Lyndall
had stressed that genuine love would occur only when women worked
and thus did not need direct economic support. However, in Lyndall,
Schreiner depicts a radical feminist who is bound into female socialization by her failure to establish any calling or vocation.

In terms derived from *Woman and Labour* (1911), Schreiner's influential study of the social and economic status of women, Lyndall
was able to reject "sex parasitism"—the iconic position of the wife in
dependency and idleness, close to the contemporaneous account by
Veblen of women as objects of conspicuous consumption or to Gilman's *Women and Economics*.[14] However, Lyndall could not voice the
enabling demand that both opens *Woman and Labour* and closes it:
"Give us labour and the training which fits for labour! We demand
this, not for ourselves alone, but for the race."[15]

Once a female hero, sure that a free choice of love would be a prelude to her achievement of power, she ends an invalid heroine, whose energies are terminated by a wasting illness. After Lyndall quarrels with her stranger and they part, she is discovered in an isolated hotel, her child dead and she herself dying. This death is provoked by a conflict between her identity as a "new woman"— independent, outspoken, purposeful, without marital subordination or economic dependence—and her already constituted psychic makeup. So in Lyndall, Schreiner has made a character who must fight against herself within herself.[16] She is split between her sensual needs and her feminist ideals, the one congruent with feminine scripts of abasement and submission, the other a criticism of that structure of desire and that psychic career.

Lyndall's dead baby, the imagery surrounding the birth, and the fact of Lyndall's death constitute as an ensemble the climax of the conflict between old and new scripts for female action.[17] It is not that Lyndall went too far, in the geopolitical terminology of the sexual terrain, but that she did not go far enough. Her despairing cry— rejecting her potential vocation as polemicist, intellectual, or political agitator—uses chrysalid, fairy-tale, and pregnancy imagery in an anatomy of various female dilemmas, from the narrative to the biological. Waldo has asked her about a "new time." In her response she rejects public and political action because she is psychologically paralyzed. "I will do nothing good for myself, nothing for the world, till someone wakes me. I am asleep, swathed, shut up in self; till I have been delivered I will deliver no one" (*SAF*, 183). The word *deliver* evokes the narrative of the sleeping beauty who must be rescued or liberated by a savior-prince. To be split between the hero, doing something for the world, and the heroine, waiting to be awakened, to be split between delivered and deliverer, is Lyndall's stalemate between romance and vocation. Further, Lyndall is torn between being a childless mother and being an unmothered child, held, mute and impotent, in an incomplete transition from the pupa. This passage predicts the death of Lyndall's child and suggests that, transposing the narratives of sexual taint, the dead child should be read as a sign of her self-division between thralldom and independence.[18]

At the beginning of the book, the character Gregory Rose had been depicted as a shallow and mannered youth, claiming to adore Em, and using an exaggerated melodramatic language in which to press his claims. "You must love me, love me better than all! . . . You were made for me, created for me! I will love you till I die!" (*SAF*, 164). But when Gregory Rose is overwhelmed with love for Lyndall, he uses almost parallel language. Naturally, he seems a comic figure with his

fickle changes, cast as a weak yet manipulative romantic youth running the gamut of stagy heartsick stances. But here too Schreiner
divests the narrative and character conventions to which she alludes.
For Gregory Rose does not want to woo a woman; he wants to be one.

Gregory Rose first finds women's clothing in the attic of the farm
and is guiltily electrified. To care for Lyndall, he dresses as a woman,
carefully shaving the beard that is his final visible point of contact with
the male sex. In his male clothes Gregory was forced into simpering
and sentimental poses; he is liberated by female clothes into passionate maternal behavior, caring for a woman damaged by conflicting
allegiances to conventional gender scripts, who dies because she cannot invent a livable version of femaleness.

In this episode of cross-dressing, Schreiner evokes homosexuality
and transvestism to contest the heterosexual dramas to which this
character does finally conform.[19] The transvestite—trapped between
male and female—nurses a dying feminist—trapped in a crossfire of
thralldom and quest: a strong tableau of sexual and social marginality.
The whole "story of" the "African farm" concerns aborted change,
dying ideologies, inchoate resistance. This combination of material
shows the author's conviction that conventional gender roles repress
human growth and social progress. In 1884, responding to a
"Woman's paper," Schreiner said, "I object to anything that divides
the two sexes. My main point is this: human development has now
reached a point at which sexual difference has become a thing of
altogether minor importance. We make too much of it; we are men
and women in the second place, human beings in the first."[20] In Gregory Rose, and in Veronica in *From Man to Man*, Schreiner presented
the suffering attendant upon sexual polarization or strictly held difference; in Lyndall and her romance plot, Schreiner dramatized the
internal self-division and damage of gender scripts.

From Man to Man also concerns the discrepancy between female
ideas and female lives. Depicted are the intellectual striving and
analysis, the emotional vulnerability, and the various forms of prostitution, marital or professional, in which the large-souled protagonists are contained and against which at least one of the sisters struggles. Rebekah's major activity besides mothering is writing in her
diary—stories, verses, and "discussions on abstract questions," "great
plans for the life that was to be lived," "passionate personal entries"
(*FMTM*, 150). One long chapter of such thoughts is called "Raindrops
in the Avenue"; the torrents of rain, analogous to her flooding
thought, are limited and socially contained by the "avenues" of
bourgeois scripts. *From Man to Man*, then, reconciles novelistic narrative with imbedded discourses, diaries, letters and meditations, and

thus is an early, though unfinished, example of the apologue form
that is used later in the century by Doris Lessing in *The Four-Gated City*
and Virginia Woolf in *The Pargiters.*

In *Woman and Labour,* Schreiner wrote the passage that could serve
as the epitaph for all her characters who were caught in material and
ideological transitions that they perceived but could not complete.

> Within the individuality itself of such persons [who are experiencing
> profound changes], goes on, in an intensified form, that very struggle,
> conflict and disco-ordination which is going on in society at large be-
> tween its different members and sections; and agonizing moments must
> arise, when the individual, seeing the necessity for adopting new courses
> of action, or for accepting new truths, or conforming to new conditions,
> will yet be tortured by the hold of traditional convictions; and the man
> or woman who attempts to adapt their life to the new material conditions
> and to harmony with the new knowledge, is almost bound at some time
> to rupture the continuity of their own psychological existence.   (*W&L,*
> 269–70)

Schreiner's way of portraying such failure and maladaptation was
to evoke stories with a powerful cultural presence, and to rupture the
continuity of their narrative existence. In the preface to *African Farm,*
she talks about deliberately undermining satisfactions of plot and
resolution by contrasting two kinds of narrative pattern. The
neatness, coherence, and closure of one is set against another: questioning, strange, unresolvable. In the exaggerated or realistic melodrama of the "stage method," "each character is duly marshalled at
first, and ticketed": there are conventional expectations assigned to
each. Thus, if you are the soprano heroine, domestic, pure-minded,
and skilled in waiting, you will be satisfied by your forthcoming nup-
tials. But Em compares her marriage to an empty box. If you are the
romantic tenor, you do not turn out happiest as a transvestite. If you
are the villain, you do not resurface, none the worse for wear. But
Bonaparte does.

Aside from her critique of these melodramas of villainy and romance, more basic elements of narrative, such as rhythm of expectation and release of tension, are also questioned, for "nothing can be
prophesied"—no action, strategy, or solution foretold (*SAF,* v). Instead
of the "immutable certainty that at the right crises each [character]
will reappear and act his part," here there is no closure, no sense of
expectation fulfilled, no satisfying accountability of story (*SAF,* v).
"There is a strange coming and going of feet. Men appear, act and re-
act upon each other, and pass away. When the crisis comes the man
who would fit it does not return. . . . When the footlights are brightest

they are blown out; and what the name of the play is no one knows" (*SAF*, v).

Childhood experiences passionately transposed, family fragmentation, the problematic of Africa, repeated crises of faith, resistance to gender socialization, disturbance about sexuality, even the mysterious seduction, and finally the marginality of place, which produces both critique and despair—all these are drawn from Schreiner's life. In particular, her confrontation with romantic thralldom after both unmothering and unfathering parents, and her fascination with religious questions provoked a double and contradictory set of responses: illness and writing. Soon after a romantic episode, her ill health, an asthmatic condition, developed, the result, her biographers speculate, of "guilts about love and attachment."[21] It is also clear, in the complete arc of Schreiner's career, that as she increasingly expressed herself in illness, her desire and ability to express herself in writing became starkly compromised. Sickness was the price she paid for "the force of her writing and of her unconventionality."[22] She felt guilt about her attempted experiments in independence and sexual attachment. She was often ill; the illness meant she did not write. Her frustration and sense of failure as a writer then contributed to her illness.

Schreiner spent her whole life struggling, as a feminist, a freethinker, a new life socialist, and a writer. Yet she held many of her positions isolated from fellow thinkers and political actors, even when she was involved with London groups. She deliberately marginalized herself—"lacking a constituency" is First and Scott's incisive summary—as if only in marginality could she recapture the powers that precipitated her career.[23] Someone who saw her after World War I remembers "the old rebellion blazing up with her championship of unpopular causes as, thumping her knees with her clenched fists, and flashing defiance, she declared: 'I'm a Freethinker, I'm a Bolshevik, I'm a Sinn Feiner!' "[24] These brave words, unattached to praxis, were necessary doses of an addiction to marginality.

Still, with the publication of *The Story of an African Farm* in 1883, Olive Schreiner originated the critique of narrative characteristic of twentieth-century writing by women. As in her own allegory the body of her work became a bridge between nineteenth- and twentieth-century projects.[25] Her accomplishment is to reject and dismantle tales of great cultural magnitude, making a whole *Story* of the critique of story, writing *finis* to three resonant narratives. She, with other women writers, "breaks the sentence" so that alternative and oppositional stories about women, men, and community can be constructed beyond the teleological formulations of quest and romance.

■

CHAPTER THREE

Breaking the Sentence; Breaking the Sequence

I am almost sure, I said to myself, that Mary Carmichael is playing a trick on us. For I feel as one feels on a switchback railway when the car, instead of sinking, as one has been led to expect, swerves up again. Mary is tampering with the expected sequence. First she broke the sentence; now she has broken the sequence. . . . Perhaps she had done this unconsciously, merely giving things their natural order, as a woman would, if she wrote like a woman. But the effect was somehow baffling; one could not see a wave heaping itself, a crisis coming round the next corner. . . . For whenever I was about to feel the usual things in the usual places, about love, about death, the annoying creature twitched me away, as if the important point were just a little further on.

VIRGINIA WOOLF
A Room of One's Own (1929)

. . . *Charlotte was gazing up into the dark eyes of Redmond. "My darling," he breathed hoarsely. Strong arms lifted her, his warm lips pressed her own.* . . .
That was the way it was supposed to go, that was the way it had always gone before, but somehow it no longer felt right. I'd taken a wrong turn somewhere; there was something, some fact or clue, that I had overlooked.

MARGARET ATWOOD
Lady Oracle (1976)

O ne approach to the feminist criticism of these modern writers is suggested in an analysis of "Mary Carmichael's first novel, *Life's Adventure*," a work and author invented by Virginia Woolf and explicated in *A Room of One's Own*.[1] This is a novel by the last of the series of ancestral mothers alluded to in the Elizabethan ballad of the Four Marys, which forms a frame for the essay. The first two are Mary Beton, with her legacy of money, and Mary Seton, who provides "room"—institutional and psychological space. Both are necessary for Mary Carmichael, the modern author, and all of them express the baffled and unmentioned Mary Hamilton, from the ages when women had no way to dissent, except through infanticide and anonymous song. Woolf scrutinizes this novel's style, plot, and purpose with

31

a diffident casualness, finding "some fact or clue" of great importance: "Mary is tampering with the expected sequence. First she broke
the sentence; now she has broken the sequence" (*AROO*, 85). In these
matching statements are telescoped a poetics of rupture and critique.

poetics of rupture r critique [margin annotation]

The sentence broken is one that expresses "the ridicule, the cen-
sure, the assurance of inferiority" about women's cultural ineptitude
and deficiencies.[2] To break the sentence rejects not grammar especially, but rhythm, pace, flow, expression: the structuring of the female voice by the male voice, female tone and manner by male expectations, female writing by male emphasis, female writing by existing
conventions of gender—in short, any way in which dominant structures shape muted ones. For a woman to write, she must experiment
with "altering and adapting the current sentence until she writes one
that takes the natural shape of her thought without crushing or dis-
torting it" (*G&R*, 81).[3]

At first it appeared as if Mary Carmichael would not be able to
break this sentence and create her own. Her style was jerky, short, and
terse, which "might mean that she was afraid of something; afraid of
being called 'sentimental' perhaps; or she remembers that women's
writing has been called flowery and so provides a superfluity of thorns
. . ." (*AROO*, 85). Here she overcompensated for femaleness in deference to existing conventions.

But eventually, facing gender in an authentic way, the writer produces "a woman's sentence," "the psychological sentence of the
feminine gender," which "is used to describe a woman's mind by a
writer [Dorothy Richardson] who is neither proud nor afraid of anything that she may discover in the psychology of her sex."[4] The sentence is "psychological" not only because it deepens external realism
with a picture of consciousness at work but also because it involves a
critique of her own consciousness, saturated as it is with discourses of
dominance.

There is nothing exclusively or essentially female about "the psychological sentence of the feminine gender," because writers of both
sexes have used that "elastic" and "enveloping" form. But it is a
"woman's sentence" because of its cultural and situational function, a
dissension stating that women's minds and concerns have been
neither completely nor accurately produced in literature as we know
it. Breaking the sentence is a way of rupturing language and tradition
sufficiently to invite a female slant, emphasis, or approach. Similarly
there is nothing innately gendered about the signifier "I," yet in *A
Room of One's Own* the speaker's "I" is both female and plural—"a
woman's voice in a patriarchal literary tradition"—and another "I,"
shadowing the page, is "polished, learned, well-fed," an explicitly
male subject speaking of and from dominance.[5]

Woolf's "woman's sentence," then, has its basis not in biology, but rather in cultural fearlessness, in the attitude of critique—a dissent from, a self-conscious marking of, dominant statement. It can be a stress shifting, the kind of realignment of emphasis noted by Nancy Miller, following Luce Irigaray: "an italicized version of what passes for the neutral or standard face . . . a way of marking what has already been said. . . ."[6]

A "woman's sentence" is Woolf's shorthand term for a writing un-afraid of gender as an issue, undeferential to male judgment while not unaware of the complex relations between male and female. A "woman's sentence" will thus be constructed in considered indiffer-ence to the fact that the writer's vision is seen as peculiar, incompe-tent, marginal. So Woolf summarizes "the first great lesson" mastered by Mary Carmichael: "she wrote as a woman, but as a woman who has forgotten that she is a woman . . ." (*AROO*, 96). The doubled emphasis on woman, yet on forgetting woman, is a significant maneuver, claim-ing freedom from a "tyranny of sex" that is nonetheless palpable and dominant, both negated and affirmed.[7]

In both *A Room of One's Own* and the related "Women and Fiction," Woolf criticizes women for "resenting the treatment of [their] sex and pleading for its rights," because, in her view, this threatens the poise a writer achieves by the transcending of "indignation" on the one hand and "resignation" on the other, the "too masculine" here and the "too feminine" there.[8] This movement between complicity and critique expresses Woolf's version of a doubled dynamic that is, as we shall see momentarily, characteristic of other women writers.[9]

What binds these writers is their oppositional stance to the social and cultural construction of gender.[10] This opposition has a number of origins. Perhaps the most suggestive is that of marginality in two arenas.[11] When a female writer is black (Alice Walker, Zora Neale Hurston, Gwendolyn Brooks, Toni Morrison), colonial (Olive Schreiner, Doris Lessing, Jean Rhys), Canadian (Margaret Atwood), of working-class origin (Tillie Olsen, Marge Piercy), of lesbian or bisexual orientation (H.D., Virginia Woolf, Adrienne Rich, Joanna Russ), or displaced and déclassé (Dorothy Richardson), double mar-ginalization can be produced. Either it compels the person to negate any possibility for a critical stance, seeking instead "conformity and inclusion" because the idea of an authoritative center is defensively affirmed, or it enlivens the potential for critique by the production of an (ambiguously) nonhegemonic person, one in marginalized dia-logue with the orders she may also affirm.[12]

The woman writers studied here are further unified by their inter-ested dissent from androcentric culture in nonfictional texts: essay, memoir, polemic, and social study. The texts will be seen, case by case, to contribute to their fictional elaborations and narrative stances.[13] Hence while hardly all of the writers would describe themselves as feminists, and some, indeed, resist that term, one may assert that any female cultural practice that makes the "meaning production process" itself "the site of struggle" may be considered feminist.[14] These authors are "feminist" because they construct a variety of oppositional strategies to the depiction of gender institutions in narrative. A writer expresses dissent from an ideological formation by attacking elements of narrative that repeat, sustain, or embody the values and attitudes in question. So after breaking the sentence, a rupture with the internalization of the authorities and voices of dominance, the woman writer will create that further rupture which is a center for this book: breaking "the sequence—the expected order" (AROO, 95).

Breaking the sequence is a rupture in habits of narrative order, that expected story told when "love was the only possible interpreter" of women's textual lives (AROO, 87). In her study of Life's Adventure, Woolf notes that the novelist Mary Carmichael alludes to "the relationship that there may be between Chloe and Roger," but this is set aside in favor of another bond, depicted "perhaps for the first time in literature" (AROO, 84, 86). "Chloe liked Olivia. They shared a laboratory together," begins Woolf (AROO, 87). The romance names with the allusions to Shakespearean transvestite characters are very suggestive, especially as opposed to the firmly heterosexual "Roger," with a whole history of slang behind him. One of these women is married, with children; the other is not. Their work—finding a cure for pernicious anemia—may suggestively beef up women's weakness of nerve with a good dose of female bonding.

The ties between Chloe and Olivia may be homosocial or, given the subsequent sexual-cultural metaphor of exploring the "serpentine cave" of women, they may be lesbian.[15] In either case, Woolf clearly presents a nonheterosexual relation nourished by the healthy vocation of women. She is also eloquent about the meaning of these changes. The women's friendship, based on their work life, will be "more varied and lasting because it will be less personal" (AROO, 88). "Personal" is Woolf's word (in essays throughout the twenties) for the privatization and exclusiveness that is part of the script of heterosexual romance. So the tie between Chloe and Olivia, a model for modern women writers, makes a critique of heterosexuality and the love plot, and offers (Woolf implies) a stronger and more positive sense of female quest. One is no longer allowed to "feel the usual things in the usual places, about love, about death" (AROO, 95). So breaking the sequence can mean delegitimating the specific narrative and cultural orders of nineteenth-century fiction—the emphasis on successful or failed romance, the subordination of quest to love, the death of the

questing female, the insertion into family life. "The important point
. . . just a little further on" that Mary Carmichael pushes her reader to
see might be such narrative strategies as reparenting, female bonding,
including lesbian ties, mother-child dyads, brother-sister pairs, familial transpositions, the multiple individual, and the transpersonal
protagonist.

This study is also designed to suggest what elements of female
identity would be drawn on to make plausible the analytic assumption
that there is a women's writing with a certain stance toward narrative.[16] The narrative strategies of twentieth-century writing by women
are the expression of two systemic elements of female identity—a
psychosexual script and a sociocultural situation, both structured by
major oscillations. The oscillations occur in the gendering process and
in the hegemonic process. Oscillation is a swinging between two positions, a touching two limits, or, alternately, a fluctuation between two
purposes, states, centers, or principles. The narrative strategies I will
present here all take basic elements of female identity, such as the
gendering sequence, and realign their components.

The possibilities for heterosexual love and romance take shape in
the object relations within the family, that is, in the ties of kinship
forged between child and parent, and in the processes of gendering,
all given very complete cultural and social support. As we know, there
is a sequence that assists these arrangements—a psychosexual script
that is one of our first dramas. The occasion of our "learning the rules
of gendering and kinship" and the apparatus for the production of
sexual personality is, of course, the oedipal crisis.[17]

Freudian theory, postulating the telos of "normal femininity" as the
proper resolution of the oedipal crisis, bears an uncanny resemblance
to the nineteenth-century endings of narrative, in which the female
hero becomes a heroine and in which the conclusion of a valid love
plot is the loss of any momentum of quest. The pitfalls to be avoided
by a woman seeking normal femininity are very consistent with the
traits of the female hero in narrative: defiance, activity, selfishness,
heroic action, and identification with other women. For Freudian
theory puts a high premium on female passivity and narcissism and
on the "end" of husband, home, and male child. As for quest or
individual aspiration, Freud poignantly realizes that the achievement
of femininity has left "no paths open to [a woman] for further development; . . . [it is] as though, in fact, the difficult development
which leads to femininity had exhausted all the possibilities of the
individual."[18] By the repressions and sacrifices involved in becoming
feminine, quest is at a dead end—a sentiment that we have seen
replicated in narrative endings.

The "original bisexuality" or "bisexual disposition" of every indi-

vidual is the major starting point for this account.[19] The oedipal crisis
is a social process of gendering that takes "bisexual, androgynous,"
libidinally active, and ungendered infants and produces girls and
boys, giving to the male future social and sexual domination, and to
the female future domesticated status within the rules of the sex-
gender system of its society.[20] Thus gender is a product. That there
must be some kind of passage of an infant "into a social human being"
is not at issue. It will involve the "[dialectical] process of struggle with
and ultimate supersession (including integration) of symbolic figures
of love, desire, and authority." As this citation from Ortner proposes,
the theoretical possibility that the oedipal crisis is historically mutable
must not be overlooked.[21] The drama might unfold with some alternate figures and some alternate products or emphases.

Another major element of the oedipal crisis for girls is the requisite
shift of object choice from "phallic" or preoedipal mother—the
mother of power—to a heterosexual object, the father. Little boys
must shift generations, but not genders, in their object choice. The
reason for the female shift has been contested. Freud postulated that
a girl will turn from her mother, sometimes with hatred and hostility,
when the mother is discovered to be bereft of the genital marker of
male power. In feminist revisions of Freud, this revelation, called
"penis envy" by Freud, has been viewed as the delivery of knowledge
well beyond the perception of sheer genital difference, the shock of
learning a whole array of psychosocial rules and orders valorizing
maleness.

To Freud, the girl's tasks in the oedipal drama involve the repression of what he calls the "little man" inside her, that active, striving,
clitoral self, and the repression of love for her mother, a person of her
own sex. Yet even the Freudian account somewhat reluctantly presents a recurring tension between the oedipal and preoedipal phases
for the female, whereas in most males (as far as the theory tells) the
oedipus complex has a linear and cumulative movement. Freud has
found that "Regressions to fixations at these pre-oedipal phases occur
very often; in many women we actually find a repeated alternation of
periods in which either masculinity or femininity has obtained the
upper hand."[22] So the oedipal crisis can extend over years and follow
an individual woman right into adulthood. Or, to say it another way,
the "feminine" or "correct" resolution of women's gender identity
comes easily unstuck and cannot be counted on.

A further elaboration of the oedipal crisis in women is available in
Nancy Chodorow's analysis of mothering as a key institution in the
social and psychic reproduction of gender. In her view, in the development of a girl, the preoedipal attachment to the mother is never

entirely given up; it persists in coloring oedipalization, in shaping problems and issues of the female ego (boundlessness and boundary problems, "lack of separation or differentiation"), and in its influence on both the fact and the way that women mother. So while the gendering process is the "arena" where the goal of heterosexuality is "negotiated," it is also where the mother-daughter dyad and female bonding are affirmed.[23]

The narrative and cultural implications of this neo-Freudian picture of gendering are staggering. With no easy or one-directional passage to "normal femininity," women as social products are characterized by unresolved and continuous alternations between allegiance to males and to females, between heterosexuality and female-identified, lesbian, or bisexual ties. The "original bisexuality" of the individual female is not easily put to rest or resolved by one early tactical episode; rather the oscillation persists and is reconstituted in her adult identity. Further, the emotional rhythms of female identity involve repeated (and possibly even simultaneous) articulations of these two principles or states, which are taken (ideologically) as opposing poles.[24]

Twentieth-century women writers undertake a reassessment of the processes of gendering by inventing narrative strategies, especially involving sequence, character, and relationship, that neutralize, minimize, or transcend any oversimplified oedipal drama. This occurs by a recognition in various elements of narrative of the "bisexual oscillation" in the psychic makeup of characters, in the resolutions of texts, in the relationships portrayed. In twentieth-century narratives, effort is devoted to depicting masculine and feminine sides in one character—in Woolf's androgyny and in similar procedures in Richardson. Original bisexuality is extended the length of a character's life in H.D. and in Woolf. Women writers readjust the maternal and paternal in ways that unbalance the univocal sequence of object choices. This is why some female quest plots, like *To the Lighthouse* and *The Four-Gated City*, loop backward to mother-child attachments. Narratives of twentieth-century women, notably their *Künstlerromane*, may invent an interplay between the mother, the father, and the hero, in a "relational triangle."[25] These changes are often accompanied by pointed remarks about the plots, characters, and situations once expected in narrative: gender polarization, patrisexual romantic love, the arrest of female quest, the "happy ending"—remarks that, as we shall see, underline the self-consciousness of this critique of narrative scripts and the psychosexual drama that forms them.[26]

These representations of gendering could be achieved irrespective of whether any of the authors were aware of the exact terms of Freud-

strategies that neutralize, minimize, or transcend any oversimplified oedipal drama

ian theory, although no doubt a number were, or whether they explicitly connected their narratives to any aspect of Freud's position
(something that does occur in Woolf's *Orlando,* in H.D.'s *Helen in Egypt*
and *Tribute to Freud,* and in Doris Lessing's *The Golden Notebook*).[27] For
women artists, this sense of "remaining in the Oedipus situation for
an indefinite period" would not have to be consciously understood.[28]
One may simply postulate that the habit of living with an "unresolved" oedipus complex would lead the bearer to a greater
identification of the unstable elements, greater intuitive knowledge of
these components of one's interior life.

Indeed, Freud suggests a massive slippage of effectiveness, so that
the learning of the rules of gender may need a good deal of extrafa-
milial reinforcement, especially where the girl is concerned. The formation of the superego—the acceptance of social rules, including
those governing gender—is the result of "educative influences, of
external intimidation threatening loss of love."[29] That is, education as
an institution of gender, and culture as a whole, including literary
products like narrative, channel the girl into dominant structures of
the sex-gender system. The romance plot in narrative thus may be
seen as a necessary extension of the processes of gendering, and the
critique of romance that we find in twentieth-century female authors,
as part of the oppositional protest lodged against both literary culture
and a psychosexual norm.

The psychosexual oscillation of the gendering process, so distinctly
theorized, interacts with another systemic aspect of female identity,
which shows the same wavering, dialogic structure: a sociocultural
oscillation of hegemonic processes. In the social and cultural arena,
there is a constant repositioning between dominant and muted, hegemonic and oppositional, central and colonial, so that a woman may be
described as (ambiguously) nonhegemonic or, with equal justice but
less drama, as (ambiguously) hegemonic if her race, class, and sexuality are dominant. Virginia Woolf envisions this oscillating consciousness in *A Room of One's Own.*

> It [the mind] can think back through its fathers or through its mothers,
> as I have said that a woman writing thinks back through her mothers.
> Again if one is a woman one is often surprised by a sudden splitting off
> of consciousness, say in walking down Whitehall, when from being the
> natural inheritor of that civilization, she becomes, on the contrary, out-
> side of it, alien and critical. (*AROO,* 101)

Note how Woolf passes from the oedipal-preoedipal division in object
relations to the social oscillation, suggesting the relation of both proc-

esses to female identity. The debate between inheritor and critic is a movement between deep identification with dominant values and deep alienation from them. Whitehall, a street in London, is a synechdoche for British civil service and administrative agreements that endure beyond changes in specific governments, and thus is a metaphor for broad sociocultural agreement.

The shifting into alternative perspectives is taken by Woolf as a phenomenon peculiarly resonant for a woman. Her use of the word *natural* as opposed to the word *critical* sums the process up. *Natural* is what every ideology happily claims it is; the beliefs, social practices, sense of the self are second nature, assumed. The word *critical,* however, has the force of a severe and transgressive dissent from cherished mental structures and social practices. This contradictory quiver, this social vibrato creates a critical sensibility: dissent from the culture by which women are partially nourished, to which they are connected.

A major originating moment of Woolf's "outsider's feeling" came, significantly enough, in her confrontation at the turn of the century with the banal but forceful social and romantic expectations represented by George Duckworth, her half-brother and self-appointed substitute parent. At issue was her green dress, unconventionally made of upholstery fabric. From the moment of his anger at her appearance, from her as yet muted defiance, Woolf crystallizes that hegemonic set: proper dress, patterned feminine behavior, "tea table training," the absolute necessity for romance, the "patriarchal machinery" creating rigid, polarized male and female personalities. What astonished Woolf most was the female role of passive, appreciative spectator and the acrobatic—almost Swiftean—jumping through hoops demanded of males; the whole "circus" or "required act" was accomplished with no irony or critical questioning.[30]

Many commentators on women as a group and on female identity have isolated as systemic some kind of dual relationship to the definitions offered by various dominant forces. Simone de Beauvoir sees the female child "hesitating between the role of *object, Other,* which is offered to her, and the assertion of her liberty" as subject.[31] John Berger argues that the "social presence" of women and their ingenuity in living in "the keeping of men" have created "two constituent yet always distinct elements of her identity as a woman": the "surveyor and the surveyed."[32] The "duality of women's position in society" is Gerda Lerner's explanation for the fact that women as a group can be both victims and upholders of the status quo: "Women live a duality—as members of the general culture and as partakers of women's culture."[33] Nancy Cott similarly views "women's group con-

dual consciousness

de Beauvoir

John Berger

Gerda Lerner

Nancy Cott

sciousness as a subculture uniquely divided against itself by ties to the
dominant culture."[34] Sheila Rowbotham describes the war of parts of
the self, given the attitudes of the dominant group on the Left. "One
part of ourselves mocked another, we joined in the ridicule of our
own aspirations. . . . Part of us leapt over into their world, part of us
stayed at home. . . . We were never all together in one place, we were
always in transit, immigrants into alien territory."[35] And Alice Walker,
in "In Search of Our Mothers' Gardens" cites Woolf's *A Room of One's
Own* to come to terms with the "contrary instincts" in certain work by
black women from Phillis Wheatley to Zora Neale Hurston.[36] In sum,
women writers as women negotiate with divided loyalties and doubled
consciousnesses, both within and without a social and cultural agreement. This, in conjunction with the psychosexual oscillation, has implications for "sentence" and "sequence"—for language, ideology,
and narrative.

Later in her career, Woolf continued her analysis of the source of
women's sociocultural oscillation. In *Three Guineas,* Woolf finds that
women's structural position enables them to take an adversarial stance
to institutions of dominance. Women, she argues, are basically outsiders, formed by their nondominant ("unpaid for") education, as
they observe the privileges of maleness and the sacrifices exacted
from women themselves for those privileges. The lived experience of
women and men even from the same social class differs so greatly that
their world views and values are irreconcilably distinct: "though we
look at the same things, we see them differently."[37]

Constituting a separate group within their social class, women
should capitalize on this built-in zone of difference to think of themselves as an interested, coherent political bloc: an actual Society of
Outsiders. They can and should refuse male society and its values
(militarism, hierarchy, authoritarianism) even as they enter formerly
all-male professions. And women have, Woolf is certain, less chance
than men for being apologists for political, economic, and social oppression so intense that—her central point—the patriarchal politics of
bourgeois liberalism is on a continuum with fascism and the authoritarian state. Being already outsiders, women should turn its negative
markers ("poverty, chastity, derision, freedom from unreal loyalties")
into positive markers of difference, and turn their marginal status to
political advantage and analytic power (*TG,* 78).

The function of *Three Guineas* is to drive a politically motivated
wedge of analysis and polemic between dominant and muted, inheritor and critic, class and gender allegiances, to try to convince
educated women no longer to cooperate with the politics of their
class. Indeed, in 1940 Woolf argued that women are in a position to

make cross-class alliances with working-class men and women because their identification as "commoners, outsiders" will override apparent class distinctions.[38]

Yet the shift to the imperative mode and the call for a vow in *Three Guineas* betray the fact that women are not purely and simply Outsiders; otherwise one would not have to exhort them to remain so. They are, however, less integrated into the dominant orders than are men of their class. Women are a muted or subordinate part of a hegemonic process. Raymond Williams suggests that seeing hegemonic processes would be a way of visualizing culture to credit the internal debate between affirmation and critique. Hegemony includes a relationship in conflictual motion between the ideologies and practices of a dominant class or social group and the alternative practices, which may be either residual or emergent, of the muted classes or groups. Any set of hegemonic assumptions—notions orthodox in a given society and historical era—are "deeply saturating" and pervasive, "organized and lived," woven into the most private areas of our lives.[39] Still the hegemonic is always in motion, being "renewed, recreated, defended and modified."[40] These hegemonic processes are a site for both sociocultural reproduction and sociocultural dissent. The debate that women experience between the critic and the inheritor, the outsider and the privileged, the oppositional and the dominant is a major example of a hegemonic process, one whose results are evident in both social and narrative texts. Constantly reaffirmed as outsiders by others and sometimes by themselves, women's loyalties to dominance remain ambiguous, for they are not themselves in control of the processes by which they are defined.

Issues of control of voice and definition, then, allow Edwin Ardener's otherwise more static model to offer a complementary set of terms to define gender relations: the articulate or dominant men and then the nondominant or muted women. The latter term recalls the muted sonority of a musical instrument—the sound different, tamped down, repressed, but still speaking, with the speech bearing the marks of partial silencing. Interestingly, giving voice to the voiceless and making visible the invisible are two prime maneuvers in feminist poetics. As Ardener would gloss this, "The muted structures are 'there' but cannot be 'realized' in the language of the dominant structure."[41] To depict these relationships, Ardener posits two almost overlapping circles, one standing for dominant vision, the other for muted. The larger uncontested space where the circles overlap is shared by men and women in a given society as parallel inhabitants of main culture. The tiny crescent-shaped band left over for women is their zone of difference. Visualizing the relationship between dominant and muted in this fashion suggests that women can oscillate between the two parts of the circle that represents them, between difference and dominance.

The concept of a "double-consciousness" that comes from one's oscillation between a main and a muted position is not, nor could it ever be, a way of describing women exclusively, but it offers a way of seeing the identity of any group that is at least partially excluded from or marginal to the historically current system of meaning, value, and power.[42] Feminist criticism, then, may be said to begin with W. E. B. DuBois, postulating for blacks this double consciousness, born in negotiation with hegemonic processes.

Ellen Moers analyzed distinctive female stances based not on innate or essential femininity but on the shared cultural experiences of secondary status—constraints on travel, education, social mediations of childhood and motherhood—and reflected in particular uses of certain cultural tropes, such as the Gothic, the monster, the landscape.[43] This postulate was given forceful statement by Elaine Showalter: that women are parallel to other minority groups in their subcultural position "relative to a dominant society" and that this position leads to a unity of "values, conventions, experiences and behaviors" from which women draw and to which they respond with various fictional and biographical strategies.[44] Following Showalter's emphasis on formal and biographical strategies of response, Sandra Gilbert and Susan Gubar pose a repeated and reinvoked struggle as the master plot for women of the nineteenth century: in a dynamic generational confrontation in which dominant culture is the father and women are either sage daughters or mad wives in relation to patriarchal power. A nineteenth-century woman writer is the site of an internalized cultural debate: her own rage that she cannot speak and her culture's rage that she can. This contradiction is resolved in a powerful fictional motif: the madwoman, in whom expression struggles with repression.[45]

Where a reading of twentieth-century materials necessarily differs from the nineteenth-century texts most profoundly analyzed by Showalter and Gilbert and Gubar is that, by the twentieth century, middle-class women are technically—on paper—rather more part of the economic world, rather less legally and politically circumscribed than they were in the nineteenth. This changed position does not alter the negotiation process, but it does mean that women have an interior identification with dominant values (traditionally expressed as a rejection of female specialness) as well as an understanding of muted alternatives. Dominant and muted may be more equally balanced opponents in the twentieth century than in the nineteenth.

Mary Jacobus has also noted, and made central to her analysis of women's writing, the split between alien critic and inheritor that I have taken as a key text for this book. Jacobus further argues that, given this situation, "at once within culture and outside it," a woman writer must simultaneously "challenge the terms and work within them."[46] This precisely parallels my argument—that woman is neither wholly "subcultural" nor, certainly, wholly main-cultural, but negotiates difference and sameness, marginality and inclusion in a constant dialogue, which takes shape variously in the various authors, but with one end—a rewriting of gender in dominant fiction. The two processes in concert—the gendering and the hegemonic process— create mutual reinforcement for the double consciousness of women writers. This is the social and sexual basis of the poetics of critique.[47]

All forms of dominant narrative, but especially romance, are tropes for the sex-gender system as a whole.[48] Given the ideological and affirmative functions of narrative, it is no surprise that the critique of story is a major aspect of the stories told by twentieth-century women writers. Having begun this discussion, in chapter 2, with a text from the 1880s, let me end with a survey of several contemporary works, to show how the critique of story is not only a thematic fact but an indication of the moral, ideological, and political desire to rescript the novel.

Toni Morrison makes plain that *The Bluest Eye* concerns desperate material conditions that create and perpetuate racism and race self-hatred. Circumstances destroy the family that cannot "breed love" without also breeding pain and destruction. And stories—with their ideologies—are one of the circumstances. *The Bluest Eye* opens with three repeated paragraphs taken from one influential text promulgating vision and values: the "Dick and Jane" readers. This banal account of suburban family bliss is a primer for denatured language and a picture book of bourgeois values (contrasting with the choral complexity of the black world).[49] This memorable American series, with its reductive repetitions ("See the dog. See the dog run") and its uncanny commands ("Laugh, Mother, laugh") is the broad ideological backdrop that Morrison evokes. She gives it first in its own graceless prose, second, with the punctuation out, lacking priority or emphasis, and finally as one gigantic run-on block of gibberish and pain: the contents of the mind of someone who sees the whole story run over her like a freight train. As epigraphs to a number of the chapters, stony blocks of the run-on Dick and Jane material make ironic introductory remarks about prime childhood categories like family, house, mother, father, and play, which contrast with the Gordian knot of Pecola's life. Blue eyes—"story book eyes"—are, she in-

[Margin notes, handwritten:]
split between alien critic + inheritor = key text for this book

Jacobus

2 processes: gendering + hegemonic

"all forms of dominant narrative = tropes for sex-gender system"

critique of story

The Bluest Eye

tuits, the answer to every problem (*TBE*, 40). She is hardly wrong. These blue eyes, the white world's norm, are the image of all niceness and rightness, all superiority and advantage whose damage Morrison measures. Pecola wants the blue eyes of whiteness so she will no longer cause disgust, revulsion, and distaste in others, but will be able to "get somebody to love her"—an announced goal from the moment she reaches menarche at the beginning of the book (*TBE*, 29).

If that primer offers one set of stories about beauty and advantage, the movies offer another set to Pecola's mother. After poverty, hard work, and an uneasy marriage undermine Pauline's sense of self, movies complete her "education," and she gives way to her own ug-liness, that is, to the rejection of any positive vision of blackness.

> Along with the idea of romantic love, she was introduced to another— physical beauty. . . . In equating physical beauty with virtue, she stripped her mind, bound it, and collected self-contempt by the heap. . . . She was never able, after her education in the movies, to look at a face and not assign it some category in the scale of absolute beauty, and the scale was one she absorbed in full from the silver screen. (*TBE*, 97)

The black and silver-white glamour of packaged romance displaces Pauline's own aesthetic and sexual experiences of "the rainbow"—all the sensuous colors she remembers from the past, the June bugs, the lemonade, the purple berry stains. Morrison shows the process by which a personality becomes socially fixed within the framework of these stories, as Pauline turns from the rich colors of blackness to the superficial pastels of the white child for whom she cares.

The story is framed in the voice of Claudia, a friend of Pecola's. When given a doll that should have represented her "fondest wish"— that is, a blond, blue-eyed, pink-skinned doll—Claudia will resist and destroy it (*TBE*, 19–22). Claudia is then one site of the critique of ideology, a break with the story of white niceness and appropriate girl behavior, exhibiting the same resistance to dominant stories that characterizes female writers and their fictional spokespeople. Claudia hates Shirley Temple, hates "white baby dolls." But she is also torn in a way we recognize—she oscillates between critique and the temptation of lightness and "good hair," the internal color line of the black com-munity.

Among the narratives of romance and the romance of narrative, the Gothic remains to this day a major organizing grid for female consciousness. It is a form of sexual feudalism: the masochistic power-lessness of the generic female confronted with the no-frills, cruel-but-tender male. The proposition that Gothic paradigms are a major

[margin handwritten note: Gothic = major organizing grid for female consciousness]

narrative ideology imbedded in female consciousness is treated com- *Lady Oracle*
ically and critically, yet seductively, in Margaret Atwood's *Lady Oracle*.
The female hero is a doubled self: Joan Foster the person and Louisa
Delacourt the writer. She is a woman self-conscious enough to write
these Gothic fictions, great suety slabs of which are cited throughout
the novel, and to manipulate these highly stylized conventions and
their banal language. On the other hand, she is still seduced by these
fictions, finding that, no matter how hard she tries—or perhaps because she tries—her life invariably falls into Gothic patterns. She
doesn't know if she is a hero or a heroine, a quester or a victim, a
woman with a career of romance writing or a career of romance. Her
double names indicate the bifurcation of possibility, and the book
oscillates between schemes that reveal her as a plotter and as the
object of others' plots. By making Joan/Louisa a writer of, and a
believer in, Gothic fictions, Atwood indicates how this narrative is an
ideology sustained in consciousness and behavior.[50]
    The doubled men of Gothic fiction (bland nice man who is un-
masked as the villain, cruel moody man who is revealed as the hero),
the murder, the senses of warning, menace, and premonition occur
constantly and are comically deflated, yet recur, toy dolls that pop up,
even when punched down. The "escape fiction" that Joan analyzes
coolly is still warmly desired, despite the fact that her invention of
mysterious disappearance, fantastic disguise, and intricate "plot" is
easily pierced, both by herself and by others. Her self-parody is so
thick that the parodic element is neutralized.
    Atwood leaves quite ambiguous the question of the main charac-
ter's complicity in the creation of Gothic from the unpromising material of life: does her life "really" fall into these shapes? Is the female
hero nudging it along? Or is her interpetive grid—narrative ideology—so powerful that it produces a Gothic script from plain old
middle-class life in twentieth-century Toronto? Even the title, *Lady
Oracle,* can be split between the compliant heroine and the myth-
piercing seer, between complicity and critique. Like a Gail Godwin
hero, a cover-illustrator for mass-market Gothics, Louisa/Joan keeps
"one foot in the door of the Unknown, the other still holding open its
place in the book of Old Plots."[51]
    Jean Rhys's concerns for the social place of women and for a cri-
tique of narrative as ideology are given dramatic shape in her final *Wide Sargasso*
novel, *Wide Sargasso Sea.*[52] Here Rhys revises Charlotte Brontë's *Jane* *Sea*
Eyre, taking the first Mrs. Rochester, Antoinette ("Bertha") Mason, as
a representative of the muted side of Brontë's story. By turning a
classic nineteenth-century novel inside out and giving its voiceless
character an explanatory story, Rhys has constructed a critical exami-

nation of romantic thralldom and marital power—internalized and external institutions that support gender inequality.

Rhys's own social background, a white woman in a black society, may have drawn her to consider the history of the heiress from the West Indies, whom we assume and accept as a figure of horror at the center of *Jane Eyre*. An interpretation from a nondominant perspective, from the eye of the other, the object, the outcast, breaks narrative *doxa* and opens a firmly closed text to heterodox questions. By the levels of passivity and fear developed in her as a child, Antoinette was readied for a savior and for a thralldom both financial and emotional. Rochester, a bourgeois male formed in a nexus of money and calculation, is making a future profit directly from the capital she provides. Antoinette's childhood history of isolation and rejection has contributed to a blank vulnerability (typical of other Rhys heroines), which brings her, devoid of a center, to a marriage without marriage contract, settlement, or legal protection. Deprived of her money, then rejected for her richly emerging sensuality, which Rochester associates with the lushness of the island and with blacks, Antoinette is driven, and then declared, mad, taken to England, and imprisoned by Rochester in an attic room, whence to haunt Brontë's novel. As Antoinette—a white and privileged but vulnerable child—she is traumatized by fire and a black uprising; as Bertha—a dark and enraged woman—she revolts by an act of destruction that mimics the arson of colonial uprisings.[53]

By a maneuver of encirclement (entering the story before) and leverage (prying the story open), Rhys ruptures *Jane Eyre*. She returns us to a framework far from the triumphant individualism of the character Jane Eyre by concentrating on the colonial situation. Through the realistic melodrama of black-white relations, Rhys allows us to see that the "personalities" of colonizer and colonized are transformed and fixed by their complementary functions.[54] So it is with the relations between the sexes in a nineteenth-century arranged marriage; a woman from a colony is a trope for the woman as a colony. *Wide Sargasso Sea* states that the closures and precisions of any tale are purchased at the expense of the muted, even unspoken narrative, which writing beyond the ending will release. ("Remember," Doris Lessing reminds us, "that for all the books we have in print, there are as many that have never reached print, have never been written down.")[55]

■

CHAPTER FOUR

"Amor Vin——":

Modifications

of Romance

in Woolf

The change which has turned the English woman from a nondescript influence, fluctuating and vague, to a voter, a wage-earner, a responsible citizen, has given her both in her life and in her art a turn toward the impersonal. Her relations now are not only emotional; they are intellectual, they are political. The old system which condemned her to squint askance at things through the eyes or through the interests of husband or brother, has given place to the direct and practical interests of one who must act for herself, and not merely influence the acts of others. Hence her attention is being directed away from the personal centre which engaged it exclusively in the past to the impersonal, and her novels naturally become more critical of society, and less analytical of individual lives.

VIRGINIA WOOLF
"Women and Fiction" (1929)

The psychological novelist has been too prone to limit psychology to the psychology of personal intercourse; we long sometimes to escape from the incessant, the remorseless analysis of falling into love and falling out of love, of what Tom feels for Judith and Judith does or does not altogether feel for Tom. We long for some more impersonal relationship. We long for ideas, for dreams, for imaginations, for poetry.

VIRGINIA WOOLF
"The Narrow Bridge of Art" (1927)

Virginia Woolf's career as a novelist makes two great lines crossing on one major problem—the formation of narrative strategies that express a more "impersonal" woman's identity by rupturing the sentences and sequences of romance. Her first two novels both draw on the traditional concerns of love plots—the production of newly joined heterosexual couples—and of quest plots—the *Bildung* of the protagonist. That is, in *The Voyage Out* (1915) and *Night and Day* (1919) Woolf considers the endings of betrothal and death.[1] After the first two novels, heterosexual romance is displaced from a controlling and privileged position in her work.[2] It will never again appear as the unique center of narrative concern; it will never again appear assumed or unquestioned. *Mrs. Dalloway* (1925) offers thematic and structural debates about romantic love. *To the Lighthouse* (1927) both idealizes and criticizes romance. *Orlando* (1928) and *Flush* (1933) close the issue of heterosexual love by drastic changes in its definition.

In her first set of novels, then, Woolf breaks the sentence by an imbedded critique of heterosexual romantic love, while in the second set, Woolf ruptures the sequence by inventing a narrative center to express postromantic relations among characters. The novels along the second major line of Woolf's career—*The Years* (1937) and *Between the Acts* (1941) as well as *The Waves* (1931)—ask the fundamental ideological and structural question, What desires will empower stories and characters if a writer does not depend on the emphases and motivations of romance? Here Woolf displaces the emotional aura and structural weight of individual quest and of hero and heroine into a communal protagonist. This protagonist—a large family, a group of friends, an audience, containing many close bonds and, not incidentally, including members of all ages and sexual persuasions— creates a structure in which couples, individuals, walls between public and private, polarized sexes, and closures in family houses are subject to strong oppositional formations. In general, Woolf separates *eros* from any forced or conventional bonds, especially such institutions as heterosexuality and marriage.

The possibility for a critique of romance began to be formulated in the earliest days of Bloomsbury, when Woolf felt an enormous liberation at being released from feminine white dresses and the façade of virginal proprieties and correct chatter, all at the service of "love and marriage." This liberation occurred because a number of the "Bloomsberries" were, as Woolf persists in calling them, "buggers"; it was not heterosexual romance and sexuality that fired their imaginations. And their stance on women, for a time refreshingly neutral, was also antimasculinist on principle.[3] So the effect of homosexuality in Bloomsbury contributed to Woolf's developing critique of romance, as did, on the other side, what she was rejecting: George Duckworth, keeper of the heterosexual flame, conventional womanhood, and the socially sanctioned "hoops" of romance and advancement. The gift of tolerance, of seeing the many fair erotic possibilities that homosexual relations called forth, thus made a contribution to Woolf's narrative choice not to give priority to heterosexual romance in her oeuvre as a whole.

This is in keeping with Woolf's sense of a change in the status of women, and thus of fiction. Newly achieved legal, economic, and political rights unfixed the modern woman from the limited "personal centre" of "husband and brother." Thus the "incessant and

change in status of ♀ + thus of fiction

remorseless analysis of falling into love and falling out of love" gives
way to a fiction "more critical of society" precisely because it is more
critical of romance.[4] Woolf's major project as a novelist—writing beyond this ending—joins her work to that of other twentieth-century
women writers who dispute the social, emotional, and narrative
charisma of romance.[5]

*from romance
to social
criticism*

In *The Voyage Out*, with Rachel Vinrace, Woolf experiments by placing a mid-nineteenth-century girl heroine in a twentieth-century context. Rachel had begun her quest under the guardianship of characters with banal and limited notions about the education and place of
women. In contrast, her aunt Helen Ambrose and her new fiancé,
Terence Hewet, are relatively free from conventional ideas of
women's duties and interests. "If [women] were properly educated I
don't see why they shouldn't be much the same as men—as satisfactory I mean; though, of course, very different."[6]

Terence and Helen agree that women should have the benefit of
free, uncensored, wide-ranging talk with men, so that men would
stimulate and challenge women as they do each other. This assumption about men as a standard reflects Woolf's early idealization and
envy of various schools for English manhood. Helen's plan for
Rachel's education, which extends fraternal male bonding to a genial
brother-and-sisterhood, attempts, in a flash, to provide a solution to
the woman question so commonsensical as to be almost flatfooted:
men should treat women as they treat men. While Helen and Terence,
as well as the acerbic Hirst, repeatedly ponder the gap of sexual
difference brought about by differential socialization, they feel that
the disability that unmarried women suffer from their prudish and
confined upbringing is fairly easily overcome. By means of this novel
and Rachel's fate, Woolf confronted herself with the impossibility of
straightforward "good faith" solutions to gender asymmetry.

The jungle voyage to a tribal settlement constitutes the central
quest of the novel. That journey reverses the relationship of art and
nature upon which these cultivated people depend; it tampers with
the ethnocentrism that they assume. And on that journey, Terence
and Rachel grow more equal and fall in love. Love at that point is
consonant with quest and seems experimental, born out of these
other critical reversals. Their constant antiphonal echoes of each
other ("We sat upon the ground" and "This is happiness") are egali-
tarian as well as tender. One "You love me?" receives "And you?" "Am
I in love—is this being in love—are we to marry each other?" (*VO*,
282, 283, 280, 281). The persistently interrogative mode is not exclusive to the lovers; the central characters use this ethical and rhetorical
tactic to show that discourse is opened, judgment is suspended, and

fixed answers are eroded. Yet a lovers' dialogue carried out in questions insists on instability and insubstantiality.

The largest question in *The Voyage Out* is asked by its largest narrative fact: the death of Rachel. Woolf shatters conventional hopes for an ending in marriage by introducing not only the dangerous illness of the main character, but a whole new set of emotional pressures, from the alienating hallucinations of Rachel to the paralysis of caretakers faced with doctors. The reader is obliged to confront the issue of death in its most "aimless and cruel" form, the sudden and gratuitous death of a young person, deaths such as Woolf herself endured in the years before her first novel was written.[7]

Using death as "the lash of a random unheeding flail" creates a dramatic rupture with many of the narrative conventions Woolf evoked.[8] Woolf may have meant this closure to be almost unassimilated and unassimilable, placing death at a tangent from all other movements and relationships so that it will never be causally tied to events, but rather will be a thing entirely apart, from another realm of experience. Thus one reads the death of Rachel as the aggressive act of the author against the hegemonic power of those narrative conventions with which the novel is, in fact, engaged—love and quest—a way of interrupting the plot "tyranny," that avalanche of events moving to "satisfactory solutions."[9] The flail of the author on her novel, the rupture with conventions of love, draws on the gratuitous flail of life on the author, the rupture of normalcy represented by death. Yet Woolf did not have unwobbling control of her critique, because she was only beginning to suspect what she would later enunciate—the relation between sentence, plot, narrative line, and gender-based ideologies and values.

At the same time, all the characters do seem to "earn" the death of Rachel Vinrace. Her death can be connected to a dialectic of rage and repression, critique and its absence, in which all parties are complicit. Rachel has had an education in chastity and avoidance such that any kind of sexual awakening is repulsive and destabilizing. When her first sexual event is the passionate kiss of Richard Dalloway, given as a response to her yearning for education, several levels of trauma and violation are set in motion. The reader feels how Rachel's education has, with a depressing swiftness, been reduced to sexuality. If this reduction—whimsical for Richard, devastating for Rachel—can be severely regarded, so too can the character's response. Because Rachel has no other context in which to put his kiss, and because she feels no other identity but the feminine and passive, it takes on the nightmare proportions of sexual trauma.

In fact, her response is a miniature version of her development in the whole book. First "life seemed to hold infinite possibilities she had never guessed at," for "something wonderful had happened," exactly like her feelings about love for Terence. She then experiences a "pallor" parallel to her whiteness in illness, and a hallucinatory dream of a deformed man, like her later dream of deformed women. Finally, the statement "still and cold as death she lay, not daring to move. . . ." strikingly prefigures her end (*VO*, 76–77).

Even if this is, as Phyllis Rose acutely suggests, a biographical reconstruction of Woolf's own associations, the "yoking of the ideas of death and sex," it may constitute Woolf's cultural criticism as well, attacking that noneducation of women, which makes Rachel so unprepared for life and sexuality that she can only punish her passion with debility and self-annihilation.[10] That mid-nineteenth century ideology of purity, by controlling her "education," has determined her fate.

If she is forced by Dalloway and beset by an internalized ideology, Rachel is also coerced by her "good" mentors. Terence is a character whose opinions on women allow the first expression of Woolf's own; the male persona gives the author permission and cover. Yet when he pursues feminist matters, he receives no response from Rachel but astonished and silent evasion. Terence is sure that Rachel should be concerned with women's status. Rachel, however, just wishes he would quit bothering her. "She was only weary of him and his questions" (*VO*, 215). At no other point but this are questions so blatantly rejected. Yet at no other point does the reader feel Rachel more talked at than in Terence's speeches to Rachel on women's potential and their anger. To break even sympathetic male sentences, women must become speaking subjects of their own discourses.

Rachel's death may accordingly be interpreted as the death of a person who evaded constitutive components of her *Bildung*—rage at her status as a woman, and the seizing of speech for herself. We must consider that Woolf meted out death as Rachel's punishment for her being insufficiently critical and vocal.[11] This death differs precisely from the tragic punishment and affirmation of Maggie Tulliver in *The Mill on the Floss,* to whom death is allotted—the social machinery of the mill dragging her under the flood—because she is too intuitively critical. For the uncritical Rachel, Woolf builds the same ending as in the Victorian novel mixing quest and love, but for an exactly opposite reason.

Woolf continues her critique of the mentors. Terence and Helen—but not Rachel—assume that marriage is the absolute and necessary outcome of the relationship. The first proposal of marriage between Terence and Rachel occurs in the absence of the bride-to-be, and thus, no matter how subtle his discussion, it lacks her informed consent. His meditations put marriage on the defensive, cataloguing the compromises it entails for women, the kinds of dishonesty that can occur when a woman must live in smooth conjunction with a person who has more social power than she.[12] As he imagines it, marriage is precisely opposed to the basic ethics of the book: frankness, honesty, questioning. Yet Terence does not take the logical, if socially drastic, step of separating love and companionship from marriage. Instead, he pursues the question of marriage and concludes that to marry Rachel would be to have a talisman of freedom. At that moment, Rachel passes from being "real" to Terence to being a symbol of Terence's desire for a controlling magnanimity.

It is by no means certain that Rachel is as swift to join love with marriage as is Terence. "Marriage?" is Rachel's repeated query to the ending that all would write for her plot. Without answering, Terence and Helen speak of "love and then of marriage" and mark their excitement with a kiss, that quasi-parental embrace over the "speechless," passive, babylike body of Rachel (VO, 281, 284, 283). This heavily revised scene has a rather scandalous aura. Learning of their love, Helen harasses Rachel, rolling her in the jungle grass, teasingly but with a good deal of lurid menace. Rachel falls to the ground in an ambiguously rendered excess of erotic violence between women.

Further, at the very moment of heterosexual embrace, Rachel is excluded. Her mentors have agreed on her proper ending. Rachel's death may then be the result of her desire to escape being written into the marriage plot in this cavalier and violent fashion. That Woolf intended something like this sense is clearer when a discarded version of the expedition scene is contrasted with this one. In the Earlier Typescript, it is Rachel who announces her impending marriage to Helen; Woolf once wanted us to feel that Rachel had consented. But not now. The version of this scene we now read ends with the embrace of mentors over the exhausted form of the bride-to-be. In this version, marriage is announced to the powerless Rachel.[13] As they congratulate themselves that their plan for Rachel's education has worked—the Victorian waif is engaged—this moment recapitulates the convention of nineteenth-century fiction in which the quest plot turns into the marriage plot as the energies and potential of the female hero are contained. At this moment romance prefigures death. Death becomes Rachel's protest against marriage and sexuality as her sole aim, against the change of a *Bildung* into a marriage plot, which powerful figures who resemble Woolf's family demand.

For the main characters in this novel are evidently displaced and realigned members of her own family: Terence resembles her brother

Thoby, the widowed Jack Hills with his fraternal interest, and her new husband, Leonard Woolf. Helen is a version of her sister Vanessa as well as their dead mother. Richard Dalloway mixes the sexual interests—even abuse—of Gerald and George Duckworth. Rachel is an amalgam at least of Stella Duckworth and Woolf herself. The novelist has brewed herself a potent draught with this mixture of desire, shame, guilt, blocked grief, incest fantasies, ambivalence to marriage, and admissions of anger and despair about women's status. It is therefore likely—this is a first novel after all—that Woolf would want an escape hatch from the culpability that she had, with difficulty, self-doubt, and mental anguish, assigned to those closest to her.

Woolf accomplishes this by the evocation of spiritual or mystical love, which she puts into the mouth of the only character unoccupied with the toils of complicity that link the central triangle. The otherwise carping St. John Hirst, who earlier in the novel could barely credit female intelligence, undergoes a gratifying, though amazing, conversion to the possibility of equality between men and women in spiritual love. The nonsexual, nonsocial, and impersonal character of that love makes an appealing compromise for the author herself, who apparently cannot decide whether the love of Rachel and Terence is a good or bad thing, whether it is manipulation or equality, whether Rachel's death occurs because she is a victim of her nineteenth-century socialization or because she is resisting being the victim of the "Victorian" ending in marriage that has been reserved for her.

Through St. John, a nimbus from Platonized Christianity comes to settle over the love plot, gives it a peace which passeth understanding, and creates the final ambiguity. One may credit the "peace" and "happiness" that Terence feels as Rachel dies as their only, poignant, and lush consummation, "the union which had been impossible while they lived" (*VO*, 353). Or one may find repulsive the necrophiliac possession of Rachel in a death-marriage about which she herself is finally puzzled: her last look being "fatigue or perplexity."

The death of Rachel expresses Woolf's oscillation between criticism and ambivalence: the criticism of narrative conventions, the shielding of masked family members among her *dramatis personae*. Insofar as Woolf metes out what her characters are owed, Rachel's death announces that they have not investigated deeply enough what they claim to question: marriage, love, gender polarization, the formation of women. Death is the vehicle for affirming the necessity for critique of the conventions governing women and narrative structures, not, as in nineteenth-century fiction, a tragic price exacted for debate and social difference.

From Katherine Mansfield on, readers of *Night and Day* have noted—sometimes in disgusted or apologetic tones—the plain fact that Woolf's second novel carefully recapitulates the "tradition of the English novel." Woolf's purpose was not uncritical homage to that tradition ("drawing from the cast—an academic exercise," she said later); nor was it only the testing of her skills ("to see if she could achieve a perfectly orthodox and conventional novel," Bell explains).[14] Like her first novel, *Night and Day* engages critically with nineteenth-century narratives of love, marriage, and quest epitomized here by the works on which Woolf evidently draws: *Emma, Pride and Prejudice,* and *Jane Eyre.* This book is a *tour de force,* simultaneously evoking a comic wedlock plot of the Austen variety and the melodramatic and hierogamic quest plot perfected by Charlotte Brontë. *Night and Day* takes up two heroes from two misallied couples, the primal stuff of the comic love plot, yet asserts that they can only affirm mutual passion because of quest. Thus love and quest are joined at narrative resolution, rather than being separated as in the nineteenth-century paradigm.

Katherine has enforced a dishonest but compelling separation in her personality between what she most deeply desires—the vocation of mathematician—and her social role of accommodating daughter and erstwhile fiancée. She has been engaged to William Rodney, a charming boy of letters. Ralph Denham, lawyer and upstart, begins the book involved with Mary Datchet, another serious, intense, independent young woman. But both Katherine and Ralph are embarked on passionless, loveless matches because they are not able to define vocation and bring day in alliance with night, comedy with quest, practicality with fantasy.[15] The night side of each involves their recognition of hidden vocations: the dogged lawyer is really a writer, the dutiful daughter, a mathematician. They yearn toward these vocations; acknowledging their desires for true work frees them for true romance.

Throughout the novel, Ralph visualizes Katherine as something connected "with vague feelings of romance and adventure such as she inspired"; moreover, this will translate into the good news for the intelligentsia that he has quit his job and will write a book (*N&D,* 131). In a precisely parallel way, Katherine, while making preparations for "a perfectly loveless marriage," maintains an interior fantasy life replete with situations from high romance and quest: "the presence of love," the "superb catastrophe in which everything was surrendered," and the possibility of riding off on an adventure with a "magnanimous hero" continually linked to Ralph (*N&D,* 107, 197). By making vocation and love draw equally on a yearning for the ideal, Woolf allows quest and love plots to be united.

This achievement is visible in the love tokens the characters share at the end, when each reads certain secret papers of the other. By the intensity of these tokens, Woolf also confesses that she accepts the narrative emphasis always implicit in heterosexual romance, of the specialness and aura of the central couple. She has not yet moved to the alteration of these established values in her formal and emotional structures.

Woolf balances these plots, and allusions to both love and quest narrative abound. The unity of the Hillbery family banquet, the poignant huff of the patriarch bested, and the mismatched lovers reassigned by an intervening magic (Mozart and Shakespeare as well as Austen in the background) are all motifs from a comic tradition.[16] The dark walks through London, the lovers' fiery excitement, their mutual thralldom, their striving souls, and a visionary daemonic presence, the mother, are motifs from quest and closely related hierogamic romance.[17] The final embrace of Katherine and Ralph balances night and day motifs, for it occurs on the threshold between the blazing light of the family house and the enchanting darkness of London, with its ideals of knowledge and achievement. They kiss on the limen between love and quest.[18]

The Austenian focus of the love plot on choice, involving an acute reading of social cues, motives, and character, is reiterated in Woolf's emphasis on honesty. In *Night and Day,* honesty is a torch passed from hand to hand; truths are spoken at considerable cost, after inner struggles to hide, repress, and prevaricate. Here, as in Austen, gnosis precedes eros, in the scene where Mary struggles with her jealousy to tell Katherine that Ralph really loves her, in the scene where Katherine informs William that he is probably in love with convenient and charming Cassandra, and in the scene where Ralph, still under the impression that Katherine is engaged, makes a passionate declaration to her. Jane Austen is matched with *Jane Eyre,* itself one of the more explosive mixtures of narrative discourses in English fiction, a hierogamic love plot based on a personal pilgrimage.

About all this, Woolf is soon dubious. As she said, rather tersely, describing Austen's plots, "A suitable marriage is, after all, the upshot of all this coming together and drawing apart. A world which so often ends in a suitable marriage is not a world to wring one's hands over."[19] Similarly, in an earlier essay on *Jane Eyre,* Woolf assumed a tone of high-handed dismissiveness that hardly accounts for the work. "Always to be a governess and always to be in love is a serious limitation in a world which is full, after all, of people who are neither one nor the other. . . ."[20] Her remarks on her sources gain credibility, if not caritas, in the context of this argument: that Woolf proposed and then struggled to achieve a way of thinking about narratives with women that was not synonymous with thinking about romance for women.

For by the time she had completed *The Voyage Out* and *Night and Day,* Woolf had also begun a critique of her own procedures and a program for another kind of fiction, in the essay "Modern Fiction" (1919). The release from the love plot and from related conventions of production is announced in this manifesto against the well-made novel. "Love interest," the thirty-two chapters, the tyranny of plot, the choices for emphasis, "catastrophe in the accepted style," conventional generic distinctions, and even the solidity of the human soul are alike questioned and challenged.[21] She addresses these conventions using the metaphor of thralldom, as if the expected narrative demands were like a romantic involvement or a spell from which one had to be released, a compelling picture of the woman writer half in love with conventions that she resisted. This tyrant of narrative, as Phyllis Rose observes, has a specifically patriarchal cast.[22] To criticize plots—especially the love-interest plot—was to criticize the cultural and narrative forces that produced women.

The critical rejections that Woolf began in "Modern Fiction" are elaborated a decade later in "Women and Fiction" (1929). Here the sentence, the plot, narrative convention, and subject matter will alike be subjected to revisionary scrutiny by the female novelist, because these narrative forms carry an ideological and interpretive freight about gender. The prevalent values of fiction are androcentric, devaluing or rendering minor and suspect female experiences.

> . . . as men are the arbiters of that [social] convention, as they have established an order of values in life, so too, since fiction is largely based on life, these values prevail there also to a very great extent.
>
> It is probable, however, that both in life and in art, the values of a woman are not the values of a man. Thus, when a woman comes to write a novel, she will find that she is perpetually wishing to alter the established values—to make serious what appears insignificant to a man, and trivial what is to him important.[23]

Therefore, trying to make fiction talk about women and their concerns, especially when a woman is the speaking subject, may necessarily lead to a critical transformation of narrative structures.

What allowed Woolf this knowledge of contradictions between dominant and nondominant interpretations of a reality, the revaluing of emphases of the trivial and the serious? One considerable source for this insight was Woolf's early experience of Leslie Stephen's unreasonable demands on his family, incidents not believed by his official biographer.[24] The division between gender and generational interests at the heart of the family and the repression of evidence offered by women marked and defined the presumably neutral, value-free truth that was told. This contradiction between the official and unofficial and the repression of one of the sides of the contradiction helped to form Woolf's project: to examine the lives of the obscure, the stories of the nondominant, the biographies of the quirky (a project accomplished in part in her *Common Reader* essays), and to examine them precisely for differences in value and emphasis. The revelation that "story" was really a product of dominant ideology and interests, and that nondominant views could nonetheless be told in oppositional narrative, helped to structure Woolf's career.

It is not surprising that these issues took shape as a debate on sexualities and on constituted authorities. Among the other structural and emotional changes that distinguish Woolf's writing after "Modern Fiction" and *Night and Day* in 1919, heterosexual romance is displaced from a privileged position in her novels and subjected to much questioning. In *Mrs. Dalloway,* the kinship of a Tory hostess and her "double" Septimus makes Woolf's structural coup, the creation of an unsexual, nonromantic central couple. "The design," she said, "is so queer and so masterful," for its emotional center is the psychic twinship between a man and a woman who never even meet, yet who share a knowledge of coercion and its antonym, ineffable "life."[25] Woolf sets their closeness against Clarissa's other relations with men: with Peter Walsh, who had courted her, and with Richard Dalloway, who married her. The design is queer because neither of the men to whom she is bound in a social, legal, or romantic sense is the man to whom she is bound in the psychic sense. This unprecedented treatment of both marriage and sexual desire displaces heterosexual love from the narrative center. Indeed, Woolf compares the prescriptive treatments for insanity that drive Septimus to suicide with the toils of romantic love in which Clarissa has been caught, constructing an attack in the strongest terms by comparing the passionate coercions of love and the desire to convert, dominate, and compel. Set in contrast are, variously, a valuable irradiating lesbian attachment between Clarissa and Sally (in the past only) and a similarly valued set of connections among people at Clarissa's party.

There are manifold subtly drawn parallels between Clarissa and Septimus, which make their kinship eerily plausible, but the most important is an attitude toward domination, which, Woolf makes quite plain, the characters share with their author.

> Suppose he [Septimus] had had the passion [for rapture], and had gone
> to Sir William Bradshaw, a great doctor yet to her obscurely evil, without

sex or lust, extremely polite to women, but capable of some indescrib-
able outrage—forcing your soul, that was it—if this young man had
gone to him, and Sir William had impressed him, like that, with his
power, might he not then have said (indeed she felt it now), Life is made
intolerable; they make life intolerable, men like that? (*MD*, 281)

Clarissa interprets the suicide as a symbolic rejection of rapacious
power relations. This is his act of resistance to authority, "holding his
treasure"—visionary ecstatic terror—intact when the forces of
medicine and law are about to possess him (*MD*, 281). Significantly,
her experience with forms of romantic and ideological thralldom allows Clarissa to make this empathetic analysis of Septimus's aims. The
allusion to rape is a point of contact between sexual and mental coercion.[26] Woolf prefigures *Three Guineas* by depicting a continuum between the political and social institutions of imperialism and religion
and the imposition of will in personal relations: all versions of that
instrumentalism which "offers help, but desires power" (*MD*, 151).
The fact that Woolf links romantic love to social and political compul-
sions means that she is no longer treating romance uncritically, as she
did in *Night and Day*, but linking it to a general analysis of power and
domination.

    "Love and religion," represented respectively by Peter Walsh and
Miss Kilman, are "the cruelest things in the world, [Clarissa] thought,
seeing them clumsy, hot, domineering, hypocritical, eavesdropping,
jealous, infinitely cruel and unscrupulous . . ." because they destroyed
"the privacy of the soul" (*MD*, 191, 192). The desire of Miss Kilman
for the Dalloway daughter, Elizabeth, is one-sided, intolerant, and
obsessive. Her sexual and relational frustrations lead her to almost
daft behavior. Likewise, in the early courtship of Clarissa, Peter was
more sexually and personally demanding of her than was Dalloway.
The knife is his sign, as the sugary cake, greedily coveted, is Miss
Kilman's. Clarissa's marriage was a resistance to his possessive and
jealous love, his sexual and psychic colonization. Peter's demand for
total possession, his disrespect for her privacy or aloofness would
have been "intolerable" (*MD*, 10). She resists any overinvestment in
that romantic love epitomized by the scenes of pursuit, fantasy, and
capture in which Peter still relentlessly engages. Such refusal is on the
one hand prudish, yet on the other, it is a choice of privacy, whose cost
is asexuality. The mutual distance and independence possible in the
Dalloway marriage and Dalloway's cool pleasantness are just saved
from the vapid because they preserve the self from emotional destruction.

    Clarissa and Septimus both experience same-sex love and passionate affection. In Septimus's case, his mourning is incomplete and his war trauma rampant because the doctors protect him from recognizing grief for a dead male companion. Similarly, Peter interrupts Clarissa's wave of joy at being kissed by Sally Seton during that courtship summer. The "infinitely precious" joy of that relationship is summed up at the moment of the kiss; there is no Miss Kilman–style aftermath of anger and frustrated desire, no Peter Walsh's "granite" of jealousy and hostility, not even the "catastrophe" (narrative climax—and damage) of marriage (*MD*, 53, 50). The kiss is able to be "the most exquisite moment of [Clarissa's] whole life," since it is not expressed in a permanent tie, nor does it suffer the temptations of power (*MD*, 52).

In this way Woolf suggests that love of women might mediate between two goods—joyous desire and tolerant privacy (*MD*, 47–48).[27] When Woolf tells of "the purity, the integrity" of Clarissa's feeling for Sally, these words express sterling values (*MD*, 50). But "this falling in love with women," the lesbian element in *Mrs. Dalloway*, has a double position in the text. The bond Clarissa and Sally make is, like the party, a network of pleasurable connections; the bond between Miss Kilman and Elizabeth is, like heterosexual thralldom, another form of bullying. If lesbianism is a nondominant form of the erotic, Woolf valorizes it; if it is yet another version of power and dominance, she satirizes it.

"Being part" of each other in a network of intense and pleasurable but unpossessive connection, in which ego is "invisible," is the counterforce, just like the kiss, to all the possessive demands criticized by the text, whether romance or power (*MD*, 12, 14). The party suggests communal values that transcend the egos of any single person: risking "one's one little point of view" for that "immeasurable delight" (*MD*, 255, 282). Instead of manipulating, the parties "create," instead of separating, they "combine"; instead of being assertions of one's class and one's power, they have (so Woolf says) no ulterior purpose but are simply "an offering for the sake of offering, perhaps" (*MD*, 185). Thus the party is a rescripting of lesbian desire, and as well solves the issue of romance. The party is like joyous tolerant desire between women extended to a wider community. One climax of the party comes when Clarissa sees her double, a woman, at the window; another comes when she can make Peter, the most pertinacious pursuer of heterosexual romance, see her simply as she is, without the overlay of jealous possessiveness. So Peter, at the very end, feels something of what Sally and Clarissa had felt long ago ("What is this terror? What is this ecstasy?" *MD* 296). Heterosexual romance has been processed and converted into what one might call neo-lesbian joy.

And the character Mrs. Dalloway proves herself a switching station for sexualities, bringing all sorts of hot individual desires into humane networks.[28]

In her party, the convergence of multiple centers of sociability and attraction, the many paths pleasurably crossing, the mutual tolerance and the joining of the characters are convincing because they have been stylistically affirmed from the beginning of the novel. The "tunnelling process" that Woolf called one of her great technical discoveries shows each character in an inner alliance with others; the similar ways each will think about leaves, life, and death join them through this "tunnel" or cave behind the surface of manners on which they many never meet or talk seriously.[29] The tunnelling process may also mute critique by showing that connections of the heart can occur despite differences in gender and status. In any event, the technique extends the aura of desire, connection, and loyalty, once confined to a couple in formation, to a widening network of characters, and is another way, added to the nonsexual central couple and the use of lesbian desire, to pose the critique of the convention of romance.

To the Lighthouse is able in a different way to express that yearning for a female bond which emerges in the Clarissa-Sally materials, by fashioning a story that displaces the heterosexual love plot in favor of the parent-child tie, a bisexual oscillation between mother and father. The yearning love of Lily for Mrs. Ramsay, which creates vision, the moment of making peace with Mr. Ramsay, which creates sociability, are both formative events, of greater importance than the traces of heterosexual courtship plots in this novel. In the first section of *To the Lighthouse,* community (the dinner party) depends extensively on couples and the bait of romance: Minta's golden haze of love helps the emotional entanglements of family life; Lily reluctantly attends to the young man whom she has been assigned, after rich meditations on refusal and rebellion. But Woolf supplants the formation of a new couple as a plot center. Lily is deliberately fabricated to avoid the romantic involvements that are proposed, and Mrs. Ramsay is explicitly criticized for proposing them. However, the book offers detailed consideration of an old couple who are always in the process of reformation and reaffirmation. Yet this couple is put in the context of many other networks, communities, and ties, involving, *inter alia*, "geniality, sisterhood, motherhood, brotherhood" (*MD,* 209). And by the death of Mrs. Ramsay at midbook, the affirmation of the romantic, polarized couple is put definitively in the past. In the third section, community and selfhood must be negotiated in the absence of the promise of couple love that once mediated them. This occurs through a concerted use of the preoedipal materials of female identity, to

dissolve the purely romantic telos of the oedipal drama. The loop in
the Lily plot (a painting untouched for ten years is begun again and
finished) expresses the peculiarities of female quest, with its loop back
through the family and the psychic stage of preoedipal attachment.[30]

In *Mrs. Dalloway* and then in *To the Lighthouse,* Woolf has expanded
the story of romance emotionally and structurally by posing the
preoedipal alternatives, lesbian bonding and the mother-child dyad,
to rupture the cultural hegemony of the love plot. *Orlando* was inspired by an energizing erotic attachment, and Woolf apparently began it to deal openly with lesbianism.[31] One can interpret the drama of
androgyny that remains as a socially compelled evasion of what Woolf
really wanted to address, or as another critical approach to heterosexuality that ruptures the couple by elaborating the sexes. *Orlando* shows
that one can have the erotic without the intense and repressive form
of gender polarization upon which the romance plot has traditionally
been built. As well, the manifold sexualities of the characters construct a cunning attack on contemporaneous theories that denigrate
homosexuality.

Orlando is at least a parodic biography, a female history of Britain, a
feminist apologue—an insouciant break with conventional norms surrounding gender, sexual identity, and narrative.[32] In this work, the
Ages of England have become the Ages of Woman, scrutinized with
two questions in mind: whether the protagonist can undertake work
and whether she can enjoy love. Until the present, these satisfactions
are divided, and love is separated from quest. The hero is originally a
man; then in a masquelike event occurring, neatly, after an anticolonial and anti-British uprising, she becomes a woman. With late adolescence, the "he"—a liberated, sensuous child—becomes the skirted,
corseted "she"—a change that shocks most women and that Orlando
herself views with anger, curiosity, and some calculation. During her
early womanhood, she mulls her spent boyish powers and her potential feminine gains, like a naïve visitor to the strange land of femaleness: a satiric voyage in an eighteenth-century mode. This section presents her swift assimilation of the rules concerning sex and
gender in her society; since they have to be learned all at once, their
social, not biological, character is clear. After a grimly educative phase
as a worshipper of a great male poet, she enters the monogamous
stolidity of marriage in the Victorian era. This is the normal closure to
a plot for a woman in narrative.

This part of *Orlando* begins with the woman's mortifying consciousness, associated with the dampening values of Victorian England, that
she is not married. Even her attempt to replace this wallowing yearning with a brisk turn to her vocation proves futile, for she can write

insipid verses only. Orlando is thus obliged to put her calling aside
and give into a craving for a wedding ring. Her "submission" to the
"spirit of the age" is paraded in rambunctious clichés of romance: "It
would be a comfort, she felt, to lean; to sit down; yes, to lie down;
never, never, never to get up again" (O, 160)—a passage that captures
the parallel closures of "couverture" in marriage and in death. This
sentiment passes to another sublime fancy, reversed but resonant in
Charlotte Brontë, and busily at work in Harlequin romances today:

> . . . she saw a man on horseback. He started. The horse stopped.
> "Madam," the man cried, leaping to the ground, "you're hurt!"
> "I'm dead, Sir!" she replied.
>
> A few minutes later, they became engaged. (O, 163)

Yet by a stroke of authorial authority, Orlando has found a man
who is a woman, just as she is a man. The institution of marriage,
which demands for a fact the legal and social fiction of strict gender
polarization (as the lawsuit establishing Orlando's sex reveals), is still
flexible enough to accommodate this ambisexual couple.[33] The marriage ceremony, which caps the Victorian era and forms a baroque
and assertive closure before the actual terminus of the book, combines middle-class propriety and romantic critique, as in the clap of
thunder that obliterates the word "Obey."

What occurs after that culturally plausible ending is Woolf's swift
panorama of the kinds of fiction and values that are now possible,
writing beyond the ending. The Hemingway novel of adventure, the
Lawrence novel of sexuality are evoked and dismissed (O, 175–76).
The only kind of writing that might answer is just like Mrs. Dalloway:
tumbling and porous. Even the innermost threads of narrative, especially ideas of emphasis, have to be reconsidered, for "the truth is that
when we write of a woman, everything is out of place—culminations
and perorations; the accent never falls where it does with a man" (O,
204). Similarly, old mottos ("Amor Vin—," which had been Love Con-
quers All) are fractured and delegitimated. Sexual norms and narrative strategies are alike the unified subject of Woolf's critical address.

Because Orlando male and Orlando female are nearly the same, so
Orlando loving Shel means, at once, men loving men, women loving
women, and women and men loving each other. "Androgyny" is
Woolf's contemporaneous description for the unconventionally gendered characters. Male and female are not polarized, but fuse and
interpenetrate. Androgynous characters cannot be assigned stable
places in hierarchies of gender status, nor do they even adhere to
physical norms: Shel is both dainty and brawny, for example.

The social constructions called male and female represent, among other features, a logical dichotomy, the dualistic division of things into A and not-A. Although biologically, sex is a spectrum, in mental structures sex is perceived as polarized. Men are men, and women are not-men. This kind of thinking simplifies the world into norm and absence or lack thereof. In *Orlando,* Woolf plays with and erodes this powerful model for thought. The Orlando figure is both A and not-A, a logical contradiction, but a narratable prototype of constant heterogeneity.[34]

By proposing androgynous selves, Woolf wants to depict characters who have stepped beyond the sex-gender system as a whole, with its claims to natural, universal status, its manners and morals, its sexual polarization, its gender asymmetry, its devaluation of the female and the homosexual. As if offhandedly, she also undercuts the prime underpinnings of its epistemology.[35] Androgyny is a critical break with ideas about sex and gender, and with interrelated narrative ideas of causality and motivation, of the uniformity of character, of the stability of time, and of the academic rules of the genre: reserve and objectivity.

We also know that by inventing these androgynous characters, Woolf treats by implication the actual bisexuality and homosexuality of key people represented in this *roman à clef.*[36] So not only the domains of gender but also the questions of "deviant" sexual identity are posed by this text. Heterosexual romance and marriage are set aside precisely in being achieved; Orlando's "dexterous deference to the spirit of the age" has let her pass through a socially demanding "customshouse" with subversive "contraband" (*O,* 174). This strategy of overt conformity allows another kind of writing beyond the ending. Orlando is released into a space not only beyond narrative conventions but also beyond sexual norms. Lesbianism is the unspoken contraband desire that marriage liberates and that itself frees writing.[37] The love of women appears with some circumspection, intermingled with the androgynous, ambisexual marriage and the doubled gender identities of Orlando. So lesbianism not only answers but extends and completes the heterosexual couple.

Given the biographical and narrative designs that make lesbianism a rich part of the discourses in *Orlando,* it is no wonder that Woolf undertakes to correct the interpretation of homosexuality as illness, deviance, or aberration. Structurally, the book presents encoded counterstatements to two current theories, both known to Woolf and her circle, about the nature of the homosexual personality. One is the "trapped soul" theory quite current in the twenties, promulgated by Havelock Ellis and other influential psychologists, and corresponding to the feelings of division and repression with which homosexuals struggled because of social taboos. The "trapped soul" postulated that the sexual container and the thing contained were not congruent— that a person could have a man's spirit and a woman's body, for example, and that one part had to struggle for expression against the other.[38] This kind of thinking could only exacerbate the body-mind dualism also paradigmatic in Western thought. The erotic, zesty tone of Orlando as well as its generic multiplicity generates the counter-idea that mixed or mingled sexual identities could be exhilarating and pleasurable. As well as being a general answer to dichotomous think-ing, the androgynous combination answers that depressing notion of a mind-body split in a homosexual personality.

Orlando's perpetual youth—at any rate, her astonishingly slow rate of growth—seems to challenge Freud's idea of the progress of the psyche from bisexual dramas to heterosexual object choice. Any adult still experiencing homosexual desire is, in Freud's terms, suffering from "arrested development," a failed transition to the proper ob-ject.[39] What better way to depict, and mock, this "arrest" than by having someone who is a sixteen-year-old in the sixteenth century age only about two decades by 1928? And even more, Woolf makes Orlan-do's youthfulness be a positive statement of the gay, aggressive verve generated by this situation. The view of Orlando as a quintessentially healthy character, of course, responds to the satanic and lurid cultural images of the lesbian prominent in turn-of-the-century "decadent" works by both Swinburne and Baudelaire.[40] The health of erotic heterogeneity and ambisexuality makes a powerful cultural text. At the midnight stroke with which the book ends, undeclared revelations are implied: of love united with quest, of the end of sexual polariza-tion, of an erotic affirmation of sexualities, and of the critique of all institutions of gender, from unmanageable dresses to narrative con-ventions.

In Flush, the final novel of this line of Woolf's development, numerous narrative and emotional allusions to the nature of romance and thralldom cap the movement away from heterosexual romance. For in Flush, romance has been reduced—no dog lover would say demeaned, just tickled out of all countenance—by emerging in a pooch. With his jealousy, desire, dependence, sublimation, loyalty, and self-sacrifice, Flush's patterns of emotional involvement and levels of pain are closest to the romance plot of Night and Day in its early glowering moments of anger, self-doubt, and unspoken passion. The dog is completely enthralled with Elizabeth Barrett; when Robert Browning interrupts their mutual love, the dog is beside himself with jealousy.

The emotions proper to the relation between Mr. Browning and Miss Barrett, which are, of course, the febrile and exciting discovery of mutual love, are displaced by being seen through the point of view of a character whose intense sense of smell, hypersensitivity to all expected tidbits and privileges, and long, fluffy ears are his strongest points. Any attention the reader would have hoped to have given to one of the officially Great Love Stories of English Letters has been baffled by the same emotions of yearning and burning apparent in interspecies desire. In sum, a Woolfean shift of emphasis from person to canine has dramatically ended the readers' and the author's thralldom to the narrative authority of the heterosexual love plot. To achieve this critical stance has been her concerted project in the novels through the central portion of her career.

■

CHAPTER FIVE

Romantic Thralldom and "Subtle Genealogies" in H.D.

She herself is the writing.

H.D.,
Helen in Egypt
(1961)

H.D. forged her oeuvre from persistent and profound struggles with cultural and narrative questions concerning sexuality and gender. She turned constantly to a recurrent pattern of perplexing personal relations: thralldom to males in romantic and spiritual love. As we have seen, romantic thralldom enters many literary plots and conventions involving love and marriage, hero and heroine, quest and vocation. It is the Jane Fairfax plot in *Emma,* the seductive capture of Maggie Tulliver, the subject of Lyndall's struggles. Thralldom is one version of conventional heterosexual narrative scripts.

Romantic thralldom is an all-encompassing, totally defining love between apparent unequals. The lover has the power of conferring self-worth and purpose upon the loved one. Such love is possessive, and while those enthralled feel it completes and even transforms them, dependency rules. The eroticism of romantic love, born of this unequal relationship, may depend for its satisfaction upon dominance and submission. Thralldom insists upon the differences between the sexes or partners, encouraging a sense of mystery surrounding the motives and powers of the lover. Because it begins and ends in polarization, the sustenance of different spheres is both a cause and an effect of romantic love. Viewed from a critical, feminist perspective, the sense of completion or transformation that often accompanies such thralldom has the high price of obliteration and paralysis. This kind of love is socially learned, and it is central and recurrent in our culture.

Both H.D.'s identity and her oeuvre were visibly formed by the transpositions she exacted from the culturally and personally sustained ideology of romantic love. Female thralldom occurs with startling, even dismal frequency throughout H.D.'s published and unpublished works. She was especially vulnerable to the power of the "héros fatal," a man whom she saw as her spiritual similar, an artist, a healer, a psychic.[1] Again and again, this figure whom she conspired to create betrayed her; again and again she was reduced to fragments from which her identity had once more to be painfully reconstructed. She states, for instance, that one famous "héros"—D. H. Lawrence— "conditioned me to deception, loss, destruction," and that another, "Lord Howell," "was the perfected Image" of this former love.[2] The many elaborate attachments she sustained to men—often to poets (Richard Aldington, Ezra Pound, Lawrence) but to others as well (Lionel Durand, Erich Heydt, Dowding)—occurred at a complex intersection of fantasy, memory, and actuality.

Yet at the same time, H.D. maintained a relationship with the novelist Winifred Bryher for fifty years, living with her through the twenties to the early forties. They became a family, for Bryher adopted Perdita, H.D.'s daughter. This sustaining relationship between "companionate women" survived more temporary arrangements: Bryher's marriages to Robert McAlmon and Kenneth Macpherson and H.D.'s affairs.[3] Even though H.D. had stabilized and perhaps solved the question of a family tie beyond or on the margins of heterosexuality, even though she was deeply committed to Bryher, lesbianism per se, platonic or sexual, was not a complete solution to the cultural problem posed by male-female ties.[4] Her personal arrangements could not obliterate obsessive performances of scripts of thralldom or reduce her transfixed attention to heterosexual romance. In fact, she was immersed in this "story" or "script" many times, in fantasy, in relationships, in narrative poems, in memoirs and autobiographical fictions, eventually constructing some strategies—my subject here—to delegitimate thralldom by inventing alternative narrative patterns. All of these were, without exception, ways of neutralizing the power of the heterosexual romance, sexual polarization, and the male "héros." As has been clear elsewhere in this study, heterosexuality is not simply or exclusively a personal, sexual issue, but also a cultural and narrative one.

The impact of sexual subordination on H.D. as woman and artist can be seen in several autobiographical novel-memoirs.[5] H.D.'s novels of identity belong to her "madrigal cycle."[6] *Bid Me to Live (A Madrigal)*, written in 1939, was until 1981, the only published volume in this series of texts, each recounting a version of her life from about 1906 to 1920, that is, from the time she left Bryn Mawr College, until after the birth of her daughter, Perdita.[7] The recently published *HERmione* joins it.[8]

The overarching story begins with a bisexual attraction, centers on loss and betrayal engendered by heterosexual relationships in a patriarchal context, and ends in the celebration of love for a woman and the almost miraculous birth of a baby girl. H.D. retold these events in the variant versions of her memoir-novels. Yet to construct the one novel that she chose to publish from the "madrigal cycle," H.D. took a segment from the story's center only.[9] *Bid Me to Live*, a *roman à clef* of a London artistic set during World War I, concerns romantic thralldom and cultural struggles for voice, validation, and space as a woman artist in relation to such encoded male figures as Aldington, Lawrence, and the music historian Cecil Gray (father of Perdita). That is, in what she chose to publish, H.D. excised or deflected attention away from Frances Gregg and Bryher, both of whom had played crucial roles in her personal and poetic development. Focusing on the heterosexual ties, she muted her lesbian bonds in deference to a strongly internalized and paradigmatic norm of heterosexuality with both narrative and social meaning.

Bid Me to Live describes a woman poet within a male-dominated bohemia. In almost every heterosexual role in which she is cast, the woman is unsatisfied and tormented: as courtesan, as deceived wife, as muse, as consort. Only at the end can she claim some happy self-recognition in the company of a man who calls her Person (Personne)—both *someone* and *no one*. With that wry half-joke, the complex male-female encounters of that novel are summarized.

The novel explores the failing attempt by Julia and Rafe Ashton to sustain a "blithe arrangement" (*BMTL*, 11). But equal adoration and equal companionship are alike put to the test because both characters face historical and personal circumstances that reduce them to sexual stereotypes. Julia has had a stillborn child before the novel begins; her grief and feelings of sexual and maternal failure, combined with depression over the war, paralyze her. In mourning, she finds sex repugnant. With Julia a depressive but still fascinating "spirit," Rafe has no trouble finding another woman ("l'autre") to serve as body. Julia becomes vulnerable, neurasthenic, needy; Rafe becomes bluff, willful, callous. Vitality in war, but death in birth evoke male- and femaleness in cruel ways, reminiscent of Andrew and Prue in *To the Lighthouse.*

Not only does Julia feel personally and sexually inadequate; she feels like a professional anomaly within the group of male artists. Indeed, inadequacies in one area create vulnerabilities in the other. Julia and Rico (based on D. H. Lawrence) have been drawn to each other in a potent mixture of sexual and spiritual attraction.[10] Julia and Rafe are alienated but sustain some worn-out hopes of companionship. Both men exacerbate Julia's sense of personal failure by turning on her artistic work; in both cases the men are protecting their turf from the woman artist. Rico had written about the poem she is composing: ". . . I don't like the second half of the Orpheus sequence as well as the first. Stick to the woman speaking. How can you know what Orpheus feels? It's your part to be woman, the woman vibration, Eurydice should be enough. You can't deal with both" (*BMTL*, 51). Julia disagrees with the absolute gender division upon which Rico insists, for he is capable of writing almost "diabolically" well about women. Rico's opinions are bold, his presence charismatic, his approval tempting, yet he has given himself permission to write freely of both sexes, while denying Julia the parallel and complementary right to "enter into the feelings of men."[11] Rico's censorship of her ideas and his desire to control her range exert a pressure on her artistic work. Her aesthetic options (of voice, subject, gender perspective) are not freely chosen but are either shaped by her personal need to please him or scarred by her struggle to write in ways that he has explicitly forbidden. ". . . Frederico, for all his acceptance of her verses, had shouted his man-is-man, his woman-is-woman at her; his shrill peacock-cry sounded a love-cry, death-cry for their generation" (*BMTL*, 136). Similarly, having sent her seductive messages of a spiritual kind, to which she was peculiarly susceptible, Rico refuses Julia's tentative sexual advance. This too asserts his power of definition, another of the rejections that shatter her identity as poet and woman.

The same demands for artistic and sexual dominance are made by Julia's husband. Rafe becomes jealous of her correspondence with Rico. Surmising that she has been inspired by him, Rafe makes judgmental remarks about the drafts: "Not so good." "A bit dramatic. . . . It's Victorian." "You might boil this one down . . . about quarter the length and cut out the *clichés*" (*BMTL*, 54, 56). Julia's response to his criticism is evasive. She insists, for example, that she's simply saved some of those drafts as scrap paper. Rafe implicitly threatens her with further loss of his love because of his wounded pride. She feels defensive and trapped. "'I told you it was only preliminary scribbling.'

There was no taut nerve in her that wanted to spring forward, she had no tragedy-queen desire to stand, facing him, hand dramatically held forward to seize the maligned page. She felt no Muse" (*BMTL*, 54).

H.D. depicts the unedifying spectacle of male poets compelling a female poet to curtail her ambition, to narrow her range, to dissolve her words, to obey gender rules, to concentrate on the item, not the oeuvre. *Bid Me to Live* shows male poets limiting the shape and force of a woman's material by using sexual and personal acceptance as a weapon. Julia's response reveals her internalization and allegiance to these demands. The encounter raises the question whether male writers, in complicity with prescribed roles for women, have helped create poetesses where there could have been poets. The stakes of the romantic thralldom with which H.D. grappled were poetic achievement itself. Thralldom to male power had to be attacked, yet it was most difficult to attack. For the bittersweet pain of heterosexual thralldom seemed to fire H.D.'s creativity as it simultaneously undercut the conditions necessary for her uncensored flowering.

The draft of the poem involving Orpheus is probably related to H.D.'s "Eurydice," a reconstruction of the myth that puts the woman as hero into the center of the story.[12] Setting the poem "Eurydice" in the semiautobiographical context provided by *Bid Me to Live,* one sees the intense anger of the hero and the challenge to her identity posed by the male poets, Aldington and Lawrence, who are covertly addressed in it. As well, the poem resists one of the most moving stories of heterosexual loyalty and love in Western culture. There is change not in the events or outline of the narrative, but rather in the meaning of each event of the sequence. H.D.'s Eurydice suffers an arousal to life and then is compelled back into death, because to be twice annihilated by the act of another is a fate that defines this mythic woman as a woman. But her lack of choice has angered her. She accuses Orpheus of "ruthlessly" seeking to regain her in order to reappropriate her presence as a muse.

Eurydice has been betrayed by his trying to save her; but she regains her autonomy in response to this act, tending the flame of her otherness to light her own way. Locked in a space she cannot avoid, she declares it not the arena of rejection, negation and loss, but the splendor of her essential self.

> At least I have the flowers of myself,
> and my thoughts, no god
> can take that;

> I have the fervour of myself for a presence
> and my own spirit for light;
>
> and my spirit with its loss
> knows this;
> though small against the black,
> small against the formless rocks,
> hell must break before I am lost;
>
> before I am lost,
> hell must open like a red rose
> for the dead to pass.
>
> (*CP,* 55)

The mysterious last lines, with their glancing reference to the Christian harrowing of hell, propose that a change of paradigms—from classical to Christian, from male to female, from heterosexual love to self-love—will make valid the other side of the story. This story's "red rose" and "the flowers of myself" recall H.D.'s major image at this time: hard-edged beauty created by resistance to a devastating force. *Sea Garden* (1916), her first book, is punctuated with poems about such flowers, which take the very image of the feminine in our cultural iconography and show its oppositional strength.[13]

An earlier version of the "madrigal cycle" story than *Bid Me to Live,* *HERmione* was also one of the censored texts (published more than fifty years after it was written), exploring a bisexual love plot as another avenue to the critique of heterosexual romance. In *HERmione,* as well as in other still unpublished novels of this group, H.D. creates a young woman hero whose quest for identity centers on the relations between vocation, marriage, and sexuality. In this work the erotic is a very complicated question indeed, for *HERmione* offers the vivid depiction not only of heterosexual desire (there is a scene of rough embracing that ends with a torn dress) but also of lesbian desire. The critique of heterosexuality and the marriage plot explores strongly articulated relations between women. By proposing a bisexual love plot in place of the normative nineteenth-century pattern, and by writing a thematically open ending in which quest takes precedence but lesbian love—the erotic and spiritual attachment between women—has been definitive in the formation of identity, H.D. has created a major revision of the texts and endings that have stood throughout this study as reference points. At the same time, like *To the Lighthouse,* this book debates the gender polarization of the author's parents' bond, evincing a yearning matrisexual desire as well as an angry rejection of the mother's domestic subservience.[14]

In *HERmione*, the romantic thralldom to the male lover is matched by thralldom to the female companion. The first part of the novel records the progression of Her's engagement to George, a character based on Ezra Pound—her agreement to marry him, her parents' opposition and then acquiesence to the impending marriage. The second part incorporates Her's growing fascination for Fayne, her disengagement from George, and the final dissolution of both relationships. George and Fayne are related antonyms: both lovers, both companions, both enthralling, both liberating.[15]

George is initially exciting, persistent, and apparently unconventional, as he holds out the promise of escape from the confinement of the bourgeois family, but Her feels increasing discomfort at the conventional unfolding of their romance. While aroused and enchanted, she also feels that the scripts of courtship are themselves inhibiting, "out of a bad novel, out of a play anyhow" (*H*, 169). As elsewhere, the metaphor of a banal narrative is used to indicate the cultural persistence of romance as an ideology, Hermione finds George's demands intense and formulaic, and when he approaches her sexually, she suddenly realizes that his kisses "smudged out" her identity (*H*, 73). George seems to recognize and encourage her as a writer, and yet he makes a more powerful, and culturally seductive, demand on her to be his muse and inspiration. In both sexual and artistic realms, she is viewed as most wonderful in the role of object, not speaking subject: "He wanted Her, but he wanted a Her that he called decorative" (*H*, 172). Thus, in the final analysis, their love impedes the vocation it had at first seemed to encourage.

Fayne represents self-love, self-identification, and a twinship between spiritual sisters. In Fayne, Hermione finds the vision for which she has yearned, and the twin soul in whose gaze she discovers identity and then language.[16] "I know her. Her. I am Her. She is Her. Knowing her, I know Her. She is some amplification of myself like amoeba giving birth, by breaking off, to amoeba. I am a sort of mother, a sort of sister to Her. *'O sister my sister O fleet sweet swallow'* " (*H*, 158).[17] An erotic mysticism and mystical eroticism draws the "sisters" together: "prophetess to prophetess on some Delphic head-land" (*H*, 180). Aroused, they merge, as H.D.'s syntax obliterates the distinction between them. "Her bent forward, face bent toward Her"—a positive portrait of narcissism in the mirroring prose (*H*, 163). Lines from Swinburne capture the ecstatic moment and contrast with the obliterating kisses of George: their kiss recalls the "metonymic responsibilities" of the passionate kiss identified by Catharine Stimpson as a motif in lesbian fiction.[18]

The name "Her" has a particular meaning bound up with these

images. Whenever H.D. writes "Her stooped" or "Her said," she uses the wrong form of the word as the subject; every time this ungrammatical usage occurs, the objective status of this speaking subject shocks. But though "her" is the objective form, the very ungainly quality of the name used as the subject of a verb also suggests the presence of some resistant, stubborn matter that will not be captured or swayed. The contradictory features of this striking nickname are resolved as Her strokes Fayne's forehead with "healing hands" and says, "I will not have her hurt. I will not have Her hurt. She is Her. I am Her. Her is Fayne. Fayne is Her. I will not let them hurt HER" (*H*, 181). The heroine learns to love her potential by caring for another woman. Self-love, lesbian love and preoedipal ties enhance female selfhood; all are ways of neutralizing heterosexual romance. Through Fayne, she is liberated from being the "decorative" object that inspires George's poems; rather she perceives her writing as something valuable to "run" for. While she follows Fayne's oracular and meddling instructions to renounce her engagement, still Fayne's trances dominate her just as George's kisses had earlier. Fayne gives Her a deeper comprehension of her poetic gifts, but at the same time her bruised egotism and spiritual domination are as demanding as were George's expansive egotism and sexual possessiveness. Yet the balance has shifted from George to Fayne because the lesbian tie is less orthodox and thus a critical negation of the norms of girlhood, musehood, and marriage that enclose her.

The heterosexual and homosexual love plots are linked at the end by a double betrayal. Hermione's reactions of confusion and muted anger produce a physical and mental breakdown, rendered in an interior monologue of striking aesthetic control and structural purpose, comparable to the passages of delirium at the end of Woolf's *The Voyage Out*. This illness serves as the final test of the *Bildung*, through which she passes to her identity.

It has snowed, and, convalescent, Her goes for a walk, which significantly takes her beyond her family's property into neighboring woods. "They were virginal for one purpose, for one Creator. Last summer the Creator had been white lightning brandished against blackness. Now the creator was Her's feet, narrow black crayon across the winter whiteness" (*H*, 223). So Hermione begins her autonomous life as a writer by hiking a track into the snow, an act paralleling yet another lightning flash, which had augured her birth and the storm of female passion for the mother of power. The narrowness of that crayon track calls attention to the tentative line of motion on a chosen path, yet, by the comparison of two Creators, the act has its grandeur and status.

At a neighbor's house, she reestablishes her friendship with young people similarly at "the end of something" (*H*, 233), who invite her to accompany them to Europe. She decides to use the money set aside for her trousseau for that journey, which she had once thought she would take as George's bride. A continuation of this quest for identity will "be my marriage," she says, referring, with revisionary panache, to the classic love plot and its traditional ending (*H*, 234).

In *Bid Me to Live* as well, art allows a resolution to the toils of sexuality. Julia was called to her vocation precisely because it seemed that as a writer she might avoid the "biological catch" of womanhood, which, "taken at any angle," meant "danger."

> You dried up and were an old maid, danger. You drifted into the affable *hausfrau*, danger. You let her rip and had operations in Paris (poor Bella), danger.
>   There was one loophole, one might be an artist. Then the danger met the danger, the woman was man-woman, the man was woman-man. (*BMTL*, 136).[19]

"Writer" is a third term, mediating between the polarized sexes. This accommodating solution of drawing on the two sides of human personality, the psychic and intellectual androgyny that Woolf explored in *A Room of One's Own* and in *Orlando*, was also H.D.'s way of transcending the antimonies of sexual polarization. Status as an artist is a way of resisting women's definitional dependence on heterosexual ties, in which one is judged by access to men.

At the end of *Bid Me to Live*, Julia suggests that the conflicts between men and women can be solved by a power that transcends the claims of romantic love. She calls this the *gloire:* spiritual vision, seeing the aura of objects, the magnetism and numinous quality of things. All this is familiar in modern and post-modern poetics. More originally, the *gloire* is identified as a way to avoid the direct polarized confrontation of male and female characteristic of the Eurydice voice.[20] H.D. is opting for another path, conceding the field, but taking up the question in a transposed form. "What did Rico matter with his blood-stream, his sex-fixations, his man-is-man, woman-is-woman? That was not true. This mood, this realm of consciousness [i.e., *gloire*] was sexless, or all sex, it was child-consciousness, it was heaven. In heaven, there is neither marriage nor giving in marriage" (*BMTL*, 62).

That is, the spiritual quest for this realm of consciousness goes beyond cultural institutions of heterosexuality. The New Testament echo ("neither marriage nor giving in marriage") signifies that H.D.

wanted to avoid both the constant subordination of woman to man in normal sexual and cultural life and the recourse to sexual difference to justify this asymmetry. In her view, men and women are equals in the spiritual realm, and there they seek not the polarized gender distinctions of sexual life, but rather a mutual suffusion of insight and wisdom.

The spiritual dimension termed *gloire* is the inner radiance of a unified object or experience, a substance beyond dualism. It is compared to a child "before it is born," that is, before it experiences sexual division and gender socialization (*BMTL*, 177). H.D. makes clear that Rico could achieve this poise in his work if only he gave up the sexual polarities for which he so eagerly and didactically proselytized.

Nondualistic thinking appears in one of H.D.'s rare general aesthetic statements, "Notes on Thought and Vision," written in 1919, almost contemporaneous with the events of *Bid Me to Live,* though not with its composition. While concerned that men develop this consciousness, she was especially interested in women's ability "to think with the womb and feel with the brain," that is, to assume a biological and cultural authority together.[21] The third consciousness—a fusion of body and mind—is fixed in the self "like a foetus in the body." Here women's biologic capacity to nourish the embryonic child bridges the sexual polarities of thralldom, because the fetus and its mother are not opposites; they are separate but fused. Instead of the dichotomous A versus not-A, a formulation as familiar to Western logic as to ideologies of gender, mother and child are more like a continuous A plus B form.[22] This vision of a nondichotomous third way will eventually take symbolic shape in the mother-child dyads in H.D.'s late poems. In the dyad, the poet could envision herself placed as either mother or child or both, a mobility and fluidity that contrasts markedly with gender polarization.

Among Aldington, Lawrence, and Pound, H.D. received no support in her attempts to resist, reconstruct, defy, or transform that sexual thralldom from which it is clear her male attachments benefited, even if her pertinacity and need stunned them in their turn. H.D.'s profound psychic damage from sexual and spiritual thralldom continued to torment her. The themes of the First World War recurred, to be resolved during World War II, which H.D. spent, by choice, in the London of the Blitz. In her own inner patterning of these events, the first war was death, and the second was rebirth. The long-awaited consummation of her poetic work did occur in *Trilogy,* for its symbols of resurrection, its vision of a new city, its invention of a new story for Mary Magdalene, constitute a cultural myth of great importance to female modernism. At the same time, however, H.D.

returned to the forms of sexual polarization and entrapment represented by the thralldom of women to men.

Why did H.D. maintain relations with men; why did she not move
entirely into the world of companionate women? Perhaps she invested
her emotional life in various men to experience their poetic and spiritual challenge. Perhaps her happiness in the world of women made
her compensate by entering painful and vulnerable relations with
men. Perhaps her view of erotic spirituality demanded the oppositional character of the masculine. Perhaps H.D. felt that men in particular (because of their recurrent war frenzy and their penchant for
authoritarian politics) needed to be converted to spiritual insight; she
cast herself as a sacrificial leader-sufferer, using love to lead them to
vision. Whatever the mixture of reasons, H.D. remained subject to
bouts of thralldom throughout her life and constructed lacerating
hopes for companion-lovers, which often ended in rejection. She was
complicit in that failure. Telling and retelling these stories of defeat
and manipulation, playing and replaying the events of the past and
studying their overlay helped H.D. control her experience.[23] If thralldom and fascination with sexual polarization are, then, a constant, so
is H.D.'s wish to find a way to write herself beyond the plot in which
she and her culture had set her.

The strategies that she designed have several things in common.
Rather than rejecting dialogue with men, they offer bridges between
men and women, third ways that mediate between the glamour and
devastation of polarization. Her strategies are more inclusive than
heterosexuality and function by neutralizing its power. These structures for narrative and emotional experience can be imagined as a
triptych: the sufficient family at the center involves transgenerational
bonds of parent to child, child to parent; the two side structures
involve peer-to-peer bonds of sibling-lovers.

A specific "case" of thralldom is associated with *Helen in Egypt* and
parallels the case of Sheri Martinelli, minor poet, artist, and
hierophant of the Pound circle. During Pound's incarceration in
St. Elizabeths, Martinelli made vows of permanent loyalty. However,
when Pound was released, he extricated himself from the relationship. Cast off, deceived, and broken, she protested to H.D. that "the
male just can't go about like that, ditching a spirit love."[24] H.D.
identified wholeheartedly because she too had been cast off—by Lord
Dowding, Britain's Air Marshal during World War II, with whom she
had a brief correspondence. She told him she was in communication
with dead RAF pilots, a psychic event he had also experienced.[25] Although she thought that these comparable visions made them spiritual equals, he insisted, following more familiar male-female patterns,

that his dead pilots came from a higher order of the spirit realm and had more complete authority than her dead pilots, thus denying the import of her messages.[26] When she writes that *Helen in Egypt* was an "attempt . . . to retain a relationship, materially 'ditched,' " it is to this relationship and rebuff that she refers.

The second part of *Helen* was similarly provoked. Erich Heydt, her friend at Kuesnacht, quarrelled with her over her claim to mediumship.[27] Heydt, who contributes considerably to the figure of Paris, could not believe in or sympathize with H.D.'s stories of communication from dead RAF airmen. Having seen Heydt as a possible convert to spiritualism, H.D. was very hurt.[28] The pattern is clear: H.D. wrote this major long poem in the aftermath of strong attraction to several men to whom she had frankly revealed bizarre psychic events and sane postwar anxieties of nuclear holocaust. She depended on their approval and collaboration. But although the poem was provoked by their rejections, within it the pattern of thralldom is broken. Nurturance and vision are achieved without sexual or spiritual damage from men.

Helen in Egypt is engaged with one particular literary "order of reality," a constitutive story of Western culture in its focus on sexual desire and tribal conquest.[29] As in "Eurydice," H.D. here gives voice to one of the female figures left voiceless and ascribed a one-sided, incomplete meaning by culture.[30] But H.D. is not writing an anti-*Iliad*, dependent on Homer's ordering of events, his cast of characters, or narrative sequence. More than a displacement to the other side of a known myth, *Helen in Egypt* will break the sequence, delegitimating the known story of the heroic conflict based on romantic passion. The poem is the archeological site where alternative stories flicker, a graphic image of the doubled vision of women in culture.

> . . . the flame
> of thoughts too deep to remember,
>
> that break through the legend,
> the fame of Achilles,
> the beauty of Helen,
>
> like fire
> through the broken pictures
> on a marble-floor.
>   (*H in E*, 258–59)

The pictures are already constituted, dominant, but also challenged— "broken" by the critical "flame."

Such a dramatic change of emphasis can occur only when the

questing Helen stops saying "by rote" the tales that culture tells about women, and the sequence of events that are said to constitute the female experience. Traditionally, Helen is sex, temptation, allure, the possessed and the possessive: a one-dimensional love goddess, victim of romantic thralldom and the victimizer of others. But in the middle of this narrative, Helen says, "I can not go on, on, on // telling the story / of the Fall of Troy," for that culturally resonant tale is not her story (*H in E*, 153). To have her story told, the writer must avoid "Apollo's snare," glossed by H.D. as "the already-written drama or script" (*H in E*, 232, 230). Instead, Helen's story calls upon "the million personal things, / things remembered, forgotten, // remembered again, assembled / and re-assembled in different order . . ." (*H in E*, 289).

So *Helen in Egypt* moves deeply into the material to which no prior attention had been paid, those memories and associations never part of the traditional telling because they were considered "trivial" and not "important," to borrow Woolf's terms about women's narrative and the alteration of values.[31]

> . . . none of these
> came into the story,
>
> it was epic, heroic and it was far
> from a basket a child upset
> and the spools that rolled to the floor. . . .
>   (*H in E*, 289)

Helen's quest for her identity is represented by the desire to decipher a hieroglyph that signifies herself.[32] Saying "She herself is the writing," meaning both one signifier and the whole new tale, H.D. suggests that Helen must become reader and writer to pierce the blandishments of the known story (*H in E*, 22, 91).[33] Described as a thought thinking itself, whose veil always wavers in the wind and eludes capture, she seeks "to unravel the tangle // that no man can ever un-knot" (*H in E*, 298). In the veil, the linear hegemony of the narrative line has been questioned, looped over onto itself. To accomplish her quest to read herself and her story, she sifts, seeks, and mulls, acting as the historian of her own unrecorded emotions. Decoding will depend on that characteristic act of the woman writer and of the heroes who extend her: the act of critique. So the repeated phrase "she herself is the writing" also summarizes the situation for women writers who begin to review and reinterpret the culturally sanctioned stories. *Helen in Egypt* rests on a poetics of critique.[34]

H.D. has replaced the sexually centered heroine and the bellicose hero with two liminal figures: Achilles, the vulnerable "New Mortal," and an incubating psyche (Helen-Thetis), a mother-child dyad still in chrysalis but also fully winged. The poet resists the culturally sanctioned characterization of their capacity for sensual love or savage war, seeing her characters as important because of their visionary abilities to crystallize the dissolved or latent meanings hidden in the former story. The characters direct attention to nonepic and nonromance material already present in culture.

In Part I, H.D. presides over a reconstruction of the hero, which begins during the Trojan War and is recorded in Achilles' retrospective meditations.[35] From being a "Destroyer," a member of the "iron-ring" of warriors in the "death-cult," Achilles breaks with conventionalized affiliations of maleness (H in E, 26, 51, 99). Even at the heart of the war, Achilles grudgingly acknowledges that Helen is an unwritten dimension of experience that challenges the soldiers so much that they simply cannot shoot her as she walks the ramparts of Troy. "Had she enchanted us // with a dream of daring, of peril, / as yet un-writ in the scrolls of history, / un-sung as yet by the poets?" (H in E, 50) As part of his increasingly postheroic stance, his rejection of the "powerful war-faction," and the melting of the "icy fortress" of a fascist perspective, Achilles will question or give up the story that he once completely believed (H in E, 18).[36]

During the war, Achilles had looked to Helen (or to her image) for a sign to judge a proposal of his fellows; by this act of allegiance to female authority, he defects from Command. For breaking the patriarchal chain from father to son and brother, Achilles is shot. Once he knows that the Command is a "lure to destruction," he has entered a reality in which "present is past, past is future"—that palimpsest calling "the whole heroic sequence" into question (H in E, 56, 57). His estrangement from the male world of force and obedience and his entrance into the female world of quest and wavering, love and death, are an inheritance from Thetis, his sea mother. Achilles becomes a postheroic man, vulnerable and questing: "the new Mortal, / shedding his glory, / limped slowly across the sand" (H in E, 10).

The second part of the poem begins with a contrast between Achilles and Paris, who, as the original lover of Helen, still views Helen as his possession and wants to seduce her yet again, making her "re-live an old story" (H in E, 223). By trying to win her from Achilles, Paris simply repeats, without transformation, his role in the traditional myth. Hence he sees Helen only as she once was—"suave" and silver-sandaled, the beautiful heroine—not as she is, the questing hierophant (H in E, 146). Because he does not acknowledge this quest, he is "defeated even upon Leuké," the magical white island (H in E,

143). Thus Helen walks away from him, barefoot, escaping from the
old erotic myth that Paris persists in believing.

In this section, Helen must avoid being trapped in the polarized
roles that the two lovers give her, while at the same time retaining
their approval. She struggles with the antagonism of Egypt and
Greece/Troy (Achilles and Paris), for one insists on the spiritual in-
itiate, Helen in Egypt, associated with the soul, death, and Eris—
discord or struggle. The other prefers the sensual fertility figure,
Helen Dendritis, associated with the body, life, and Eros. Further,
Paris and Achilles are the slayer and the slain, and she must reconcile
the two men whom she has loved, one of whom has killed the other.

Making Achilles and Helen into brother-sister questers is the first
move in H.D.'s strategy to break with the script of romantic thralldom.
The quests of Helen and Achilles are finally not journeys toward love
for each other, but quests to identify the source: the mother. Further,
Helen avoids a replay of the drama of sexual thralldom by asking
Paris, as well, to join her on a brother-sister quest. Then, amazingly to
the uninitiated reader, Paris is transposed into Helen's child by
Achilles; for another way to handle the lover, displaced from
dominance in the plot of thralldom, is to return him to the role of a
child. As Helen says, the "first lover [Paris], was created by my last
[Achilles]" (*H in E,* 185). The boy-child is the place where the exas-
perating lover may be usefully put; such a son-consort, while fascinating, cannot dominate or entrap the woman. H.D. has contained his
sexual power by demoting him generationally.

However, by the time Helen has relived the experiences of Achilles
and Paris in their untransformed states, she is "weary of War" and of
love stories as well (*H in E,* 157–58, 149–150. "Only the Quest remains," guided by Theseus, the character based on Freud, to reorder
her memories and to work through both the romantic and heroic
scripts.[37] At the absolute center of the poem, Helen enters the white
world-egg, a version of her original site of birth; she is assisted by the
paternal/maternal figure of Theseus, acting as inseminator, mother,
and midwife. Theseus is a literal psychopomp, for he instructs Helen
to reenter the cocoon that he has woven for her out of the "bright
threads" of his own accomplished quest—the invention of
psychoanalysis (*H in E,* 169):

> . . . here is soft woven wool;
> wrapped in this shawl, my butterfly,
>
> my Psyche, disappear into the web,
> the shell, re-integrate,
> nor fear to recall

the shock of the iron-Ram,
the break in the Wall,
the flaming Towers,

shouting and desecration
of the altars; you are safe here;
remember if you wish to remember,

or forget. . . .

(*H in E*, 170–71)

If Achilles is a New Mortal, Helen is the embryonic, dazed psyche, attempting throughout, with fascinating violence to the biological process, to incorporate the butterfly and the chrysalid in one constantly liminal unit. H.D. wanted to evoke the amount of backward integration necessary to female *Bildung;* she shows Helen reentering the cocoon because her formation needs extra dimensions, or because her formation is not complete. This corresponds to the mingling of backward-moving memory and forward-moving quest in the structure of the poem, to the small loops between poetry and prose creating textures that double and texts that question. In Helen's ". . . wavering / like a Psyche / with half-dried wings," the subject is a particularly vulnerable moment in the life-cycle of butterflies (*H in E*, 166). When adult insects first emerge damp from the chrysalis, they must wait until their wing structures dry and stiffen before they can fly. So Helen is the winged psyche at the exact moment when it cannot use its wings, caught in the transition between two stages. In short, with these psyche images, H.D. makes every effort to exaggerate the vulnerable transitions, the wavering double directions of the female quest.

Helen transcends opposite lovers and opposing identities because the mediation of Theseus reparents her. He acts as both mother and father, healing the gender divisions found in the traditional nuclear family. Theseus also offers her a "subtle genealogy," a family and sexual drama that rearranges these prime ties into a new pattern (*H in E*, 184).

The third section is dominated by a little wooden idol of Thetis, which Achilles had carved when a boy. Like Helen as psyche in the Theseus section, the eidolon (image) of Thetis is both pupa and butterfly. Thetis is the swaddled soul and her own psychopomp, or soul bearer.[38] That is the mystery of the psyche figure, who, according to the old myth, is pregnant on her quest of soul-making. She bears both herself and her child in a double incubation. Similarly, during a portion of her quest, Helen, like Psyche, is pregnant with Achilles' child:

"a treasure beyond a treasure . . . the gift I forced from him" (*H in E*, 282–83). But it is not the child (actually a twin or double child) as consummation of male-female relations that is emphasized, but the fraternal-sororal bond of Achilles and Helen, and then the mother-child chain of the linked dyads (Thetis-Helen, Helen-Euphorion, Euphorion as Achilles/Helen). So *Helen in Egypt* ends with the appearance of a mother-child chain: Helen as avatar of the mother, Thetis; Helen as mother of the double child; Helen as a girl child in the arms of a goddess who is also herself.[39]

The mystery of the nenuphar or waterlily, the flower beacon, revealed to be the hieroglyphic sign given to Helen to decode, is the "subtle genealogy" of both sibling pairs and parent-child dyads.

> father, brother, son, lover,
> sister, husband and child;
>
> beyond all other, the Child,
> the child in the father,
> the child in the mother,
>
> the child-mother, yourself. . . .
>   (*H in E*, 187)

Especially the "child-mother, yourself" surpasses both war and romantic love, both the strains of the heroic and the romantic scripts. Helen is at once the Great Mother and the baby in her mother's arms. "Helen in Hellas forever" is the climactic, reverberating phrase, which suggests an ongoing exchange of force in the closed circuit of mother-child-mother (*H in E*, 190). This closure in reparenting solves for H.D. the needs and themes of her major work—the needs for undamaging nurturance and undamaging powers.[40] Helen is the complete family represented by the petals of the nenuphar, but most particularly she is "the child in the mother," nurtured by Theseus and Thetis, and the child-mother herself, the climactic eidolon Helen-Thetis, which she both represents and worships.

So the defining moment of rupture with the known Helen story of romance is thus a defining moment of rupture with a more concealed story—of romance's origin in the linear resolution of the female oedipal crisis. In its alternative resolution, the poem elaborates the originating bond, the mother-child dyad. This is postulated as the central telos, offering the satisfactions of closure, with other familial bonds petalled around that calyx.

A parallel muting of the lover to enhance the mother-child chain occurs in "Winter Love," a "coda" to *Helen in Egypt*.[41] In "Winter Love," Bryher—the sister as mother—and Pound—the male "lover"—are both encoded in relation to the figure of Helen in a way that makes this poem an extension of the motifs and meanings of *HERmione* as well as a continuation of *Helen in Egypt*. In "Winter Love," a child of Helen's belongs as much to Sage Femme, the Bryher figure, as to Odysseus, encoding Pound. Both have conceived the baby, one in sexual passion, the other in maternal wisdom. By using childbirth agony, resentment, revulsion, and ecstasy as the climax of the poem, and by making the child come equally from the insemination by man and the life-giving salvation by woman, H.D. has created a bisexual structure that gives the woman weight and force in her poetic universe. H.D.'s "subtle genealogy" and subtler genetics, again the center of the poem, answer romantic thralldom and the valorization of maleness with the mother-child dyad.

Reparenting as a narrative strategy is the return by the female hero to parental figures in order to forge an alternative fictional resolution to the oedipal crisis that these parent figures evoke. The resolution *Helen in Egypt* proposes is the enhanced, majestic mother-child dyad, liberated by a maternal father and a critical female reader. By rewriting the telos of the oedipal crisis in the strategy of reparenting, H.D. was attempting to end her submission to sexual polarization and romance, to construct from available male and female roles, sibling and parent-child ties, some set of relationships that would be less emotionally damaging to her as a woman than those she had actually experienced—and helped to construct—with men. To do this, she created a female quest plot whose final answer was the revelation of mother and child. The "thousand-petalled lily" contains and presents all the relations of the sufficient family—sufficient because it answers female trauma in romance with the emotional satisfactions of a narrative that engages the preoedipal dyad (*H in E*, 104). This dyad is a major strategy for breaking the sequence.

■

CHAPTER SIX

To "bear my mother's name": *Künstlerromane* by Women Writers

No song or poem will bear my mother's name. . . . Perhaps she was herself a poet— though only her daughter's name is signed to the poems that we know.
ALICE WALKER
"In Search of Our Mothers' Gardens" (1974)

The love plot and *Bildungs* plot are fused in a particular fictional strategy, a figure emerging in a range of narratives from Elizabeth Barrett Browning's *Aurora Leigh* to Margaret Atwood's *Surfacing*. And the central struggle between designated role and meaningful vocation is negotiated by different narrative tactics in nineteenth- and twentieth-century texts.[1] The figure of a female artist encodes the conflict between any empowered woman and the barriers to her achievement.[2] Using the female artist as a literary motif dramatizes and heightens the already-present contradiction in bourgeois ideology between the ideals of striving, improvement, and visible public works, and the feminine version of that formula: passivity, "accomplishments," and invisible private acts.

For bourgeois women, torn between their class values and the subset of values historically affirmed for their gender caste, the figure of the female artist expressed the doubled experience of a dominant ideology that was supposed to be muted in them and that therefore became oppositional for their gender. Making a female character be a "woman of genius" sets in motion not only conventional notions of womanhood but also conventional romantic notions of the genius, the person apart, who, because unique and gifted, could be released from social ties and expectations.[3] Genius theory is a particular exaggeration of bourgeois individualism, and its evocation increases the tension between middle-class women as a special group and the dominant assumptions of their class. Because it is precisely expression and the desire to refuse silence that are at issue in artistic creation, the contradiction between dominant and muted areas can also be played out in the motif of the imbedded artwork, another narrative marker of these *Künstlerromane*.

motif of the imbedded artwork

Aurora Leigh (1856) by Elizabeth Barrett Browning is the mid-century text of an emergent ideological formation, as *Ruth Hall* (1855), a sweet American book, is that of dominant sentiments. *Aurora Leigh* is a booklength narrative poem about the fusing of artist and woman, and the testing of values surrounding class and spiritual vision.[4] In the final moments of this work, the artist Aurora accepts her suitor in marriage, having discovered that all her notable successes are compromised without affection.[5]

> Passioned to exalt
> The artist's instinct in me at the cost
> Of putting down the woman's, I forgot
> No perfect artist is developed here
> From any imperfect woman.
>   (*AL*, 380)

Aurora's expostulation of Love's primacy at the end of the work ("Art is much, but Love is more. / O Art, my Art, thou'rt much, but Love is more!" *AL*, 381) is well separated from the even more powerful statements of her allegiance to art and her meditations on craft, in Books II and V, which describe the upsurge of her passionate inspiration as the "lava-lymph" (*AL*, 195).

> Never flinch,
> But still, unscrupulously epic, catch
> Upon the burning lava of a song
> The full-veined, heaving, double-breasted Age:
> That, when the next shall come, the men of that
> May touch the impress with reverent hand, and say
> "Behold,—behold the paps we all have sucked!"
>   (*AL*, 201–202)

Aurora Leigh is irrepressibly rich in imagery of volcanoes and breasts, of maternal power to nourish; and by evoking the physical female, the poem claims both biological and cultural authority to speak.[6]

Heterosexual love may have moral and ideological primacy in *Aurora Leigh,* as articulated at the end, but vocation, itself bound with maternal bliss and the power of love/hate relations among women, has textual primacy.[7] Vocation, asserted early and often, is, moreover, stated in the critical context of a beady-eyed analysis of female education for domesticity, acquiesence, and superficiality. Aurora's choice of vocation is made against the will of her closest relatives, including Romney. She asserts female right to a profession not because of financial exigency or family crisis, but out of sheer desire and for the sake of sheer power. Her ecstatic commitment to the vocation of poet and her achievement tend to make valid the ideology of striving and success that she embodies, joining that set of values to female possibility.[8]

Between the beginning and the end, Romney and Aurora have exchanged roles, in a chiastic move that tends to make their marriage somewhat credible, despite the plot mechanism that has him involved with three women, representing three social classes and three female types. Aurora has seen the centrality of love, he the vitality of her art. While he had, in Book II, been the fountainhead of smugly discouraging statements about women as artists ("We get no Christ from you,—and verily / We shall not get a poet, in my mind," *AL,* 81), at the end he comes to recognize that her achievement was more vital than his in inducing the conversion experiences that are the real root of any social change. This readjustment takes shape in a distinct and punitive shock to his views. For Romney, like an escapee from *Jane Eyre,* is first rejected, like St. John Rivers, and then, like Rochester, blinded. This wounding of male heroes is, according to Elaine Showalter, a symbolic way of making them experience the passivity, dependency, and powerlessness associated with women's experiences of gender.[9] And, as in Brontë's *Shirley,* the rebellious lower orders express, in unacceptable form, the rancor and hostility of all the powerless, women included. For Romney's blindness is direct punishment for his political theories. A mean-spirited, animalistic rebellion causes the accident that blinds him. The poor have been so brutalized that their souls are nasty, unawakened, unspiritual; their true awakening will be brought about only by poetry and God, not by politics.

Because he can no longer continue these handicapped reformist activities, the private sphere of love and the cosmic sphere of religion become the world in which all his needs can—must—be satisfied. So the man is made to live in the "separate sphere," in the feminine culture of love and God. The creation of Romney's short-fall, his "castration" by the malicious verve of the unwashed masses, creates a power vacuum where the upper-class or upper-middle-class hero

See also Juliet Mitchell on romanticism

again, like Rochester

used to be. Aurora is then available to claim both masculine and feminine rewards—the hero's reward of success and the heroine's reward of marriage—in a rescripting of nineteenth-century motifs that joins romantic love to the public sphere of vocataion.

> Shine out for two, Aurora, and fulfil
> My falling-short that must be! work for two,
> As I, though thus restrained, for two, shall love!
> (*AL*, 389)

Since Aurora had offered to sacrifice and to be used (*AL* 381), what more aggrandizing way to fulfill her desire for abasement than to demand that she do twice as often and twice as intensely what she has already proven she can do very well. Being an artist is, at the end, reinterpreted as self-sacrifice for the woman, and thus is aligned with feminine ideology. This work, then, created a powerful reference point, but it did not change the nineteenth-century convention of representation that saw the price of artistic ambition as the loss of femininity.

Most of the nineteenth-century works with female artists as heroes observe the pieties, putting their final emphasis on the woman, not the genius; the narratives are lacerated with conflicts between femininity and ambition. There are works in which the only reason for an artistic vocation is the utterly desperate and melodramatic destitution of the main character—say a widow with young children, cast out from her sanctimonious, petty family. Such is the case with Fanny Fern's *Ruth Hall: A Domestic Tale of the Present Time,* published (in America) a year before *Aurora Leigh.* In this work, when a child asks, "When I get to be a woman shall I write books, Momma?" the proper answer is clearly Ruth's "God forbid . . . no happy woman ever writes. From Harry's grave sprang Floy [her pen name]."[10] This statement may be taken as the mid-century base line of attitudes, in which a woman's entry into public discourse elicits a shudder of self-disgust and is allowable only if it is undertaken in mourning and domesticity.

Self-realization and ambition as a female crime, and the absolute separation of love and vocation are also grimly coded into a moral tale by Rebecca Harding Davis (1864).[11] An older woman, Hetty, vividly discontented with the dullness and ordinary struggles of her life, is alienated from her new baby and from her husband. The focus of her discontent is her ambition to succeed in the public world with "fame and an accomplished deed in life" ("TWS," 10). The climax of this conflict comes in a sequence that we later learn is a hallucinatory dream of an artist's life. She is hissed on stage, sexually exposed,

homeless, mistaken for a prostitute, and responsible for her husband's death from grief: surely an intense catalogue of punishments
for the crime of ambition. This transposition of desire for vocation to
shame and disgust is achieved by Davis's manipulation of the dual
connotations of the artist as soul and body. At first her ambition is
boldly justified as "the highest soul-utterance," a "mission," "a true
action of the creative power," but the sordid intervention of a "greasy"
impresario refracts these spiritual claims and collapses them. There is
no third or mediating way out of the paradox that the apparently
romantic aspirations have a sordid reality, while humdrum domestic
life is, instead, the real sphere of divine mission. Here, as in *Aurora
Leigh,* class questions subtly shift the ground: the preindustrial farm
in which all participate, the family work in unity and interdepen-
dence, is clearly better than the protocapitalist exploitation of artist/
woman by impresario/man, a relationship all too suggestive of prostitute to pimp. Reunited with family, baby, and husband, Hetty thanks
God that she was purged of selfishness, willful dreams, and her delu-
sive claims to talent. "A woman has no better work in life than the one
she has taken up: to make herself a visible Providence to her husband
and child" ("TWS," 19). God is usefully recruited to bolster the solution. The public sphere is tempting but shallow; the transcendent
"Self" without ties is desolate; the private sphere, rather than stultifying and "mawkish," is a cozy and ennobling realm of human love
("TWS," 15, 8). The either/or ending of love versus vocation is
created with a newly honed edge in this tale. Although it does offer a
pointed vocabulary of critique, the narrative just as pointedly dis-
credits it.

   Kate Chopin's *The Awakening* (1899) summarizes these nineteenth-
century motifs, working them allusively, testing their limits, considering how they might be broken.[12] The way the life of the artist can
be mistaken for the life of the demimondaine, the way "the children"
come in and are narratively presented, and an allusion to the sa-
credness of home ties by a woman suffering in childbed are motifs
shared with Rebecca Harding Davis. The death of Edna Pontellier as
an artist figure is a plain statement that the character rejects the
binary, either/or convention of love versus vocation. However, the fact
that her rejection of complicity takes the form of suicide attacks the
binary division between selves only by the monism of obliteration.
Chopin hints that there might be some socially plausible, if marginalized, third way open to Edna, who is too attached to her privileges of class (the dovecote, the smart set) and gender (her beauty) to
pursue it. In this narrative the binary choice still has force, but not
finality; the main character cannot experiment further and punishes

herself for her mixture of ambition to transcend feminine norms and complicity with them by an act (swimming) that both celebrates and destroys that awakening.

The sentiment about impropriety, the loss of a sense of feminine coherence, and a tremendous ambivalence toward a profession appear in another turn-of-the-century work, Sarah Grand's *The Beth Book* (1897).[13] An artistic vocation for this spirited person would seem highly desirable, given her sexually degraded, emotionally sterile marriage. Yet ambivalence toward the female artist is again present, and the norms of femininity are carefully elaborated. Beth writes a book only after trying the feminine vocation of needlewoman. When she does write, she becomes lax and less ladylike, in tiny bits of symbolic degeneration like not keeping the Sabbath, overindulging in coffee, and neglecting to wash her face. Nursing a fellow artist back to health, she sacrifices her meager money, her health, her dresses, and even her hair in a feminine orgy of charity, not even knowing meantime that her book "achieved a very respectable success" (*TBB*, 517). At the end, she gives up writing to become an orator; this occurs in part because speechmaking is presented as her "natural gift," so that any suspicion of effort could be disabused (*TBB*, 525). Further, her knight, the fellow artist in the garret, does come. All these motifs of feminine modification of the plot occur in the final third of the book; the descriptions of power and frustration make up the major part. Allocation of narrative force points in one direction; the ideological priorities set in the resolution point in another. The description of genius offers a vocabulary of passionate and frustrated striving; the events of the plot offer the conciliations and closures demanded by the femaleness of the artist.

The Story of Avis (1877) by the prolific American writer Elizabeth Stuart Phelps Ward takes up the challenge of *Aurora Leigh* to examine the relation of a woman to artistic vocation after the declaration of love and the marriage that conclude Browning's poem. This deft book is formed like a quilt of neatly fitted and boldly colored discourses—sentimental, realistic, and, of course, allegorical (the death of a bird [Latin: avis] given to her future husband for safekeeping).

Avis is another of the large-spirited and gifted artist heroes torn between human energy and feminine ideology. Phelps Ward's version of a tragicomic wedlock plot will show that marriage and vocation should not be combined for women.

Success—for a woman—means absolute surrender, in whatever direction. Whether she paints a picture, or loves a man, there is no division of labor possible in her economy. To the attainment of any end worth living

for, a symmetrical sacrifice of her nature is compulsory upon her. I do
not say that this was meant to be so. I do not think we know what was
meant for women. It is enough that it *is* so.[14]

Women are trained to a personality, formed by social constraints that
compel an undivided commitment to one path; allusions to the psychological economy of romance make change seem impossible. Avis
argues that even a woman of genius cannot break that imposed pattern of sacrifice, of an either/or choice. Her future husband claims
that a talented and dynamic woman painter, once married, would be
able to create and housekeep in fair and equal balance. He is, not
incidentally, feckless, although persuasive. The book is built to test
their opposing propositions; Avis "wins" the argument by losing her
art, a plot mechanism that recapitulates the double bind of femininity
and vocation.[15]

Shrewdly observed details of daily life in a household that does not
compromise its bourgeois solidity make the novel a study in frustration.[16] Not only the arrival of children but, in sharply executed scenes,
their behavior—seductive tantrums outside the studio door—
dramatizes the conflicts that daily impede the practice of her talent.
Her paints grow dusty; domesticity encroaches constantly. Then the
home itself falters: one child dies, the husband is invalided by tuberculosis, the marriage is an alienating stalemate. The author's attention
shifts to the prevention of the spiritual and emotional divorce she has
so cunningly suggested, as if Avis would be dishonored as a character
if she could not recapture love or respect for her husband. With this
shift of attention, the burden of the novel falls on the wedlock plot,
and the *Bildung* of the female artist is put aside. But even her husband's death does not set Avis free. In a conservative scene of surrender, the character discovers that being married had "eaten into and
eaten out the core of her life, left her a riddled, withered thing, spent
and rent" (*SA*, 447). She can no longer create, for her genius has been
used up in love; she is reduced to teaching art school. This mercantil-
ist view of the psychic economy of women suggests that a fixed
amount of energy exists in her life; what is spent is never replenished
or recreated. Hence the either/or choice persists and controls the
character.

The book ends by the generational displacement of the mother's
ambition onto her daughter.[17] The mother reads her child the story of
the Quest for the Holy Grail, and we understand that while the first
generation (Sir Lancelot) failed, the second, purer generation of seek-
ers will achieve the quest. The thwarted mother bequeathes her ambi-

tion to the child, and that emergent daughter becomes, as we shall see, the main character of the twentieth-century *Künstlerroman*.[18]

Avis's two major art works embody the conflict between vocation and love. One is the catalyst for her marriage, a portrait of her future husband. The other is the sphinx, a work of a thwarted artist, encoding both the powers and failures of her genius.[19] In the sphinx is depicted the muted, riddling, and inarticulate drive of woman artists in particular and of women in general, suggesting vocation and its erosion, potential speech and actual silencing, the whole "mutilated actuality" of her career (*SA*, 150).

In a number of works that center on female artists, characters from the conventional heterosexual love plot, loving males as well as carefully domestic aunts *(The Story of Avis, Aurora Leigh)* or dim, rejecting mothers *(The Beth Book)*, make strong demands for conformity to exactingly interpreted feminine roles. Thus lover and maternal figures compel the processes of silencing and thwart the preternatural articulateness of the female artists. In the nineteenth-century works, the husband or suitor is the major problem for the artistic career. The husband/suitor's concerted disapproval of the artist's vocation *(Aurora Leigh,* until the end), his lack of sustained understanding of the nature of her needs *(The Story of Avis),* his view of wife as bourgeois possession *(The Awakening),* his fraudulent unworthiness *(The Beth Book),* and his controlling of her artistic and intellectual activity (as we shall see in "The Yellow Wallpaper") are some of the motifs.

The major modulation from the nineteenth- to the twentieth-century *Künstlerroman* involves the position of heterosexual love and the couple within the narrative. The romance plot, which often turns into a stalemate, is displaced in twentieth-century narratives and replaced by a triangular plot of nurturance offered to an emergent daughter by a parental couple. Whenever the heterosexual bond remains central to the main character, she is usually a "thwarted mother" type of artist. Charlotte Perkins Gilman's "The Yellow Wallpaper" may be taken as a transitional work; the nurturing that the potential artist receives is a form of social and emotional control, repressive tolerance at its shrewdest. But Gilman's text is transitional because, instead of submitting to the complicity or battered resignation we see in *The Beth Book* or *The Story of Avis,* Gilman's hero performs the act signaling a shift in female narrative politics, the critique of narrative and ideology by writing beyond the ending.

"The Yellow Wallpaper" is an obdurate account of the conflict between an artist's calling and external constraints, telling of the literal entrapment of a potential writer in the room in which she is suffering

from a breakdown.[20] Her journal of self-analysis (the work is constructed as a diary) is written furtively, under her husband's ban. The
external controls on the woman's activity are very persistent, so her
creative energy is baffled except for one completed document—the
text we hold.

The room of her imprisonment epitomizes the doubled public and
private power characteristic of the social pressures brought to bear on
women. As the marital bedroom, it recalls love and trust; with its bars
and fixed furniture, it mimics such impersonal corrective institutions
as jails and asylums. In the double character of the husband/doctor,
Gilman has expressed this nexus of patriarchal love, power, and
force; he combines the professional authority of the physician with
the legal and emotional authority of the husband.[21] The cause of the
character's worsening depression is written—and with the proper
eyes can be read—in the yellow wallpaper of the sickroom and in the
diary secretly kept by the woman.

The symptoms have a double impact, involving her fixation on the
wallpaper and her decoding of it. In the inability of the trained professional to read her symptoms (but in his power to enforce his interpretation), in the ability of the untrained patient to understand the
semiology of her illness (but her powerlessness to have her reading
credited), Gilman has constructed a dramatic statement illustrating
the difficulty of the muted group to "deny or reverse a universal
assumption."[22] When the ill woman makes the climactic separation of
the wallpaper's front pattern and its hidden female figure, she makes
the crucial analytic distinction between a muted ("creeping") woman
and the "central, effective and dominant system of meanings" in her
society.[23] By making the wallpaper pattern represent the patterns of
androcentric society, Gilman underscores the dailiness and omnipres-
ence of the universal assumption of male dominance, its apparent
banality and harmlessness—just one modest feature of home décor.
But like any system of social and ideological dominance, it is pervasive, extensive, and saturating.[24] All who live within this fixed pattern
of institutions and values are affected by it, no matter what their social
benefits or sufferings or how "careful" they are; Gilman reports that
"the paper stained everything it touched" ("YWP," 27).

At the ending, depending on one's interpretive paradigm, two contradictory opinions about the main character can be held. The conflicting judgments are simultaneously present, as the narrator, tearing
the wallpaper, tries to release her double, the muted subtext with its
unsaid meanings. "Much Madness is divinest Sense" here. But from
the standpoint of "Much Sense—the starkest Madness—" that is, from
the perspective of normalcy, her statement demanding freedom for

the muted meanings looks like irrationality and delusion.[25] By an ending that calls attention to interpretive paradigms and powers, Gilman highlights the politics of narrative.

The autobiographical sources of this short story have been well-documented, from the breakdown itself to the infantalizing rest cure, prescribed by an eminent Philadelphia doctor.[26] As Gilman was massaged and fattened, she could "Have but two hours' intellectual life a day. And never touch pen, brush or pencil as long as you live." "The Yellow Wallpaper," dramatizing the mental cruelty of that dependent inactivity, was written with an explicitly didactic purpose—"to reach Dr. S. Weir Mitchell, and convince him of the error of his ways."[27] It is less noted that the inspiration for this story parallels the provocation of *The Story of Avis:* a compensatory defense of a thwarted mother and a highly critical eye cast at the institution of heterosexual romance and marriage—in Gilman's case both the marriage of her parents and her own first marriage.[28]

The motif in which the maternal parent becomes the muse for the daughter has more than fictional status; we can trace it through the biographies of women authors from Virginia Woolf and H. D. to Alice Walker. In a Woolfean essay, Walker "thinks back," tracing the sources of her art to the parent whose artistry is vital.

> Whatever she planted grew as if by magic, and her fame as a grower of flowers spread over three counties. . . . And I remember people coming to my mother's yard to be given cuttings from her flowers; I hear again the praise showered on her because whatever rocky soil she landed on, she turned into a garden. A garden so brilliant with colors, so original in its design, so magnificent with life and creativity, that to this day people drive by our house in Georgia—perfect strangers and imperfect strangers—and ask to stand or walk among my mother's art.[29]

Judging from the evidence in Gilman, Phelps Ward, Woolf, and Walker, there seems to be a specific biographical drama that has entered and shaped *Künstlerromane* by women. Such a narrative is engaged with a maternal figure and, on a biographical level, is often compensatory for her losses (which may themselves be imaginatively heightened by being remembered by her child). The daughter becomes an artist to extend, reveal, and elaborate her mother's often thwarted talents. "No song or poem will bear my mother's name" ("SMG," 240). Still, "perhaps she was herself a poet," summarizes Walker, "though only her daughter's name is signed to the poems that we know" ("SMG," 243).

The younger artist's future project as a creator lies in completing the fragmentary and potential work of the mother; the mother is the daughter's muse, but in more than a passive sense. For the mother is also an artist. She has written, sung, made, or created, but her work, because in unconventional media, is muted and unrecognized. The media in which she works are often the materials of "everyday use" (to borrow a phrase from Alice Walker), and her works are artisanal.[30] The traditional notion of a muse is a figure who gives access to feeling or knowledge that she herself cannot formulate. In contrast, this maternal muse struggles with her condition to forge a work, usually one unique, unrepeatable work—an event, a gesture, an atmosphere—a work of synthesis and artistry that is consumed or used.

By entering and expressing herself in some more dominant art form (poem, not garden, painting, not cuisine, novel, not parlor piano playing) the daughter can make prominent the work both have achieved. Mother and daughter are thus collaborators, coauthors separated by a generation. Because only the daughter's work is perceived as art within conventional definitions, it will challenge these formulations of decorum, so the mother or muted parent too can be seen as the artist s/he was.[31] This intellectual, aesthetic, and ethical defense of the mother becomes involved with the evocation of the preoedipal dyad, matrisexuality, or a bisexual oscillation deep in the gendering process. In these works, the female artist is given a way of looping back and reenacting childhood ties, to achieve not the culturally approved ending in heterosexual romance, but rather the reparenting necessary to her second birth as an artist.

In the nineteenth-century texts sampled here, heterosexual ties and the marriage relation come under considerable critical scrutiny, but no change in narrative modes occurs. In twentieth-century texts, the proportion of successful artist figures increases, by virtue of a keen change in the terms of the conflict between role and vocation. Instead of meaning marriage, motherhood, and housewifery, "role" comes to mean the filial completion of a thwarted parent's task. The daughter artist and the blocked, usually maternal, parent are, then, the central characters of twentieth-century women's *Künstlerromane*. The maternal or parental muse and the reparenting motifs are strategies that erode, transpose, and reject narratives of heterosexual love and romantic thralldom.

Precisely this is at stake in Virginia Woolf's *To the Lighthouse*, which concerns Lily Briscoe's long development, revealed through the interrupted process of completing her painting over the ten years in which the novel is set. The painting, a vivid formulation of the novel's themes in an imaginary plastic structure, is "about" a mother and child, Mrs. Ramsay and James, or even Lily herself, poised between strong opposing forces representing male and female—Mr. and Mrs. Ramsay. The creation of that dynamic poise has been the central aesthetic struggle for Lily.[32]

Because of her double and contradictory status, Mrs. Ramsay exists twice in Lily's painting, first as one of the two conventional sides that must be balanced, but then as the inspiration for the revelatory stroke in the middle. For Mrs. Ramsay is central to the two systems: she is the stereotypical feminine side of that dichotomy between male and female which will be superseded, yet at the same time she is the final line at the center of the painting: the dome of the mother-child dyad, the lighthouse of quest-love, the wedge-shaped mark of life infused with the void of oceanic death.

The Ramsays present a closed circuit of gender-stereotyped traits: transience and permanence, intuition and reason, caring and intellection, diffuseness and structure, being and ambition, yielding and principle. The balance of functions has made this a brilliantly successful couple, which sums up a whole family ideology in its interdependent gender divisions. In order for Lily to move into her future, she must renounce the polarized parents as models and reject the system of heterosexual bonding and the division of emotional labor that these parents uphold. Thus she cannot and will not marry, although matchmaking is one of the pretexts for the collection of characters at the summer house.[33]

The division of labor between the sexes is forcefully depicted. Mr. Ramsay is a system builder, struggling in vain to reach the elusive letter in the linear alphabet of knowledge—the R, which he cannot grasp without accepting the personal and the subjective. He wants achievement and fame, yet fears failure as measured by some unyielding norm. One of his oft-muttered mottoes comes from the compelling and unsettling "Charge of the Light Brigade," a poem concerning a heroic blunder that first kills and then immortalizes. For Woolf, Mr. Ramsay stands for male culture at its best and most vulnerable.

In contrast—and the contrasts are everywhere—Mrs. Ramsay creates a woman's culture in the anthropological sense, working in the media of food and relationships, especially new couples; her works are subject to time, change, and decay and are always studiedly unmonumental—a dinner, a casual letter, an atmosphere. It is typical of Woolf's tricky commentary on their relationship—her letter to his letter—that Mrs. Ramsay's art of life answers the philosophical problem upon which Mr. Ramsay has long been working: "subject and object and the nature of reality," or "think of a kitchen table . . . when you're not there" (*TTL*, 38). While the table may have objective, possibly verifiable existence on its own, still without us it has no meaning, and may therefore be said to depend on us for its reality. Without humanizing acts involving the perception of needs, there is nothing out there but meaningless wooden boards over which time destructively plays. The second part, "Time Passes," offers proof that things depend for their meaning specifically on a feminine construction of subjective memory and coherence as well as on the hard female work of preservation and maintenance. In this way, Woolf's narrative politics value the apparently trivial, not the apparently heroic.

As we have seen, "What an admirable idea! They must marry!" is a solution that grows unconvincing to Woolf as a creator of narrative (*TTL*, 109). By the midpoint of the novel, both of the traditional endings—marriage and death—have occurred, a sharp critical statement on Woolf's part that clears the ground of any rival solutions to Lily's plot. The third part of *To the Lighthouse* surpasses these classic resolutions, moving beyond the endings they propose, to brother-sister links, to male-female friendship, and, even more, to a vision that overwhelms all the binary systems on which the novel has been built. The final stroke, the placement of Lily's last line, an abstraction of the mother-child dyad wedged into the divided picture, makes her work emotionally complete and aesthetically unified. The either/or division between masculine and feminine reaches a both/and resolution in the art work of the female artist, who joins oedipal to preoedipal materials and expresses the hive, dome, and secret hieroglyphs of matrisexual passion.[34] This synthesis of polarities is even recorded in Woolf's response to her text: on one hand she can characterize it as a "hard muscular book," yet she can also see it as "soft and pliable, and I think deep. . . ."[35]

In the first part of the novel, Lily opts for the pure quest plot of artistic ambition. But this quest is not focused on the social career of the artist. Indeed, Woolf has so completely deemphasized the ambition, the program, the career of the artist that readers are sometimes deceived about Lily's seriousness. In an offhand critique of the genius theory, Woolf has Lily simply state that "she would always go on painting, because it interested her" (*TTL*, 110). When oppressed with imposed polarities of male-female etiquette and the niceties of courtships, Lily "remembered, all of a sudden as if she had found a treasure, that she had her work" (*TTL*, 128). That simile recalls the traditional reward of quest. Lily eloquently opts for her vocation: "she need not marry, thank Heaven: she need not undergo that degradation. She was saved from that dilution. She would move the tree rather more to the middle" (*TTL*, 154). Yet despite her certainty and such intense words as "degradation," Lily cannot finish her painting, not because "women can't paint, women can't write"—Tansley's taunt and an external goad—but because she has split her formalist vision from her emotional life (*TTL*, 238). Woolf further insists that Lily's painting can be completed only if she immerses herself in vulnerability, need, exposure, and grief, only through empathy—a set of feelings usually called womanly—and not through exclusive attention to aesthetics in a vacuum. The point is illustrated in the later scene with Mr. Ramsay, when "The sympathy she had not given him weighed her down. It made it difficult for her to paint" (*TTL*, 254). In short, the painting can be achieved only through the fusion of love with quest.

The love here is not of the classic novelistic kind: Lily's helpful and genuine admiration for Mr. Ramsay's boots, saving him from yet another depressive attack, is hardly a prelude to their courtship. But love it is, alluding to familial love, friendly love, comradely ties, some "of those unclassified affections of which there are so many" (*TTL*, 157). She helps him without dissolving into romantic thralldom or powerful self-abnegation, an important distinction from Mrs. Ramsay's way. Not only in offering affection to him but in admitting vulnerability to love and loss in herself, Lily is able to complete her painting. Thus love enables quest; quest is given meaning because of love. The two arcing and interconnected actions that complete the novel—Mr. Ramsay's sail across the bay with his children and Lily's completion of the painting—are both journeys that had been becalmed until love, grief, and need were admitted.[36]

Hence the solution to the aesthetic problem that Lily's painting had always presented—the joining of the two sides—could never have been found by aesthetic or formal means alone, but rather lay in her vulnerability to feelings of emptiness and baffled desire.[37] Woolf makes us feel that with every brush stroke disparate forces are being fused, and that the painting is the site of psychic resolutions: between love and death, presence and emptiness, grief and joy, past and present, memory and amnesia, as well as between male and female, mother and child. Her triple cries to Mrs. Ramsay, admissions of love and of mourning, enable the painting to take shape. Each new stage of vulnerability, then, contributes to the painting's development. So in its attitudes, preparations, and achievements, Lily's art is much closer to the model Mrs. Ramsay had presented, despite Lily's rejection of some of the feminine social duties she encourages. In contrast to some distinctive male artist heroes in the modern period, who "have a common insistence that the artist *as artist* must turn his back on life," the art works of these fictional female artists are immersed in the human relations basic to each character.[38]

Vita Sackville-West's novel *All Passion Spent* (1931) has similar mother-daughter motifs, expressed through the relationship between

the thwarted artist, Lady Slane, and her great-granddaughter, Deborah. When Lady Slane remembers her past, she focuses on the
defining conflict between vocation and love. She had wanted to run
off, dressed as a boy, but really as "a sexless creature," to become a
painter.[39] Instead of following her desire, Lady Slane marries a prominent public man and leads an upper-class life. Channeled into the
engagement that she regards as a joke, she suddenly realizes that
everyone has entered "into the general conspiracy to defraud her of
her chosen life" (*APS*, 158). This story, narrated in the aftermath of
her marriage, long wifedom, and her husband's death—after the
official story is told—is again an act of writing beyond the ending to
construct an oppositional view of the plot—meaning both narrative
and conspiracy—that traps women in a conventional role. The daughter artist, a reborn version of Lady Slane ("this other self, this projection of herself," *APS*, 280), has broken her engagement in order to
become a musician. The novel ends with a matrisexual connection
between daughter-singer and the Lady, which repeats Lily and Mrs.
Ramsay's embrace. The exchange inspires both Deborah's composition and her defiance of marriage. The thwarted "mother" dies, having given life to the "daughter," who steps beyond the frame of the
story.

Similarly, on the last page of *Surfacing* (1972) by Margaret Atwood,
the narrator hovers between past and future, between her dead parents and her unborn child, between meretricious commercial art and
the art she promises to make. *Surfacing* also shows an emergent
daughter who focuses the heritage of both parents in order to bring
herself to maturity. The man in the book, a woodsy impregnator, is set
aside when his task is done. The art work is a ritual performance piece
that the protagonist constructs in order to gain access to her parental,
Canadian, mythic (especially matriarchal) roots. Through this performance ritual, she sloughs off the victimization and deadness of
nationality and gender. Alone in the wilderness, the protagonist
choreographs visions of her parents, dreams, and symbolic acts, like
eating or not, into a unity both aesthetic and transformative. The
ritual functions in this character's life much as Lily's painting did,
closing the past and readying the self for the future. The liminal
ending in which the narrator crosses over into love (for her unborn
child) and achievement (her unborn art) mingles quest and love; the
acceptance of female role—the pregnancy was deliberately sought—
is, like the scenes of empathy in *To the Lighthouse*, the enabling act.[40]

Despite my use of the words "mother" and "daughter" to characterize the preoedipal implications of this reparenting, some of these
figures are either displaced by some generations or are not the biolog-

ical daughters of the mothers they seek. The generational displacement in the twentieth-century works covertly announces that the mother might be less than inspiring. Hence the mother may die in the story, as she does in Woolf, Sackville-West, and Tillie Olsen. In Christina Stead's novel *The Man Who Loved Children* (1940), the daughter artist Louie has even murdered Henny, her mother, with Henny's complicit understanding. Louie then emerges from her family, having broken the grip of the two embattled parents, escaping beyond the frame of the book in a liminal ending: "I have gone for a walk round the world."[41] The death or generational displacement of the mother in plots involving a daughter artist may be the writer's way of solving one form of the conflict between role and vocation, between the mutual costs, in Jane Flax's terms, of maternal nurturance and filial autonomy. The narrative death is a cold-blooded if necessary enabling act, which distinguishes the useful from the damaging in the maternal heritage. The useful part—empathy and symbiosis—is placed in the daughter's art work; the damaging part—envelopment and paralysis—lies buried in the grave.[42]

The doubled story in Tillie Olsen's "Tell Me a Riddle" is based on the complementary characters of artists who are thwarted and emergent, mother and daughter, dying and living. One major riddle—"How was it that soft reaching tendrils also became blows that knocked?"—refers in general to the ceaseless dialogue between possibility and betrayal that is carried on over a woman's lifetime, and in specific to the conflict between motherhood and Eva's political and artistic vocations.[43] The lifelong impoverishment of Eva's complex spirit, a narrowing carried out in the private realm of family life as well as in the public, historical realm, with its failure of revolutionary hopes, has made her a rancorous old lady. Eva is deaf, deliberately, bitterly silent, and filled with hostility and resentment: a paradigmatically muted figure.

During the story, she and her husband leave their house, site of many contentious and thematic issues about the meaning of home and family, and visit three "daughters." The first returns to the past, with her ghettoized emphasis on Jewish particularism; the second lives a life like her mother's, with its ever-present claims and pressures of children "intensely and now" ("TMR," 84). The third figure, the grandchild Jeannie, completes the pattern, offering future promise. Resembling the revolutionary woman who taught Eva to read more than fifty years before, Jeannie expresses a continuity between the battered ideals of the century's struggles and the unknown future in which these revolutionary possibilities might be realized.

At the last stage of her journey, with her death from cancer immi-

nent, Eva becomes the point upon which past, present, and future
converge. She recovers her long-repressed identity as "First mother,
singing mother," beginning her "incessant words," which resemble
the *Sprechstimme* of modernist musical style ("TMR," 107, 103).[44] Her
suffering and her memories crack her open; her voicing makes a
broken, poetic song-speech with a pedal-point of unanswerable rid-
dles: "So strong for what? To rot not grow"; "Man . . . we'll destroy
ourselves?" ("TMR," 99). Like the pageant music in Woolf's *Between
the Acts,* Eva's song is a communal one, and her individual person is
like a conduit through which a collectivity chants: "night and day,
asleep or awake . . . the songs and the phrases leaping" ("TMR," 108).
In Eva's cantata of voices, memories, stories, bits of speeches and
books, Olsen makes a manifesto of long-muted voices, a political and
aesthetic statement of power from the apparently powerless, who
sometimes can hear the music of human struggle and destiny.

The granddaughter Jeannie, a Visiting Nurse, only gradually
emerges as an artist in the course of the story. For if Jeannie is a muse
for Eva, the reverse is also true: the grandmother's vision will reorient
the younger woman. In the sketch of her grandmother "coiled . . . like
an ear," Jeannie shows she has understood Eva's essence: sensitivity to
the music of struggling humanity ("TMR," 102). Another of Jeannie's
sketches, of her grandparents lying, hands "clasped, feeding each
other," makes the grandfather forgive Eva for her bitterness ("TMR,"
115). Jeannie "remarries" them at their last moments together. So,
like Eva's, her art is a moral and didactic act.

Human creativity in its boldest and broadest senses inspires Eva's
cantata. The collective strength and "zest" of voices at a community
chorale break through her defenses. The stories of Chekhov and
Balzac are high cultural sources; a Pan del Muerto—folk-art cookie
for a dead child—comes from popular culture. "Like art," this decorated cookie recalls the songs of Anon in *Between the Acts,* the moment
"almost like a work of art" in *To the Lighthouse,* and "my mother's art"
of the garden for Alice Walker ("TMR" 100). Like Woolf and Walker,
Olsen obliterates the distinction between high culture and folk art in
the array of Eva's sources.[45] Yet while immersion in the human condition compels artistic expression, such an immersion also prevents it.
Olsen's own career is a negotiation with this contradiction. She
chooses to look for the unsaid, absent, or missing elements, constructing a literary and political stance "dark with silences" of the unspoken.[46] Olsen has testified to the thematic and moral center provided
by her recognition, like Woolf's in *A Room of One's Own,* of the social,
material, and emotional circumstances that prevent, or give a certain
twisted cast to, fruition and achievement.

If, in these women writers, the function of the artist with the tools of dominant culture is to embody muted experiences, then the figure of the female artist counters the modernist tradition of exile, alienation, and refusal of social roles—the *non serviam* of the classic artist hero, Stephen Dedalus. The woman writer creates the ethical role of the artist by making her imaginatively depict and try to change the life in which she is also immersed. This differentiates the figure in the female *Künstlerromane* from the fantasies of social untouchability or superiority that are prevalent in modernist depictions. These issues of change and stasis emerge in Doris Lessing's *The Golden Notebook* (1962). A published writer of a book that she now regards with contempt, Anna Wulf can no longer "write," but keeps four notebooks, separated explanations for the political and sexual strains that caused her professional stalemate. The major formal project of Lessing's book is to explore and surpass meretricious, abandoned, or incomplete stories, sometimes love plots, but also a whole novel called *Free Women,* in order to arrive at some precious dialectical "golden" amalgam, through which a more dynamic statement about history, politics, and personal relations can be articulated.[47]

Free Women is a tidy, third-person "autobiographical" work. This deliberately provincial novel is like the "small, quite lively, intelligent novels" of the fifties in Britain, which Lessing regards with "despair" because they are ignorant of change and of the "world-mind, or world ethic" to which they do not contribute.[48] *The Golden Notebook* records Anna Wulf's choice between affirmative culture—an art work like *Free Women* that affirms existing social relations—and the negating act of criticism. Indeed, Lessing even offers two resolutions, the dominant and the critical. In one, the end of *Free Women,* the character decides not to write, but rather to do "matrimonial welfare work," an act of social reproduction, helping things limp along as usual. Whereas in the "Golden Notebook" section, the Saul-Anna couple, having undergone a tempering in the destructive and pleasurable postures of heterosexual love, renounces those designs to write the novels whose first lines are a gift each has provided to the other, in their most meaningful act beyond thralldom. "To put the short novel *Free Women* as a summary and condensation of all that mass of material was to say something about the conventional novel," Lessing stated, the "something" being how its univocal neatness fails to capture the "rough" and "apparently formless and unshaped" experiences.[49] The physical end of *The Golden Notebook* stands only to be eroded by the tidal rip of notebooks swelling around it, each of whose acts of containment are criticized by the presence of the others, for each constructs a reality that tries to exclude the others.

The contrast Lessing faces between her artist's formless questions, embodied in the relations between the notebooks, and the proper novel is reminiscent of Woolf's "Modern Fiction" essay, with its similar contrast between "life" and the tidiness of novels, and its impatience to combat the closures of fictional tradition.[50] Lessing's critique of conventional novels is also joined, as it sometimes is in Woolf, to a general dissent from the rituals of bourgeois cultural production: the regarding of talent as "commodity," the extolling of submission to authority, the denial of divergent values and assumptions, the exclusion of originality or unconformity by a powerful "social mechanism."[51] Almost half of the "Preface to *The Golden Notebook*" is devoted to a radical critique of cultural institutions, whose arguments about authority and whose rhetorical intransigence bear comparison to *Three Guineas.* In Lessing, then, the critique of narrative is one part of a general attack on affirmative ideologies. This is the "story" that she rejects; in *The Golden Notebook* as a totality she writes beyond that ending.

Anna had argued endlessly that it is impossible to create art, since the only wholeness people exhibit occurs by virtue of pastiche and ersatz imitations of order. She learns that it is not art that should be rejected but a limiting conception of artistic order. Thus another kind of narrative must be invented—the multivocal, palimpsestic, personal, autobiographical, documentary, analytic, essayistic diary-novel. This is not the encylopedic form of the authoritative *summa* but something that has switched the poles of authority—an encyclopedia with its categories unformed, its indices unmade, its alphabets unorganized, without fixed grids of judgment, exclusion, concision, or categorization. Anna has found that to write fiction as it was once written would constitute a premature resolution of conflict, confining contradictions rather than releasing them the length and breadth of the work. Narrative based on nostalgia, on manipulative transpositions, on small-minded, riskless reaches into the expressive are obsessively set forth and rejected. Thus the novel is an encyclopedia of the critique of narrative and hegemonic orders.

Ideological and personal inclusiveness play an ethical role in *The Golden Notebook,* because only by holding everything (the "chaos" about which Anna defensively talks) can basic ways of seeing and fictionalizing be called into question. This process of delegitimation has its own muse. At the bottom of a casket seen in a dream lies "joy-in-spite" or "joy-in-destruction," a gnome who is the critical sensibility animating the work of piercing normal politics, society, sexuality, and narrative. This joy in destruction is the muse of critique. Lessing said about her work, referring at once to *The Golden Notebook*'s complex poetics of domestic values - nurturance, community building, inclusiveness, empathetic care.

Künstlerromane by Women Writers   103

structure, to the assumptions that it addressed, and to the stories it delegitimated, that it was "an attempt to break a form; to break certain forms of consciousness and go beyond them."[52] Thus Lessing's contribution to the critique of ideology and narrative in writing beyond the ending.

The fictional art work, distinctively described in these works, has a poetics of domestic values—nurturance, community building, inclusiveness, empathetic care.[53] The poetics of the fictional art work begins with its ethics, not its aesthetics; it has its source in human ties and its end in human change. The work is described as having a clear ethical function and is not severed from the personal or social needs that are its source—for example, the mourning or rage expressed by the characters. This art work can only be made with an immersion in personal vulnerability, a breakdown, or a breakthrough, as in Gilman, Lessing, and Atwood, or as an articulation of long-repressed grief or love, usually the experiences of a daughter in relation to parents, as in Woolf and Olsen.[54] This saturation in buried, even taboo emotions, first resisted, then sought, and finally claimed, is the preferred process by which the fictional artist comes into her own. Since this art work annuls aesthetic distance and is based on vulnerability and need, it is very like "life."[55]

But the work is not exclusively expressive in its poetics. While often begun in situations of psychic desperation, these works are not satisfied simply to confess this fact, or to transform the fictional artist through her knowledge. In contradistinction to purely expressive theories of art, here sincerity is valued because it clarifies the ethical and social bases of the experience. Expression, in the fictional art works, is informed with critical purpose. Anna Wulf's breakdown, the subject of her most dramatic and fructifying notebook, is a decisive rupture with the paradigms of intellectual and emotional order in which she once believed. Eva's cantata begins in hostile anger and ends with a vision of social and revolutionary hope. The hero of "The Yellow Wallpaper" resists the definitional grids that imprison her double in the wallpaper.

The depicted art work is charged with the conditions of its own creation. Maintaining self-reflexive emphasis on the process of creation, this art work is not presented as an artifact free from the stresses and limits of the time in which it was formed. Instead, it is both fabricated from and immersed in the temporal, social, and psychic conditions of muted female life that we are compelled to understand in reading the work: interruptions, blockage, long censorship, derision, self-hatred, internalized repression. Nor does the art work seek the status of a masterpiece or great work, which will be severed from

Gubar calls this 'revisionary domestic ideology'

poetics of domestic values

✳

its everyday connections, stored in a museum or gallery, published or sold. The imaginary art work takes its cue from the artisanal experience, in which the object is made for use and has its existence in the realm of necessity, as an expression of ties or needs. Art defined in this fashion is not a property dependent upon its market price and the level of rarity or specialness that it has attained. The fictional art work, drawing on the artisanal, not only expresses its connection with the parental or maternal handicrafter but also registers a protest against art as a salable commodity. The thing precious only because it is hoarded, saved, unconsumed is rejected. Instead, craft (gardening, cooking, storytelling, singing, quilting) and art (painting, sculpting, writing) are viewed as varient parts of one spectrum of human production. This pointed fusion of craft and high art makes a critical assessment of the value placed on activities elevated above the material and conflictual realm.[56]

The division between high and decorative arts is a historical construct, not a universal, and it can be linked to the view of the artist as a separated, isolated genius. By inserting the artist in a social group, the family—but a family reconceptualized so that parental and especially maternal ties are a nurturing source, not an impediment—and by structuring an ethics of emotional service, the idea of the artist as social outcast is contested.

So the fictional art works are carefully built to end what Theodor Adorno calls "the pure autonomy of mind" in the relation of art to culture. Culture—high bourgeois culture—"originates in the radical separation of mental and physical work. It is from this separation, the original sin, as it were, that culture draws it strength."[57] William Morris also points to the historical specificity of the moment when "the great and lesser arts" separate, the one to become "ingenious toys" for the rich, the other to become trivial and unintelligent.[58] It is clear that the fusion of the artisanal and high art has been an analytic dream for radical thinkers. The ideological importance of this fusion for solving the narrative dilemma of role and vocation is apparent when one remembers the completely binary alternatives of the nineteenth-century texts—either domestic life or artistic life. The twentieth-century female *Künstlerromane* solve that binary opposition between work and domesticity by having the fictional art work function as a labor of love, a continuation of the artisanal impulse of a thwarted parent, an emotional gift for family, child, self, or others. This may or may not be realistic, but it is a compelling narrative solution to a prime contradiction. In their artist novels, women writers present a radical oppositional aesthetics criticizing dominance.

■

CHAPTER SEVEN

"Perceiving the other-side of everything": Tactics of Revisionary Mythopoesis

Because Perseus looked and rescued her, she would have to be grateful to him all her life and smile and be Mrs. Perseus.
DOROTHY RICHARDSON
Honeycomb (1917), *Pilgrimage*

I may be breathing naturally but I have the feeling of holding my breath under water. As if I were searching under water for some priceless treasure, and if I bobbed up to the surface the clue to its whereabouts would be lost forever. So I, though seated upright, am in a sense diving, head-down under water—in another element, and as I seem now so near to getting the answer or finding the treasure, I feel that my whole life, my whole being, will be blighted forever if I miss this chance. I must not lose grip, I must not lose the end of the picture and so miss the meaning of the whole, so far painfully perceived. I must hold on here or the picture will blur over and the sequence be lost. In a sense, it seems I am drowning; already half-drowned to the ordinary dimensions of space and time, I know that I must drown, as it were, completely in order to come out on the other side of things (like Alice with her looking-glass or Perseus with his mirror). I must drown completely and come out on the other side, or rise to the surface after the third time down, not dead to this life but with a new set of values, my treasure dredged from the depth. I must be born again or break utterly.
H.D.
Tribute to Freud (1956)

Twentieth-century women poets turn again and again to rewrite, reinterpret, or reenvision classical myths and other culturally resonant materials, such as biblical stories or folk tales. They are reformulating a special kind of persistent narrative that is the repository of many dimensions of representation. Roland Barthes has historicized the question of myth and the related question of an eternal essence for Woman.

Are there objects which are *inevitably* a source of suggestiveness, as Baudelaire suggested about Woman? Certainly not: one can conceive of very ancient myths, but there are no eternal ones; for it is human history which converts reality into speech, and it alone rules the life and death of mythical language. Ancient or not, mythology can only have an historical foundation, for myth is a type of speech chosen by history: it cannot possibly evolve from the 'nature' of things.[1]

But a historicized sense of myth is normally lost; for myth is built on and claims the denial of history, transforming "history into nature."[2] Myth best demonstrates its ideological character by refusing to acknowledge that it ever had any truck with the nonuniversal or the nontranscendent.[3] Of all our stories, myths are considered the most universal, describing deep structures of human need and evincing the most cunning knowledge of "mankind." Likewise, myths are held to offer exclusive narrative coverage, saying every vital thing that could be imagined about a character or an event, providing a repertoire of causes and effects, stimuli and responses, that are not only paradigmatic but timeless.

When a woman writer chooses myth as her subject, she is faced with material that is indifferent or, more often, actively hostile to historical considerations of gender, claiming as it does universal, humanistic, natural, or even archetypal status. To face myth as a woman writer is, putting things at their most extreme, to stand at the impact point of a strong system of interpretation masked as representation, and to rehearse one's own colonization or "iconization" through the materials one's culture considers powerful and primary.

Myth is a story that, regardless of its loose ends, states cultural agreement and coherence. Thus when a writer dissents from that agreement, or oscillates between being a member and a critic of her culture, she can turn to a myth because she can thereby attain a maximum tension with and maximum seduction by dominant stories.

The special status of myth for women writers has much to do with institutions of cultural recruitment: canons sacred or secular, censorship, schooling. The classics are a tool of social consolidation: knowing or not knowing the Graeco-Roman classics in the original had highly symbolic status as a social marker of both class and gender caste.[4] Although Woolf struggled in her early adult years to learn Greek, during her first breakdown, even the birds seemed to speak that language naturally. H.D.'s mastery of the Greek lyric, approximately contemporaneous with Woolf's, constituted her statement that she had accumulated enough cultural authority to work as a poet.[5]

The special status of Judeo-Christian myths hardly needs elaborating. These literally canonical, sacred texts on which are built man's highest and perhaps most redeeming ideals have constituted ideologies surrounding and defining women as evil, duplicitous, closer to nature, disallowed from speech, thought, or debate. The consequent anxiety of the blasphemous female author, traced by Sandra Gilbert and Susan Gubar, might be a little less intense for a woman facing the classics, for they only bear the authority of school, not God.[6] However, the classics still seem to have induced that mixture of defensive paralysis and assertive transformation characteristic of a female position in culture, the defensive situation on the margins of speech and culture and the assertive repossession of voice when oppositional narratives are invented.

Women poets invent revisionary myths in the attempt to forge an anticolonial mythopoesis, an attack on cultural hegemony as it is, which necessarily has included a vision of gender. Such a poet, in Alicia Ostriker's words, "deconstructs a prior 'myth' or 'story' and constructs a new one which includes, instead of excluding, herself."[7] But even the desire to produce a critical mythopoesis is a project fraught with some irony, since one of the social functions of mythic narrative is precisely the solidification, consolidation, and affirmation of a hegemony—the "operative, iterative, and validatory" functions of myth, in Geoffrey Kirk's terms.[8] Myth may provide a charter for certain kinds of institutional authority by excluding stories that tell the "wrong" tale from the canon; by cementing or palliating contradictions; by assimilating the narrative of conquered peoples to the myths of a conquering nation. In short, making a critical mythopoesis goes against the grain of a major function of myth: the affirmation of dominant culture. Thus we can see why a critical mythic act, aware of the political implications of narrative, might cross over into a "liberated" mythopoesis—the claim that one or another group is the privileged site of noncolonial consciousness. For this claim simply recapitulates one of the affirmative functions of myth and applies it to the muted group.

The whole revisionary project critical of existing cultural agreements has been summed up by Adrienne Rich in a deservedly noted statement, of which I cite a part.

> Re-vision—the act of looking back, of seeing with fresh eyes, of entering an old text from a new critical direction—is for women more than a chapter in cultural history: it is an act of survival. Until we can understand the assumptions in which we are drenched we cannot know ourselves. . . . We need to know the writing of the past, and know it differently than we have ever known it; not to pass on a tradition but to break its hold over us.[9]

The rewriting of myths is, then, "revisionary," critical of existing culture and values. Within this overarching term, one can distinguish two related ways of remaking mythic stories.

The poet's attitude toward the tale as given determines whether there will be a displacement of attention to the other side of the story, or a delegitimation of the known tale, a critique even unto sequences and priorities of narrative. Narrative displacement is like breaking the sentence, because it offers the possibility of speech to the female in the case, giving voice to the muted. Narrative delegitimation "breaks the sequence"; a realignment that puts the last first and the first last has always ruptured conventional morality, politics, and narrative.[10]

Displacement is a committed identification with Otherness—a participant observer's investigation of the claims of those parts of culture and personality that are taboo, despised, marginalized. The new "sentence" comes from the "other-side of everything," articulating things "not . . . noticed before, or, if noticed . . . guiltily suppressed."[11] Sometimes with displacement, the other side seems the only right side, and the poet claims to have found the nugget of absolute truth at the far-away bottom of the fiction. In "An Ancient Gesture," Edna St. Vincent Millay insists that Penelope "really" cried, while Ulysses only pretended to; her act is "authentic," his, just a "gesture."[12] The contention of authenticity or truth finally unburied helps give power to the retold tale and authority to the teller, both necessary for confronting the cultural weight of Western civilization.

For defection from paradigmatic ways of seeing, there are the useful simplicities of Robin Morgan's statement:

> May I realize that I
>   am a
>   monster. I am
>   a
>   monster
> I am a monster.
>
> And I am proud.

Here the process of bringing the full, unfragmented statement to the left margin indicates first the tentative, then the bold, claim to a reversal of values.[13]

The question whether a "Medusa" is paralyzed or paralyzing is given curious resonance by the relative blockage of Louise Bogan's own poetic career.[14]

> When the bare eyes were before me
> And the hissing hair,
> Held up at a window, seen through a door.
> The stiff bald eyes, the serpents on the forehead
> Formed in the air.

> This is a dead scene forever now.
> Nothing will ever stir.

The poet's muse can be that "other side" found in the displacement of the myth. The mirror that Medusa provides here allows May Sarton to postulate her repressed anger as subject.

> I turn your face around! It is my face.
> That frozen rage is what I must explore—
> Oh secret, self-enclosed, and ravaged place!
> This is the gift I thank Medusa for.[15]

In Sylvia Plath's work, Medusa—like the monsters in sci-fi movies of the 1950s—is a blob with a distinctly maternal character. As the controlling phallic mother she interrupts and ruins the heterosexual love plot.[16]

> I didn't call you.
> I didn't call you at all.
> Nevertheless, nevertheless
> You steamed to me over the sea,
> Fat and red, a placenta
>
> Paralyzing the kicking lovers.
> . . . .
> Green as eunuchs, your wishes
> Hiss at my sins.
> Off, off, eely tentacle!
>
> There is nothing between us.

The otherness of Medusa, with its Gorgonesque infinitation of possibilities, and its anger, expressed and repressed, are paradigmatic of all the things one may find when one turns to the "other side" of a story. A change of point of view reveals the implicit politics of narrative: the choice of the teller or the perspective will alter its core assumptions and one's sense of the tale.[17] By putting the female eye, ego, and voice at the center of the tale, displacement asks the kind of questions that certain feminist historians have, in parallel ways, put forth: How do events, selves, and grids for understanding look when viewed by a female subject evaluated in ways she chooses?[18]

This narrative displacement to the "other side" of the story can occur whenever a well-known story is accepted but told from some noncanonical perspective. So if a poet is writing about Eurydice or Calypso, as H.D. did, those stories' sequences are taken as absolutes. But, as noted earlier, the poet reveals the emotions of the female protagonist under these circumstances; different causes and different responses occur in precisely the same plot.

H.D. points to Eurydice's bitter resentment at having to hope for release and then be forcibly returned to death. H.D.'s retelling pivots from powerlessness to female power, a thematic displacement vivid in the poem, while accepting the major feature of the plot—that Orpheus does turn back to look at Eurydice and thus loses her. But while the plot's sequence is, point for point, the same as the classic tale, the critical view from the "other side" demands eight times to know what indeed was his motivation in turning, for the usual explanation (his great love) is not acceptable.

> why did you turn back,
> that hell should be reinhabited
> of myself thus
> swept into nothingness?
>
> why did you turn?
> why did you glance back?
> why did you hesitate for that moment?
> [etc.]
>
> (*CP,* 51–52)

A displacement to the other side provides the poem's turning point and conclusion: "I tell you this: // such loss is no loss." Values are reversed: the "loss" of the earth, the light, the man, and other "live souls" is redefined as "no loss." Indeed, H.D.'s "Eurydice" is a paradigmatic poem of displacement, because it negates the negative parts of the story, and because its very setting—death, the underworld—is the other side dramatically envisioned.[19]

Margaret Atwood's street-smart sequence "Circe/Mud Poems" in *You Are Happy* uses both revisionary strategies; based mainly on the poetics of displacement, it moves toward delegitimation, the critical creation of an unexpected story, in attempts to gain release from a colonial tale.[20] Although Circe begins by spending "days with my head pressed to the earth," attempting to gather a "few muted syllables" in a bare landscape, she gives up this oppositional pursuit of new speech rather easily, as soon as the Odyssean antagonist is washed up on her island ("C/MP," 49). Then Circe bitterly acts her inevitable script. The old romantic story dominates, and the promising critique of story and language is debased to a withering tongue-lashing:

> One day you simply appeared in your stupid boat,
> your killer's hands, your disjointed body, jagged
> as a shipwreck . . .
>
> ("C/MP," 50)

The decision of Circe and Odysseus to become lovers seems to engage the woman in a foreknown sequence predicted brusquely. "To be feared, to be despised, / These are your choices," she says to Odysseus, criticizing his participation in this foreordained tale:

> Don't you get tired of killing
> those whose deaths have been predicted
> and are therefore dead already?
>   ("C/MP," 51)

Both characters are "in the clutch of" a "story" synonymous with a "disease," and both are "helpless" ("C/MP," 64).

At this point in the poem, the man has been only the bearer of the old Homeric plot, while the woman, in a way that we should recognize, inhabits two plots, dominant and muted. Seduced—the term is used advisedly—by the man and the coherence of the romantic part, yet drawn to the "monsters" of the muted tale, Circe wavers between the inevitable and the inarticulate ("C/MP," 64). Indeed, the alternatives presented in Atwood's title, with its interesting virgule of opposition and relation, sum up this oscillating female stance. Circe as transformative magician-physician dispenses curative letters of the nonhegemonic speech to the needy; Circe as mud lies passively, and men build and enter her.

> It's the story that counts. No use telling me this isn't a story, or not the same story. . . . In the story the boat disappears one day over the horizon, just disappears, and it doesn't say what happens then. On the island, that is. It's the animals I'm afraid of, they weren't part of the bargain. . . . Don't evade, don't pretend you won't leave after all: you leave in the story and the story is ruthless. ("C/MP," 68)

In this prose passage, the narratives debate, yet essentially the outline of the known story is "ruthless," unstoppable.

At the end of this sequence, Atwood's final statement, "There are two islands," designates two ways of telling a story as well as two kinds of love. In the first, the couple is complicit with patterns of thralldom.

>   we proceed
>   as usual, we watch for
>   omens, we are sad
>
>   and so forth, it is over,
>   I am right, it starts again,
>   jerkier this time and faster,

and she ends this rerun, "I could recite it backwards" ("C/MP," 69). No matter the variations; in the metaphor of a film so banalized that the

narrator has it memorized, the myth is affirmed. Somehow the narrative must be altered further, the very outlines and telos of the story
changed; bluntly, this possibility is sketchy at best. "The second I
know nothing about / because it never happened."

Decolonization of narrative may be described in the Memmiesque
schemata that Atwood presents in *Survival*. There are four stages in a
transition from an internalized colonial mentality to an anticolonial
world view; "the positions," she dryly reminds us, "are the same
whether you are a victimized country, a victimized minority group or
a victimized individual" (*S*, 36).[21] The denial of victimhood or the
naming of fate or nature as its cause is comparable to the tactic of
displacement. To speak as a natural, dumb, animalistic, nontech-
nological, primitive other is a linguistic maneuver to express what the
colonizer saw as a voiceless nonentity: Circe as Mud. Here the inheritor of muteness, embracing the despised side, affirms that she can
define and voice that Otherness. The next social strategies, "to refuse
to accept the assumption that the role is inevitable," or to achieve a
change of consciousness, might correspond to the active rupture with
a narrative order, the tactic of delegitimation (*S*, 37). Because if "you
are able to accept your own experience for what it is, rather than
having to distort it to make it correspond with others' versions of it
. . . ," then you are producing a new story (*S*, 39). That this story is still
based on dialogues between the margin and the center is suggested by
Atwood's review of black American women writers. "If you are a
member of an imperial culture, a Roman rather than a Gaul, you can
take things for granted, to the point of ignorance or amnesia, in a way
that the Gauls cannot. Black American women are, paradoxically,
both Gauls and Romans, but these writers identify most of the time
with the Gauls."[22]

A "Roman" turns into a "Gaul" in works by the black American
poet Gwendolyn Brooks. Her critique of myth shows again that
stories are ideologies that shape our sense of reality—indeed, that
stories themselves can colonize. Gwendolyn Brooks's poem "A
Bronzeville Mother Loiters in Mississippi. Meanwhile, a Mississippi
Mother Burns Bacon." takes up the ballad imbedded in a white
woman's mind and confronts it with the reality: her complicit guilt in
a lynching.[23]

When the protagonist tries to live inside a mythic narrative about a
villain, a maiden, and a hero, the poet homes in on that self-
justificatory belief.

From the first it had been like a
Ballad. It had the beat inevitable. It had the blood.

A wildness cut up, and tied in little bunches,
Like the four-line stanzas of the ballads she had never quite
Understood—the ballads they had set her to, in school.

Herself: the milk-white maid, the "maid mild"
Of the ballad. Pursued
By the Dark Villain. Rescued by the Fine Prince.
The Happiness-Ever-After.

                                                   (*SP,* 75)

The "Villain," a fourteen-year-old black youth, is accused by the white woman of some crime that she cannot exactly name to herself. The wife had a script to damn the youth that was complete, dominant, and enthralling. However, that story comes completely undone. The inevitability of the narrative, with its stereotypes of hero and heroine, meets the historical truth of what indeed occurred: a white husband, asserting his power and place, has killed a black youth and has been acquitted. The fairy-tale narrative of Dark Villain, Fair Maiden, and Hero falsifies the encounter of black and white, male and female, power and powerless, whose bold strokes are beholden to an intersection of race and gender and a specific history of black and white that is evoked in the resonant name "Emmett Till," unstated until the second poem in Brooks's sequence.[24]

To reveal the break with her interpretive framework, Brooks shows her character stunned by the disintegrating "composition" and disgusted at the power relations of race and gender that have made "the pattern prevail" (*SP,* 77). At this moment of rupture, the husband or prince comes. The murderous violence of this man's dominance is marked by a domestic incident apparently far from the headlines and protests that marked his acquittal. But, as we have seen before, the erasure of the dualism of public and private spheres is one part of the critique of ideology in women's writing. So the man's public trial recurs in a private judgment. He slaps his child fiercely, leaving a red mark, the mark—Brooks is quite explicit—of patriarchal racial and gender violence. Seeing her child so marked precipitates the woman's stunned meditation on the blood-red stain perpetually following his "Hand."

In her revulsion, she is able to visualize her counterpart: the black mother of the youth her husband "hacked." Both women have been silenced, castrated, and unvoiced by male power. Neither can protect her child from his violence. The relation and division of these two women is expressed by the lengthy title of the poem, with its combination of parallels ("mother" and "Mississippi") and separation (complete, even wearying, sentences punctuated with periods).

The ballad in the white woman's mind had once operated as "the ending"—the ending of all questions, the ending in satisfaction: "The Happiness-Ever-After." But the realities of male and white power have forced her beyond the ending. The paradigm shifts, and the picture in her mind changes. Instead of seeing a Fine Prince, we see a domineering Hand and a mouth, the naked violence that the fairy tale had mystified.

> The last bleak news of the ballad.
> The rest of the rugged music.
> The last quatrain
>
> (*SP*, 80)

is the delegitimated story.

For in a strong maneuver, Brooks proceeds to write the poem beyond the ending of "Bronzeville Mother," creating an oblique brief statement about the mourning black woman. Taken together, the poems make a critique of myths by the tactics of displacement and delegitimation, expressed in the revulsion of the two silenced mothers.

This second poem, "The Last Quatrain of the Ballad of Emmett Till," refers to the griefs hidden in that actual case yet does not touch its details in any way. The feelings evoked in this poem come from a range of geographical and experiential marginality that cannot be put directly into words. The restraint of this poem is an act of desperate power on Brooks's part, denying narration altogether by a series of symbolic descriptions focused by the title. The poem offers that strange sense of destabilization achieved when every detail is too nice, too restrained.

> Emmett's mother is a pretty-faced thing;
>   the tint of pulled taffy.
> She sits in a red room,
>   drinking black coffee.
> She kisses her killed boy.
>   And she is sorry.
> Chaos in windy grays
>   through a red prairie.
>
> (*SP*, 81)

Such pointed allusions to color are a motif in black writing in general and may also continue and draw upon ambiguities in Angelina Weld Grimké's "Tenebris."[25]

Brooks's poetics draws on the marginality and the historically constructed situation of blackness. Discussing the idea that a black writer will see things differently from a white one, her argument offers subtle evidence of the way seeing from the other side rejects conventional images and natural truths.

In an interview of 1969, the interviewer cites a 1950 statement for Brooks's comment.

> At the present time, poets who happen also to be Negroes are twice-tried. They have to write poetry, and they have to remember that they are Negroes. . . . *They* are likely to find significances in those subjects not instantly obvious to their fairer fellows. The raindrop may seem to them to represent racial tears. . . . The golden sun might remind them that they are burning.

Brooks responds:

> That's carrying it a stretch too far, as poets will do, I suppose; but at least in Chicago we [the Black Arts Movement] have had spirited conversations about whether a black poet has the right to deal with trees, to concern himself with trees. And one of the things that I've always said was, certainly, certainly a black poet may be involved in a concern for trees, if only because when he looks at one he thinks of how his ancestors have been lynched thereon.[26]

The interviewer, shocked at this departure from the universality of a natural fact notes that "it is, of course, possible for anyone to look at a tree and see just a tree. . . ." But Brooks insists on the anticolonial poetics of displacement and delegitimation: "It is possible, but if a black person looks *long* enough, he just might think of other things that a white person might not. . . . " She then goes on to cite "horrific" pictures of lynchings, to prove that people's mental associations draw on historically different formations. This is the same kind of doubled consciousness that generates all the contradictions of a marginal group, between the Roman and the Gaul, between insider and outsider, between dominant and muted of any paradigm—whether gender or race.

Although the poet H.D. was a member of a dominant group in class and race, several other social practices, especially sexuality, sexual preference, and exile, contribute to her sense of marginality in dialogue with dominance. H.D. oscillated between heterosexual and lesbian ties; "perfect bi——" described the doubled identity she affirmed.[27] This perspective led to critical analysis of the sexual and cultural dominance of males. Female and occult materials of culture, religion, narrative, and the psyche had been buried, to the detriment of history itself. Indeed, as her visionary autobiography, *The Gift,* traces, H.D. even found such hidden materials within her own family's history: a visionary capacity of social and political use for a redemptive drama. Repossession of this gift, a syncretic worship of the holy spirit, would lead to mutual tolerance among all tribes and nations, and thus to an end to war. H.D. felt that it was the writer's task, for her own quest and, given the impact of World War II, for the sake of Western culture, to remember these materials, raising them to full and effective status.

H.D. spoke throughout her career, and, as Susan Friedman shows, paradigmatically in her relation with Freud, of the muted alternatives that she represented: art, the visionary, the antimaterialist, and the female. To enunciate these muted alternatives is the project of H.D.'s *Trilogy* (1944–46), a major work of revisionary mythopoesis, dissenting from the ideology presented in sacred stories and inventing another story and another kind of prophet to give narrative coherence to the muted values.[28]

H.D. works with the Christian story but opens the tale to reveal the occulted myth of the mother goddess, so that Jesus himself and Christianity itself are seen as expressions of the Great Mother.[29] H.D. reads the Gospels with a keen eye for the anti-institutional character of the early followers of Jesus: "the twisted or the tortured individuals, // out of line, out of step with world so-called progress," persons such as "an unbalanced, neurotic woman" and "an outcast and a vagabond" (*FR, CP,* 586). Christianity as a charismatic movement of the Mother Goddess spoke to these muted outcasts, and most particularly to a certain "Mary the Jewess," whose story *The Flowering of the Rod* will tell.[30]

Even when the male-centered God the father exudes his rays, at the beginning of the poem, the question of the female reinserts itself in history and myth. She is the wall that does not fall at the bomb site with which H.D. begins the poem. *The Walls Do Not Fall* shows that war is a battle against the life force. The names of Isis and other mother goddesses break into this section of *Trilogy,* as if no matter which way the speaker turns, the female element surprises by its muted presence. The first poem is, in the main, about Amen, the father God, an androgynous version of a patriarch, "not at all like Jehovah" (*WDNF, CP,* 523). Although the patriarch has been feminized by H.D.'s evocation of the "new Sun" behind Christ, Sirus and Osiris, behind the Sire of Western religion, this concession is not enough (*WDNF, CP,* 524). Similarly, the iconography of the caduceus (rod and lily bud) announces a mingling of maternal and paternal forces, yet these are still rearrangements of existing imagery and known traditions, the "story" with which the poet is already familiar. In sum, *The Walls Do Not Fall* attempts to normalize some of the irruptive female force while attempting to forge a new way to worship the "world-father / father of past aeons" (*WDNF, CP,* 523).

But this text gives way to a growing subtext; affirmation yields to displacement. A seed is planted in the poet's heart, and it produces a tree, a motif long associated with mother goddesses. What she has known of the male gods must be "re-valued" (*WDNF, CP,* 538). Hence the poet begins a voyage into "the unrecorded (*WDNF, CP,* 543). That existing, but unspoken, story is marked by the presence of muted voices in H.D. herself, which she discovers by an examination of her poetic manner. Her stylistic self-criticism—". . . rhyme, jingle, / over-worked assonance, nonsense, / juxtaposition of words for words' sake," and "inconsequent syllables, / too malleable, too brittle, / / over-sensitive, under-definitive / clash of opposites"—is repossessed and affirmed as a ludic and fecund source for culturally hidden material (*WDNF, CP,* 534–35).

> I know, I feel
> the meaning that words hide;
>
> they are anagrams, cryptograms,
> little boxes, conditioned
>
> to hatch butterflies . . .
> (*WDNF, CP,* 540)

These repeated confrontations with the suggestive presence of alternative perspectives, alternative signifieds, have made H.D. cite and examine the locus classicus of monotheistic affirmation, *"Thou shalt have none other gods but me,"* and ask, "or shall we?" (*WDNF, CP,* 538–39). The radical, most destabilizing question has been posed, and the other side of the story comes in its wake. *Trilogy* begins a massive pivoting, so that the subtext of Section I will become the dominant text by Section III.

The second section, *Tribute to the Angels,* still attempts consciously to assert the male principles (the thrones and powers of angelic orders) about which the poet has set herself the task of writing. The first unit ends with thanks to the angel Uriel, the second to Anneal, but suddenly the progressive appearance of the angels is drastically altered. This narrative expectation has been surprised, ruptured by a vision that takes the poet beyond the story and sequences that she herself set up.

> I had thought
> to address him [Gabriel] as I had the others,
> Uriel, Anneal;

> how could I imagine
> the lady would come instead?
>   (*TA, CP,* 564)

H.D. then writes a three-section explanation listing all the culturally available images of Mary in painting and icon, with the repeated
phrase "we have seen her" pinpointing strategies of representation.

> We have seen her head bowed down
> with the weight of a domed crown,
>
> or we have seen her, a wisp of a girl
> trapped in a golden halo. . . .
>   (*TA, CP,* 564)

The painters who "missed never a line / of the suave turn of the head /
or subtle shade of lowered eye-lid" have provided an apparently com-
prehensive picture of this figure (*TA, CP,* 565). However, H.D. argues,
their comprehensiveness is a fiction; the "universal" truth is incomplete. In this assertion is the critical pivot of this section and of *Trilogy*
as a whole:

> But none of these, none of these
> suggest her as I saw her.
>   (*TA, CP,* 566)

Although the poet kindly engages in a dialogue with a whole tradition
of depiction, acknowledging "you have done very well by her," H.D.
still insists that "she wasn't" any of the images sanctioned by tradition
(*TA, CP,* 569). If the mainstream image will not suffice, the occult ones
to which H.D. was evidently attracted are also insufficient: "not *vas
spirituale* / not *rosa mystica* even" (*TA, CP,* 574). So H.D.'s critical revaluation of Mary displaces the story and the iconography that belong to
all of our cultural apparatus.

In an image strangely reminiscent of "The Yellow Wallpaper" in its
release of an imagined woman from the strictures that confine her,
H.D. refers to the Mary Madonna in stained glass.

> she is not
>
> imprisoned in leaden bars
> in a coloured window;
>
> she is Psyche, the butterfly,
> out of the cocoon.
>   (*TA, CP,* 570)

Psyche is the aspect of the story never articulated before this poem: the spirit of transformation and quest symbolized as a mother-child dyad.

The apocalyptic material from Revelations that H.D. displaces is a studied debasement of the images of the mother goddesses in the polytheistic cults of the Fertile Crescent, whose icons and social practices haunt the monotheistic father cults.[31] Jezebel, priest and prophet, as the "mother of Harlots" (Rev. 17:5), sacred sexual acts as "fornication," the golden cup and the scarlet blood—control of fertility and increase (Rev. 18:3)—as her "sorceries" and "abominations": all these terms characterize a despised religion. H.D. turns John's derogatory vision around, so that the "other-side of everything" is visible.[32] Further, John has announced that his prophecy is final, untamperable. In an echo of the injunction to worship no other gods, this prophet declares that there shall be no prophets after him. H.D. demurs, proceeding to recast not only John's misogynist interpretations but also his authoritarian voice.

H.D.'s Lady "bore / none of her usual attributes; / the Child was not with her" (*TA, CP,* 597). Not simply the conduit for God's incarnation, Mary is carrying a book, as if she herself were prophet, scribe, or lawgiver. The final whiteness of this Mary is not the sexual purity of the virgin birth but the textual plurality of the virginal page; her book has no story whatsoever.

> She carries a book but it is not
> the tome of the ancient wisdom,
>
> the pages, I imagine, are the blank pages
> of the unwritten volume of the new. . . .
> (*TA, CP,* 570)

So her book resists assimilation into the past and its authority relations. It contains neither a hierarchic doctrine nor the most open-ended statement. Blank, unwritten, the "text" is complete potentiality. For if the existence of any text involves a series of choices and exclusions, which necessarily and inescapably limit its statements to a perspective, then H.D.'s imagined book, by not containing any writing, remains the plural, ideal, unlimited statement. Furthermore, "we," in all our plurality, are invited to fill these pages. In contrast, biblical materials come from the revealed or dictated word of God. The plural and multivocal substitute for the univocal, as Mary, "not awe-inspiring . . . not even over-whelming" is a humanization of the divine and a renunciation of the hieratic (*TA, CP,* 572).

The communion with this figure will produce a book of a memorable, wavering character, fluid and alterable.

> written
> or unwritten, its pages will reveal
>
> a tale of a Fisherman,
> a tale of a jar or jars,
>
> the same—different—the same attributes,
> different yet the same as before.
>
> (*TA, CP,* 571)

H.D.'s version of the oscillation between dominant and muted values in women's identity expresses itself in this passage. She debates whether narrative will be genuinely new—a complete rupture with the dominant and an empowering of the silenced—or whether it recovers these muted truths perpetually hidden at the core of dominant values.

In *Trilogy*'s final poem, *The Flowering of the Rod,* the project of delegitimation is completed; the picture of the Madonna that ends the poem adjusts the narrative and the theology of Christianity. The story told in Section III "is not on record," although H.D. says everyone knows it (*FR, CP,* 587). As an unwritten narrative, it suggests, by marginality to dominant culture, its status as a secret truth. The hidden narrative is H.D.'s invention, based on a suggestion in the Gospels about the Mary who "anointed the Lord with ointment [myrrh] and wiped his feet with her hair."[33] The occulted interpretation of this event places Christianity in a matrifocal religious tradition.

H.D. tells how Mary Magdalene purchased a second jar of myrrh from Kaspar, the same person who had offered the first jar to the Christ child, and narrates his conversion to antipatriarchal thinking because of this confrontation with Mary. The fabrication of this narrative, joining two different New Testament stories that incorporate myrrh (Christ's birth and the Last Supper), is an act of critical delegitimation of culturally sacred narratives, because it inserts a line of causation where no such relation had existed, thereby making a new sequence. The story also depicts Mary Magdalene as teacher and missionary, much as do certain "Gnostic Gospels."[34]

Such a narrative criticizes male characters as well as tradition for their incomplete story, based on repression of memory, loss of connection with matriarchal religion, and disgust at the sensuality and independence of women. Kaspar had tried to refuse Mary's purchase, "but the un-maidenly woman did not take the hint," unaffected by his derision and disgust (*FR, CP,* 588). In the same way that she will not respond to his social cues, she is not containable in narrative scripts, or versions of propriety. When she unbraids "her extraordinary hair" at H.D.'s telling of the Last Supper and kisses Christ's feet, Simon, the host, is embarrassed and revolted, because "she looked like a heathen // picture or carved idol / from a forbidden sea-temple," a Mediterranean great goddess like "Isis, Astarte, Cypris . . . / Ge-meter, De-meter, earth-mother / or Venus / in a star" (*FR, CP,* 594, 594–95, 596).

However, there is a legend "contained in old signs and symbols," which Kaspar the Mage remembers suddenly, a vision of the maternal presence crucially necessary to that "parched, dying man" (*FR, CP,* 600, 591). And in the recovery of his long-repressed memory, Kaspar also understands marginality. For this third Mage was an outsider. "His part in this ritual / was almost negligible"; moreover, because of his very choice of a gift, he has been riddled with doubt about his generosity (*FR, CP,* 612). His vision is brought on by a stunned realization that through the despised woman, Mary Magdalene, his half-forgotten vow to give the other precious jar of ointment to Christ has been fulfilled.

The sensuous principle of Mary Magdalene and the vision to which she gives access do not add a dimension to myth, offering a more complete picture by the addition of some details. Rather, access to that "trivial" part causes the transformation of the story by major readjustments of its effect and weight. The incarnate Godhead central to the Christian world view has become a function of numinous maternal love. Christ himself may be no more than a perfumed balm, like the sheaf of flowers or wheat held by pagan Bona Dea.

Trilogy presents three massive portals, as in a new Notre Dame cathedral. The first celebrates a revised paternal god. The second, central, portal meditates on the whiteness and mystery of Mary and on her unifying, Godlike force. The third suggests a syncretic Christianity, rejecting the male and neuter trinity for the mother-son dyad, rejecting male for female prophet. As a rediscovery of the muted matrifocal and polytheistic religions of Old Europe, the dying and reborn son, the Great Mother, and the Elusinian resurrection of the flower, H.D.'s Christianity is "different, yet the same as before."

In H.D.'s memoirs also, subtle memories and muted stories are prevalent. What appears in these memoirs, as sometimes in the poetry, to be an infinite retardation of narrative telos is instead another kind of story, with the definition of what has finally "happened" never completed, always capable of modification, always doubling and questioning itself. These narrative tactics bring this muted female area into focus, as it slowly emerges into speech.

In *The Gift,* a memoir that just precedes *Trilogy,* H.D. builds to the revelation of a mysterious story transmitted as a gift from Mamalie, her grandmother, to the child Hilda.[35] Mamalie reveals a hidden, politically repressed moment of American history when Moravian settlers and Shawnee Indians met in a ritual of shamanistic and pentecostal dimensions, bringing the "ancient secrets of Europe and the ancient secrets of America into a single union of power and spirit, a united brotherhood" (*G,* 135). This noncolonial compact with the Indians, transmitted by Mamalie from secret materials, stands in H.D.'s mind ever after for its rejection of political hierarchy and dominance: a unity of creeds and races through similar spiritual gifts. H.D. parses her own title: "The Gift, I think must have been this Gift of understanding, of linking up all the mysteries through time, in all lands and for all people."[36] The gift in itself is the power to know and to serve a muted story, transmitted by female apostolic succession. H.D.'s gift serves a function parallel to Atwood's cultural understanding of Canada as a colonial nation and Brooks's critique of the racial hegemony of presumably universal symbols. All three writers rectify narrative by major attention to muted stories. The messages, political knowledge, or alteration of spiritual consciousness from the "other-side of everything" are tools to transform hegemonic society and the tales it tells.

■

CHAPTER EIGHT

The Critique of Consciousness and Myth in Levertov, Rich, and Rukeyser

I want to be able to separate in myself what is old and cyclic, the recurring history, the myth, from what is new, what I feel or think that might be new. . . .
DORIS LESSING
The Golden Notebook (1962)

In the decade and a half that saw the anticolonial, black, Vietnamese, and women's movements flourish, three women poets, Adrienne Rich, Muriel Rukeyser, and Denise Levertov, invented self-exploratory and culturally reevaluative quest plots, so that the act of cultural criticism became their central lyric act, from the critique of language and consciousness to its necessary extension, the discussion of the individual in history.

The poets saw themselves contributing to the undermining of cultural structures repressive of women first by reevaluating canons of proper language and proper subject. With their deliberate use of taboo words, and with the thematic purpose these words symbolize, the poets provided support for an argument made in "Professions for Women."[1] Virginia Woolf traces the process by which a woman creates from her life and the contradictions of her consciousness the new context in which she has permission to speak and act in autonomous, fearless ways. First, she must "kill the angel in the house," that self-sacrificing, charming, flirtatious phantom who always pleases others, never herself. The death of the angel of self-repression, that is, the critique of old consciousness, hypothetically insures that there will be no sex-linked taboos on women's self-exploration.

In "Hypocrite Women," Denise Levertov asks what specific female constraints can prevent or inhibit one's choosing to make life a pilgrimage.[2] The answer: women repress whatever they feel—even their own self-doubt—to preserve a generous, unruffled surface, while they "mother man in his doubt," encouraging the nuances and moods necessary for his self-expression. The women really feel cold, moonstruck, self-absorbed: in a word, "unwomanly." To hide the paradox of "unwomanliness," they assume the mask their culture has long made available: flirtation used as self-repression. In doing so, they also hide the intensity of the conflict from themselves. The judgment "Whorishly with the psychopomp / we play and plead—" alerts us to what is at stake. This traditional guide of souls from Greek mythology, crucial to spiritual development, is assailed by a teasing display of charm, which the women use as a deliberate strategy of refusal, rejecting their capacity for growth and denying their inmost selves. Key terms such as "to mother" and "whorishly," and the image of cutting dreams "like ends of split hair," are linguistic allegories criticizing women who, concerned simply with pleasing men, tailor their responses to ignore messages of myth and dream, always so vital in Levertov. By self-censorship, women deny themselves the challenge of soul-making.

The women have agreed with the man that they—that their "cunts"—are ugly. But in this poem, the word *cunt* has been used openly and carefully as a counterstrategy of affirmation. The explicit naming of sexual organs and bodily functions in this and contemporaneous poems by women uncensors taboo words, and by so doing, constructs a critique of the cultural values of propriety and complicity that have kept these words—and females themselves—unspeakable.

Muriel Rukeyser's "Despisals"[3] likewise poses forbidden words like "asshole," "shit," and "clitoris" to explore the social implications of self-hatred. Rukeyser argues that the ghettoization of parts of the body precedes and in some way has caused the ghettoes of the city. Through the creation of individual consciousness, reproduced in the upbringing of every child, an intolerant, destructive society is also formed. The poem studies the continuity of repression from the individual psyche to the collective city.

Through the flat, bold words of "Despisals," Rukeyser has also dramatized the power of the reader's assumptions. For a person is likely to be startled at the forbidden words, shocked that the poet did not censor herself. Since the poem concerns the rejection of shame and contempt, readers find that their internalized expectations for the poem's tone or diction are a version of the "despisals" criticized therein. The poem causes the reader to examine the repressive function of canons of right language by its delegitimation of linguistic taboos.

In order for a woman to accomplish Woolf's second task, aggressive truth-telling from female experiences, she must rejoin the internal struggle between censorship—respect for dominant ideology—and expression of muted insights. The expression of a woman's feelings can be achieved only by delegitimating narrative patterns embodying the social practices and mental structures that repress women. The writer must "break the sentence" of beliefs and the sequence of plot structures that express them.

Adrienne Rich's "Snapshots of a Daughter-in-Law" (1958–60) is an outstanding example of this critique of consciousness. As Rukeyser and Levertov confront canons of respectable language, so Rich has to pit herself against acceptable canons of subject: "I had been taught that poetry should be 'universal,' which meant, of course, non-female."[4] As an act of self-defense, she excludes the pronoun "I" from the work (although she ends with "we"), uses allusions to expert opinion, and chooses a title with ironic reference to "feminine" sources of authority: her marital status and family relationships.

Indeed, like a feminist *Waste Land* in its "loaded gun" allusiveness, the poem answers, sometimes in a relentlessly dismissive way, some of the problems posed by male culture. Rich even uses *The Second Sex* of Simone de Beauvoir the way T. S. Eliot used Jesse Weston. There is a tissue of reference to such classic modernist texts as Yeats's "Leda and the Swan." When Yeats asks, "Did she put on his knowledge with his power / before the indifferent beak could let her drop?" Rich responds, "A thinking woman sleeps with monsters. / The beak that grips her, she becomes," turning the question back, and showing an ambivalent judgment about the possession of phallic power and knowledge. Anger, rupture, and a wounding self-initiation define this text.

The three poems of the first section discuss the intricate but limited patterns of behavior of women in Rich's own family. They have few options. The mother lives through memories of past elegance; yet because she does not think, but only feels, all her experience is "useless."[5] The daughter-in-law hears and, with a deep self-denying perversity, represses unseen voices that call on her to rebel or to be selfish, demands she cannot begin to fulfill. The third poem exposes sisters without sisterhood, who express the monstrous dimensions of their self-hatred through hostility toward each other. At one and the same time, the poet is isolated from other women and implicated in their paralysis, anger, and disintegration. She is torn between her sense of being exceptional and her protofeminist identification with women as a structurally separate group. Such a bleak sketch of the options available to women—frustration taking shape as vagueness, madness, bitchiness—demands some causal explanation, which the poet discovers in the next section by referring to and analyzing classic literary texts that evoke the history of women's condition and the fate of their gifts.

When a woman as gifted as Emily Dickinson appears—an image of Rich herself—she is compelled to pursue her ideas and images in the interstices of domestic life, a life that exists in diffuse, interruptible contrast to explosive power.[6] Alternately, endless domestic tasks will give shape to a woman's life. She will put all her energy into upkeep, not into living, "dusting everything on the whatnot every day of life."

If domesticity is one social expectation that shapes a woman's personality and to which her gifts must conform, the demands of beauty are another. The woman is idol, objectified by the necessity of preserving a sleek and beautiful surface, and powerless because of artifice.

The section that follows, with its oblique citation from Campion, argues that courtship also immobilizes women.[7] The accomplished woman bending over a lute is not immersed in art for its sake or for hers; song is one of the ornaments of her beauty; art enhances her as an icon. Love, along with domesticity and beauty, is the third term creating the traditional boundaries that mold and define women. Woman is a social construct, not, as in much lyric, an idealized vision. Each of these three terms of women's condition creates typical traits: the combination of repressed power and actual powerlessness; the bitterness of a person prevented from full fruition; a "keenness" about nature and human relationships that comes from dependence on love.

Having summed up the classic expectations, Rich turns to modern touchstones of cultural attitudes toward women, identifying in each case, with concision and subtlety, the complex psychological paralysis and kinds of failure that have been the lot of women who internalize or are controlled by male opinion. She recalls how Mary Wollstonecraft was reviled by men for her analyses of the status of women. But Diderot's praise of their lush flowering arouses women to self-pity and infinite regrets for their past potential; they are tacitly forgiven for a lack of accomplishments.

Rich caustically challenges both majority opinion about women and women's complicity with it.

Our blight has been our sinecure:
mere talent was enough for us—
glitter in fragments and rough drafts.

Sigh no more, ladies.
                        Time is male
and in his cups drinks to the fair.
Bemused by gallantry, we hear
our mediocrities over-praised,
indolence read as abnegation,
slattern thought styled intuition,
every lapse forgiven, our crime
only to cast too bold a shadow
or smash the mould straight off.

For that, solitary confinement,
tear gas, attrition shelling,
Few applicants for that honor.
                        (*PSN*, 50)

Women are praised precisely because their work has not called male
"superiority" and male analysis into question. Safe and childlike, mental invalids, women may be patronized generously because of their
failure to grow and to persevere. Rich exposes the double face of the
prevailing culture: its paternal protection of female mediocrity and its
destructive attack on female boldness.

Given what she says, any woman must reinvent herself; hence at
the end of the poem, she is compared to the helicopter, half bird, half
knife. To construct her new consciousness, the woman must at one
and the same time sever her allegiance to the destructive views of the
past and transcend the presence of destructive ideologies in herself,
producing that critique distinctive of twentieth-century women
writers, "not to pass on a tradition, but to break its hold over us."[8]

Levertov, Rich, and Rukeyser share a concern for individual mental structures and their cultural roots. They see that the contents of
consciousness curtail the work of the imagination. Therefore, they
mount a critical attack on dominant patterns of perception and practice.

Both for historical reasons and to extend their analysis of consciousness further, all three poets write about political situations—the
Vietnam War, and, in Rukeyser's case, the two World Wars. The same
concern to investigate, to criticize, to protest against the common-
places of perception and behavior that animates their poems about
women leads the poets to examine political forces and power relations

that inform individual consciousness. The Vietnam War becomes a
focal issue, since, in a historical sense, it is the concrete political reality
in which they feel implicated, and, in a symbolic sense, it epitomizes
the destructive values and acts that the old consciousness can produce. The Vietnam War also demystified the colonial-imperial relation. This swift delegitimation of a national mission made the process
of critique especially sharp, a development that had, in turn, two
intellectual effects on the generations to which these poets belonged:
continual attention to the critical analysis of ideology on one hand,
and, on the other hand, the spiritual hope for an ungridded area of
human activity without ideology—giving access to an epiphanal or
purely experiential truth. These two effects are, of course, contradictory.

   As a group, the poems that comment on the war and talk about
political protests ask how the individual psyche is related to history. To
phrase the question somewhat differently, they ask how to apply the
model of personal changes of consciousness to produce social change.
In "Breaking Open," Rukeyser documents a series of linked conver-
sions and communions that extend personal change outward to small
groups.[9] In her terms, "breaking open," will result from a knowledge
of our historical and our personal moments and must lead to a transformation of both—history through psyche and psyche through history. Another meditative political poem of recent years, Levertov's
"Staying Alive," longs for the revolutionary "life that / wants to live,"
as opposed to the deadly "unlived life."[10] Social change begins—as in
Rukeyser—with individual witnesses to the new life, who try to dem-
onstrate in the present the values and relationships the changed society would bring. Levertov and Rukeyser share one response to the
question of changing society.[11] They go deeper into themselves, not as
an act of rejection or a declaration of autonomy, but from a belief that
inwardness is one necessary path to social transformation. Their
documentary poems about politics and the war return dramatically to
a concern for consciousness and changes in the self.

   In poems contemporaneous with the Vietnam War, Adrienne Rich
linked male sexuality and personal life to war. In "The Phenomenology of Anger" Rich is a combatant, and the battlefield is her consciousness. War parallels the patriarchal oppression of women. Domination, depersonalization, and dehumanization are the vectors of the
patriarchal psyche; multiplied and extended on a national scale, these
male traits are, in Rich's view, an ur-political explanation for the Vietnam War and its atrocities.[12] Social dislocation and war stem from an
estrangement, at some original moment, between "female" and
"male" components of the human psyche. Rich pursues this split,

conducting an examination of psychic life to trace the colonial relation to its origins.

On one level Rukeyser's "Breaking Open," Levertov's "Staying
Alive," and Rich's "The Phenomenology of Anger" record an im-
passe: the near impossibility of creating social change only through
changing consciousness. However, the poets write as if continuing to
know more and feel more—rage in Rich, communion in Rukeyser,
participation in Levertov—could create social change by the explosive
needs of consciousness itself. But in another sense, these poems about
the interaction of history and consciousness reveal that nothing—not
the most hidden aspects of the psychic life of the individual—exists
apart from the pressures of a historical era.

The gendered, historically sculpted person, realizing the dimensions of her opposition to dominant ideologies, breaks the repeating
sentences and sequences of that dominance in myths of critique.
These myths entail critical perceptions about the nature of women.
They recast long-sanctified plots, especially quest patterns, and reenvision such familiar figures as the hero, the lady, and the reborn god.
The poems are so strongly reevaluative that they may even appear
antimythological ("No more masks! No more mythologies!"), precisely because they record the realization that certain prime myths are
invalid and crippling for women: "a book of myths / in which / our
names do not appear." Indeed, the poems are often self-evaluative,
recasting the poet's prior work.

One of the most curious is Rukeyser's "The Poem as Mask."[13] Explicitly antimythological, the poem is also an act of self-criticism, written in direct opposition to an earlier "Orpheus."[14] The older poem,
constructed like a court masque of English tradition, uses the power
of music as organizing symbol, centers on a static drama of transformation, and ends with a song of unity. The figure of Orpheus—the
poet reborn as a god, the fragments of the human reunited as the
divine, a transcendent experience that gives power to the self—is a
motif of great resonance for Rukeyser.[15] Yet in "The Poem as Mask,"
she brings her earlier poem into question by deliberate acts of self-
examination and self-criticism, showing that the myth she had so
lovingly chosen and carefully shaped is an impediment to her quest.
"The Poem as Mask" states that she had censored her feelings, writing
him, god, myth, when she meant *me, human, my life.* As a woman, she had
been unable to affirm her "torn life"—the loss of love, a dangerous
birth, the rescue of self and newborn child. Her former use of the
myth blunted her sense of personal reality; it was a "mask" of cover-
ing, not a "masque" of unity and joy. So she makes a vow at the end of
the poem: "No more masks! No more mythologies!" But while this

vow is understandably antimythological, a cry against alien patterns imposed on women's lives, the poem's final lines present a renewed myth based on concrete feelings of peace, blessing, and wholeness. The new myth comes from within the self, as the orphic experiences in the historical life of the poet that offer inspiration and rebirth.

Another matching set of mythopoetic works by Rukeyser concerns Oedipus and the sphinx: "Private Life of the Sphinx" from *The Green Wave* (1948) and "Myth" from *Breaking Open* (1973).[16] Both poems work with revisionary strategies. The first makes a serious, pulsing lyrical displacement to the sphinx's side of things; she redefines herself away from male power in order to become a perpetual questioner. However, this early version of the myth accepts that the answer to her riddle must still be *man*. This is exactly the answer delegitimated by Rukeyser's later, jokey, joyous "Myth," in which the universal is abruptly particularized and the answer that "everyone knows" is called into question (*CP,* 278, 498). Rukeyser plays on the generic "mankind" by having her sphinx pointedly note that, despite Oedipus's assumption, the abstract noun in question does not, from her perspective, include womankind. The sphinx's deflating reduction of universal assumption to untenable opinion makes the poem a critique of consciousness through critical allusions not only to the classical story but to an earlier poem.

Denise Levertov's major mythopoetic work, "Relearning the Alphabet," chronicles a journey of the self and a rediscovery of the roots of vision.[17] The loss of contact with sources is solved by a pilgrimage in which each letter of the alphabet marks the route. The form is thus a primer of meaning, teaching the reader to attend to concrete experience that bears a special resonance or pitch. To the loss of both self and love, Levertov first proposes a false solution: the will, imagistically related to the cold moon. But inner avatars, who take the form of men, compel her to stop. Only by retracing the steps of her journey, that is, by a self-critical reassessment, can the true path be found. The "U" section states:

> Relearn the alphabet,
> relearn the world, the world
> understood anew only in doing, under-
> stood only as
> looked-up-into out of earth
>
> (*RA,* 119)

The focus on *under-stood* is a call for a return to basic detail, to the event rooted in concrete, daily life. For this understanding, the poet forges the syntactically entangled set of prepositions ("up-into out of"), situating herself in the real at that moment, always decisive in Levertov, when its inner energy is known.

In "Relearning the Alphabet," the hero is a woman, and it appears that she is also her own prize or treasure, for she rediscovers that authentic self.

> In childhood dream-play I was always
> the knight or squire, not
> the lady:
> quester, petitioner, win or lose, not
> she who was sought.
> The initial of quest or question
> branded itself long since on the flank
> of my Pegasus.
>
> (*RA*, 116)

Yet although the poem can be read as a myth of the woman-hero finding the woman-captive and freeing her, Levertov is not comfortable with this. She states that she is only the knight or quester and rejects the implicit role of the captive self or muted lady.

The formal use of the alphabet is also a measure of how far Levertov allows herself to go into critique. As the poem's significant action is the "relearning" of the most ordinary things, what is more basic than the alphabet, what more ubiquitous, or more taken for granted? So the alphabet form focuses subtle attention on building blocks of consciousness: here the form works critically. However, the alphabet is a self-limited area for critique, since the letters must finally be put back into the accustomed order. The material of reality is "relearned," not revised; the alphabet is the sign of that familiar order, reinvested with wonder, but not called into question. As a corollary, Levertov remains engaged with cyclic and archetypal patterns, unlike the other two poets.

Adrienne Rich's work during this period also centers on a critique of the stories and meanings that have patterned a dominant perspective. "Diving into the Wreck," specifically antimythological, perturbed by the existing cultural "book of myths," creates a new myth, similar to Rukeyser's in its focus on the act of criticism and in its centering on reality.[18]

In "Diving into the Wreck," descent, detection, and exploration are metaphors for the acts of criticism. The poet, as an undersea diver, takes a journey down to an individual and collective past, where some mysterious, challenging "wreck" occurred that no prior research or instruction can clarify. We discover that the wreck is the personal and

cultural foundering of the relations between the sexes. Her exploration moves to the unembellished and apparently unmediated perception of

> the thing I came for:
> the wreck and not the story of the wreck
> the thing itself and not the myth.
>   (*PSN*, 197)

Like Rukeyser, but in a darker tone, Rich places her emphasis beyond
the culturally validated frames of story and myth, on the absolute and
concrete perception of the seeker. The diver spends much of the
poem in descent to arrive at dissent, moving deeper than the surface
of meanings and atmospheres in which it is "natural" to be the way we
are. Further, the diver goes beyond the "ending" of the implied story
of a wreck to examine clues to alternative stories that—first unnoticed—would otherwise be doomed to be permanently muted. The
"book of myths" contains sentences and sequences that do not name
properly, keeping things invisible or unspoken. But if explored from
this muted experiential perspective without the scripts of narrative,
the wreck will yield alternative meaning.

  In the act of detection, the analysis of the wreck, the poet discovers
that she has herself become the object of the search: "I am she: I am
he // whose drowned face sleeps with open eyes . . . " (*PSN*, 198). This
discovery of multiple, androgynous, unifying identities is part of the
truth of the wreck. The holistic "one" who is revealed underwater is
constructed of opposites before their split: I and we, she and he, dead
and living, speaker and spoken, individual and collective, cargo and
instruments, seeker and sought.

  In this poem of journey and transformation, Rich is tapping the
plots of myth while reenvisioning the content. While there is a hero, a
quest, and a buried treasure, the hero is a woman; the quest is a
critique of old myths; the treasure is the whole buried knowledge of
the relations between the sexes that cannot yet be brought to the
surface, and a self-definition won only through the act of criticism.[19]

  In a traditional "transformation myth," according to Erich Neumann, a male hero (like Perseus) engages in a struggle or quest to
liberate a captive woman, and possibly a treasure, from a female
monster. At the successful end of the struggle, the hero marries the
captive, having extricated her from the coils of the "terrible mother,"
a snake or dragon, who represents the captive's own dangerous and
despised matriarchal past. The captive woman is the necessary con-
tributor to the hero's development, representing a fruitfulness and

creativity that he appropriates and that transforms him. The hero severs (or rescues) the creative, supportive, enriching aspects of the female from the baleful, destructive, devouring aspects, becoming the custodian of the "good" and the repressor of the "wicked" aspects of female power. "With the freeing of the captive and the founding of a new kingdom, the patriarchal age comes into force."[20] This kind of tale offers marriage to its female character, quest and control to its male, and, in addition, makes the female relatively impotent.

The ultimate intention of "Diving into the Wreck" is to call this patriarchal myth into question. Rich does so by constructing her oppositional version of the origin and history of consciousness. If we were to take Rich's myth as a simple reversal of Neumann's model, it would be easy to say that in the underwater journey of the self, she too finds her opposite. But displacement is not her aim. Unlike the fecund captive-treasure of the patriarchial myth, this character is dead, arrested in the strained posture of unfulfilled searching. Far from being the answer, s/he is one complex part of the question the wreck poses. The new "fruitful center" in Rich's myth has become the creative antagonism of the woman-hero to traditional consciousness and old patterns of myth—an antagonism aroused by the fact that the book of stories and explanations excludes her. In the course of her journey, a new woman has been invented, one appropriating her own fruitfulness and power. She is both hero and treasure, a unity not achieved by heterosexual bonding but by anticolonial quest.[21]

Besides being critiques, the myths of Rich and Rukeyser in this period of work are nonstatic and nonarchetypal. Rejecting the unchanging, unhistorical types—hero, captive, treasure, reborn god—the poets make these new myths historically specific inventions. They are lyric documents entailing perceptions of a changing self in a historical context, reinterpreting elements of the quest or motifs of rebirth by a reevaluation of who the poets are, the time and place they have entered, and the cultural stances their lives were expected to embody. In both poets, the rupture of sequences, the "splitting open" and delegitimation of constituted stories, occurs oppositionally outside "the guidelines of orthodoxy," as Rich said of Dickinson.[22] This is why the critiques of consciousness are a necessary first step to the poems that reevaluate myth.

Further, these myths replace archetypes with prototypes. They do not investigate moments of eternal recurrence, but rather break with the idea of an essentially unchanging reality. Prototypes are original, model forms on which to base the self and its action—forms open to transformation, and forms, unlike archetypes, that offer similar patterns of experience *to* others, rather than imposing these patterns *on*

others. A dictionary definition reveals the significant distinction between the words.[23] While both archetype and prototype "denote original models," an archetype "is usually construed as an ideal form that
establishes an unchanging pattern for all things of its kind." However,
"what develops from a prototype may represent significant
modification from the original." A prototype is not a binding, timeless
pattern, but one critically open to the possibility, even the necessity, of
its transformation. Thinking in terms of prototypes historicizes myth.

Criticizing the nature of myth is one of the reevaluations that
women writers consciously undertake, for their own lives allow them
to see the culturally repressive functions of archetypes, and their own
experiences of personal and social change, recorded in poems about
consciousness and politics, belie the illusion of a timeless, unhistorical
pattern that controls reality.

Reassessment by an intense examination of conscience is characteristic of these mythic poems as a group. At the same time, it marks the
intense self-questioning and internal debate of Rich's coming out as a
lesbian.[24] Since about 1974, Rich has adopted a lesbian feminist perspective to situate this critical examination of culture, trying thereby
to create an irrevocable distance between dominant and alternative/
oppositional social practices. So, in part, Rich uses the term "lesbian
feminist" as we have been using the terms "feminist" or "critical"
throughout this study, to describe a person who has made an analytic
severing from certain patriarchal cultural practices, whose acts of
oppositional deliberation have brought her to "the other-side of
everything"—to the questioning of primary institutions of social, sexual, and cultural organization.[25] Rich's lesbian stance is consistant with
the perspective of all the writers who are the subject of this study.

Rich's most theoretical statement on sexuality criticizes heterosexuality, showing how it is one institution of the sex-gender system,
psychosexually and socially produced. Although heterosexuality has
seemed like a part of nature, it can be called into question by a critical
approach that deuniversalizes it, taking it from the realm of biology
and setting it into the realm of politics.[26] The rhetorical purpose of the
essay is to shift the relative weights of dominant and alternative sexualities, so that, by the end, the "lesbian continuum" seems dominant
as well as attractive, while heterosexuality seems not only a minor
position for species survival, but an unpalatable one. Rich redefines
the category of lesbian to include not only women who are sexually
and erotically bound (what she calls "lesbian existence") but also
women who are in any way affiliated with other women or not connected to men—single women, independent women, women who aid
other women—as well as any activity of nurturance and support in
which women are mutually engaged. Thus the term "lesbian con-

tinuum" broadens the meaning from a sexual minority to an oppositional and women-identified behavior whose scope is much greater
than had been suspected. The poles of dominant and alternative are
shifted; more than a delegitimation of main culture by an oppositional stance, this is a capture of centrality by a perspective once
falsely or ignorantly considered of only secondary importance.

Shifting the term *lesbian* from the purely sexual to a widely social
and cultural arena still preserves the depth charge of shock inherent
in what had been a deeply taboo sexual affiliation. Rich has, in fact,
always been concerned to find a stance that cannot possibly be appropriated by main culture because it embodies such a definitive critical
negation of the status quo. Rich's use of the term lesbian, and choice
of lesbianism, satisfied her as a way of publicly establishing the most
radical outsider status in relation to such institutions of gendering as
the oedipal crisis and heterosexuality.[27]

Self-revisionary poems followed Rich's declaration of lesbian existence. "Natural Resources," one of the important poems in *The Dream
of a Common Language,* reassesses earlier stages of Rich's work, represented by "Snapshots of a Daughter-in-Law" and "Diving into the
Wreck" respectively.[28] "Natural Resources" begins with the image of a
descent to a treasure, with evident parallels to the earlier poem.
There is a palpable difference, however, between the well-equipped,
technologically supported but brilliantly isolated scuba diver, and the
miner in this poem, who more clearly suffers the consequences of her
labor: body bent, lungs filled with dust. The miner is an ordinary
woman; the diver had been exceptional. Rich insists, rejecting the
allegorical nature of her diver, that this miner is "no metaphor" (*DCL*,
60).

The treasure in "Diving into the Wreck" was found with the recognition of the essential human identity of the two sexes, which, once
present, had been severed in a primeval event whose meanings rever-
berate through history and psyche. Hence the treasure is a buried but
pulsing presence of wholeness in the androgynous unity of the sexes.
In contrast, the treasures of "Natural Resources" are the constant and
perpetual acts of female labor, which preserve and remake "a universe of humble things" (*DCL*, 66).

These acts are depicted, with a lacerating vision, as the acts of
women uniquely, in distinction to men.

> I am tired of faintheartedness,
> their having to be *exceptional*
>
> to do what an ordinary woman
> does in the course of things.
>   (*DCL*, 64)

Domestic tasks, once seen by Rich as debilitating and grating taxes on female talent, are here pensively celebrated as virtually the only stay against male aggression and destructiveness.

In addition, "Natural Resources" shows an entirely different definition of "culture" than did "Snapshots"—more anthropological and social than specifically literary and artistic, the culture of workers, not literati. This argues that women produce civilization, in ordinary and communal acts. It is not surprising that the only literary allusion in "Natural Resources" (one remembers that "Snapshots" was filled with citations) occurs when the poet speaks of men, as if the strategy of citation helps identify the tedium of these repeated notions from high culture. The turn from a "botched civilization"—it is Ezra Pound's "Hugh Selwyn Mauberley" that is cited—seems to complete a movement that began with the modernist response to World War II, and that has various manifestations in the Woolf of *Three Guineas,* the H.D. of *The Gift,* and the Lessing of *Four-Gated City.*

Rich's anger, explored for several of the poem's sections, emerges in the stern declaration exactly opposed to "Diving into the Wreck": "there are words I cannot choose again; / *humanism androgyny.*"[29] In "Natural Resources," then, the poet no longer seeks a term in which the positive elements of male and female can be reconciled, or, indeed, any term in which "man" is taken as the center, or part of the center, of the universe.[30] But more than that, debate about the permanent validity of humanism is current among radical thinkers, both socialist and feminist. It is not that this antihumanism implies nonhumanitarian behaviors, but rather that the universalizing assumptions of humanism about the needs and aspirations of all "(hu)mankind" are found to be bereft of meaning because they do not acknowledge people's formation as specific, historically rooted subjects. In her exposition of Louis Althusser's antihumanist position, Janet Wolff provides a gloss that can apply to Rich as well: that humanism wrongly posits people "who somehow pre-exist the contingencies of their material and social lives."[31]

But Rich's antihumanism has also coexisted with an unmediated appeal to myth. The debate between archetype and prototype—mythic and social dimensions of narrative—may recur in oscillation because these terms sum up two fundamental positions. Myth can be seen as a sacred or primal verity touched within the poem, a statement that by its very nature offers an unmediated gist beyond social grids and ideological expectations; indeed, it is construed as a way to transcend these. Mediation of any sort, including the social practices of language and literary convention, tends then to be overlooked or minimized. Language is seen as a function of nature or the body, both of which are treated as entities whose essential part is hardly touched by culture. Alternatively, myth can be viewed as narrative that is at root historically occasioned, related to questions of power and ideology, performing certain functions: "language generat[ing] reality in the inescapable context of power," in Donna Haraway's phrase.[32] The two positions are separated by their views of the possibility for historical change in narrative. These positions both come into Rich's work in the books of poetry (to date) that she has published since the appearance of *Poems Selected and New* in 1974, and are the subject of intense debate.[33]

These works also make specific reference to romance, among other plots and images by which women are culturally produced. *The Dream of a Common Language* draws on a new love relationship in the poet's life. And indeed, early poems in both *The Dream of a Common Language* and *A Wild Patience* present the two-woman couple in ways ranging from pure sensuality to wary marginality. Despite the power of this bond, the poems do not so much celebrate passion and yearning (for "*Tristan und Isolde* is scarcely the story," *DCL*, 33) as stand as a warning, even in the midst of personal bliss, not to make of that lesbian bond a *solitude à deux*, a thralldom, a privileged world. For, Rich says, even about passion and growing trust, "I can't call it life until we start to move / beyond this secret circle of fire. . ." (*DCL*, 9). The 1981 and 1983 volumes use the lesbian couple as an ethical and intellectual situation in which probing questions can be asked by women together in a "laboratory," like Woolf's Chloe and Olivia. Typically, the poet establishes a bond not of coupledom but of "twainship" with other women, intellectually passionate and demanding of both herself and this sister a commitment to understanding and to struggle. So the lesbian couple is not a new form of romance, and the sexual tie is not its sole justification. "Women are made taboo to women—not just sexually, but as comrades, cocreators, coinspirators."[34] The passion in these poems is, then, not primarily for sensual fulfillment, but rather for creating the kind of social and community fulfillment among women that responds critically to that nineteenth-century narrative paradigm evoked in the allusion to the *Liebestod* of Tristan and Isolde.

Yet there is a subtle debate between two of the books as well, which rejoins the themes that have concerned us here. Some of the most ecstatic moments of *The Dream of a Common Language* and *A Wild Patience* are also their most ecstatic temptation: to be free of speech altogether, for it is a tainting script.[35] This setting aside of language comes at the contact of a daughter with a mythic mother: the Minoan snake goddess in "The Image"; the Eleusinian sprouting wheat in "Cartographies of Silence"; the "homesick" contact with the mother in

"Transcendental Etude." Speechlessness, the intuitive grasp of the body's codes and of nurturing, beautiful objects, all associated with the mother-daughter bond, are such a temptation because they seem safer and truer than a speech that has been culturally contaminated. To be free of speech is, of course, impossible, yet the yearning is still affirmed through the mythic imagination and the maternal body.

Rich's ideas about language express and are related to the search for a bond that is pre-gridded, natural, and therefore authentic. She hopes to know and speak from a voice of pure gesture and sensation:

> If you can read and understand this poem
> send something back: a burning strand of hair
> a still-warm, still-liquid drop of blood . . .
> (WP, 7)

As one part of this enterprise, Rich has outlined in "Sibling Mysteries" an alternative path out of the oedipal crisis, an account that does not equalize the maternal with the paternal in a bisexual oscillation. Rich postulates that the maternal is and can remain the parent of authority. The argument hopes to affirm a purely natural bond that exists between female bodies before culture has severed it, and to which one could return, if the veneer of oedipalization were stripped.

> The daughters never were
> true brides of the father
>
> the daughters were to begin with
> brides of the mother
>
> then brides of each other
> under a different law . . .
> (DCL, 52)

The sense that better learning and knowing will occur in natural language inspires the end of *The Dream of a Common Language*, in which a woman walks away from "argument and jargon" and begins to piece together a quiltlike amalgam of natural materials, a witch's brew contrived for the white magic of female transformation.

Yet even a work of art that claims this natural discourse of silks, whiskers, and shells, insofar as it is made or constructed, insofar as acts of intention draw it together, is in contradiction to the poetics on which it claims to be based. The call for "no masks" and "no mythologies" is, after all, made up of acts of displacement to another story or the delegitimating of a dominant narrative in favor of the fictions of the muted. As Margaret Homans shrewdly notes, even

"Diving into the Wreck," with its pointed rejection of the "book of myths," still shows the speaker's life dependent on her mediating face mask.[36] One may equally well note that Rukeyser's comments rejecting myths lead simply to a more pluralistic music and choreography, rejecting the modernist use of myth as scaffolding and the separation of mythopoesis and history in favor of an equally potent myth of immanence.[37]

Homans's criticism of certain contemporary women writers, Rich among them, is based on an argument about the inherent fictiveness of language. Language in its innermost structure (the relation of signifier to signified) draws on dualism and division; there is never any direct or natural correlation between word and thing, but only a set of conventional attachments, learned behaviors subtly deployed. Homans argues that there develop certain constructs based on this law of twos: opposition, which may valorize one side, not the other; hierarchy, setting one side above the other; appropriation, assimilating one side to the other. Faced with these formulations and struck by the fact that, as women, they are always the other side in dualistic systems, some women poets may try to exorcise these dualisms by fiat, declaring that they have done with their position in otherness, and therefore with fictiveness. They henceforth propose to live happily ever after in a unitary world where word does equal thing, and where women "tell the truth" about their lives as if a "truth" that exists beyond the fictions and languages in which it is told could be reached by special folk (in this case, females).[38] Homans's statement of the problem is elegantly accomplished.

With the search for a natural language being so thwarted by the nature of language itself, one may well ask why poets are thus tempted when they will inevitably be so deceived in the search for a pure discourse of things. Rich's activity in defining a female poetics offers some suggestion. Such a search seems to signal a rupture with the conventionalized correlations of word and thing, because the poet becomes aware of muted words that cannot be said, like "lesbian," aware of invisible things that are unaccounted for, like feelings in motherhood, or bonding between women. Such a poetics is, therefore, a signal of frustration with convention and a sign of ideological dissent, a desire to rewrite culture by the critical examination of the "natural": that is, by uncovering that which our current social and linguistic practices currently exclude. The postulating of monistic discourse is, then, a poetics that signals ideological critique, the valorizing of oppositional in contrast to dominant.

The debate between gesture and language in Rich quickens in *A Wild Patience* and culminates in "Turning the Wheel," its final poem,

where the debate is affiliated with archetypal mythic quest on one
hand and prototypical historical research on the other, the spiritual
truth tested by historical skepticism. The very title of this self-
reflective poem indicates a change of direction. The poem is set in the
Southwest, and, despite the Indians and the landscape, it conscien-
tiously avoids primitivism and nostalgia, rejecting "an archetypal
blur" of history turned into myth, the "false history" of a woman who
does not have the courage to ask of texts and artifacts her particularist
questions (*AWP*, 54, 53). Rather than making one-dimensional pictures of the Indian women who survive, colonized, half powerful and
half self-hating, Rich instructs herself to "forget the archetypes . . . do
not pursue / the ready-made abstraction, do not peer for symbols"
(*AWP*, 56). Instead she evokes a flawed and self-contradictory reality.

   This rejection of universals rejoins the theme of the book as a
whole, continuing the twinning ties to women, yet examining difference, anger, pain, resistance, in order not to romanticize any kind of
tie between women. Indeed, there are a number of overtly self-critical
remarks in which Rich draws herself back from romanticizing women
(as in the poem about Ethel Rosenberg), and there are as well poems
that notably contain rifts or misunderstandings, or are critical of female heroes.

   It is therefore consistent that at the end of "Turning the Wheel,"
Rich turns away and refuses to visit the majestic and intransigent
Grand Canyon, "the female core of a continent." A visit to the Grand
Canyon had seemed obligatory, because of the force that site had in
Rich's imagination.

> Seeing those rocks   that road   in dreams   I know
> it is happening again   as twice while waking
> I am travelling to the edge   to meet the face
> of annihilating and impersonal time
> stained in the colors of a woman's genitals.
>   (*AWP*, 59)

While she begins by driving eagerly to this mythic place, willing to be
transfixed by its massive symbol of time, sexuality, and gender, still on
this one day, the journey is rejected: "Today I turned the wheel refused that journey" (*AWP*, 59). The reasons for the refusal are particular, intimate, immersed in a specific life's history, the discovery that
the "world beyond time" would be too taxing to confront. When Rich
makes the refusal of this iconic meeting, the debate between the prototypical and the archetypal seems (perhaps temporarily) to have re-

solved in favor of the historically and personally specific, not the symbolic.

The same concern to reassert continual journeys and the provisional in a meditative context of self-reflection and in the context of chosen communities occurs in *Sources;* even though it would be easy and gratifying to "rest among the beautiful and common weeds I cán name," the task of such naming and journeying is ceaseless. "There is no finite knowing, no such rest" (*S,* 35). Rich is concerned here to reestablish the primacy for her work of the New England tradition of self-scrutiny, joined with an acknowledgment of the Jewish community, to which she had silently belonged. Self-scrutiny is one part of Rich's generally existentialist project: the lived ethics of "transcendence"—de Beauvoir's challenge in *The Second Sex* that women should claim choice, liberty, and enterprise and thereby transform the static polarization of (male) Self and (female) Other that has structured Western ideology. This claim of choice has been recast by Rich to end *Sources:*

> I mean knowing the world, and my place in it, not in
> order to stare with bitterness or detachment, but as a
> powerful and womanly series of choices: and here I
> write the words, in their fullness:
> powerful;   womanly.
>
> (*S,* 35)

At the same time, by writing the word *womanly* with all that it implies of immanence and rootedness in matter, Rich disaffiliates from the pure transcendence that de Beauvoir idealized.[39]

As becomes especially clear from Rich's self-critical poems and from her lyrical discussions of history and myth, the debate between the true and the fictive, between a spiritual and historical stance, between "experience" and mediation, and between archetype and prototype has long structured Rich's work and may continue to express her versions of the project of twentieth-century women's writing.

CHAPTER NINE

"Beyond the hard visible horizon"

They, these women, then were the only people who *knew*. Their smile was the smile of these wide vistas, wrought and shaped, held back by the pity they turned towards the blind life of men; but it was *alone* in its vision of the spaces opening beyond the world of daily life.

The open scene, that seemed at once without her and within, beckoned and claimed her, extending for ever, without horizons. . . . Here was the path of advance. But, pursuing it, she must be always alone; supported in the turmoil of life that drove the haunting scene [of conventional romance and beauty] away, hidden beyond the hard visible horizon, by the remembered signs and smiles of these far-off lonely women.

DOROTHY RICHARDSON
Deadlock (1921)

She had been getting ready for her great journey to the horizons in search of *people;* it was important to all the world that she should find them and they find her.

ZORA NEALE HURSTON
Their Eyes Were Watching God
(1937)

The quest plots of twentieth-century women writers incorporate a critical response both to the ending in death and to the ending in marriage, once obligatory goals for the female protagonist. This nineteenth-century ending in death had offered muted yet resonant elements of symbolic protest, often referring back to brief moments of social integration, expressed energy, and personal triumph, from Maggie Tulliver like a great maternal spirit to Lily Bart, on her aesthetic, self-arranged bier, and Edna Pontellier powerfully swimming out to death. In twentieth-century narratives by Richardson, Hurston, and Walker, female quests end differently.[1] The hero is a representative of a striving community, breaking with individualism in her rupture from gender-based ends. She encompasses opposites and can represent both sociocultural debates and a psychic interplay between boundaries and boundlessness. In the distinctive narrative strategy of the multiple individual, the female hero fuses with a complex and contradictory group; her power is articulated in and continued through a community that is formed in direct answer to the claims of love and romance.

Pilgrimage by Dorothy Richardson (1873–1957) is a wayward and prolix narrative during which the female protagonist, Miriam Henderson, slowly achieves two related goals: vocation as a woman writer and spiritual community in a "lay convent" of Friends.[2] Richardson first created herself as a person and writer and then re-created herself as the main character and solipsistic point of view of her massive novel, a work looping back through a series of memorable encounters, professions, groups, loves, and desires. As a writer, Richardson is like the mother of a daughter whom she is and whom she has produced. She then exists twice, in and through her book; that double existence is both homage to and erasure of the mother whose suicide, the defining trauma of her life, is so absently narrated in *Pilgrimage* that biographical glosses must be used to find it. Dyadic issues of envelopment and separation thus mark the whole body of this text and provide the ground from which its major ambition springs.

Since *Pilgrimage* is a novel about a fascinating and attractive woman very often in love, it appears as if the story will end in marriage. Yet the text protests continually against the master plot of romance. Resistance to conventional varieties of romance and resistance to conventional narrative are exactly congruent in Richardson. Her "feminine equivalent of the current masculine realism"—a phrase she used in 1938 to define her aims for the book—tracks consciousness in the untidy, contradictory stops and starts of meditation, and contests any idea of narrative as inception, motivation, and completion.[3] And with many tactics, Richardson insists that whatever the sexual and emotional blandishments, and many are catalogued, Miriam will not succumb to any marriage whatsoever.[4] Further, the erotic relationships pursued in the book are, by their very bulk and sequences, an answer to the downfall quest plot of the nineteenth-century tradition, which, no matter what the female hero's yearning, refocuses itself on sexuality and, when undifferentiated yearning causes the inevitable (sometimes even misconstrued) slip, makes clear that social obloquy and death come tumbling after. *Pilgrimage* shrugs off these well-charted narrative areas of sexuality and death.

Miriam also enters manipulative relations with women like Miss Holland or Miss Dear, which are themselves grotesque rewritings of heterosexuality. With Miss Dear, a predatory, clinging invalid, mistress of tricks and concealments, Miriam compares herself to a husband with a dependent wife, a man to "household women" (*Tr*, III, 412). From the array of characters with whom Miriam is friendly, one pattern emerges: few are mainstream or conventional. Rather, all are marginals—a lesbian couple (Jan and Mag),[5] a bohemian writer (Hypo Wilson), a fast set of artists, various "emancipated people"

(*Tun,* II, 116). In addition, Mr. Mendizabal, Miss Szigmondy, and Mr. Shatov are all Jews. Even the mentally ill are included. All characters and relationships are hedges against suitable male partners who want to pursue flirtations or marriage. Miriam's eventual entry into the Society of Friends climaxes her booklong search for a healthy marginality, providing a critique of bourgeois values from a spiritual perspective, as her emancipated friends had from a social perspective. Despite its concern with sexuality and romance, the book contests the basis of the romance plot: gender asymmetry and the gross inequality of women, on which dominant culture, as well as narrative plots are built.

Given the autobiographical origins of *Pilgrimage,* the significance of its main defection is all the more striking. The half of Richardson's life closely described in *Pilgrimage* actually ended in marriage. The book emphatically does not. Although Miriam knows that one "Mr. Noble" (suggesting Alan Odle, Richardson's future husband) is staying at her boarding house, no meeting is engineered, and he is seen only as obliging and silent. Richardson avoids for the narrative telos of *Pilgrimage* the transformative act she chose for herself.[6]

Richardson married in 1917 to nurture a man fifteen years younger than herself whom she thought was dying of tuberculosis. Odle was like one of her works. For him she made the space, time, and atmosphere that allowed him to create. He was, in fact, a compulsive worker; correspondingly she attenuated her drive. Not only did she do all the domestic and financial chores, she also plotted his life and his experiences with the strong will of an author. Writing of his first trip to Switzerland in 1923, she noted, "He must see his first mountains in the early morning light & then be kept quietly browsing inactive and speechless in the charm of his new surroundings till he's had a day or two sitting about by or on the lake."[7] One might compare her to a mother with a sensitive and fractious child, or to a child with a sensitive and fractious mother. Indeed, Odle is a version of her mother, and she rescripts her life by her heroic salvage of him, filled with, as Gloria Fromm says, "self-imposed—and ritualistic—obligations."[8]

Mrs. Richardson's suicidal depression was witnessed by the young Dorothy. The mother's actual death occurred in Richardson's momentary absence. Her failure to prevent that suicide left her guilty and stunned; saving Odle redeemed her.[9] Preserving him allowed her to rewrite her life so that it did not end with blame for maternal death. In fact, the final words of *Pilgrimage* not only avoid marriage but resurrect the mother-child dyad; Miriam holds Amabel and Shatov's baby in her happy arms with a sense of "serenity" and "fulfillment" (*MM,* IV, 658).[10] The versions of mother-child relations represented by her marriage link *Pilgrimage* to other *Künstlerromane* by women.

Romance, representing an ideology about women, is a cultural phenomenon that Richardson writes to resist. She was shocked at her critique, feeling it "monstrous" in its dismissal of the materials and narratives that dominant culture had heretofore provided.[11] But she was even more stunned by prevalent misogynist assumptions. Miriam's shock (in *The Tunnel,* a book that Woolf reviewed) at reading an encyclopedia entry under *Woman* is fiercer and more desperate than even Woolf's parallel scenes in *A Room of One's Own.* In Richardson, the thoroughness of the prejudice against women provokes both tremendous revulsion to men and a suicidal fantasy from induced self-hatred. Miriam has found the classics, the works of every field of knowledge—"all the conceptual space"—saturated with the opinion that women "stopped being people"; women are part of nature, limited to gynecological functions; they are stigmatized as "half-human," as "inferior," as "undeveloped man"[12] (*Tun,* II, 220).

> If one could only burn all the volumes [of the encyclopedia]; stop the publication of them. But it was all books, all the literature in the world, right back to Juvenal . . . whatever happened, if it could all be avenged by somebody in some way, there was all that . . . the classics, the finest literature—'unsurpassed.' Education would always mean coming in contact with all that. [. . .] *How* could Newnham and Girton women endure it? [. . .] If, by one thought, all the men in the world could be stopped, shaken, and slapped. There *must,* somewhere, be some power that could avenge it all . . . but if these men were right, there was not. Nothing but Nature and her decrees. (*Tun,* II, 219–20)

The character Miriam is, then, constructed as a one-woman experiment, in the sense that the term is used in naturalism, to prove that these decrees of "nature" are masculinist ideology and to attack nothing less than Western culture's production of the female. The monumental—really excessive—length of *Pilgrimage* may indeed be attributable to Richardson's desire for vengeance on culture, for a female alternative to the cultural bulk of "the finest literature," and for a massive mountain of narrative to be placed between the main character and the hegemonic stories and opinion that haunted her. The invention of a novel spoken completely from the point of view of the main character—female—by an author whose life doubled her—female—protagonist's certainly creates a way of representing "women only in relation to the world as known to women."[13] "If women had been the recorders of things from the beginning it would all have been the other way round . . ." (*Tun*, II, 251). This alternative to hegemonic stories offered an uncribbed and uncurbed consciousness, speaking from its own center, devoid of an explanatory framework from narrator or prior narrative conventions. Richardson's obdurate decision to make a growing girl her center, catching that girl in phases from the dopey to the empowered, made an important statement about "the other way round." For the narrative marginality of teeming, uncontrolled thoughts and the gender marginality of the "new woman" were constantly connected tropes.[14]

Both contest the romance of culture and the culture of romance, two conventional versions of female meaning, struggle, and end. For Miriam to refuse to charm others is to doubt the social telos for herself as a very nubile girl. Cleverness and charm, "grimacing" and brightness are dissected by Miriam and her sisters as tactics to catch husbands, an apparent necessity for the newly impoverished Henderson sisters (*PR*, I, 165–66). The "old and stricken" looks of her sisters as they later endure their double marriage ceremony become associated with the suicide of their mother and provide the double ending of the first volume of *Pilgrimage*, which, like Woolf's first two novels, disposes of the endings in marriage and death (*H*, I, 462).

"Story"—narrative as expected—is interestingly associated in Miriam's mind with "flirtation"—tricks to please and entrap men. For Richardson as novelist, story resistance expresses in narrative poetics what Miriam's marriage resistance expresses in theme: both deny the force of the heterosexual love plot and of polarized gender hierarchies. "People thought it was silly, almost wrong to look [ahead] at the end of a book. But if it spoilt a book, there was something wrong about the book. If it was finished and the interest gone when you know who married who, what was the good of reading at all? It was a sort of trick, a sell" (*H*, I, 384).

Hence to refuse story in a novel is to refuse a major aspect of feminine charm. At the same time, clever books, like clever talk, are "mannish." If writing meant "rows and rows of 'fine' books; nothing but men sitting in studies doing something cleverly, being very important, 'men of letters'; and looking out for approbation. If writing meant that, it was not worth doing" (*Tun*, II, 130). Stereotypically female, stereotypically male, stories are doubly taxed by their affiliation with the group women, which she loathes for its charming masquerades, and the group men, which she condemns for its clever self-importance. There is a third, synthetic, way sought by this pilgrim between the Scylla and the Charybdis of the polarized sexes: liminality (similar to Woolf's androgyny), with its both/and appeal to multiplicity.

Pilgrimage is structured by a progress from very simple types of men—the Eliotic, idiotic clerk at Brighton, the banal German pastor pursuing an impressionable foreign teenager—toward the more complex: a solid Canadian physician, a married writer/womanizer, an unassimilated Orthodox Jew, an unfrocked French monk after his nervous breakdown. There are also side flirtations. But because most of the men eventually propose gender asymmetry or misogyny, and because the courtship context proposes what Miriam repeatedly calls the "plot" or the "novel" of sexual scripts, she will never consent to make any tie permanent. Her control is expressed by escaping just when each man feels she is his.

The dismissive investigation of the marriage plot occurs repeatedly. Wooed (in *The Tunnel*) by a Mr. Tremayne, Miriam is seduced by the role yet offers this parodic script of the rake's conversion by love:

> She was a very religious, very womanly woman, the ideal wife and mother and he was a bad fast man who wanted to be saved. It was such an easy part to play. She could go on playing it to the end of her life, . . . making the home a sanctuary of rest and refreshment and religious aspiration. . . . And if she kept out of the conversation and listened and smiled a little, he would go away adoring. (*Tun*, II, 27–28)

Instead, playing Beethoven loudly and passionately, "banging" the piano "till her hair nearly came down," she deliberately drives Mr. Tremayne away. Subsequently, over the protests of many men, she ferrets from her psyche any vestige of feminine passivity and charm and proceeds to violate norms of behavior with considerable gusto.

With Mr. Hancock at the Academy of Science, bitter at his admiration of a self-consciously feminine woman, she is blunt about the "trick and the whole advertising manner" underpinning charm and wiles, understanding with disgust how men demand this performance, yet feeling guilty that Hancock falls asleep—if she is insufficiently entertaining. Any romantic situation means "hiding so much, letting so much go; all the real things" (*Tun*, II, 105–108). The "so much" and the "real" cut from the romantic situation reemerge in the choice of poetics; that attempt to produce a novel where nothing "has to be left out" is exactly oppositional to the social conventions of gender and romance.

Bohemia demands the same tactics from its women: they must say "clever things in a high bright voice," either "imitating the clever sayings of men, or flattering them" (*Tun*, II, 113, 117). In another social context, set in a "shrine" and worshipped as "an object of romantic veneration" by the Canadian Haber, Miriam feels as if she were "part of a novel," which leaves her with a "haunting familiar sense of unreality" (*In,* II, 389). "Perhaps in Canada there were old-fashioned women who *were* objects of romantic veneration all their lives, living all the time as if they were Maud or some other woman from Tennyson." Courted ostentatiously by the Jew Mendizabal, she is accused of unfeminine fascination with such a dubious creature. Everyone at the boarding house gossips about her, for his mind is "a French novel" (*In,* II, 432). Thinking about all this, she considers the renunciatory remark of Schreiner's Lyndall—as Richardson did, thinking about poetics: "A woman must march with her regiment"— that is, conform to mandated expectations. "What for? What was the plot for? There's a *word . . . coercion,* that's the word. Better any sort of free life" (*In,* II, 434–35). In this allusion to Schreiner, one can again see how marriage resistance and resistance to narrative scripts are equivalent. Whether the demands are those of purity or its opposite, whether the homage is noble or fast, the various certainties of romance are stultifying for both character and author. In response, "Miriam felt she must get into the open and go far on and on and on" (*In,* II, 390). *Pilgrimage* is a quest away from cultural scripts of love and plot for hero and author.

Indeed, one of the longer and more sustained ties depicted is broken definitively when Michael Shatov makes some (unnarrated) glancing misogynist remark about "women in the mass," the kind of opinion that, for Miriam, "turned life into a nightmare" (*D,* III, 214). But such are her powers of escape that even the ultimate fall fails to trap her. Pregnant with the married Hypo Wilson's child, she rejects, at once, Shatov's offer of marriage as a refuge and Hypo's own smug response: that "booked for maternity" she must now "stand aside" from the flow of life (*CH,* IV, 321). In her turn, she declares that having a baby is "neither the beginning nor the end of feminine being" (*CH,* IV, 331). Both character and author are spared, by an autobiographical miscarriage, the task of writing in, and with, a real baby.

In short, throughout the book, to its final episode of marriage resistance with Richard Roscorla, "to marry would be actually to become, as far as the outside world could see, exactly the creature men described. To go into complete solitude, marked for life as a segregated female whose whole range of activities was known . . ." (*RL,* III, 302). The resistance to marriage was the resistance to the production of women by gender polarization, gender asymmetry, gender limitations.

The repetitive episodes of avoiding heterosexual romance are jointed later by an intense attraction between women. The sexual choices are clear: continued adulterous relations with that bohemian writer modeled on H. G. Wells, marriage to a solid citizen, refused for the second time, and a woman-identified bond with Amabel, similar to the lesbian tie between Hermione and Fayne in *HERmione* or to the ecstatic kiss of young Mrs. Dalloway and Sally Seton in *Mrs. Dalloway*. *Dawn's Left Hand* is a booklong debate about which sex to love; still, any romance plot is found to limit the quest of the main character, who remains plural and mobile. But this strong an attraction to a woman liberates Miriam in another sense from heterosexual romance, because it rouses memories of personal and spiritual joy, which lead to narrative understanding.[15]

Sleeping in Amabel's presence, Miriam awakens to see a vision of herself as a child in a flowering garden. Through this love, their "wordless communion," and this ecstatic contact with her past self, Miriam realizes, "All my life, since the beginning, I've left things standing on the horizon" (*DLH,* IV, 245, 253). It is that communal joy to which she wants to return. The influence of Amabel translates into the gift of speech as well as theme. The physical aspect of Amabel's love letter, even to the spaces between the strokes of the pen, gives Miriam an intimation of a new style involving response between reader and writer, a collective effort between them (*DLH,* IV, 214–15). This style, she affirms, is gender-inflected. Male writers offer only pictures of themselves (that intrusive "I" to which Woolf also had several occasions to refer); female writers are themselves "the medium of expression" (*DLH,* IV, 215).

Thus the erotic and emotional intensity of women's friendship cuts the Gordian knots of both heterosexuality and narrative convention. Here, as in the lives and works of H.D. and Woolf, the "continuous blossoming" of the writer depends on same-sex attraction (*DLH,* IV, 217). At the same time, Miriam deliberately marries Amabel off to her own Jewish suitor, Michael Shatov, in the manipulative act of a novelist, scripting others' realities with the conventional ending she rejects for herself. For Miriam, the lesbian moment is broadly absorbed as it is refused in specifics; it contributes to a sensibility of continuous pilgrimage to the group women. Women are "the only people who *knew*"; women are an answer beyond "the blind life of men": it is women who are "hidden beyond the hard visible horizon" (*D,* III, 198).

Liminality is central to the alternative sex-gender system this novel proposes, and it might be interpreted as an encoded version of the lesbian moment by virtue of its both/and fluidity: "harvesting the lively thought that comes when one is neither here nor there" (*Tr,* III, 416). Like the androgyny metaphor that Woolf offers at the end of the twenties to discuss the formation of personal and artistic identity, and like the synthesis made by the "daughter" artist of two "parental" sides discussed in chapter 6, Richardson's analysis proposes Miriam as a new person, "something between a man and a woman; looking both ways" (*Tun*, II, 187). This Janus-Janean figure combines the assertive, active, and "overbearing" quality of one sex with the "larger, bigger, deeper, less wordy and clever" presence of the other (*Tun*, II, 188). Miriam resists man's consciousness but desires his freedom of movement: *Pilgrimage* honors the "always getting away" characteristic of men and the immanent, radiant atmosphere, a special creation of women (*RL*, III, 257–58). The new psychic and social type of permanent liminality can be seen as female because it accepts all, judges nothing, has a totalizing both/and vision. " 'Shapeless' shapeliness" is, Richardson argues, "the unique gift of the feminine psyche," in "its power to do what the shapely mentalities of men appear incapable of doing for themselves, to act as a focus for divergent points of view."[16] Liminality—constant transition that does not crystallize into any "state" (married or single, male or female, one opinion versus another)—ends gender scripts by dissolving alternative, polarized, either/or possibilities into infinite potentiality.[17]

Hence the already existing plots and presuppositions of the "romantic and the realistic novel alike" are, Richardson stated, inappropriate for "the material that moved me to write."

> Each [kind of novel], so it seemed to me, left out certain essentials and dramatised life misleadingly. Horizontally. Assembling their characters, the novelists developed situations, devised events, climax and conclusion. I could not accept their finalities. Always for charm or repulsion, for good or ill, one was aware of the author and applauding, or deploring, his manipulations.[18]

In a way consistent with other writers studied here, Richardson holds that narrative conventions are simply an organization of the fantasies of the dominant culture and are "dependent on a whole questionable set of agreements and assumptions between reader and writer."[19] Richardson, like Schreiner and Woolf, and indeed responding to the same cultural matrix, condemned "the dramatic novel complete with plot, set scenes, beginning, middle, climax, and curtain," for this well-made work, with its "deliberately imposed narrative, incidents and figures," did not begin to account for "the mass lying unexpressed."[20] She is keen to read novels like fields, from any point to any other point, rather than sequentially ("horizontally").[21] Richardson's dissenting remarks about the linearity of the novel, themselves characteristic of the poetics of modernism, were at the same time bound up with questions about the depiction of gender that linearity implied. Gender issues for Richardson, as for Woolf and H.D., were frozen versions of social habits that no longer had a unique claim to dominance. Stages of a female romantic plot were rigid in light of greater social possibility. The narrative telos in marriage was therefore brought under intense scrutiny. Richardson goes so far as to identify and to reject the sexual rhythms of narrative conventions, their "frothy excitement (a prime source of the moralist's condemnation)."[22] She thus sought to revise even the pace of novels, breaking their allegiance to a sexuality perceived only as arousal and climax.

In her portrait of Miriam's development into a writer, Richardson shows a project about women as a gender group hidden inside of, and partially masked by, novelistic structures of sex and sentiment that are more instantaneously gratifying. When Bob Graville insists Miriam could "write the confessions of a modern woman," he means a kind of soft-core "sensational" or pulp fiction; Miriam responds by criticizing that kind of narrative appeal. She says that to write as a woman, one writes "from the other side, the woman's side," revising the dominant book, where "everything would be left out that is always there, preceding and accompanying and surviving the drama of human relationships" (DH, IV, 524–25). Like Woolf's use of the term "personal," this is a way of insisting that certain mandated ties to others are only part of the story. That woman's side offers a third way, beyond the antinomies of gender polarization, between "masculine novels" stigmatized as "irrelevant" and "the feminine ones far too much influ[enced] by magic traditions, and too much set upon exploiting the sex motif as hitherto seen and depicted by men. . . ."[23]

The enormous lack of a "story" in this novel is then a serious, deeply held, and justifiable element of Richardson's poetics of fiction, given the fact that "story" for women has typically meant plots of seduction, courtship, the energies of quest deflected into sexual downfall, the choice of a marriage partner, the melodramas of beginning, middle, and end, the trajectories of sexual arousal and release. Even telling an amusing tale is a capitulation to flirtatious mannerisms. But when "story" means meaningful sequence or formal generalization, its lack becomes rather more nerve-wracking: provoking, not provocative. For kinds of formal patterning involving priority, weight, cause and effect, connection, sequence, and meaning are undermined in a casual but drastic way by Pilgrimage. Because of this radical feminist dissolution of categories, one can readily understand all manner of testy remarks about the novel, including May Sinclair's mix of wonder and annoyance, which generated the original use of the term *stream of consciousness:* "there is no drama, no situation, no set scene. Nothing happens. It is just life going on and on. It is Miriam Henderson's stream of consciousness going on and on."[24]

The rupture with conventional narrative occurs on all scales in *Pilgrimage,* and the qualified success of such strategies creates a clear problem for Virginia Woolf, who proposes something very similar—the critique of romance—for similar reasons—its social, psychic, and narrative limitations. Among all the exposition in *The Tunnel,* Woolf highlights the poetics that comes from the critique of romance. She cites Hypo Wilson's prediction, "There will be books with all that cut out—him and her—all that sort of thing."[25] We have seen how, in Richardson, the romance plot is inextricably tied to and is a symbol of the "shapeliness of the old accepted forms."[26] Woolf too connects the formal and the ideological aspects of the critique—the link between conventional narrative on the one hand and normative expectations for female life on the other.

> So "him and her" are cut out, and with them goes the old deliberate business: the chapters that lead up and the chapters that lead down; the characters who are always characteristic; the scenes that are passionate and the scenes that are humorous; the elaborate construction of reality; the conception that shapes and surrounds the whole. All these things are cast away. . . .[27]

In these reviews, Woolf formulates something that becomes central to her criticism and praxis: the "uncomfortable" idea that narrative emphasis changes when one focuses on gender, and on the twentieth-century woman, not the nineteenth-century plot. "The accent upon the emotions has shifted. What was emphatic is smoothed away. What was important to Maggie Tulliver no longer matters to Miriam Henderson."[28]

Woolf's consideration of Richardson began as she finished *Night and Day,* her second novel, which synthesizes versions of the nineteenth-century marriage plot as, in a stranger way, her first novel worked with the link between marriage and death that textures many classic novels. Woolf had announced her vocation, as we saw in chapter 4, by writing, with ambivalence and desire, variant kinds of "heroine's texts." As she distanced herself from these kinds of plots, she discovered Richardson's work. Woolf uses Richardson as her scout, to establish and valorize a framework in which the inflection of gender within narrative can be examined. It may even be a case of the Woolfean angel fearing to tread, yet entering into a greater narrative boldness, signaled to her by the Richardsonian fool.[29]

In clearing the novel of "story," Richardson invents a positive strategy to rupture the telos of romance, a strategy I am calling the "multiple individual." Richardson postulates that one could separate heterosexual romance, "him and her," and sexual polarization from the special component that makes the love story so attractive. "Something that justified the sentimental books they all jeered at; a light that had come suddenly, . . . bringing wide thoughts and sympathies; centering in the girl; breaking down barriers so completely that for a while they all seemed to exchange personalities" (*RL*, III, 275). Just as late nineteenth-century free-thinking movements desired to refine an ethics out of the dross of institutionalized religion, so Richardson wants to refine empathetic communion from sentimental narrative—the romance and marriage plots that she found both derisory and controlling. "The girl" can be the symbolic center of these concerns not simply because she incarnates the narrative dilemma of the female protagonist, but because, to Richardson, women have a special capacity for pluralism, heterogeneity, and a tolerant, multiple caritas.

"It is that women can hold all opinions at once, or any, or none" (*RL*, III, 259). In Richardson's view, women are gifted to see the "million sides to every question" (*Tun*, II, 189). The female perspective is holistic, synthetic, totalizing, rather than instrumental, calculating, rational. In a memorable scene, Miriam argues with a lawyer that his conventionalized identification of immediate causes involves judgments and priorities that falsify the analysis of an accident. She, instead, would look for "the sum total of *all* the circumstances," going backwards and around, making a nonteleological constellation that tries to account, in no privileged fashion, for causal multiplicity (*H*, I, 442–43). Their capacity for fusing opposite perspectives, for seeing things from so many viewpoints, for understanding multiple and divergent opinions, makes women multiple individuals.[30] But further, as individuals, they have less-defined boundaries and stronger desires for these plural identifications. Hence women are the privileged site of a desire to move "beyond the hard visible horizon" of the bounded self and to express a "communal consciousness" (*D*, III, 198, and *CH*, IV, 334).

Quite early in her life, just after returning from her first job as a teacher in Germany, Richardson became "convinced that many of the evils besetting the world originated in the enclosed particularist home and in the institutions [i.e. schools] preparing women for such homes."[31] As she rejected that family-centered private home (even giving up teaching as a tainted undertaking), so she rejected the ideology of privatization and its narrative embodiment.

Indeed, boarding houses are residences of choice in *Pilgrimage*, because they are liminal spaces between the family house and the international, professional city. One of Miriam's first journeys is a climb to the top of a boarding house to gain the half-dingy, half-translucent space of a room that she claims for her independent self, and whose vista over the city she liberates by removing its window lattice (*Tun,* II, 13). An impersonal possession of space is here, as in Woolf's famous title, a symbol of freedom precisely in its rejection of female obligations: "no interruption, no one watching or speculating or treating one in some particular way that had to be met" (*Tun,* II, 17).

Instead, the city of London becomes a significant "character"—one offering a substitute for heterosexual romance. ". . . What London can mean as a companion, I have tried to set down in *Pilgrimage.*"[32] The greatest kinds of bliss occur in this collective space: London under fog, at dusk, and at dawn, London seen at a strange angle from her window, is irradiated with a joy even better than love: "the lovely, strange, unconscious life of London . . . holding the secret of the fellowship of its inhabitants" (*CH,* IV, 334).

The city is never claustrophobic or binding, but rather open and choral. Fusing public and private spaces in the city of many intersecting groups, as Woolf would do later in *The Years,* allows Richardson to veto one of the central conventions of the novel, one that exerts particular force on a heroine's text: the idea that an elsewhere is impossible to find. The claustrophobia of *The Mill on the Floss, The House of Mirth,* or *Portrait of a Lady* occurs when the novelist constructs a world to insist that there are no alternative places to go, no ways of leaving, no other relationships or circles of friends—and judges—than the terrible ones to which the female hero is bound. In contrast in *Pilgrimage* there are many characters and groups. No group's morality or limitations capture Miriam permanently; no one group can inhibit her wacky notions. Richardson herself had found the interlocking worlds with which she made contact, from science and religion to art and politics, arranged like an "archipelago." "I found all these islands to be the habitations of fascinating secret societies, to each of which in turn I wished to belong and yet was held back, returning to solitude and to nowhere, where alone I could be everywhere at once, hearing all the voices in chorus."[33] In community, the "hard visible horizon" of the lone individual or the unique couple is overpassed; the individual is at once single and choral.

As well as in the city of London, that horizon is met and surpassed in the pastoral Quaker retreat at Dimple Hill. Miriam feels kinship with the Quaker community because her energetic pilgrimage outward through London and its groups has always been given value by recurrent moments of meditative understanding, when she goes "down through the layers of her surface being," and by vivid moments of illumination, when outer and inner lives are fused (*DH*, IV, 498).[34] What this community of lay mystics and its "spiritual rhythm" offers can be gauged by her response to a communal dinner, in which "she saw upon each face a radiance recalling the look of a happy lover" (*DH*, IV, 470). Thus the community is an extension of—and substitute for—exclusive romance.[35]

Quaker attitudes are deeply implicated in questions of gender. Because Friends do not institutionalize that "angry, jealous, selfish male God of the patriarchate," Miriam is free to establish her own female sense of the divine. Further, because the "inner life of the [Friends'] meeting was more fully with the women" and their "pure, live atmosphere," The Society of Friends becomes an institutional way of stating one's belief in female values and female difference, yet one that, quite deliberately, avoided feminism (*RL*, III, 328, 329). For Miriam ends up, in contemporary parlance, a postfeminist. She rummages around "in the archives of her intermittent feminism" and finds that she no longer cares about the sexist opinions that had formerly incensed her (*DH*, IV, 503–504). Instead she finds "the misty dawn of a conviction, new and startling and bringing, as it cleared and took shape, a return of the sense of unity with those about her." By this maneuver, Richardson transposes those traits of cultural value, identified throughout as female, to the sphere of spiritual and communal knowledge. So in many ways, the final valorizing of the Quaker community is the answer to and the substitute for Miriam's preoccupation with gender institutions.

For the deepest "reality of feminism" is that women are blessed because they are the peacemakers, a neo-Christian formulation that completes and balances her earlier, Judaistic implication that they were the chosen people.[36] In both formulations, Richardson is reclaimed by main-cultural terms for the representation of gender that she had, in the bulk of her text, gone far to delegitimate: woman is intuitive, woman is unconflictual. Feminism's reality is flattened, from critique of the production of gendered people in narrative and in institutions organizing sexuality, to a paean to an essentialist femininity and its spiritual gifts, embodied in the maternal and generous Rachel Mary, a name doubly marked by motherly allusions.[37]

In any event, making the narrative center be the multiple individual is a strategy expressing the psychic oscillation between boundaries and boundlessness, characteristic of the mother-child dyad, and the social oscillation between pluralist positions and between the lone individual and an endless array of fascinating groups. This is an op-

positional narrative strategy, denying the force of marriage as an end
as well as death and judgment. It is a strategy invented as well by
other women writers, working in the Afro-American tradition,
writers "preoccupied with the spiritual survival, the survival *whole* of
my people," to cite Alice Walker.[38]

One of the functions of the multiple individual as a strategy would
be to absorb and present the plural, contradictory universe in an
inclusive, not selective, fashion. This may be thought of as a way of
achieving a doubled vision. The function is shaped differently in each
author, but there remains a resemblance between Richardson's both/
and liminality of the psyche moving beyond the horizon, Zora Neale
Hurston's horizon vision, and Alice Walker's dramatization of social
and spiritual contradiction. Hurston's Janie, after her quest: "Ah
done been tuh de horizon and back and now Ah kin set heah in mah
house and live by comparisons."[39] In Hurston, the horizon indicates
not only expansive possibility but a way of breaking the frame of
individual consciousness. Hurston ends her book with that kind of
evocation: "She pulled in her horizon like a great fish-net. Pulled it
from around the waist of the world and draped it over her shoulder.
So much of life in its meshes! She called in her soul to come and see"
(*TEWWG*, 286). The world's multiplicity becomes Janie's possession.

Earlier, Hurston's image of the horizon is used in a way that makes
the quest to plurality clearer. Janie's "great journey to the horizons"—
in the plural—occurs because the main character is "in search of
people" (*TEWWG*, 138). She breaks out of the narrow definitions of
womanhood understandably bequeathed by the rigid and fearful ex-
slave, her grandmother, and out of the narrow definitions of marriage
and sexuality that structured her romantic life, first with the
significantly named Killicks and then with Jody Stark.

Stark is an authoritarian and an egotist; this second marriage alien-
ates her from a vision of pleasure—he "took the bloom off" by being
judge and punisher (*TEWWG*, 70). His store is a metaphor for his
vision of the world: ownership, superiority, control. The vocal, amusing group of folk storytellers and "liars" hanging around the porch
opens this closed world to multiple commentary, tales, and jibes.
Janie's alienation from her marriage is marked by her growing
identification with folk life, its contests and rituals, its pleasures and its
narrative skills.

After Stark's death, Janie is courted by, and marries, a young man
named Tea Cake, sensual and amusing. On one level, their heady
sexuality hardly represents a critique of romance, since Janie experiences a blissful love that is broken only when Tea Cake, bitten by a
rabid dog, must be tragically killed by Janie herself, in self-defense.

Much as H.D. was incited to begin *Helen in Egypt* by a bout of romantic thralldom and a need to examine this desire, so Hurston wrote *Their Eyes Were Watching God* to discuss with herself a thoroughgoing romance "soaked . . . in ecstasy," "the real love affair of my life," a love alternately arousing and shaming, as her desire for autonomous work ("my real self") conflicted with her desire for complete romantic possession.[40] Hurston later said, "I tried to embalm all the tenderness of my passion for him in *Their Eyes Were Watching God*"; the double-edged word *embalm* bespeaks the volcanic ambivalence that makes her invention of Janie and Tea Cake fit within one febrile tradition of romance and yet transpose that thralldom to another arena. Not only his death but also the fact that Tea Cake gives Janie access to black folk life is Hurston's fictional resolution of the contradiction between her own work as an anthropologist and the intensity of her feelings for "AWP."[41]

So the romance plot becomes communitarian and Janie a multiple individual through Tea Cake's love. Through Tea Cake, Janie becomes one with the black folk community; indeed, marrying Tea Cake is a way of marrying that community. A dark man, opposed in his very body to those who want, in shallow self-hatred, to "lighten up de race," Tea Cake takes Janie as an agricultural worker to "the muck"— a rich, fertile region in the Florida Everglades (*TEWWG*, 209). Because it is explicitly stated that "The muck meant Tea Cake. . . ," he is more than one man or a sexual partner, but rather the representative of fecund blackness itself, the fulfillment of a yearning for organic and vocal community (*TEWWG*, 283).

Not only is Tea Cake a man of the people, with all their virtues and vices; he has a sense of fairness and equality with his wife that contrasts definitively to Janie's other husbands. So in her depiction of this folk hero, Hurston doubly criticizes both sexism and black self-hatred. Instead of being owned like a slave by one man, forbidden to participate in the tales and jokes of a "trashy people," through Tea Cake, Janie becomes part of a community, defends the "mingled people" of color, and participates herself, as an equal, in the tale-telling and folk rumination of the porch sitters that is the moral center of Hurston's work (*TEWWG*, 85, 210). The passage from a voiceless, repressed Janie to Janie as a "delegate to de big 'ssociation of life" shows how the formation of the self in this novel is resolved not in individualistic terms but by Janie's identification with blackness and black culture (*TEWWG*, 18).[42]

For Hurston, a community of blackness was a creative source, a source of the pleasure (to cite Alice Walker's appreciative remarks) "of each other's loquacious and *bodacious* company," and the generative power of "blues made and used right on the spot" (*TEWWG*, 197).[43] Hurston was a practicing anthropologist who did field research on black culture in the American South and in the Carribean. With a white male scholar, Franz Boas, and a white woman, Mrs. R. Osgood Mason, as reparenting mentors, Hurston defined her vocation within anthropology as making black cultural life an object of analytic and aesthetic attention. "Godmother" Mason was an amateur folklorist, whose romantic fascination with the "sincerity" of folk life gave Hurston the permission she needed to investigate it: "I must tell the tales, sing the songs, do the dances, and repeat the raucous sayings and doings of the Negro farthest down."[44] "LET THE PEOPLE SING, was and is my motto," as through the singular hero the community speaks.[45]

Meridian (1976) by Alice Walker similarly creates a pluralist spiritual and political vision for her single, questing protagonist, Meridian Hill. The story seems to be Meridian's biography, telling of her growth through childhood, marriage, and motherhood, her subsequent attendance at Saxon, a nice black women's college, and then her political work. Yet hardly organized individualistically or chronologically, it is even more a retrospective study of black women and black civil rights workers, among whom Meridian is situated and from whom she emerges. So *Meridian* is, in fact, a collective biography of a multiple individual, who articulates social and spiritual questions.[46]

Walker's specific use of the multiple individual may be a narrative response to a particular circumstance of black "mainstreaming" eloquently analyzed by Mary Helen Washington, in which one family member is chosen to escape racial limitations, given the best possible education, and given, as well, permission to leave her family and her people, to deny and resist that identification with class, race, and social identity which would otherwise have been a heritage.[47] This cultural strategy is delegitimated by Walker's narrative practice, which tells the stories of many women along with Meridian's own single tale, and thus relocates the individual hero in a narrative multiplicity that is both matrifocal and conflictual, registering the heritage of debates and struggles among the women who are detailed. Mrs. Hill, Meridian's spotless, angry mother; Feather Mae, whose ecstatic visions within the Indian serpent mound are a model for Meridian's trances; Wile Chile, the despised thirteen-year-old garbage picker, pregnant, soon to die; Fast Mary of the Tower (certainly the fourth Mary of the ballad on which Woolf also drew), a college student who commits infanticide and then suicide—these are the multiple women from whom Meridian emerges and whose passionate conflicts define her. For poetics, Walker retells a Procne-Philomela myth in Louvinie, the slave whose tongue was cut out for storytelling. Her tongue, buried at the roots of a magnolia, makes that tree, "Sojourner," magnificent.

Triumph over many forms of violation is a major theme. When the Saxon women riot on campus, at first their rage turns inward, and they destroy the sheltering symbol of their own ancestral spirit of marginality and voice: Sojourner itself. History and Walker conspire to offer black women another chance; at the end of the novel, that ruined magnolia has begun to sprout—the Old South destroyed, the New South perhaps a viable shoot. With this collective biography, vision, pain, sexual crime and punishment, and the cost of talent are explored as the conflictual heritage of black women. All the characters are equally the narrative subject; the "progress" of each and all is intertwined. Further, within this multiplicity no character goes unchanged, unexamined, unforgiven, even in the brutal cross-racial hostility of the shooting of Tommy Odds, the rape of Lynne, and the murder of the biracial child Camara. While villainous and ugly acts are constantly performed, Walker rejects any "black-white" melodrama of political judgment and summary categories.

The collective struggle of the Civil Rights Movement of the 1960s offers Meridian a second life, a way of beginning her "story" again—a story that had seemed stalemated in a nineteenth-century ending.[48] At the beginning Walker briefly presents conventional scripts for narratives about women: a carnival exhibit of an actual mummified woman in all her pickled roles—Obedient Daughter, Devoted Wife, Adoring Mother, and . . . Gone Wrong.[49] Throughout, Walker makes the reader stare hard at a series of conventional endings, which Meridian as multiple individual will painfully displace from narrative hegemony.

Caught young with a child in a limiting marriage, Meridian understands that the dim life she lives had an origin in the drama of heterosexual romance, which girls continue to act.

> [The girls] simply did not know they were living their own lives—
> between twelve and fifteen—but assumed they lived someone else's.
> They tried to live the lives of their movie idols; and those lives were
> fantasy. . . . So they moved, did the young girls outside her window, in
> the dream of happy endings: of women who had everything, of men
> who ran the world. (*M*, 75)

Caught almost as young having just aborted another child of another man, she thinks of the classic ending for the sexual plots in which she has been almost permanently locked. The ending for her kind of guilty sin is death. A chapter called "The Recurring Dream" opens with a passage whose first paragraph is repeated three times (I shall cite it only once) in order to emphasize the personal stalemate as well as the culturally reiterated nature of this resolution.

> She dreamed she was a character in a novel and that her existence presented an insoluble problem, one that would be solved only by her death at the end.
>
> Even when she gave up reading novels that encouraged such a solution—and nearly all of them did—the dream did not cease. (*M*, 117)

So do dominant scripts enter one's unconscious life.

At the end of *Meridian,* both the love and the death plots resurface in more elegant forms. Truman appeals to her: "I want you to love me" (*M*, 216). And the reader also considers that this heterosexual couple, after all their suffering, could make a confirming resolution. But Walker rejects compromise. "My love for you changed," says Meridian, and by that statement the author announces the creation of an alternative male/female unit—sister-brother questers, a form of relation that displaces the heterosexual couple in H.D.'s *Helen in Egypt,* in Lessing's *Landlocked,* in Schreiner's *The Story of an African Farm.* In the final paragraphs, Truman becomes a new Meridian, infused with the same "illness"—an epileptic dizziness that is the experience of contradiction, a paralysis that is a form of mourning. When Meridian leaves him, Truman gets into her chrysalid sleeping bag, dons her visored cap, and begins his first shaking spell. She has passed on her conflict, like a torch. Meridian's life is, in its singularity, a collective mission; always alone, she is the avatar of a people who will "one day gather at the river" (*M*, 220).

But no suggestion of the older structuring plots is as difficult to avoid as death. Parallel narrative traditions on which Walker draws— the Christian and black traditions, mutually reinforcing—suggest martyrdom as an end. Martyrdom is Meridian's greatest temptation; she is, after all, introduced staring down a white tank filled with white policemen, thinking "*she's* God," as an early informant drily says, but being in truth "so burnt out and weird" (*M*, 22, 21). For one primary question the novel poses is how the characters focus their social passion and rage for justice. Will it be in perverse rectifications of racial hostilities—self-mutilation, violence against others, rape, murder? Will it be in martyrdom? " 'The only new thing now,' she had said to herself . . . 'would be the refusal of Christ to accept crucifixion. King,' she had said, turning down a muddy lane, 'should have refused. Malcolm, too, should have refused' " (*M*, 151). With scrupulous attention to conventional narrative resolution and the statements made therein, Walker takes Meridian beyond all the endings of romance and death in a final section, cunningly entitled "Ending." What is the nature of her opposition? " 'All those characters in all those novels that require death to end the book should refuse. All saints should walk away. Do their bit, then—just walk away. See Europe, visit Hawaii, become agronomists or raise Dalmations.' She didn't care what they did, but they should do it" (*M*, 151).

She has become the multiple individual, in a new plot, not the saint in an old. Sainthood, with its self-denial, its testing by suffering, its personal superiority, is turned inside out in the multiple individual.[50] Instead of one person's taking on the guilt of the collective, a conflictory collective offers its "spiritual work" to the individual (*M*, 89). She understands that it is neither in punitive or transcendent individual love, nor in punitive or transcendent individual death that her "ending" will be written, but in a "communal spirit, togetherness, righteous convergence," which has both a spiritual and a political meaning (*M*, 199).

■

CHAPTER TEN

"'I' rejected; 'We' substituted": The Later Novels of Woolf

. . . to form—new combinations?
VIRGINIA WOOLF
The Years (1937)

The choral or group protagonist is, as we have seen, another major strategy of female modernism, a means of empowering narrative if one chooses to depend neither upon the romance and personal *Bildungs* plots nor upon some of the assumptions (beginning with gender polarization and the dichotomy of male and female, public and private spheres, and moving to hero and heroine and the "hard visible horizon" of the isolated individual) underlying those plots.

At the end of Woolf's second novel, *Night and Day,* the romantic couple try to visit the Schreineresque single woman, yet can only stand, paralyzed, on her doorstep. Left unmated, Mary is sacrificed to the symmetry of the narrative solutions. Indeed, to construct these solutions, Mary's public, political, and practical tasks are even made to appear less complete and more marginal than Katherine's private, visionary, and romantic vocation. But Mary cannot be assimilated to this resolution for another reason. Mary is one first indication of a nonheroic figure assimilated within a nonromance network, like Bernard and the friends, Eleanor and the family, La Trobe and the pageant. An even earlier suggestion of this figure, Rosamond Merridew, historian, makes clear the continuity between professional women, critically examining social institutions, and the choral protagonist. There is a thematic, structural, and ideological continuity among these early spinster researchers, the later choral novels, and Woolf's critical examinations of women in culture and society.

Woolf explains that women writers are influenced by the social changes that women as a group have undergone. Because women are now (in general) wage earners and citizens, they need no longer be overdependent upon winning love to achieve self-worth, economic status, and class position. Their narratives will show a corresponding change. No longer "pinned down / by love" as "the only natural action," women writers and their creations will have greater scope.[1]

For example, "[the] men and women [characters of women writers] will not be observed wholly in relation to each other emotionally, but as they cohere and clash in groups and classes and races."[2] This muting of the "emotional" is Woolf's code for deemphasis of the plot of romance. Woolf thus suggests a direct correlation between women's critique of romance and their professional status. When a woman writer has no means of support beyond marriage, no personal legacy, no earning power, she will tamp down her capacity for critical analysis, but if she has achieved social and economic freedom, her novels will be "naturally [sic] more critical of society."[3]

Her late novels correspond to a design Woolf set forth in 1927, suggesting that in ten or fifteen years (exactly on the mark), a new intergeneric novel would fuse poetry, prose, and drama. In this programmatic prophecy, it is vital to note that these intergeneric works will reject the realistic sociological novel of facts, incomes, and environment; the psychological novel with "the incessant, the remorseless analysis of falling into love and falling out of love. . . ," plots, in short, of quests ending in success or failure and of romance.[4] Both late novels substitute for these discredited narratives the invention of a communal protagonist and a collective language.

The communal protagonist is a way of organizing the work so that neither the development of an individual against a backdrop of supporting characters nor the formation of a heterosexual couple is central to the novel. As a further development from the multiple individual considered in the preceding chapter, the choral protagonist makes the group, not the individual, the central character.[5] Not based on individual *Bildung* or romance, but rather on a collective *Bildung* and communal affect, the novel can suggest the structures of social change in the structures of narrative.[6] The communal protagonist operates, then, as a critique both of the hierarchies and authoritarian practice of gender and of the narrative practice that selects and honors only major figures.

The promotion of any given character to a position of greatest importance in a narrative indicates dominant values and marks social hierarchies.[7] To discredit this social practice of narrative, in *The Years* and *Between the Acts,* Woolf has equalized the characters. No one stands higher in the plot than any other: the final conveyor of value is plural. Several of Woolf's discarded titles for *The Years* express this: *The Caravan* is a collective ramshackle journeying, *Ordinary People* evokes the multiple and humdrum at once.[8]

Between the Acts, Woolf's last novel, extends the social parable of *The Years* to the question of what unifies all of us, and explores intersecting groups to answer, "We live in others."[9] The establishing of collective identity in the experience of the pageant is the major action; the communal protagonist recognizes itself in the mirror the play provides. History, language, heritage, tensions, truisms, and a batty tolerance are shown to be manifold expressions of "'We' the composed of many different things . . . we all life, all art, all waifs and strays. . . ."[10]

Between the Acts sees romance as the most rigid and masquelike operation: pursuit, lust, rape fantasy, love-hate ambivalence. The work incorporates these dramas, especially of Giles and Isa, as flashy desperate moments in an encompassing setting of communal ties. Just a few pages before "the curtain rose" on their ultimate sexual struggle, Isa thinks, "Love and hate—how they tore her asunder! Surely it was time someone invented a new plot, or that the author came out from the bushes . . ." (*BA,* 215). She is a character in just such a novel. The author in the bushes, Miss La Trobe, has invented this new plot, not of "I" nor of "her and him" but of "We." Indeed, Woolf was examining what ties bound this "We" together, in part by reading "Freud on Groups" during the composition of *Between the Acts.*[11]

In "Group Psychology and the Analysis of the Ego" (1921), Freud widens his idea that the sexual instinct underlies human behavior by incorporating this drive into a larger framework called *libido*— including much more than sexual connection: love for parents and children, love for friends, love for humanity. Libidinal ties are broader and more encompassing than romance. However, much as H.D. reprocessed Freud's ideas, so Woolf was selective here, for Freud also postulated that these libidinal ties were focused by a political leader who served as the desired object for the mass, and who thereby created group cohesion. Instead, Woolf depicted broad, horizontal connections and—a process especially marked in *The Years*—rejected any vestige of status or hierarchy for her libidinal groups.

The Years chronicles three major changes, from the patriarchal, repressive family, to relatively fluid and reactive fraternal-sororal ties, to a critical group of visionary outsiders: three modulations of the communal protagonist. Repetition as a rhetorical tactic marks the debate between the status quo and change. Dominant insistence on social reproduction is conveyed by Woolf in a chronic use of repetition, especially of boring comments and insights. With dissent from social reproduction and the longing for "a new world," the use of repetition occurs to highlight a dreamy collective vision of change.

The bourgeois family is an institution that most members are happiest leaving (even little Rose flees, disastrously, into the evening) and gloomiest when returning to (Eleanor: "broody"; Abel Pargiter: "out of temper"). Those who cannot leave wait for the kettle to boil. The participants in family life seem to be united only by shared negativity: concealments, hostility, resentment, guilt—in short, "the atmosphere of suppressed emotion."[12] Guilty stains such as Rose's dirty pinafore, Delia's anger at her mother's lingering death, and Abel's sordid mistress are always hidden to protect a banal surface. But even Col. Pargiter's sexual adventures are coopted to domesticity; his mistress is mechanical, financially dependent.

Gender stereotypes each character. For lack of purpose except waiting for male attention, Milly and Delia are enormously bored—Delia indulging in the compensatory fantasies of sexual romance and political adventure to which Florence Nightingale knowingly alluded in "Cassandra."[13] As for the brothers, whether willing or unwilling, suited or not, each of the Pargiter males is prepared for a classic profession: law, university, army. Even though Rose is more militant than the reluctant Martin, and Eleanor more fascinated by law than the brother who becomes a judge, women are barred from public life. This limpid critique of the bourgeois family underlines the discrepancy between the polarized gender sets in one social class.

At first, the system of social reproduction seems forceful and intact, quite impervious to change, and the novel seems parodic, a tribute to stasis. By midbook, *The Years* has achieved a calibrated optimism of the will, showing a change not only cosmic, cyclic, and chronic (like the seasons and the day, which are, not incidentally, deconstructed by being taken out of their expected order) but evolutionary. Woolf harnesses the endless cycles of family life for a defining change. By the end, the critique of social replication becomes intense. For in the title *The Years,* Woolf captures the Shelleyan radicalism of the "Ode to the West Wind," which makes the inevitability of the seasons into the prophecy of transformation.

In a similar way, Woolf makes the inevitability of social clichés and banalities become the key to meaningful change in *Between the Acts.* The humble apologetic speech of a diffident and almost unrecognized *raisonneur* figure, Rev. Streatfield, delivers the meaning of the novel in shy clichés. "We are members of one another," he says; com-

munity does exist and has been affirmed by the mummers' performance. Our unity in dispersion is manifest: "We act different parts; but
are the same" (*BA*, 192). Further, all creatures have participated; we
are not the exclusive or ruling inhabitants of our world: "Dare we . . .
limit life to ourselves?" Because of our common values and self-
recognition, "Surely, we should unite?"

In *The Years*, the closing up of the house in 1913 marks the end of
the patriarchal family, a change that Eleanor embraces and the servant Crosby mourns, breaking illusions of family unity and cross-class
similarity.[14] At this moment is revealed what had been partially concealed earlier: that within the same family, one might have radically
different interests. The smelly old family dog to which Crosby is
overly loyal gets intermingled in the prosings of everyday speech with
the death of one old patriarch himself: "He ought to have been put
down long ago" suspiciously takes in both, revealing long-repressed
hostilities (*Y*, 219).

The unspoken and long repressed have both structural and critical
meaning. Virtually everything that could have been grist for a "plot,"
with its crises, discoveries, shocks, renunciations, and causal connections, Woolf has dropped. For example, Rose is forever unable to talk
about an exhibitionist, and the narrative shows the power of that
childhood trauma by having it be completely repressed, except for an
unpleasant aura attached to the red erect mailbox. Connections are,
in short, deliberately unsaid, unmade, like half-thoughts that pass
before they can be captured. The art of the book—to look deshabille,
uncrafted, a little dim—sustains the final picture of the unclosed,
never fully measured capacities of time, people, history. But these
carefully achieved loose connections also sustain an alternative reading of permanent repression and stasis. The lack of connectedness is a
deliberate risk on Woolf's part, expressing the deepest of alternatives:
stasis and change.

The "story" becomes the unsaid at countless junctures. When
someone says, "I'll tell you the true story one of these days," it never
happens; stories are postponed—forever, and the reader barely remembers that they were promised (*Y*, 143). "There was a story—" is
definitively interrupted (*Y*, 153). "Tell me . . ." evokes no response (*Y*,
180). "I saw . . . ," says Eleanor about Spain, and as she is poised to tell
about it, her sister-in-law saves her the trouble in a way typical of the
book: "You must tell me all about it afterwards" (*Y*, 197). Instead, the
book concentrates on lapse, gap, space, tacitness, and repression. The
ellipsis is favored in punctuation, and Woolf will repeatedly narrate in
detail the phatic and awkward moments before a conversation begins,

but neglect to record ongoing talk freely flowing. Because so many stories are only alluded to, the novel becomes a story of missing stories. Like stasis in relation to change, the unsaid because repressed and the unsaid because incipient vie in the same narrative space, creating an oscillation between dominant presence and muted potential.

Throughout the book, characters constantly question the substantiality, effect, and borders of the ego: "What's 'I'?" and "What would the world be . . . without 'I' in it?" (Y, 140, 242). That is, to achieve the choral protagonist that can tell her privileged story, Woolf must insist on the disintegration of the individual ego. Characters are constituted by the flickering of time and tide; "I" and "she" is just something temporary that may happen, the way an individual lady is actually, like a postimpressionist painting, "composed of lozenges of floating colours" or "caught in a net of light" (Y, 241).

"What's 'I'?" and "Are we one, or are we separate?" become important questions in the scene between Maggie and her sister Sara, which is capped by a solo dance by their mother for the entranced daughters (Y, 140). This communion and charmed performance is interrupted by the "querulous" calls of the husband, peremptorily claiming the prerogatives of locks and swords and property (Y, 144). The interruption, by a heterosexual and generational exclusivity of the blissful relation between women, makes a clear comment. Questions of oneness and separation, so suggestive in this mother-daughter dyad, intimate that the fluid ego boundaries of the preoedipal bond are one source for the communal protagonist.[15] But the dissolving borders of the self ("He had a feeling that he was no one and nowhere in particular") are not simply or only statements about personal psychology, experiences of private consciousness, or that generative void continuous in Woolf's characters since Rachel Vinrace; in this novel the dissolution of the ego is "deeply political" (Y, 311).[16] If the soul "wishes to expand; to adventure; to form—new combinations," individual egos must lose their tendencies for aggrandizement and dominance (Y, 296).

Of two social gatherings at midbook, one looks backward to the tensions of upper middle-class life, the other forward to "new combinations." Kitty's high-season soirée of 1914 is formal, mannered, and elegant. Concealment reigns; when wine is spilled down a woman's dress, all pretend not to notice. Some exhibit "the beautiful breeding that simulated at least human charity" (Y, 259). Yet at the end, even the hostess wants to be elsewhere. She catches the night train to her country house, where she can be released not only from specific social obligations, but, on that remarkable journey, from governing assumptions, for "she seemed to be passing from one world to another; this was the moment of transition" (*Y,* 270).

The contrasting dinner party, given by René and Maggie, is small and inelegant. Brusqueness, worry, and bitterness are exposed, and "things seemed to have lost their skins; to be freed from some surface hardness . . ." (*Y,* 287). In this bohemian and middle-class company occurs one of the first moments of pleasure and intimacy as a group, commemorated with the toast "to the new world," celebrated with wine, and teasingly noted in the call for a speech, which is as teasingly rejected. Eleanor visualizes her new sense of possibility as a Mediterranean hill town with all the roof grouped together, a classical image, neither outrageous nor threatening (*Y,* 294). From golden wine and missing speeches to the central idea of a communal vision, this party foreshadows the climactic gathering at the end.

Woolf makes community plausible by the tactic of interpenetrating choral remarks so that each character is continuing, adding, intuiting, and humorously modifying the other's longing.

> "But how . . ." she began, ". . . how can we improve ourselves . . . live more . . ." she dropped her voice as if she were afraid of waking sleepers, " . . . live more naturally . . . better . . . How can we?"
>
> "It is only a question," he said—he stopped. He drew himself close to her—"of learning. The soul . . ." Again he stopped.
>
> "Yes—the soul?" she prompted him.
>
> "The soul—the whole being," he explained. He hollowed his hands as if to enclose a circle. "It wishes to expand; to adventure; to form—new combinations?" (*Y,* 296)

And what prevents this expansive, interrogated possibility? "Each is his own little cubicle; each with his own cross or holy books; each with his fire, his wife . . ." (*Y,* 296). Allegiances to particular romance, private property, and defensively maintained values are the barriers to "new combinations"; it is the business of *The Years* not to attack but rather to dissolve these barriers, whose knotlike bastion is the private sphere. Hence a narrative dissolution of the institution that produces a private/public dichotomy, related to and upheld by conventions of gender, becomes central to the novel.

By transforming the family into a group protagonist, Woolf goes to the heart of the Victorian ideology of the dichotomous division of the world into separate and opposing spheres: public/social and private/domestic, which are, in apparently natural fashion, allocated to the sexes in a division of labor and activities. Yet the realms are interconnected, interlocked; the world of domesticity is not a "natural, moral, and essentially unchanging private realm," exclusively female, opposed to the fluid, historical, progressive, and evolving public world.[17] The family, Woolf shows, is the institution that reveals the interpenetration of public and private, "the tyrannies and servilities of the one are the tyrannies and servilities of the other" (*TG*, 142). She dedicates the very texture of her novel to elaborating the inseparable connection and to contesting the ideology of separate spheres.

So after the 1880 section, the narrative often takes place in a space formed by the dissolution of the patriarchal house, a liminal space between public and private. The more settled and elegant houses (like Kitty's, or Milly and Hugh's) are only traveled toward and left; Sara and Maggie, like Miriam Henderson, live in rooms, open to street noises and neighborhood connections. When characters meet, they often use public spaces—the park, taxicabs, restaurants. Houses are exposed to public and political strife; thus a dinner party occurs during a zeppelin raid. Finally, as if to underline the dissolution of the patriarchal family, the climactic party is held in rented rooms that formerly were the headquarters of a radical or feminist group.

At this gathering, the communal protagonist takes two forms. First, "gathered in a group, were the old brothers and sisters" (*Y*, 432). Not only are these characters aged, but they represent an outmoded group. In its wealthy clothes, by its motionlessness, this group has become static, like "statues," and represents the culturally dominant aspect of the novel (*Y*, 432–33). The characters (Milly and her husband Hugh) who represent changeless reproduction are "not interested in other people's children, . . . only in their own; their own property; their own flesh and blood . . ." (*Y*, 378). Woolf treats this old guard with measured wit.

The divisions between the groups become acute at the moment when Rose, always stentorian, demands silence for the speech, a silence in which she asserts, "I'm proud of my family; proud of my country," and adds, when reminded, her sex, too (*Y*, 416). These parochial commemorations are exactly what the alternative group rejects.[18] By sexual orientation, ranges of foreignness, personal marginality, gender, and nonhegemonic social identity, all the characters in the vanguard of outsiders have ceased to idealize the dominant center represented by other family members; all are united in their longing for "a new world" or "another kind of civlization."[19] Indeed, the action of the long final section of *The Years* is a reaffirmation, after a hiatus of perhaps twenty years, of the glimmer of "a new world" felt at the 1917 dinner. To this hope are recruited two members of the younger generation, Peggy and North, joining Eleanor, Nicholas, and possibly Sara in a kinship more potent than blood: "a chorus, a general statement, a song for four voices."[20]

Eleanor is an "educated man's daughter," to cite the pointed phrase from *Three Guineas,* her upper middle-class position definitively modified by gender. Therefore, she sees things differently from her more stolid brothers. Her sense of community has always begun with a feminine empathy, whether within the family or from a sense of shared social good, as in a passage she admires from Dante. Although she is the eldest Pargiter, with more links to the past, she has always looked to the future and never wants to think back on her youth in the 1880s, which her niece Peggy wrongly assumes was "so peaceful and so safe" (*Y,* 326). In response to Peggy, Eleanor makes her position clear: a ceaseless hope for social transformation. "'What I want to see before I die . . . is something different. . . .' She waved her hand out of the window. They were passing public buildings; offices of some sort. '. . . another kind of civilization'" (*Y,* 335). During the party, Eleanor becomes more excited, as if the enjoyment here, the reverberating "happy in this world—happy with living people" could be translated into the radical energies that would bring about real change (*Y,* 387).

Peggy illustrates Woolf's lucid and optimistic proposition in *Three Guineas:* since the opening of professions to women in 1919, with the gain of earning power and independence, a woman need no longer be beholden to either father or husband for her personal needs and economic keep. Because her social identity is more self-defined, she does not depend on the wiles of traditional womanhood. In Eleanor and Peggy, Woolf has factored out the precarious analytic compound that distinguishes *Three Guineas:* women free from unreal loyalties because historically marked by the denial of access to education, professions, and sociocultural power, yet, when given this access and integrated into a male-centered world, retaining the mark of gender exclusion, suppression, and prejudice to belong to society in a different way, with a different valence from men. Outsiders who are not integrated into the institutions of assimilation and social control are depicted by Woolf as more disinterested, less seduced by reward systems or power hierarchies, not obedient to the rituals of power and privilege. As she describes them, with one economic foot in and one ethical foot out of the dominant ethos, outsiders are dialogic, oscillating, in the terms this study has used. They are critical inheritors.

During the party, Peggy, like Eleanor, has her hope for change renewed in a parallel social vision, "in which there was real laughter, real happiness, and this fractured world was whole; whole, vast and free" (*Y*, 390). Her statement, finally attempted, comes out wrong, and involves a personal attack on her brother North, predicting that he will compromise with a commonplace life, "instead of living . . . living differently, differently" (*Y*, 391). Still, North eventually understands in his turn.

After a long sojourn as a farmer in imperial Africa, North has returned to the mother country and the metropole with a sense of distance, interrogation, and perspective ("he felt an outsider"), which he sums up in the cool phrase "money and politics" (*Y*, 317, 318). North may be Woolf's peculiar stand-in for the laboring classes, for he has, after all, farmed and been "in control of a herd of sheep" (*Y*, 404). Sheep aside, at least he is aware of the class character of the soirée, for he notes the absence of "the Sweeps and the Sewer-men, the Seamstresses and the Stevedores," and understands the limitations of upper middle-class experience at Oxford and Harrow, which are immodestly and snobbishly taken as the whole world by some other of the younger guests (*Y*, 404).

Despite her unpracticed, derisive formulation about him, North captures exactly the spirit of his sister's remark about "living differently." "He felt her feeling now; it was not about him; it was about other people; about another world, a new world . . ." (*Y*, 422). The echo of the yearning phrase from the 1917 party shows North inventing the same communal and porous self to which each of these outsiders awakens: "make a new ripple in human consciousness, be the bubble and the stream, the stream and the bubble—myself and the world together—he raised his glass. Anonymously, he said, looking at the clear yellow liquid" (*Y*, 410).

First, he rejects "societies"—one thinks of Woolf's sometimes acid portraits of reformers—and sees the decided limitations of the "priests" of authority (*Y*, 409). Then he rejects being mobilized by fascism: "Not black shirts, green shirts, red shirts—always posing in the public eye; that's all poppycock" (*Y*, 410). Correspondingly, he rejects the "one mass," "a rice pudding world, a white counterpane world," how socialism appeared in its leveling. So although Woolf was seeking a transpersonal "new combination," she held to a sense of individual rights and liberties. The "anonymous" self she evokes is, then, probably a resolution of the contradiction between individualism, voluntarily allowing itself not to be known, and the mass that must be rejected. Woolf's third way preserves the specialness and specific textures of individual life, though rejecting aggressive defensiveness and power to dominate others.

Nicholas is a foreigner and a homosexual, his "criminal" sexuality pointedly underlined yet only momentarily shocking. Throughout the novel he too has struggled to articulate a social vision. Woolf deliberately includes a male homosexual and possibly a lesbian in each of the communal protagonists in the final books, first because she identified with sexual marginality both for herself and for her friends.[21] Second, homosexual/lesbian characters criticize the narrow system of economically based love, expressed in marriage and sexual polarization. This in turn depends on the fact that Woolf never chooses to show the homosexual characters with their erotic or life partners, but depicts them either in watchful, analytic isolation or in friendly, sustaining ties with others—one branch of the "new combinations." Finally, Woolf's program of tolerance intends to depict affective diversity: "these immensely composite and wide flung passions," as she says in a letter to Ethel Smyth.[22] A homosexual character becomes an occasion not for an alternative eros of exclusivity and thralldom but for an oppositional expansion of individual passions to libidinal ties among a collectivity.

The passage through possible rejection and disgust to the heightened community of chosen tolerance is negotiated more precariously with Jews. Sara, a fellow lodger in a boarding house with that symbolic Jew, is a character whose visionary chants pose challenges to dominant ways of seeing, prefiguring Lynda in Doris Lessing's *The Four-Gated City*.[23] Without father, husband, or profession, Sara is declassé, alienated from the sexual roles and class privileges of her compatriots. Her first defining moment of rage and vision occurs when an upper-class couple in a Rolls Royce drives across a bridge on which she is walking (*Y,* 321–22). Her rejection of wealth, charm and fashion, power and conventional blandishments of sexuality, along with the intense allusions to high modernist voices, define her as an outsider.

The Jew in the bath in Sara's boarding house is a second test for her chosen identification as socially marginal. For the Jew is the ultimate outsider in this novel, as elsewhere in the thirties, and presents its most intense dilemma. If she does not join the "conspiracy" of unthinking service to unexamined values, presented in an Eliotic image of the "unreal City," she must accept kinship with people like the Jew, described in physically revolting terms—his animal grease, his sexual hairs (*Y,* 340). If she cannot accept this Jew, she is, consciously or not, part of the world of a "clean-shaven, rosy-gilled, mutton-fed" man, whose first statement, "'I knew your father at Oxford,'" invokes inescapable ties to class, father, and nonpluralist nation (*Y,* 342, 341).

One assumes that Sara will choose the outsiders with whom she is already structurally linked as a visionary and a woman. But for this to occur, Woolf insists—with an image that borders on the anti-Semitism from which we are asked to flinch—more than a pallid effort is required. One must overcome violent physical revulsion toward whomever one assumes is the lowest, dirtiest, most foreign, and repugnant embodiment of Otherness. To be an outsider is not simply to hold patronizing, dismissive attitudes toward patriarchy, power, and authority, or "poppycock," the recurrent, punning, supercilious word (*Y*, 322). To join with outsiders requires both a critical perspective— the distancing from the world as it is—and a spiritual commitment to the world as it might be, through a forgiving identification and participation in all its members. One is reminded here, as with Lucy Swithin in *Between the Acts*, of a revisionary remark Woolf made about Christianity in her search for ways to describe, without delimiting, the changes in consciousness and society that she sought. Outsiders "would attempt to free the religious spirit from its present servitude and would help, if need be, to create a new religion based, it might well be, upon the New Testament, but, it might well be, very different from the religion now erected upon that basis" (*TG*, 113).[24] This subtle clue to an Antigonesque religious spirit pervades the end of *The Years* as well. Antigone was, for Woolf, like Christ before the letter: " 'Tis not my nature to join in hating, but in loving." Believers want "not to break the laws, but to find the law" that opposed dictatorship, patriarchal power, servile obedience, and uncritical assent to political tyranny (*TG*, 138).

The creation of this new religious spirit is at issue in the pageant of *Between the Acts*. Like the daughter's art work influenced by a maternal vision, discussed in chapter 6, Miss La Trobe's pageant embodies values for which Mrs. Swithin is noted—"one-making," empathy, sacramental and loving tolerance, and a somewhat batty bricolage. Consequently, Mrs. Swithin can be thanked as the "author" when Miss La Trobe will not be, for the pageant is a secular ritual of "one-making" (*BA*, 175). The word troop can be used as much for flocks of animals, especially the pastoral sheep so dear to Christian iconography, as for performers. Although Miss La Trobe is the initiator, she melds back into the troop also, wishing, "it seems to remain anonymous" (*BA*, 194). Here, as in *The Years*, anonymity is a term to suggest a mediation between the poles of individual assertion and group similarity.[25]

The actors are individually a little querulous, complaining, pushy, "swathed in conventions," yet when inside the pageant, they represent communality: a unity of dispersion or diversity, simultaneously "undisp" (Woolf's repeating neologism), losing their aggressive edges but not their personal quirks (*BA*, 64). Again, an oscillating balance distinguishes the thematic concept. So the family and their guests individually are dim and needy; when they become the audience, they gain resonance in the group affirmation. Here, as in *The Years,* division, ego, rank, distinction, and hierarchy are attacked; "I" is rejected; "We" substituted.

In *The Years,* Nicholas's interrupted and undelivered speech corresponds perfectly to the theme of missed connections, gaps of communication, lapses, and ellipses. And the refusal to speechify is also a way to refuse the idealization, lies, and glissades almost inevitably required on such public occasions. But fundamentally, Nicholas cannot finish his speech because any such assumption of authority, summing up the fluid, porous, and historical, is an act that collapses from its own ridiculous presumption. Maggie, too, refuses to speak, laughing all the while, and she seems to be saying something that North also understands: "no idols, no idols," meaning the denial of authoritative closure and all hierarchies of power (*Y,* 425).

Yet when Kitty realizes that she does want to hear "something," "But not the past—not memories. The present; the future—that was what she wanted," Nicholas faces her privately, not publicly, and drinks to the human race, "now in its infancy, may it grow to maturity" (*Y,* 425–26). Woolf has engineered a closure *malgré soi,* simultaneously engaging with two structural ideologies that express alternative visions of porousness and power. In her critique of romance, with its icon of couple formation, its idealization of the family house, the private sphere for women, and the hierarchy of the sexes, Woolf has formulated an ideological and narrative strategy of the collective protagonist. She does so to allow inheritor and critic to coexist in one narrative space.

For in *The Years* and in *Between the Acts,* while Woolf wanted to suggest the value of the ideas and attitudes of the vanguard, nonetheless this new center of vision remains in a willing dialogue with hegemonic values and characters, desiring not to coerce but to welcome them. This is why Nicholas never makes a public celebratory speech, but responds to Kitty's individual need for a toast; it is why the novel ends as Eleanor extends welcoming hands to her brother Morris and inquires, "And now?" having seen from the window yet another bourgeois house close with a thud on yet another young couple. Woolf constructs the work so that the choral protagonist may include both vanguard outsiders and the "old brothers and sisters," and all may step into the postbourgeois world together.

In keeping with this dialogic stance, the text does not privilege its own ideological positions. This explains why *The Years* looks a little unconstructed in its nonforceful resistance of unitary focus, and can also explain Woolf's very wrenching rejection of a brilliant mixed-genre design for the novel—*The Pargiters* design, which alternated didactic essay with narrative.[26] For a contradictory response to sociocultural identity also marks the history of the composition of *The Years,* with its conflicting pulls between Antigone's feminist tolerance and Creon's dogmatic absolutism.

During the long and painful process of composition of *The Years,* Woolf engaged in an intense debate about its "narrative politics," asking how to bring the dominant order into question without being tainted by dominant values.[27] At first glance, it appears that the essays of *The Pargiters*—precise, contained, and bitter analyses of family life—are satisfactorily critical. For example, Woolf shows the father owning his family's opinion and priorities by controlling money. She discusses "street love"—sexual harassment—as a form of social control. She shows the way differential assumptions about womanhood are factored by divisions even within the middle class, and how one cannot assume "that the laws of [female] conduct [are] fixed" (*P,* 151). Yet Woolf seems to have felt that her critique, the dramatic, passionate depiction of female oppression in the family, was at the same time authoritarian. The values she wanted the work to express were being undermined by the otherwise promising novel-essay form. Tonally, the work was built from the patriarchal voice to which she was ideologically opposed.

Furthermore, the dramatic split between novel and essay in *The Pargiters* flattened the characters and tended to put them at the service of the author's conception, making the narrative illustrative, the writer authoritative. Using a narrative to forward an idea or a proposition made the author behave like the egotistical "I" of the male party-goer in *The Years* or the male novelist in *A Room of One's Own:* it created that univocal vision that brooked no opposition. "The didactic" and "propaganda" were code words Woolf used to identify her fear of falling into assertion.[28] Despite the fact that she had amassed much historical evidence, she did not want to use the novel form to hector, polemicize, or compel others to believe these points. This was why the first hint of the dreadful difficulties of writing this novel came with the "hinge" scene of Elvira [Sara] in her bed reading Antigone's pleas for tolerance and forgiveness against rigid dogmatism. Woolf feared that *The Pargiters* had been Creonesque: commanding assent, making it possible to interpret certain incidents only one way, brooking no argument.[29] In contrast, Woolf projected an Antigonesque narrative: tolerant, humane, forgiving.

So she reformulated the vexing question of this novel: "There are to be millions of ideas but no preaching—history, politics, feminism, art, literature—in short a summing up of all I know, feel, laugh at, despise, like, admire, hate and so on."[30] She decided to make the characters discuss issues of a concrete social and sexual character. Eleanor sees birth control devices; Rose, Elvira [Sara], and Maggie discuss contraception; Eleanor tries to debate her own mixed motives for serving the poor as a social worker and begins to criticize herself for seeking power; Eleanor feels guilt and complicity at the death of a naval officer in the war. However, all of these interesting scenes were cut at the galley-proof stage from the final version of *The Years*. Grace Radin, the critic who has studied these changes most comprehensively, sadly notes "the extent to which feminist, pacifist, and sexual themes have been deleted, obscured, or attenuated."[31]

Woolf might have felt that the "new world" was more convincing as unfleshed, even mystical, rather than forged from contemporary issues. This is the same Woolf who finds a feminist call for "Justice, Equality, Liberty" too much of a slogan and is more attracted to the looser, less specific, more evocative appeal of Antigone's higher law (*TG*, 138). This is the same Woolf who, as Susan Squier has found, revises the essays on the London scene to mute critical comments, present in her drafts, about class and gender.[32] And this is the same Woolf who, in "Professions for Women," confesses ambivalent inability to tell "the truth about my own experiences as a body."[33] Sometimes, in the internalized dialogue that marked Woolf as an inheritor and a critic, being an inheritor was more compelling.

The language of *Between the Acts* comes as a grand invention, for it recasts the issue of dominant and muted, and the dialectic between them, by representing perpetual "betweenness" itself. The point at which *un* and *disp* are one generates the fecund language of rhyme and chime, half doggrel, half sublime, that Anon speaks through the novel. The voice of this novel, a collage of "scraps, orts and fragments" unifying the poetic and the mundane, is a major expression of the communal protagonist, for it takes dominant clichés and finds their muted utopian content (*BA*, 188, 192).

The voice of *Between the Acts* is a development from the interruptions and conversational bridges in *The Years:* quick phrasal intercuts, ranging from the humdrum and banal to the lyric, precious, and fancy: "a new style—to mix."[34] Part of the critique made in *Between the Acts* occurs through its language, which breaks both sentence and sequence, showing the way high culture is indebted to the luscious babble that seems to join us all in undifferentiated voicing. The babble Woolf allows to structure this work is like the "The-tis, sea-tis," hypnagogic punning of H.D.'s *Helen in Egypt:* it allows access to another arena of meaning, to complete the "story" told by dominant culture.[35]

The babble, the ballads, the lullabies and folk voices have always been vital to Woolf, visible at climactic moments in her works. When she confronts an individual with positive dissolution into crowd, city, folk, or life itself, the moment is often marked with popular ballad or song. The ballad singer and her "old bubbling, burbling song" in *Mrs. Dalloway,* the "voix d'enfants chantant" and their allusion to nonhegemonic Celtic counting-out rhymes and Cockney dialect and hegemonic Latin in *The Years,* the almost anonymous "Lurianna, Lurilee" in *To the Lighthouse,* the structuring allusion to the ballad of the Four Marys in *A Room of One's Own,* and many tunes and turns in *Between the Acts,* tropes presided over by La Trobe—all these are ways of posing a common heritage, bypassing the makers of high art (*MD,* 123).

The cackle, rattle, and yaffle stretches the whole length of the text (*BA,* 183). And that "voice that was no one's voice" engineers a dissent from some of the major tenets of dominant ideology: that the individual triumphs over the many, that the context is a catapult for that individual, that public and private are distinct and not interpenetrating (*BA,* 181). This *vox populi* is a way—Woolf's final way—of rejecting "I" and substituting "We."

■

CHAPTER ELEVEN

"Kin with each other": Speculative Consciousness and Collective Protagonists

We are all of us made kin with each other and with everything in the world because of the kinship of possible destruction.
DORIS LESSING
"The Small Personal Voice"
(1957)

Raising the issue of the future is another tactic for writing beyond the ending, especially as that ending has functioned in the classic novel: as closure of historical movement and therefore as the end of development. Having been posed as an experiment in change and choice, a novel typically ends by asserting that choice is over and that the growth of character or the capacity for a defining action has ceased. If "happily ever after" means anything, it means that pleasurable illusion of stasis.

Most novels begin in the past and end just at, or just before, the present, with a highly choreographed, controlled glance at the future. The present (where the reader sits reading) and the future (outside of both book and reader) are felt to be unsullied, untouchable, and in about the same political and moral key as today. But if a novel travels through the present into the future, then social or character development can no longer be felt as complete, or our space as readers perceived as untrammeled.

A critique of the ideologies implied in plots always involves some critical response to the rules of the world, since narrative structures are saturated in these rules. Such a critique can involve the visualization of the world as it could be. This interest informs fictions by some women across the century who, from Charlotte Perkins Gilman to Doris Lessing, challenge the world as we know it by a resolute imagining of other times and other customs. This group of novels may have speculative, fantasy, or "science fiction" elements, such as time travel, telepathic communication, the discovery of a utopian civilization, or the sense of a world parallel to ours. The allusions to science fiction are made didactically, to estrange readers from the rules of the world as known—both laws of physics and laws of society, everything from causality to propriety.[1]

Works like Gilman's *Herland* (1915) and Joanna Russ's *The Female Man* (1975) are bound by their critical and inventive stances toward deep assumptions. For example, these fictions contain embedded elements from "assertive discourse"—genres like sermon, manifesto, tract, fable—to guide or inform the action.[2] In line with the general use of the narrative as a teaching story, elements like character and plot function mainly as the bearers of propositions or moral arguments, whose function is to persuade. The characters may be flat because they represent compendia of typical traits, or because they function like manifestos, bringing undiscussable messages. Characters in these teaching stories are like Socratic questions; the ideas, not the characters, are well rounded. The fiction establishes a dialogue with habitual structures of satisfaction, ranges of feeling, and response.

The collective protagonist in speculative fiction is both formally and thematically central. These fictions replace individual heroes or sealed couples with groups, which have a sense of purpose and identity, and whose growth occurs in mutual collaboration. The use of a collective protagonist may imply that problems or issues that we see as individually based are in fact social in cause and in cure: Lessing's view of madness is an example. This protagonist is an avatar of new values in a dramatic and narrative form, suggesting that individual conflict and resolution are completed and absorbed by communal growth, and that collective survival is an essential goal.

The poetics of estrangement dissolves assumptions about the way our world works by confronting its norms with another outlook or world view, "implying a new set of norms."[3] Women's science fictions provide an intermingling of two kinds of estrangement, one empirical and the other fantastic, supernatural. Social and political transformation may be depicted through realistic projections of contemporary life and through uncanny, spiritual realms. These female authors seem especially interested in portraying changes of consciousness that call into play the spiritual and unverifiable. The authors construct as an arena of debate and site of action the dominant or normal consciousness and proceed to rupture its continuity and its expectations. Breakthroughs to future consciousness, telepathic communication, lives parallel to ours are ways of narrating muted alternatives to psychological and social forms that are embedded in personal consciousness.

At about the same time that Woolf and H.D. began their writing careers, Charlotte Perkins Gilman wrote two tract novels about a recently discovered earthly paradise without males, in which the center of emotional and political life was (parthenogenetic) motherhood. *Herland* (1915) and *With Her in Ourland* (1916), both serialized in Gilman's artisanal journal, *Forerunner,* chronicle the discovery of this hidden land by three male explorers, one of whom idealizes women, one of whom denigrates them, and one of whom treats them as equals.[4] "Maternal thinking," Sara Ruddick's term for the ideology to which certain mothering practices give rise, extends through all the social institutions—agriculture, education, defense—and pervades all habits of mind.[5] "A motherliness" of protection, care, and judicious choices, wise, sweet, and reasonable, is at once the idea and the tone.

Herland is a collectivized sisterhood where the powers of mother and sister love, "united action" without competition, produces a whole nation serving all "our children" (*H,* 129). Gilman evokes a kin or family model for the public sphere. "The country was a unit—it was Theirs. They themselves were a unit, a conscious group; they thought in terms of the community" (*H,* 184). "All the surrendering devotion our women have put into their private families, these women put into their country and race. All the loyalty and service men expect of wives, they gave, not singly to men, but collectively to one another" (*H,* 213). The comment that romance is an impediment to social development could not be clearer. This merging of what we consider public and private is one of the consistent aims of the collective protagonist. One cunning result in Herland is that the women classify the field of "psychology with history—not with personal life," using the information to improve the generations (*H,* 242). The specifically eugenicist cast shows Gilman's allegiance to one strand of nineteenth-century modernizing thought, but a similar emphasis on human perfectability will animate Doris Lessing's five-volume work as well. With consciousness not fixed, but being part of a historical process, basic embedded structures of belief can change.

The interest of the book lies in its critique of values, especially privatization *as* the female sphere. Gilman subtitutes nonpossessive, nonromantic love, and valorizes "racial [public sphere] motherhood" over biological.[6] She argues by inference that without the superimposition of the narratives and assumptions of masculinity and without extreme gender polarization (plots of courtship, sexual passion, jealousy, adventure, ambition, struggle between unequals), then women's innate natures could flower unimpeded. This innate nature was absolutely maternal and nonsexual (*H,* 238). Sex-feeling, a form of private possession, can, to Gilman's evident relief, be replaced by friendship and affection, forms of community.

All this is consistent with her discovery of the "root error" of our civilization, which Herland has cured—private property, including the private possession of children and women in the patriarchal family. "It all comes down to that absurd root error of the proprietary family. . . . That old Boss Father is behind God. . . . The personal concept of God as a father, with his special children, his benign patronage, his quick rage, long anger, and eternal vengeance . . . is an ugly picture" (*WHO,* 181). *Herland* and *With Her in Ourland* solve the problem of public/private dichotomy by annexing the public sphere to the maternal realm, substituting the Benevolent Mother for the Boss Father.

Gilman's critique of ideology is not matched with any literary articulation of the collective protagonist. Although the work discusses, even eulogizes, the collective, *Herland* is not constructed to show how it functions, nor is the "conscious group" made a narrative center in any way. The story's center is singular, one representative from Herland named Ellador, with whom the nice male hero falls in love. The courtship is a conversion to the female-centered world view, a conversion to critique. But, although the work talks about changes in narrative, it still offers unwitting proof that "Love, Combat, or Danger" (all, in Gilman's view, requiring men) might well remain necessary for interesting literature, at least as far as the author's imagination carried her (*H,* 128). Import men into Herland, and one indeed has a plot with a little love, a little danger, a tad of suspense; however, these flurries of action are generally neutralized by the natives, as if plot were just too much childish excitement, and mothers knew best how to handle that.

But if her narrative skills here are simple, Gilman's critical sensibility still is consistent with what we have discovered about many women writers. She argues that "Love, Combat, and Danger" have reflected the values of "our androcentric culture." Within this "masculine literature," the ceaseless repetiton of stories of love and war gives people a false impression of life.[7] The "humanizing of women" will, in Gilman's view, change the nature of fiction. She identifies several new types of plots, some of which will be used subsequently, but chooses for *Herland* the most dated and moralistic: the curbing of the sex drive with the "high standards of conscious motherhood."[8] So the ideology of maternalism, which in the late nineteenth century was actually accompanied by a "loss of control" by women over the management of motherhood, is, in Gilman, reprocessed in a compensatory fashion, so that women retain control.[9]

The same critical view of social and narrative convention, the same interest in new plots, occurs in Joanna Russ's acerbic and analytic manifesto "What Can a Heroine Do? or Why Women Can't Write."[10] The Russ article argues that plots are "dramatic embodiments of what a culture believes to be true": "that of all the possible actions people can do in fiction, very few can be done by women."[11] There is virtually only one occupation for a female protagonist—love, of course—which our culture uses to absorb all possible *Bildung*, success/failure, learning, education, and transition to adulthood. Seeing that "culture is male [and] our literary myths are for heroes, not heroines," Russ suggests that writers employ plots "which have nothing to do with our accepted gender roles"—detective stories, supernatural fiction, and science fiction.[12]

Joanna Russ's *The Female Man* carries out the contesting of gender in narrative as devastatingly and wittily as *Orlando*, its spiritual foremother.[13] A visitor from outer space, a place called Whileaway, time-travels to Earth and studies our quaint sexual customs. Janet gradually meets Jeannine and Joanna (all three of their names mean God's precious gift) and Jael, a biblical woman warrior. These four J's are either alternative selves in one person or, as types of the genus Woman, alternative strategies for dealing with the same kind of social givens that Gilman called the Man-Made World.

The multiple protagonist is a major feature of this work because it bears the intellectual weight—the analysis of the various ways one can be a female man—and because it is a way of building conflicting perspectives into the work to express women's social identity as critic and inheritor. In Russ, the cluster protagonist represents the divided consciousness of contemporary women.[14] Jeannine is a sweet hangover from the late 1930s, suffering a permanent Depression. A fuzzy, dependent, rather hopeless woman, Jeannine is a librarian guarding, but not transforming, the past. She has a brief quest, which quickly collapses into "I want to get married": the old answer and ending to plots and risks in women's lives. But the moment when Jeannine allows the angry Jael to build military bases on her world, she begins to awaken. Jeannine is seen as a "female man" because she is male-

identified. She "turns into a man" by subsuming herself in male demands, by identifying with her oppression and oppressor. Thus she is
a "man"—seeing herself completely through male eyes.

Joanna—it has escaped no one that she bears the author's given
name—is closest to ourselves: the woman who stands in a puddle of
water, grasping two alternating electrical currents, trying to fuse
them. She lives in an oscillating contradiction: between woman and
man, feminist and phallocrat, joy and rage. "If you let yourself
through yourself and into yourself and out of yourself, turn yourself
inside out, give yourself the kiss of reconciliation, marry yourself, love
yourself—Well, I turned into a man" (*FM*, 139). Joanna did not turn
into a member of the male gender or sex, but she did turn into a
generic man—or, as one might translate the term, a human, a person.
Russ richochets between man as male and man as human until we are
astir and enraged again at the appropriation of all personhood by the
term *man*. But women are part of mankind, or so we have been told;
Joanna proposes to take this truism at its face value. "If we are all
Mankind, it follows to my interested and righteous and rightnow very
bright and beady little eyes, that I too am a Man and not at all a
Woman . . . " (*FM*, 140).

If the production of "woman" is one primary task of the society we
know, the production of any other kind of "woman" will thus involve
other worlds, other rules. The world invented, Whileaway, is perhaps
the Anglo-Saxon translation of "estrangement." Janet Everson (JE, an
allusion both to selfhood and to a well-known nineteenth-century
quester) comes from Whileaway, or Earth many years hence. Janet no
longer feels the slightest tincture of forced and socialized inferiority
("self-effacement training, deference training," *FM*, 151). This is because on Whileaway there is no sexism, there is no asymmetry or
polarization between the sexes, because there are not two sexes but
only one—the collective woman. It is a devastating syllogism.

Now Whileaway is described, with a certain bravura, tongue-in-
cheek quality, as a new Earth. Technology, art, some social institutions,
geography, history, and details of travel are given as if this were science fiction, and as if Janet came from the future. But the sci-fi
material is presented to dress up, or even camp up the essential truth
about Whileaway. It is not a future place or future time, but a mental
place in the present. One gains access to Whileaway through consciousness turned away from the assumptions, priorities, and order-
ings of the world we know.[15] So Whileaway is a topos that exists in
one's mind after a person experiences the estranging paradigm shift
of a feminist conversion.

What will join these women and cause their mutual self-recognition? Jael, or murderous rage. Her name is taken from the biblical hero in the Book of Judges who nailed a spike into the head of her enemy. Jael attacks the head, rather than the body, because it is man's consciousness that needs to be murdered. Jael does to macho and patriarchal consciousness (with gusto) what Woolf does to feminine consciousness in killing the Angel in the House. Jael is a reversal; she is the woman-as-man: an assassin, a sexual aggressor, a way of paying men back for violence and dominance. Jael is jury, judge, and executioner at once because she lives in the era of relentless and unending sex war. Her values are the emergency values of the war for which she is a major strategist.

Like a Socratic question to which Russ knows the answer, Jael shows how lurid, disquieting, and vulgar are our normal levels of sexual hostility and sexual dominance. However revolting Jael is—and she is not pleasant—she is the mirror image of the glib, patronizing, and equally murderous patterns of the socially acceptable relations between the sexes. Through Jael, Russ argues that anger is the only antidote to every cultural situation that women experience: silence, voicelessness, invisibility, loss of identity, passivity, rape. Anger fuses the women's fragmented consciousness and is the recognition that binds the collective protagonist.

Marge Piercy's book *Woman on the Edge of Time* (1976) is another speculative fiction in which the writer attempts to identify psychology with history, individual with group. Here too consciousness is an active setting. Consuelo Ramos, the main character, has been wrongly imprisoned in a mental institution and becomes the subject of a research experiment that will surgically insert computer-monitored electrodes in her brain in order to control behavior. Connie is found by, or imagines, the future; she time-travels to Mattapoisett, an attractive utopia whose values and achievements represent the best of Movement projects: it is communitarian, feminist, ecological, culturally nuanced, and creative. The "scientific" experiment to which Connie is forced to submit is a crossroads for the political and social use of mental pacification, and she takes an incisive step, murder, to stop the experiment from continuing.[16]

Connie Ramos is a typical Chicana, indeed somewhat overloaded with typicality by Piercy. She is a primer of the brutality of poverty, of a social psychology caused by oppression. Rape is the book's metaphor for the double oppression of racism and sexism. Piercy presents the thesis that to be a woman is to suffer a constant, ceaseless, humiliating rape, which culminates in the attempted rape of one's consciousness. The major dictate of the world given to women is to acquiesce to violation. If the women do not acquiesce, they are defined as crazy and legally raped. Piercy moves the reader to ask questions of power and value: Whose system is this? Whose perceptions of reality are upheld by bureaucratic institutions of power and prestige? The perception that Connie is violent depends on an invisible, "natural" context of gender power.

Piercy shows how politicized anger becomes the final outpost that hegemonic society attempts to colonize. Consciousness itself—epitomized by Connie's mental powers of "receiving" messages from the future—could be controlled in a final solution to all forms of anger and nonconformity. The mind-control claims to control violence, but Percy unmasks that rationalization and shows how, under the guise of curing, therapeutic arts can be directed to the political manipulation of consciousness.

Connie, the name, condenses associations that make this point: words from knowing and learning *(canny, conning, consciousness, kenning)*, words that suggest victimization *(conned)* and critique *(con—* oppositional—and *cunning)*. Indeed, Connie Ramos's initials, CR, offer almost as fine a hint of possibilities as Charlotte Brontë's JE. CR—consciousness raising, consciousness "flowering" (for *ramos* means "frond" or "branch" in Spanish)—is an allusion to the small-group process of understanding in the women's movement in the seventies, which connected one's personal and individual situation with the status and issues confronted by all members of a nondominant group. CR is a way for the individual to see herself as a member of a collective, an insight that is directly translated into narrative terms with this use of the collective protagonist: mutually supportive and enlightening.[17]

This book is an argument that utopia (the *eu-topos,* or good place that is found nowhere, *u-topos*) can still be visualized, that one can project a communitarian, nonsexist, productive, democratic society. By her vivid and coherent descriptions of social institutions, Piercy has answered the challenge of the two famous Cold War dystopias so influential in the fifties—*1984* and *Brave New World*—which powerfully and convincingly describe totalitarian societies but give no tools for imagining alternatives.[18]

When Connie is "in" the future, she becomes part of a transpersonal protagonist—something between an affinity group and a family. As Connie grows more and more alienated from relationships in the present, since she now has an alternative against which to measure them, she grows more attached to the collectivity in the future. This future world contains characters quite parallel to those people whom she had loved. For example, Bee, her lover in the future, is as warm and solid as her lover Claude, but Bee is fulfilled in his work, while

Claude was a hustler. A reader could view this doubling of characters as a signal that Connie is hallucinating when she thinks of the future, but Piercy is, I think, presenting a richer and more didactic point: that we can have much more human and social fulfillment with the same types of people who inhabit our world.

Speculative fiction by women visualizes a world where muted groups, values, and institutions become dominant, and, at least in these cases, seems particularly interested in visualizing alternatives to the nuclear family and to consciousness. These fictions reverse the ratio of dominant to muted, until the values that had been socially repressed in our time—Gilman's motherhood, Russ's feminist vision, Piercy's Movement ideas, Lessing's subculture of "mad" hearers and seers—gain hegemony in another time, another space.

Doris Lessing's view of the double function of the artist, as critic and prophet, "strengthening a vision of a good," makes her, too, create a critique of ideology and narrative consistent with the practice of other women and engagé writers. Her concerns, she has made clear, intersect with feminism but are not bounded by women's rights.[19] Still, her career can be related to those of other women writers similarly disenchanted with the construction of the female in narratives defending the sex-gender system and the private family sphere.

Lessing's *The Children of Violence* offers a considerable version of the communal protagonist, making an appeal to a change of consciousness to forge a path out of the couple and the individual, and relating ideology to narrative practices. In this *Bildungsroman,* Lessing puts Martha Quest, the hero of her five novels, at the crossroads of such large historical forces that Martha's personal desire for social change is eventually satisfied by a cataclysmic and collective change of worldwide proportions.[20]

Lessing traces her ordinary hero from Africa to London, from individual to collective mind, and from pre–World War II, the breakup of the colonial empire, the Cold War, and the sixties, through to the millennium, in which catastrophic political and ecological events have decisively changed life on earth. The critique of social reproduction—sheer replication of personalities, institutions, and functions—is Lessing's subject; to engage it, she engineers a rupture with narrative expectations and the repetitive affirmation of dominant values.

This one of Lessing's ambitions was galvanized by Olive Schreiner: to write a book like *The Story of an African Farm,* "on the frontier of the human mind," a book whose very title evokes the moment of reading when one's "deepest self was touched," and touched by changes in consciousness.[21]

The search for a way to touch this "frontier" motivates Lessing's rupture of narrative, her unique way of having done with "the 'plot' and the characters." After almost the whole of five novels has been told in an empirical realism that depends on conventional frames of time and space, on an understanding of the limits and shapes of consciousness, and on agreements about characters' boundaries, Lessing breaks with these strategies. Notably, she contests the sense of the fictional itself and its center in the bounded individual. She moves the fiction into the future, postulating a growth in the telepathic potential of individual consciousness. Because a new (and better) grasp of reality supersedes the old one, and new consciousness supersedes old at the resolution, the book has estranged its readers from the inner norms of the genre as well as of the world.

Lessing has said, in a characteristically blunt way, that *Children of Violence* is "a study of the individual conscience in its relations with the collective."[22] In the context of the essay in which it was stated, an uncompromising anti–Cold War aesthetic, this formulation announces Lessing's desire to enunciate a third way, given the two ideological and political poles between which she felt herself situated: the bourgeois, capitalist West, with its literature of psychic despair, and the antibourgeois, Communist East, with its literature of banal optimism.[23] Both are innocent, limited, and escapist, parallel in their narrowness of focus on either the "helpless and solitary" individual or the saccharine collective. For her third way, Lessing, like Woolf, has appropriated a bourgeois concern for free will and individual nuance and a socialist concern for a collective transformation.

For this reason, Lessing expands the *Bildung* of *Children of Violence* beyond the bounds of individual character, with its goals of success or social integration.[24] This narrative move into a collective center is her way of writing beyond the ending. Lessing foresees the possibility for "a world-mind, a world-ethic," something that both Marxism and "the formal religions" had attempted; the ending of *The Four-Gated City* draws on both the organization of a social collective and the spiritually tuned individual seers and hearers to postulate a synthesis as massive in its materials in struggle (Marxism/religion) as it is grand in its evolutionary reading of many contemporary trends.[25]

The early novels of the series undertake the discrediting of the conventional life of women—in romance, marriages, affairs, motherhood, the nuclear family, and other family ties. Love of all sorts is coolly examined as Martha the quester moves unflaggingly down mandated paths to female success: being attractive, marrying well, becoming a mother. The main tension in Martha Quest, announced by her name, is between her housekeeping and tending side and her seeking and inquiring one, between the maintenance of normalcy and a transformation large enough (global and cataclysmic, as it happens) to ensure that the bourgeois family, traditional male-female, parent-child, and black-white ties, colonial society and its counterpart in the metropole will no longer exist to form others as she was formed.

Literature gives Martha a peculiar sense of the norm: the English countryside against her African farm; "Blithe heroes and heroines" of novels against her bitter adolescence; her mother's manipulative and dated ideas of nice English girls, as against Martha's social status and even her physical development (*MQ*, 7). There are many points at which Martha herself adheres to literary and attitudinal scripts of womanhood: her release from "imprisonment" on the farm by a letter "like the kiss of the prince in the fairy tales"; or a man's touch to release the imprisoned self (*MQ*, 197). This concern for scripts and their incompleteness or compromised failure continues in *Proper Marriage*, in which the couple tries to make love correctly by following a "book of words" (*PM*, 28). Martha finds that literature offers structures and resolutions that bear no resemblance to her life as a woman.

> If you read novels and diaries, women didn't seem to have these problems. Is it really conceivable that we should have turned into something quite different in the space of about fifty years? Or do you suppose they didn't tell the truth, the novelists? In the books, the young and idealistic girl gets married, has a baby—she at once turns into something quite different; and she is perfectly happy to spend her whole life bringing up children with a tedious husband. (*PM*, 205–206)

Given her sense of imposing frameworks and her troubled marginality, given her immersion and her potential for contesting norms, Martha feels a contradictory "gap between herself and the past," expressed in two defining visions, one of an ancient utopian city and one of organic wholeness, human integration into the natural world (*MQ*, 10). The city, four-gated, shows community among races, ages, peoples—emphatically the opposite of the Africa she knows. The pleasure, poise and mutuality of the citizens and the beauty of the place hint at its double valence: the city represents at once social peace and psychic integration. The "sound of flutes" further prefigures the "sweetness" and the "fine high air" of the space that Martha does ultimately find, where dichotomies of inner and outer, body and spirit no longer have power (*MQ*, 11). Throughout the series, Martha feels "as if something new was demanding conception, with her flesh as host"; these visions of possibility resonate throughout the novels (*MQ*, 53).[26]

The desire for difference, rebellion, resistance to the life of her parents had led her to the fast set in town; yet these fast young men know (as do their employers, their waiters, and their parents) that they are simply the next generation of civil servants and lawyers. So they are treated with a squeamish deference despite their antics. Among the avenues for breaking the endless replication of society, marriage into the sundowner set will not succeed, as Martha realizes even before the ceremony that makes her "Knowell" that the cycles of life have not yet been broken. By the end of the first book, Martha feels "cheated," "lost and afraid," because the difference she seeks has turned into a petty and provincial version of conventionality that the next book will activate under the rubric of "a proper marriage," into which Martha is affianced wearing her mother's engagement ring (*MQ*, 241, 235).

No romance plot will henceforth be viable in itself, a similarity between Lessing and the other writers included in this study. Marriage for social acceptability, propriety, and property is discredited. But so is another kind of marriage, that which uses the nature of the institution to legitimate the status of the foreigner Anton Hesse, who would otherwise be deported. Both marriages distance her from herself. So this is a *Bildungsroman* away from "her old enemy, the hound Repetition, snapping at her heels," away, that is, from social insertion, social replication. This is not a book about the learning or creating of one's place in society, but a narrative that shows "I don't know anything about anything yet . ." and that suggests human ties and potentials that have not yet been activated (*RS*, 172).

The logic of social replication—the fact that variants exist but change does not occur—is marked by the extraordinary doubling of A/M names in the books, in which women often have *M* initials (Martha, Marjorie, Maisie, Millicent, Marnie, later Margaret, Milly, and the mother May), and the men have initial *A* names (Anton, Andrew, Athen, and the father Alfred). This is also a tactic for stating that even with one center, one protagonist, still, parallel plots have occurred, and one's experience is neither so exclusive nor so unique as narrative forms seem to make it. The alliterative repetitions foreshadow the transpersonal protagonist.[27]

Comfortable, provincial, stolid and petty life Lessing symbolizes by a ferris wheel that whirls outside the window of the young Knowell couple. It is a concrete analogue to "the great bourgeois monster, the nightmare *repetition*," an inevitable cyclic process of replicating the people, functions, classes, and ideology from one generation to the next (*PM*, 77, 95). That ferris wheel's "flickering cycle seemed a revelation of an appalling and intimate truth," comprising at once biology and society, pregnancy, marriage, the cycle of family and class (*PM*,

98). Seeing it makes Martha vow never to bear a child—a vain vow indeed, for she is unknowingly pregnant from the first page of *A Proper Marriage*. And it is in this book that Martha's quest becomes clear: it is to break the chain of social replication, that "fatality" in which she is immersed (*PM*, 95).

Women, as Lessing makes Martha richly aware, are the point of production of this replica building: this is the major text of *A Proper Marriage* (during which the husband is more off the stage than on, appropriately in the "phony war"). From Martha's naïve "Do you mean to say that a woman's not entitled to decide whether she's going to have a baby or not?" the book's subjects are Martha's pregnancy and birth—a striking rendering—and the early childhood of Caroline, during which the battles of infant and parent begin to make Martha over into her own querulous, demanding, furtive, and angry mother (*PM*, 18). The result is Martha's calculated resistance to starting a second child, for that choice would signal her conscious, knowledgeable acquiescence to the bourgeois life of a provincial wife and mother, in a world like "a Victorian novel" (*PM*, 187). The second baby becomes an issue between Douglas and Martha, and among the various choral families as well, the Quests, the Talbots, and others who act in collusion to make her want the child. So Martha begins to break repetition by the choice of nonpregnancy at the end of *A Proper Marriage*, matching the nonchoice of pregnancy that opens the book.

Three plausible but not sufficient possibilities are offered to break the cycle of things happening "the same way over and over again": the war ("the war will break it up, it won't survive the war"), a hope scotched by memories of the two veterans of the first war, Mr. Maynard and Mr. Quest; romantic love, with William, simply set aside; and finally the Communist Party, with the attendant political conversion and transformative fervor (*PM*, 49, 187). Revolution, of course, promises a decisive rupture with the past and is sought exactly because of its promise to change everything.

Ripple from the Storm and *Landlocked* compose a two-novel disquisition and analysis of the efficacy of political agitation to bring about change on the scale that racial, sexual, familial, and social relations seem to demand. This theme is announced by Anton's eloquent inspirational speech to the Communist Party group early in *Ripple*, in which Martha is released from "the nightmare of recurring and fated evil" into a collectivity that seems to touch and use "the moments of experience which seemed to her enduring and true; the moments of illumination and belief" (*RS*, 54).

Although Lessing offers a canny and informed portrait of political organizing in a historical context, she is after something more. At the very end of *Landlocked,* two novels later, a matching scene occurs, in which three women from the old, now dissolved communist group have been invited to a new socialist cadre. They discover that the infrastructure, the texture, the jokes, the cast of characters are an exact replica of their failed group. In every way, from laughter to the lack of political perspective, the groups are equivalent in their smugness. History repeats, as Lessing unflinchingly announces: there is a "Jackie Bolton," an "Anton Hesse," an "Andrew McGrew." And "If the dramatis personae were the same, presumably the plot was also . . ." (*L,* 275)—a plot based on the interplay between the visionary and his two "restraining influences," a plot that already had a fixed shape and a certain outcome in the failure of their political action. The demonstration is complete; its force has something to do with the weight Lessing puts on the concept of change—that it be a break with "the Old Villain, which is a name for the patterns of conditioned thinking which form the prison in which we all live."[28] To put it in other terms, there has to be a degree of change that is not susceptible to the ironic, accurate choral commentary of Mr. Maynard, a commentary deployed throughout the four African novels to punctuate, and puncture, Martha's first quests. He is both that "Old Villain" personified and an accurate registrar of Martha's illusions.

So the hope for revolution, as Lessing shapes it, is another kind of romance, filled with the illusions of complete transformation without pain or struggle. Lessing interweaves the two romances—sexual and political—to make sure this is perfectly understood. Both romantic love and revolution involve much frenetic, exhausting, and uplifting activity, from the personal honeymoons to the honeymoon of the Popular Front.

Of the forces that have combined to call the politics of the Left into question, Lessing pinpoints several: a lack of understanding of their interpersonal dynamics; a refusal to credit intuitions that involve decodings of psychosocial needs; a forcing of lockstep "logic" or "analysis" on situations; an inability to read messages in unexpected places, like dreams of increasing premonitory accuracy, gestures, hallucinations, and breakdowns. Lessing underlines that feelings and intuitions not only matter in a perfunctory sense, but indeed brought about one new policy (cooperation with the Labour Party) that facilitated the only political event with permanent impact: the "meeting in the location" with both Africans and whites (*RS,* 158). Often the elements denied by "politics" are factors involving personal life, such as the apparently trivial question of whether the female comrades should look attractive.

Landlocked, with its idyllic sexual bond with Thomas, could be read as a fulfillment of Martha's female desire for "someone who would unify her elements, a man [who] would be like a roof, or like a fire burning in the centre of the empty space" (*L*, 30). But while the plot of the book offers an affair with such a man, neither the physical fire of Thomas nor the political fire of Athen holds her together. Lessing has chosen this novel, with its most seductive possibilities of hierogamic romance, as the vehicle to show the energy animating desire and violence: a "sensation of sinking deeper and deeper into light" (*L*, 153). If attuned either by desire or by the transfiguring political choice of death, individuals become a tunnel through which the past and future go coursing. By the end of the first half of *Four-Gated City*, the search for men and love in the form of heterosexual romance "ceased to be an exploration into unknown possibilities," and Martha makes a tactical decision not to seek marriage or love but to pursue that work which is light or transfiguration without the mediation of either romance or politics (*FGC*, 287).

Ripple from the Storm and *Landlocked* strengthen attention to another aspect of reality, a hint of "mutation" or evolutionary growth, which develops further in *Four-Gated City* (*L*, 116). There are several intense, but quickly overridden allusions to forces or looks or feelings, all relatively ineffable, and all suggesting that "something new is trying to get born through our thick skins" (*L*, 116). Love has been cast in a broadened role; Lessing sees sexuality as one way of tapping into a force or an energy, and once again a new practice displaces intense romantic connection. It is not idyllic sexuality or hierogamy that Lessing emphasizes but the forces the couple taps: "something happened between us—I mean, not just loving each other" (*L*, 219).

Thomas's manuscript and Mrs. Van's black coat (maternal, protective, and alluding to Africa) are the only two objects brought forward from the first novels to *Four-Gated City*. Talismanic and premonitory, the objects predict Martha's two functions: as middle-aged housekeeper/caretaker, "careful and troubled about many things" (Luke 10:38–42), and as visionary worker, finally piercing another dimension and power of mind that serves the world. Thomas's manuscript is a peculiar nexus of dominant and muted discourses, the broadcasting of a conflictual nest of stories. For "there were notes, comments, scribbled over and across and on the margins of the original text, in red pencil. These, hard to decipher, were in themselves a different story or, at least, made of the original a different story" (*L*, 269).

The Four-Gated City makes of the other novels a different story, for conventional narrative is displaced here. In the hundred pages before Martha settles in the Coldridge household, she is an alien, outside of the rules, accents, and class codes that structure postwar English society. Lessing has Martha try on three kinds of social identity (and hints herself at three delegitimated narratives—"angry young man" naturalism, Murdochian symbolism, and a Lessingesque realism to which she bids farewell).[29] Working-class life has a tough honesty, some goodwill, and political shrewdness, as well as being community oriented, but it brings out giggling, inane "Matty," a personality Martha does not want to recover. Middle-class life demands the same drugged consciousness as did Martha's ocean voyage to England on a bourgeois ship of fools. Jack's bohemian life (like life with the now dead Thomas) offers visionary experiences and a sense of postnormal consciousness. Therefore it is the only one of the three prologue lives to which she returns during the novel, yet its sensual energy is eventually rechanneled into manipulative sex. The miniature quest for a situation that integrates, calls upon, and deepens the self is ended when she finds both class identification and a group through whom history will work. She joins the upper middle-class intelligentsia of a left-wing variety, dissolving individual identity into "an extraordinary household . . . containing such a variety of attitudes, positions! A whole" (*FGC*, 211).

The relation between Mark and Lynda, the originating Coldridge family, reveals the chronic problem of male-female gender polarization and romantic thralldom. The issue is so intense for Mark that even in the postcataclysm world he still returns to "Lynda, and then Lynda, and then Lynda," and cannot stop seeking her smile in others (*FGC*, 613). The group protagonist is a way of writing beyond this morbid, touching, painful heterosexual romance, and beyond the bourgeois house.

In a very subtle scene, Martha remembers her daughter Caroline and the stupidity of thinking she was liberating the girl from social replication just by deserting her. This is a "debt" that Martha must pay back to the bourgeois house, to motherhood and to the family, using these institutions not as an end but as a probe (*FGC*, 38, 431). The hysteria of realizing that she must again reenter the family is patent: "She was worried, anxious: but she held the fort, she manned defenses" (*FGC*, 68, 71). So she loops back into motherhood in a very troubled household, repeating what she once evaded, in the great looping-back motion that we have seen elsewhere in the female quest.

Lessing often reiterates as a principle of psychic economy that one cannot evade but must "go through" or "fight out of" the troubling anxiety. If in the earlier books the critique of bourgeois life, love, and the family is that they do not understand their public and social functions, and the critique of leftist movements is that they do not valorize private life, then for the synthesis, Lessing must invent an institution that does fuse public and private, psychic and political, sexual and social life. The household, with its washes of politics and personality, and particularly Martha-Mark-Lynda, makes that synthesis by becoming a collective protagonist.[30]

The collective protagonist is announced at the Aldermaston March against nuclear weapons in 1961, when Martha, Lynda, and Mark watch themselves in various other triplets as "variations on a theme." The sexual or romantic character of these individuals is clearly set aside in the shrugged response to Margaret's pointed gibe that they make "a charming *ménage à trois*" (*FGC*, 397, 398). The real project of this protagonist is enunciated by Brandon, an angelic guide who appears just once in 600 pages: how to bring about change that really changes things.

Those who do not survive to ask are stuck in time, their particular set of qualities either fixed by one era or useful only to one era. Sally-Sarah has been fixed as a refugee in the forties; Colin by the Cold War politics of the fifties; Paul, their son, by the pop London of the early sixties. The survivors, a parallel family of Martha, Lynda, and Mark/Francis, seem to change, even startlingly, with their eras. For the women and boy, Lessing uses fashion or physical appearance to signal this flexibility, but it is a flexibility bending to that core problem: how to prevent social replication.

Mar/k/tha explore exterior time, political choices, historical action, utopian possibilities; Lynd/Marth/a work with a transhistorical stratum, probe psychological depths, and experience madness. The quests for political insight and psychic communication alternate structurally. The three have begun to function impersonally and chorally by the latter part of the novel. This has a number of effects. By being set free into the impersonal, they become the magnet for a varied assortment of adolescents escaping from the heavy-handed family house. This access to external crises allows the novel to continue while the three discuss and editorialize; the results of their conversation are summarized by Lessing in "reports." The prose becomes cooler, more documentary; this disconnects the reader from any personal feeling for the characters. By a number of these tactics of pattern and tone, Lessing helps us recognize the new protagonist. Together they break the central structuring dualisms of bourgeois hegemony. The split between public and private is explored by Mark-Martha and climaxes in Mark's study, with its mapped walls charting the areas for the coming ecological disaster. The split between inner and outer worlds, explored by Lynda and Martha, climaxes in their ability to bring a new faculty of mind to human consciousness. The split between romantic thralldom and the kin-based community is explored in the difference between Mark and Francis, for Francis later replaces Mark within the collective protagonist. The new group protagonist is a way for Lessing to express an ideological critique of dualisms through the narrative structure.

But this collective protagonist has two routes to the "city," which, it slowly emerges, are contradictory in their sense of priorities. Thus, at the end, two sites of rescue are presented. The hierarchic refugee camp in the desert, run by Mark, remakes the symbols of the good life; Faris, the island in the sea, with a diffuse power center, has values based on transindividual psychic powers of seeing and hearing.[31]

Mark sums up his parochial "stupidity" in the last pages of the novel. Because of paternalism and because of a refusal to stop "still thinking" in the old way, Mark rests in the pathos of social replication even after the cataclysm, stuck with "Bristol sherry" from Brazil (indicator of privatization and property), with a high-level rank in the bureaucracy (indicating prestige and patronage), and with an intemperate romantic thralldom. So romantic love is left at the absolute end as a symbol of resistance to change.[32] In contrast, Martha, from her city vision, Lynda, because of her madness, and Francis, because of adopting "kin," are all able to resist social replication. Two generations of men (Mark to Francis) are necessary to match one generation of women. Lessing, like H.D., Rich, and others, depicts female visionaries as a vanguard, and female bonding as one of the essential conditions for learning and for change.[33]

A good deal of *Landlocked* and all of *The Four-Gated City* are devoted to the recurrent, slowly consolidated discovery of another space or world, found through intensities of sexuality, rage, and madness. Because this "space" is a radically different experience from natural phenomena, it is elusive, hard to hold; it is, however, in grandest outlines, positive, a "sweet truth . . . once . . . sucked in like air through [the] pores" (*FGC*, 578). Lessing examines the social identity of a group of persons, bound neither by race, by class, by nationality, nor by gender, whose abilities bring them into contact with this space. In "the mad," Lessing identifies a social group that bridges the public and the private. Those set aside as mad have, in her view, two kinds of capabilities: they can hear what people think and can see what might occur. They function as antennae, picking up information that consciousness (possibly future consciousness) somehow sends through channels beyond what we now "know." In focusing on this fringe group, Lessing is trying to postulate a real social basis for change and for rupture with the rules of the world.[34] Lessing does not idealize madness per se, but a visionary capability. The focus on madness occurs to develop that social group which can bear the burden of estrangement while it develops the faculties that are of use to the whole human race. Madness, in short, is not an exaggerated kind of individualism, but a distorted expression of *communitas.*

Lessing's identification with Sufi wisdom literature, established in, say, epigrams to *The Four-Gated City,* was an "intensification" of ideas she has always held about a material evolution of humanity, a "conscious self-development" that will "serve mankind in its path of planned evolution."[35] Because some people have "certain faculties in embryo" by which they can get to a "country which lay just beyond or alongside, or within the landscape they could see and touch," Lessing insists that human progress will occur; in these allegorical constructs, one hears proud and un-ironic echoes of some of Schreiner's quest parables (*FGC,* 496, 355).

These new visionary capacities are a way of having individual liberty and the rights of conscience built into the human race. Instead of being acquired, and thus potentially compromised and weak, certain moral and ethical stances would be as natural, as biologically and materially based, as heartbeats. Thus "revolution" would occur in an "untouchable" form because it "was in the structure of life's substance" (*FGC,* 586, 396) This improvement in consciousness would automatically bring to an end the totalitarian tendencies of the modern state (that "iron heel" part of her novel that she thinks is a "true prophecy").[36] Brain waves, forging an oppositional collective, can outstrip all authorities, from the secret police to the overt government. Hence a major political change can be accomplished permanently without aggression, hostilities, coup, or election, by the further evolution of the mind.

Consciousness is, then, the ground for a number of these speculative fictions. And their emphasis on consciousness has to do with the nature and locus of female power—and powerlessness—a fact made plain by Virginia Woolf in "Thoughts on Peace in an Air Raid."[37] One of the major powers of the muted is to think against the current. However, among the powers of the powerful is the embedding of structures of seeing, feeling, knowing, and telling—including the telling of stories—that repeat the narratives of dominance. Woolf's meditation on peace and freedom in the midst of war and enslavement leads her to understand that a great change of consciousness must occur in all people to rid any individual of the "voices in himself" [herself] formed by education, tradition, training, and "ancient instincts."

In the twentieth century, legal, economic, and social struggles have succeeded in winning very significant gains in the external aspects of women's lives. But interior barriers in gender-linked and gender-producing institutions—among them dominant narrative—are persistent. In order to have a change in the world of the scale and effect proposed by Woolf in *The Years* or Lessing in *The Four-Gated City*, consciousness must be a prime site for the activity. To change ideas about the world, and to depict such a change, it is logical that narrative, as a site of ideology, should focus on mind, as a site of ideology. These quests of consciousness have, moreover, as their major action the changing of seeing, perceiving, and understanding for characters.

The didactic and hortatory nature of these speculative fictions calls attention to the production of alternative rather than acquiescent ideas. To write a narrative that includes future vision is, even crudely, to break the reproduction of the status quo. The focus on consciousness is a way of dramatizing a rupture from the normal rules of the world. Such fictions are another way of writing beyond the ending.

NOTES

1. Endings and Contradictions

1. Raymond Williams, *Marxism and Literature* (Oxford: Oxford University Press, 1977), p. 212.

2. The "sex-gender system" is Gayle Rubin's definitional term for the social relations of gender; Gayle Rubin, "The Traffic in Women: Notes on the 'Political Economy' of Sex," in *Toward an Anthropology of Women*, ed. Rayna [Rapp] Reiter (New York: Monthly Review Press, 1975), p. 168.

3. This is not my subject here; interested readers are directed to Judith Lowder Newton, *Women, Power and Subversion: Social Strategies in British Fiction, 1778–1860* (Athens: The University of Georgia Press, 1981); Igor Webb, *From Custom to Capital: The English Novel and the Industrial Revolution* (Ithaca: Cornell University Press, 1981); Mary Poovey, *The Proper Lady and The Woman Writer* (Forthcoming, University of Chicago Press). There is some evidence that the marital bond (and its parallel the romance plot) grew in importance during the nineteenth century, eroding the emotional ties to kin and neighborhood. See Ellen Ross, "Women and Family," in "Examining Family History," *Feminist Studies* 5, 1 (Spring 1979): 181–89.

4. Michèle Barrett, *Women's Oppression Today: Problems in Marxist Feminist Analysis* (London: Verso and New Left Books, 1980), p. 97.

5. John H. Gagnon and William Simon, *Sexual Conduct: The Social Sources of Human Sexuality* (Chicago: Aldine Publishing Company, 1973), pp. 19–26.

6. Ibid., p. 9.

7. This argument has clearly been influenced by Raymond Williams: "For it is of the essence of a convention that it ratifies an assumption or a point of view, so that the work can be made and received. . . . The reality of conventions as the mode of junction of social position and literary practice remains central." *Marxism and Literature*, p. 179.

8. Woolf and Forster, "The New Censorship," *Nation & Athenaeum*, Sept. 8, 1928, p. 726.

9. Louis Althusser, *For Marx*, trans. Ben Brewster (London: New Left Books, 1977), p. 233. This understanding of Althusser has been aided by a paper by Stephen Zelnick, Temple University, "Ideology as Narrative: Critical Approaches to *Robinson Crusoe.*"

10. In general this position draws on Pierre Macherey, *A Theory of Literary Production* (London: Routledge and Kegan Paul, 1978).

11. This either/or choice was the subject of considerable comment; for

example, Mona Caird, *The Morality of Marriage* (London: Redway, 1897): In the future "women will no longer have to choose between freedom and the affections of the home—now the stern alternatives," p. 145. In the early twentieth century, married women represented only 14 percent of all working women: Lee Holcombe, *Victorian Ladies at Work: Middle Class Working Women in England and Wales, 1850–1914* (London: David and Charles Newton Abbot, 1973), p. 217.

12. There are many historical reasons, again not my subject, to situate the 1880s in England as a significant moment for these narrative ruptures. The "earliest critiques of 'Victorianism' can be situated in this period," as well as the final consolidation of The Married Women's Property Act (1882), which gave wives a legal identity and the right to keep their own earnings. During this period the role of the state increased, making family, sexuality (including "sexual unorthodoxies") and the division of labor by gender into public, juridical and legal matters. Also during this period, the reorganization of divorce and separation procedures occurred and the circulation of birth-control materials was relatively unimpeded. Jeffrey Weeks, *Sex, Politics and Society: The Regulation of Sexuality since 1800* (London: Longman, 1981), pp. 23, 81–84. *cf Patricia Boumelha* ←

13. Nancy K. Miller, *The Heroine's Text: Readings in the French and English Novel, 1722–1782* (New York: Columbia University Press, 1980), pp. xi, 151, 157.

14. The fact that these social changes have been a long-term project for female commentators and thinkers can be represented by two texts, one from 1859 and one from 1925. Barbara Bodichon, the American sculptor, urges that women be trained for professions and be able to earn an income, for only then could they form "equal unions." "We ardently desire that women should not make love their profession." *Women and Work* (New York: C. S. Francis, 1859), pp. 19, 27. In a debate in the mid-1920s between a feminist and an antifeminist, Dora Russell notes the persistence of economic and social norms that force women to that either/or choice between their vocation (earning money, utilizing their talents in society) and love with marriage. "This choice is not feminism—feminists have fought it persistently—it is medieval Christianity." *Hypatia; or, Woman and Knowledge* (New York: E. P. Dutton and Co., 1925), p. 31.

15. Anne Sexton, "Cinderella," *Transformations* (Boston: Houghton Mifflin Company, 1971), pp. 56–57.

16. Virginia Woolf, *Three Guineas* (New York: Harcourt, Brace and World, Inc., 1938), p. 143.

17. Virginia Woolf, *Orlando* (New York: The New American Library, 1960; first published 1928), p. 190.

18. In "Women and Fiction," Woolf points out that her title can be "read in two ways: it may allude to women and the fiction that they write, or to women and the fiction that is written about them." *Granite and Rainbow* (New York: Harcourt, Brace and Company, 1958), p. 76. The beauty of the Mary Carmichael trope in *A Room of One's Own* (the text for which "Women and Fiction" was the seed) is that Woolf has created at once an imaginary writer and an imaginary character, so that she becomes a complete instance of the issue of women and fiction.

19. Virginia Woolf, *A Room of One's Own* (New York: Harcourt, Brace and World, Inc., 1929), pp. 87, 89.

20. Dorothy Richardson, *Backwater* (1916), in *Pilgrimage* (New York: Popular Library, 1976), p. 284.

21. Nina Auerbach, *Communities of Women: An Idea in Fiction* (Cambridge, Mass.: Harvard University Press, 1978); Alan Friedman, *The Turn of the Novel* (New York: Oxford University Press, 1966).

22. A note on terms. What I mean by the female hero is a central character whose activities, growth, and insight are given much narrative attention and much authorial interest. When I mean heroine—the object of male attention or rescue—I will use that term. A quest plot may be any progressive, goal-oriented search with stages, obstacles, and "battles," which in general involves self-realization, mastery, and the expression of energy, where this may be at the service of a larger ideology (e.g., in *Pilgrim's Progress* or in *Parcival*). What I call a romance or marriage plot is the use of conjugal love as a telos and of the developing heterosexual love relation as a major, if not the only major, element in organizing the narrative action. In its more virulent or purest strain, the romance plot asserts that *amor vincit omnia* (a phrase to which Woolf alludes in Orlando, and which, in her form, is the title of chapter 4 of the present study).

23. Jean Kennard has briskly summed up this kind of thing. "The very structure of the novel places [the male hero] as leader, [the female protagonist] as follower. For her, maturity lies in learning that her ideals are fantasies, that happiness lies in approximating the male reality and in denying much of what had seemed to be herself." *Victims of Convention* (Hamden, Ct.: Archon Books, 1978), p. 14. Kennard's formulations also link ideology to structure, but more normatively than I will do.

24. Jane Austen, *Emma* (New York: W. W. Norton and Company, Inc., 1972), p. 297. Further citations in the text, abbreviated as *E*.

25. The voluntary and profound good sense in marriage that comes to the female hero is often contrasted with a conventionally feminine character. For the female protagonists tend to triumph, by their moral depths and willed choices, over the shallow, superficial, and even designing versions of femininity depicted in the novels. This type of character may even exact a malicious or deceitful revenge for her powerlessness, while at the same time, being incapable of nobility: Rosamond in *Middlemarch*, Ginevra in *Villette*, Blanche Ingram in *Jane Eyre*.

26. This is Gilbert and Gubar's argument in *The Madwoman in the Attic: The Woman Writer and the Nineteenth-Century Literary Imagination* (New Haven: Yale University Press, 1979). They say this in the context of the identification of a major contradiction in nineteenth-century texts between the work and its conventions and the female author for whom the culture is inimical to what she wants to say. In Austen, the social hegemony that the text presents is, in their view, a "cover story," while anger and pride in assertion of the female imagination are encoded variously in Austen's and others' works. This encoded anger and assertion is the "madwoman in the attic," the irruption of a monster woman or Satanic Eve that expresses at once a muted feminist desire for critique and the anxiety of a female author confronting male cultural tradition. By looking at the encodings of revolt and rage, Gilbert and Gubar discuss the nature and sources of destabilizing subtexts. By looking at the nature and functions of resolution in these texts, I am studying the ideological statements and contradictions that constitute dominant narrative. For the

nineteenth century, Gilbert and Gubar emphasize the subversive; I emphasize the dominant.

27. The Marxist Feminist Literature Collective discusses the way that, in "post-1848" nineteenth-century novels, the heroines can be placed outside of "normative kinship patterns" and the ways that the Gothic elements encode the otherwise "'unspeakable' sexual desires of women." Marxist Feminist Literature Collective, "Women's Writing: Jane Eyre, Shirley, Villette, Aurora Leigh," in *1848: The Sociology of Literature,* ed. Francis Barker (Colchester: University of Essex, 1978): pp. 185–206.

28. For the terminology in which to discuss the types of marriage plot, I am drawing here, as elsewhere, on Evelyn Hinz, "Hierogamy versus Wedlock: Types of Marriage Plots and Their Relationship to Genres of Prose Fiction," *PMLA* 91, 5 (October 1976): 900–13. Briefly, *wed*lock is the comedic, social marriage; wed*lock* is the tragicomic; hierogamy is the sacred marriage of beauty and the beast, sky and earth. For Hinz, the first terms mark the "novel," the last, the "romance," a distinction over which I glide, for it seems to oversimplify the often multiple discourses in a narrative.

29. Bertha has received brilliant and provocative critical attention. Helene Moglen sees her as "the monstrous embodiment of psychosexual conflicts which are intrinsic to the romance predicament." *Charlotte Brontë: The Self Conceived* (New York: W. W. Norton and Company, Inc., 1976), p. 24. Elaine Showalter notes the connection between the sexual appetite in Bertha and the menstrual cycle: *A Literature of Their Own* (Princeton: Princeton University Press, 1977), pp. 119–21. Gilbert and Gubar take Bertha's angry and irruptive presence as the paradigmatic figure of enraged female selfhood, the madwoman in the attic, and the double of the woman writer.

30. David Goldknopf, *The Life of the Novel* (Chicago: University of Chicago Press, 1972) makes very clear the degree to which any use of coincidence was a deliberate choice.

31. Charlotte Brontë, *Villette* (London: Dent, 1974), p. 329.

32. In this reading I am at odds with several distinguished critics of Brontë who hold that the ending criticizes the inadequacy of the happy ending convention; in my view both *Jane Eyre* and *Villette* can be assimilated to the either/or choice between romance and vocation. *Jane Eyre* offers romance as its final term, *Villette* offers vocation, and in both there is a sense of something missing.

33. George Eliot, *Middlemarch* (New York: W. W. Norton and Company, Inc., 1977), p. 522. Further references in text, abbreviated as *M.*

34. John Stuart Mill and Harriet Taylor Mill, "The Subjugation of Women" (1869), in *Essays on Sex Equality,* ed. Alice S. Rossi (Chicago: The University of Chicago Press, 1970), p. 141.

35. Frances Power Cobbe, "The Final Cause of Woman," *Women's Work and Women's Culture,* ed. Josephine E. Butler (London: Macmillan and Co., 1869), p. 6.

36. Rachel Brownstein has written about the self-mirroring and educative relation between female reader and heroine, the former learning from the latter self-consciousness, irony, wholeness, as well as female rites of passage. Brownstein's emphasis falls on the heroic heroine of aspiration and integrity, yet also on the persistence of romance, showing how the heroine's self-awareness serves the plot. Agreeing with the persistence of romance at resolu-

tion, my emphasis falls on the rescripting of that kind of resolution by twentieth-century women writers. Rachel M. Brownstein, *Becoming a Heroine: Reading About Women in Novels* (New York: The Viking Press, 1982).

37. Webb, *From Custom to Capital*, pp. 171, 168.

38. Ibid., p. 175.

39. Newton, *Women, Power, and Subversion*, pp. 10–11.

40. Gillian Beer argues that if the price of forward growth for women is a cramped, narrow sphere, then death may rescue her from these determining bonds. "Beyond Determinism: George Eliot and Virginia Woolf," in *Women Writing and Writing about Women*, ed. Mary Jacobus (London: Croom Helm, 1979), pp. 80–99.

41. George Eliot, *The Mill on the Floss* (Boston: Houghton Mifflin Company, 1961), p. 252. Further references in the text, abbreviated as *MotF.*

42. The figure is, in Fredric Jameson's term (from Julia Kristeva), an "ideologeme," that is, "a historically determinate conceptual or semic complex which can project itself variously in the form of a 'value system' or 'philosophic concept,' or in the form of a protonarrative, a private or collective narrative fantasy." *The Political Unconscious: Narrative as a Socially Symbolic Act* (Ithaca: Cornell University Press, 1981), p. 115. Also, an "ideologeme itself is a form of social praxis, that is . . . a symbolic resolution to a concrete historical situation," p. 117.

2. The Rupture of Story

1. Raymond Williams, *Marxism and Literature* (Oxford: Oxford University Press, 1977), p. 112. Indeed, the term "experience" for any event, for a specific sexual experience, and for the impingement of reality on a person, all taken innocently as unmediated, is in truth a measure of our satisfaction with the "second natural," or the things that go without saying. Thus the concept of experience is, as Raymond Williams has succinctly said, "the most common form of ideology." "Marxism, Structuralism and Literary Analysis," *New Left Review* 129 (Sept.-Oct. 1981): 63.

2. Virginia Woolf, "Phases of Fiction," in *Granite and Rainbow* (New York: Harcourt, Brace and Company, 1958), pp. 101–102.

3. In a passage undoubtedly known to Virginia Woolf, Olive Schreiner began, "We have a Shakespeare; but what of the possible Shakespeares we might have had, who passed their life from youth upward brewing currant wine and making pastries for fat country squires to eat, with no glimpse of the freedom of life and action, necessary even to poach on deer in the green forests, stifled out without one line written, simply because, being of the weaker sex, life gave no room for action and grasp on life?" These are part of Rebekah's written meditations in *From Man to Man* (1927) (Chicago: Academy Press Limited, 1977), p. 195.

4. Olive Schreiner, *The Story of an African Farm*, with an introduction by Doris Lessing (New York: Schocken Books, 1976); abbreviated in the text as *SAF.* In making the claim of coherence of purpose, I am in conflict with the major—virtually the only—critical response to this novel to date. Beyond its relevance to the debates of its time (emancipated heroine, religious speculation), the book has been taxed for its awkwardness. For example: Schreiner's "only 'finished' novel is a clumsy, uneven book," or "the labors of construction and plotting were beyond her" (respectively, Vineta Colby, *The Singular Anomaly: Women Novelists of the Nineteenth Century* [New York: New York University

Press, 1970], p. 48, and Elaine Showalter, *A Literature of Their Own* [Princeton: Princeton University Press, 1977], p. 198). While critics generally agree about the passion and evocativeness of the work, they have all been apologetic about the text.

5. Critics have sometimes commented that the racial question is virtually excluded from this story. Blacks are present as choral backdrop only, and historically accurate racist epithets are not stinted. However, I think a concern for racial oppression enters covertly. Waldo "is" the black African. He is despised in an analogous way, and his inventions are broken. He is described as wild and unkempt, paralleling descriptions of the tribal blacks. He does the work assigned to the native and also makes wood carvings reminiscent of African art. Finally, he is described as muttering like a "Kaffir."

Yes.
also
Michael K

6. See Henry Louis Gates, Jr., "The 'Blackness of Blackness': A Critique of the Sign and the Signifying Monkey," *Critical Inquiry* 9, 4 (June 1983): 685–723.

7. Jerome Buckley, *Season of Youth: The Bildungsroman from Dickens to Golding* (Cambridge, Mass.: Harvard University Press, 1974).

8. This study will take up the two occasions upon which Dorothy Richardson alludes to this formulation; see chap. 9.

9. Here is the brief allegory:

> I saw a woman sleeping. In her sleep she dreamt Life stood before her, and held in each hand a gift—in the one love, in the other Freedom. And she said to the woman, "Choose!"
>
> And the woman waited long: and she said, "Freedom!"
>
> And Life said, "Thou hast well chosen. If thou hadst said, "Love," I would have given thee that thou didst ask for; and I would have gone from thee, and returned to thee no more. Now, the day will come when I shall return. In that day I shall bear both gifts in one hand."
>
> I heard the woman laugh in her sleep.

"Life's Gifts," in *Dreams* (Boston: Roberts Brothers, 1891), pp. 115–16.

10. Evelyn Hinz, "Hierogamy versus Wedlock: Types of Marriage Plots and Their Relationship to Genres of Prose Fiction," *PMLA* 91, 5 (October 1976): 900–13.

11. All biographical information draws on the extraordinary work of Ruth First and Ann Scott, *Olive Schreiner* (New York: Schocken Books, 1980). Biographers are divided on whether Schreiner was in fact seduced but are clear that her confrontation with love, desire, and possibly dishonor in the Julius Gau incident (1872) was "highly destructive." First and Scott, p. 61.

12. For example, the character who embodies norms associated with the social and comedic marriage plot is the thrice-married Tant' Sannie. Because the character is negligible, Schreiner can dismiss money, status, morality, marriage, and property with ease.

13. This argument is made by Robin Morgan, "The Politics of Sado-Masochistic Fantasies," in *Going Too Far* (New York: Random House, 1977), pp. 227–40.

14. Charlotte Perkins Gilman saw that femininity and true womanhood were not freely chosen or natural but were the result of the economic dependence of women on men, and that these were ideologies with material roots. *Women and Economics: A Study of the Economic Relation Between Men and Women*

as a Factor in Social Evolution (1898) (New York: Harper and Row Publishers, 1966).

15. Olive Schreiner, *Women and Labour* (1889; London: Virago Ltd, 1978), pp. 33 and 283, and also as a motif, *passim.*

16. Schreiner knew that one feminist goal is the dismantling of these internal, obdurate structures of feeling: "It is not against men we have to fight but against ourselves within ourselves." Letter of 1889, in *The Letters of Olive Schreiner, 1876–1920,* ed. S. C. Cronwright-Schreiner (Boston: Little, Brown and Company, 1924), p. 151.

17. The fate of Lyndall even presents an uncanny premonition of Schreiner's problematic career, her dead baby, and her sense of aborted quest.

18. Schreiner, too, insisted that Lyndall's death was not a punishment for a sexual sin but was involved with a more general struggle of human nature. S. C. Cronwright-Schreiner, *The Life of Olive Schreiner* (London: Unwin, 1924), p. 189.

19. The scenes with Gregory Rose in women's clothing have some resemblance to a brief scene in *From Man to Man,* written from 1873 to 1920, first published after Schreiner's death, in 1927. In this scene, an unlovable and manipulative character named Veronica secretly visits a man's room and touches his clothing with fascination (*FMtM,* 100–101). With this furtive spying upon a man's clothing, Schreiner comments on repressed sexuality and the moral and emotional destruction it will wreak. About this scene, Schreiner said, "I don't know how it came into my head," although earlier in the same year, 1884, she herself had expressed the desire "to wear boy's clothes and *will* as soon as I can get other women to join me. Boy's knickerbockers, but not coats, I think they are ugly." *Letters of Olive Schreiner,* pp. 49 and 39. Later in *From Man to Man,* Rebekah, the thoroughly sympathetic main character, expresses a desire to be a man, in part so she could care for the weak, but especially because of "the great freedom opened to her, no place shut off from her, the long chain broken, all work possible for her, no law to say this and this is for women . . ." (*FMtM,* 202). For a study of female cross-dressing in its literary and social implications, see Susan Gubar, "Blessings in Disguise: Cross Dressing as Re-Dressing for Female Modernists," *The Massachusetts Review* XXII, 3 (Autumn 1981): 477–508.

20. *Letters of Olive Schreiner,* p. 51. Compare this statement from *Woman and Labour:* that the Woman's Movement is "part of a great movement of the sexes towards each other, a movement towards common occupations, common interests, common ideals, and towards an emotional sympathy between the sexes more deeply founded and more indestructible than any the world has yet seen" (*W&L,* 259).

21. First and Scott, *Olive Schreiner,* p. 68. As yet unpublished research by Yaffa Draznin also suggests that the normal medical treatment for her condition considerably worsened Schreiner's health.

22. Ibid., p. 336.

23. Ibid., p. 340.

24. Louis Hermann, "Woman in Revolt," *Literary Guide* 70, 3 (March 1955): 28. The article was written for the centenary of Schreiner's birth.

25. "Over that bridge which shall be built with our bodies, who will pass?" The answer epitomizes Schreiner's optimism of the will. "He said, '*The entire human race.*'" "Three Dreams in a Desert," in *Dreams,* p. 83.

3. Breaking the Sentence; Breaking the Sequence

1. Virginia Woolf, *A Room of One's Own* (New York: Harcourt, Brace and World, Inc., 1957); abbreviated in the text as *AROO.* The epigraphs come from pp. 85 and 95.

2. Virginia Woolf, "Women and Fiction" (1929), in *Granite and Rainbow* (New York: Harcourt, Brace and Company, 1958), p. 80; abbreviated as *G&R.*

3. The sentence is further qualified as being "too loose, too heavy, too pompous for a woman's use" (*G&R,* 81). A parallel, but slightly softened, statement about the sentence is found in *AROO,* 79, and an elaboration in the 1923 review of Dorothy Richardson, "Romance and the Heart," reprinted in *Contemporary Writers: Essays on Twentieth Century Books and Authors* (New York: Harcourt Brace Jovanovich, 1965), pp. 123–25. Working with these passages, Josephine Donovan also notes that the differences between "male" and "female" sentences exist in the tone of authority, the declaration of the insider in one, the under-the-surface life in the other, which rejects the authoritarian. Donovan also links Woolf's achievements in subjective realism to her critique of gender ideologies in narrative. "Feminist Style Criticism," in *Images of Women in Fiction: Feminist Perspectives,* ed. Susan Koppelman Cornillon (Bowling Green: Bowling Green University Popular Press, 1972), pp. 339–52. A further note on the analysis of Woolf's "sentence." In this study as a whole, I am carefully (too?) agnostic on the subject of those actual disruptions of syntax, grammar, and words more characteristic of, say, Gertrude Stein; however, what Julia Kristeva calls the semiotic and symbolic registers may be another oscillation of dominant discourse in dialogue with marginality.

4. "Romance and the Heart," *Contemporary Writers,* pp. 124–25.

5. This is Nelly Furman's argument. "Textual Feminism," in *Women and Language in Literature and Society,* ed. Sally McConnell-Ginet, Ruth Borker, and Nelly Furman (New York: Praeger, 1980), pp. 50–51.

6. Nancy Miller, "Emphasis Added: Plots and Plausibilities in Women's Fiction," *PMLA* 96,1 (January 1981): 38.

7. "Women Novelists," reprinted in *Contemporary Writers,* p. 25.

8. *Granite and Rainbow,* p. 80.

9. Here in the twenties, Woolf holds in conflictive tension her materialist and idealist views of writing. She argues that through art one may—indeed one must—transcend the cultural conditions of one's own formation. So in *A Room of One's Own,* Woolf combines a materialist analysis of the conditions that determine a woman's identity and capacity for work and an idealist vision of androgyny, a unity of the warring and unequal genders in luminous serenity. This point is made by Michèle Barrett in her introduction to a collection of essays by Virginia Woolf, *Women and Writing* (New York: Harcourt Brace Jovanovich, 1979), pp. 20, 22.

10. For example, Woolf compared living with the institutions of gender as they are to living in "half-civilized barbarism," a slap at the meliorism of liberal ideology. Reply to "Affable Hawk" from the *New Statesman* of 1920, in *The Diary of Virginia Woolf, Volume Two: 1920–1924,* ed. Anne Olivier Bell and Andrew McNeillie (New York: Harcourt Brace Jovanovich, 1978), p. 342.

11. Carolyn G. Heilbrun points toward the role of double determining when she suggests that "to be a feminist one had to have an experience of being an outsider more extreme than merely being a woman." *Reinventing Womanhood* (New York: W. W. Norton and Company, 1979), pp. 20–24. Ad-

rienne Rich describes that tension leading to a doubled vision: "Born a white woman, Jewish or of curious mind / —twice an outsider, still believing in inclusion—" *A Wild Patience Has Taken Me This Far* (New York: W. W. Norton and Company, 1981), p 39.

12. Myra Jehlen, "Archimedes and the Paradox of Feminist Criticism," *Signs* 6, 4 (Summer 1981): 594. Jehlen makes this point about nineteenth-century American women, attempting to explain the literature of sentiment and limited challenge that they produced. " . . . in this society, women stand outside any of the definitions of complete being; hence perhaps the appeal to them of a literature of conformity and inclusion." "(Ambiguously) nonhege-monic" from my essay "For the Etruscans: Sexual Difference and Artistic Production—the Debate over a Female Aesthetic," in *The Future of Difference,* ed. Hester Eisenstein and Alice Jardine (Boston: G. K. Hall & Co., 1980). A further development of the phrase "(ambiguously) nonhegamonic" is found in Margaret Homans, " 'Her Very Own Howl': The Ambiguities of Repre-sentation in Recent Women's Fiction," *Signs* 9, 2 (Winter 1983): 186–205. Homans suggests that "there is a specifically gender-based alienation from language" visible in thematic treatments of language in women's fiction, which derives from "the special ambiguity of women's simultaneous participa-tion in and exclusion from a hegemonic group. . . ," p. 205.

13. For example: Olive Schreiner, *Women and Labour;* Charlotte Perkins Gilman, *The Man-Made World; or, Our Androcentric Culture* and *Women and Economics;* Virginia Woolf, *Three Guineas, A Room of One's Own,* and various essays; H.D., *Tribute to Freud, End to Torment* and *The Gift;* Dorothy Richardson, essays on women; Adrienne Rich, *Of Woman Born* and *On Lies, Secrets and Silence;* Tillie Olsen, *Silences;* Doris Lessing, *A Small Personal Voice;* Alice Wal-ker, *In Search of Our Mother's Gardens.*

14. Annette Kuhn, *Women's Pictures: Feminism and Cinema* (London: Rout-ledge and Kegan Paul, 1982), p. 17. The first chapter is a sterling exposition of feminist analysis of culture.

15. In the course of her research on the draft of *A Room of One's Own,* Alice Fox communicated to Jane Marcus that Woolf originally, wittily left a blank unfilled by the word *laboratory.* "Then she wrote that she was afraid to turn the page to see what they shared, and she thought of the obscenity trial for a novel." The allusion made and excised is to the contemporaneous trial of *The Well of Loneliness;* the implication that Woolf handled differently in her pub-lished text is that homophobic censorship and self-censorship alike conspire to mute discussion of relational ties between women. Jane Marcus, "Liberty, Sorority, Misogyny," in *The Representation of Women in Fiction,* ed. Carolyn G. Heilbrun and Margaret R. Higonnet (Baltimore: Johns Hopkins University Press, 1983), p. 82.

16. Elaine Showalter proposes "that the specificity of women's writing [is] not . . . a transient by-product of sexism but [is] a fundamentally and continu-ally determining reality." "Feminist Criticism in the Wilderness," *Critical In-quiry* 8, 2 (Winter 1981): 205.

17. Gayle Rubin, "The Traffic in Women: Notes on the 'Political Economy' of Sex," in *Toward an Anthropology of Women,* ed. Rayna [Rapp] Reiter (New York: Monthly Review Press, 1975): pp. 157–210.

18. Sigmund Freud, "The Psychology of Women" (1933), in *New Introduc-tory Lectures on Psycho-Analysis,* trans. W. J. H. Sprott (New York: W. W. Norton and Company, Inc., 1933), p. 184. The same essay is called "Femininity" in

The Standard Edition of the Complete Psychological Works of Sigmund Freud, vol. xxii, trans. James Strachey (London: The Hogarth Press and The Institute of Psychoanalysis, 1964).

19. Freud, "The Psychology of Women," p. 158.

20. Gayle Rubin, "The Traffic in Women," p. 185.

21. Sherry B. Ortner, "Oedipal Father, Mother's Brother, and The Penis: A Review of Juliet Mitchell's *Psychoanalysis and Feminism," Feminist Studies* II, 2/3 (1975): 179. As Michèle Barrett has remarked, "no substantial work has yet been produced that historicizes the [gendering] processes outlined in psychoanalytic theory." *Women's Oppression Today: Problems in Marxist Feminist Analysis* (London: Verso and New Left Books, 1980), p. 197.

22. Freud, "The Psychology of Women," p. 179. By female masculinity is meant the pre-oedipal object choice of a female; by femininity is meant the oedipal object choice of a male.

23. Nancy Chodorow, *The Reproduction of Mothering: Psychoanalysis and the Sociology of Gender* (Berkeley: University of California Press, 1978), p. 112.

24. Chodorow summarizes the female's "emotional, if not erotic bisexual oscillation between mother and father—between preoccupation with 'mother-child' issues and 'male-female' issues." *The Reproduction of Mothering,* p. 168. I am indebted to Chodorow for the concept of oscillation.

25. "The asymmetrical structure of parenting generates a female oedipus complex . . . characterized by the continuation of preoedipal attachments and preoccupations, sexual oscillation in an oedipal triangle, and the lack of either absolute change of love object or absolute oedipal resolution." Chodorow, *The Reproduction of Mothering,* pp. 133–34.

26. In an analysis related to my point here, Elizabeth Abel sees the theme and presence of same-sex friendship in literary works by women as an expression of female identity and the particularities of female oedipalization. As well, Abel offers striking remarks on the theory of literary influence that can be derived from Chodorow. "(E) Merging Identities: The Dynamics of Female Friendship in Contemporary Fiction by Women," *Signs* 6, 3 (Spring 1981): 413–35.

27. For example, H.D. was psychoanalyzed by Freud, and engaged, according to Susan Friedman, in a constant interior debate with Freud on several issues, including gender. *Psyche Reborn: The Emergence of H.D.* (Bloomington: Indiana University Press, 1981). Virginia Woolf noted her "very amateurish knowledge of Freud and the psychoanalysts" and admitted that "my knowledge is merely from superficial talk." In her circle, however, the talkers might have included James Strachey, the translator of Freud's *Complete Psychological Works,* cited in note 18. *The Letters of Virginia Woolf, Volume Five, 1932–1935,* ed. Nigel Nicolson and Joanne Trautmann (New York: Harcourt Brace Jovanovich, 1979), 36 and 91.

28. Freud, "The Psychology of Women," p. 177.

29. Freud, "The Passing of the Oedipus-Complex," in *Collected Papers, Volume II* (London: The Hogarth Press, 1957), p. 275. The paper dates from 1924.

30. Virginia Woolf, *Moments of Being,* ed. Jeanne Schulkind (New York: Harcourt Brace Jovanovich, 1978), pp. 132, 129, 132.

31. Simone de Beauvoir, *The Second Sex,* trans. H. M. Parshley (New York: Bantam Books, 1972), p. 47.

32. John Berger, *Ways of Seeing* (New York: Viking Press, 1972), p. 46.

33. Gerda Lerner, *The Majority Finds its Past: Placing Women in History* (Oxford: Oxford University Press, 1979), pp. xxi, 52.

34. Nancy Cott, "Introduction," *Root of Bitterness: Documents of the Social History of American Women* (New York: E. P. Dutton and Co., 1972), p. 3.

35. Sheila Rowbotham, *Women's Consciousness, Man's World* (London: Penguin, 1973), pp. 30–31.

36. Alice Walker, "In Search of Our Mothers' Gardens," in *In Search of Our Mothers' Gardens* (San Diego: Harcourt Brace Jovanovich, 1983), p. 235.

37. Virginia Woolf, *Three Guineas* (New York: Harcourt, Brace and World, Inc., 1938), p. 5. Abbreviated in the text as *TG.*

38. Virginia Woolf, "The Leaning Tower," in *The Moment and Other Essays* (New York: Harcourt Brace Jovanovich, 1948), p. 154.

39. Raymond Williams, "Base and Superstucture in Marxist Cultural Theory," *New Left Review* 82 (Nov.–Dec. 1973): 7.

40. Raymond Williams, *Marxism and Literature* (Oxford: Oxford University Press, 1977), p. 112.

41. Edwin Ardener, "The 'Problem' Revisited," a coda to "Belief and the Problem of Women," in *Perceiving Women,* ed. Shirley Ardener (New York: John Wiley and Sons, 1975), p. 22. Elaine Showalter made Ardener's analysis available to feminist criticism in "Feminist Criticism in the Wildnerness," *Critical Inquiry* 8, 2 (Winter 1981), especially 199–201.

42. "Double-consciousness" is, in fact, the influential formulation of black identity made in 1903 by W. E. B. DuBois in *The Souls of Black Folk* (in *Three Negro Classics,* ed. John Hope Franklin [New York: Avon Books, 1965], p. 215). "It is a peculiar sensation, the double-consciousness, this sense of always looking at one's self through the eyes of others, of measuring one's soul by the tape of a world that looks on in amused contempt and pity. One ever feels his twoness—an American, a Negro; two souls, two thoughts, two unreconciled strivings; two warring ideals in one dark body, whose dogged strength alone keeps it from being torn asunder." Richard Wright made a similar point in 1956: "First of all, my position is a split one. I'm black. I'm a man of the West. These hard facts condition, to some degree, my outlook . . ." (*Présence Africaine* [November 1956], cited in *The Black Writer in Africa and the Americas,* ed. Lloyd W. Brown [Los Angeles: Hennessey & Ingalls, Inc., 1973], p. 27).

43. Ellen Moers, *Literary Women: The Great Writers* (Garden City, N.Y.: Doubleday and Company, Inc., 1976).

44. Elaine Showalter, *A Literature of Their Own: British Women Novelists from Brontë to Lessing* (Princeton, N.J.: Princeton University Press, 1977), p. 11. The postulation of "unity" is also generally assumed in this study. However, other perspectives on women's writing might make other assumptions, now that "women's writing" is an accepted critical category.

45. Sandra M. Gilbert and Susan Gubar, *The Madwoman in the Attic: The Woman Writer and the Nineteenth-Century Literary Imagination* (New Haven: Yale University Press, 1979), p. 49.

46. Mary Jacobus, "The Difference of View," in *Women Writing and Writing about Women,* ed. Mary Jacobus (London: Croom Helm, 1979), pp. 19–20.

47. Myra Jehlen's summary of the relationship of women to culture is exemplary.

> Women (and perhaps some men not of the universal kind) must deal with their situation as a *pre*condition for writing about it. They have to confront the assumptions that render them a kind of fiction in themselves in that they are

defined by others, as components of the language and thought of others. It hardly matters at this prior stage what a woman wants to write; its political nature is implicit in the fact that it is she (a "she") who will do it. All women's writing would thus be congenitally defiant and universally characterized by the blasphemous argument it makes in coming into being. And this would mean that the autonomous individuality of a woman's story or poem is framed by engagement, the engagement of its denial of dependence. We might think of the form this necessary denial takes (however it is individually interpreted, whether conciliatory or assertive) as analogous to genre, in being an issue, not of content, but of the structural formulation of the work's relationship to the inherently formally patriarchal language which is the only language we have.

"Archimedes," p. 582. The proposal this book makes for the "structural formulation" analogous to genre is the act of critique, drawing on the oscillations of female identity.

48. The sex-gender system involves a linked chain of institutions such as the sexual division of labor in production and in the socialization of children, valorized heterosexuality and the constraint on female sexuality, marriage and kinship, sexual object choice and desire, gender asymmetry and polarization.

49. Toni Morrison, *The Bluest Eye* (1970) (New York: Pocket Books, 1972). Abbreviated in the text as *TBE*.

50. Margaret Atwood, *Lady Oracle* (New York: Avon Books, 1976). Atwood has herself noted, in discussions of her poetry, the tensions between examination by lens and presentation by mirrors, which give a "backward reflection." This split is analogous to critical analysis and scrutiny on one hand, and remystification, the backward reflection, on the other. Karla Hammond, "An Interview with Margaret Atwood," *The American Poetry Review* (Sept.–Oct. 1979): 27. Atwood has also considered the woman question over the years from 1960 to the present, always in a demystifying tone. Her position can be exactly characterized by the oscillation between membership in the group *woman*, with all that means in terms of cultural stereotypes and limitations (for she uses a Woolfean trope of herself as a "graduate studentess" at Harvard, attempting to enter Widener Library in the early 1960s), and, on the other hand, membership in the group *human*, with a bluff impatience with any writer's version of reality, whether masculinist or liberationist, that puts the "capital W" on "Woman." *Second Words: Selected Critical Prose* (Toronto: House of Anansi Press, 1982), pp. 329, 227.

51. Gail Godwin, *Violet Clay* (New York: Alfred A. Knopf, 1978), p. 45.

52. Jean Rhys, *Wide Sargasso Sea* (1966) (London: Penguin Books, 1968).

53. Elizabeth Baer makes this point. "The Sisterhood of Jane Eyre and Antoinette Cosway," in *The Voyage In: Fictions of Female Development*, ed. Elizabeth Abel, Marianne Hirsch, and Elizabeth Langland (Hanover: University Press of New England, 1983).

54. Analyses such as Albert Memmi, *The Colonizer and the Colonized* (Boston: Beacon Press, 1967).

55. Doris Lessing, "The Preface to *The Golden Notebook*," in *A Small Personal Voice* (New York: Alfred A. Knopf, 1974), p. 39.

4. "Amor Vin———"

1. The editions of Woolf's novels used are as follows: *The Voyage Out* (abbreviated in the text as *VO*) (the 1920 Doran edition; New York: Harcourt,

Brace and World, Inc., 1948); *Night and Day (N&D)* (1919; New York: Harcourt Brace Jovanovich, 1973); *Mrs. Dalloway (MD)* (New York: Harcourt, Brace and World, Inc., 1925); *Orlando (O)* (New York: The New American Library, 1928); *Flush: A Biography* (New York: Harcourt, Brace and Company, 1933). *Jacob's Room* (1922), which I do not discuss, could be seen as the symbolic death of the male hero, which clears the way for the female hero and her plot.

  2. Woolf investigates where to put romance even at the absolute beginning of her writing career, in "The Journal of Mistress Joan Martyn" (1906). The narrator escapes marriage by being a scholar; the fifteenth-century heroine dies before a limited marriage; her mother, the nation-builder, survives. The work contrasts the attraction of Tristan and Iseult or Helen of Troy stories as models for romance with the managerial stolidity of marriage as her mother knows it. Although unfinished, the work asks questions that Woolf's whole oeuvre answers. "The Journal of Mistress Joan Martyn," ed. Susan M. Squier and Louise A. DeSalvo, *Twentieth Century Literature* 25, 3/4 (Fall/ Winter 1979): 237–69.

  3. Virginia Woolf, *Moments of Being,* ed. Jeanne Schulkind (New York: Harcourt Brace Jovanovich, 1976), p. 169. Carolyn Heilbrun has analyzed the critique of masculinist values, especially sexual polarization and bellicose phallicism, that distinguished Bloomsbury's ethical vision of androgynous people. *Toward a Recognition of Androgyny* (New York: Harper and Row, Publishers, 1973), p. 126.

  4. Woolf speaks of this change in her essay "Women and Fiction," stating that in novels in the future, "men and women will not be observed wholly in relation to each other emotionally, but as they cohere and clash in groups and classes and races." The citations, from the essays cited as epigrams: "The Narrow Bridge of Art" and "Women and Fiction," in *Granite and Rainbow* (New York: Harcourt, Brace and Company, 1958), pp. 19, 83.

  5. The interpretation views the delegitimation of the romance plot as a conscious act of expression; it might be well to note Mark Spilka's analysis. He views the absence of romance as one of the unintended results of unexpressed grief and feels that Woolf longed to uphold a "faith in romantic love" but that her life's circumstances impeded her. *Virginia Woolf's Quarrel with Grieving* (Lincoln: University of Nebraska Press, 1980), pp. 72–73.

  6. This essayistic set piece (*VO,* 96), a letter of Helen's, was troublesome writing for Woolf, who even herself felt it to be "an experiment." Yet she did not solve the compositional problems by cutting this section out (Quentin Bell, *Virginia Woolf: A Biography,* vol. I [London: The Hogarth Press, 1972], p. 211). Quite the contrary; she needed these opinions to be stated by a sympathetic character and not questioned, as they might have been if offered in conversation.

  7. *The Letters of Virginia Woolf, Volume One, 1888–1912 (Virginia Stephen),* ed. Nigel Nicolson and Joanne Trautmann (New York: Harcourt Brace Jovanovich, 1975), letter #187, 1 Nov. 1904, p. 150. The story of the deaths is harrowing no matter how often it is told. There is no doubt that Woolf is here transposing some of the material and pain from her early family life, including the deaths of Stella Duckworth, her half-sister, three months after her marriage (1897), and of Thoby Stephen, her brother, dead of typhoid contracted on a journey (1906), not to speak of her mother's (1895) and her father's (1904). Each death, save perhaps her father's, was more senseless and

unexpected than the last. In three of the illnesses, as Bell points out, there was a strong retrospective sense of a case bungled by the attending physician (Bell, *Biography*, vol. I, p. 110). This, too, enters into *The Voyage Out;* the French doctor, belatedly summoned, could never cure what the hairy Spanish doctor had exacerbated as a spreader of infection.

8. "A Sketch of the Past," in *Moments of Being: Unpublished Autobiographical Writings*, ed. Jeanne Schulkind (New York: Harcourt Brace Jovanovich, 1976), p. 117.

9. "Tyranny" (actually "tyrant") from "Modern Fiction," in *The Common Reader* (New York: Harcourt, Brace and World, Inc., 1925), p. 153; "satisfactory solutions" from *A Writer's Diary*, ed. Leonard Woolf (New York: Harcourt, Brace and Company, 1953), p. 10. As Woolf viewed the matter soon after completing *Night and Day*, her originality lay in the rejection of the "happy answers" or "satisfactory solutions" of social insertion and successful quest, not answers "one would accept, if one had the least respect for one's soul."

10. Phyllis Rose, *Woman of Letters: A Life of Virginia Woolf* (New York: Oxford University Press, 1978), p. 15. Rose also points to the nineteenth-century education that Rachel has received.

11. This aspect of my interpretation—death because of the repressions of patriarchal education, and therefore Rachel's incomplete entrance into critique—should be distinguished from Mitchell Leaska's interpretation of "self-willed death," a suicide of escape from pressures, to protect Rachel's core identity and to avoid sexuality. Mitchell A. Leaska, *The Novels of Virginia Woolf: From Beginning to End* (New York: John Jay Press, 1977), p. 38.

12. For example, "All the most individual and humane of his friends were bachelors and spinsters; indeed he was surprised to find that the women he most admired and knew best were unmarried women. Marriage seemed to be worse for them than it was for men" (*VO*, 241).

13. The composition process, its taxing cost, and its possible meanings are scrupulously traced in Louise DeSalvo, *Virginia Woolf's First Voyage: A Novel in the Making* (Totowa, N.J.: Rowman and Littlefield, 1980). These revisions have received a good deal of forceful comment from both DeSalvo and Leaska. The Earlier Typescript reads: "'Oh Helen, Helen!' She could hear Rachel gasping as she rolled her, 'Don't! For God sake! Stop! I'll tell you a secret! I'm going—to—be—married!' Helen paused with one hand upon Rachel's throat holding her head down among the grasses. 'You think I didn't know that!' she cried." But the final version (here the 1920 Doran edition) reads, "[Rachel] thought she heard them speak of love and then of marriage" (*VO* 284). The Earlier Typescript cited from Leaska, *The Novels of Virginia Woolf*, pp. 35–36.

14. Katherine Mansfield review, *Athenaeum*, 21 Nov. 1919, reprinted in *Virginia Woolf: The Critical Heritage*, ed. Robin Majumdar and Allen McLaurin (London: Routledge & Kegan Paul, 1975), p. 82. Mansfield concludes, "In the midst of our admiration, it makes us feel old and chill. . . . " Woolf knew the review, was "irritated" by it, and struggled with her jealous but not foolish sense of a quota system for public recognition of the women writers with whom she was most engaged: Mansfield and Dorothy Richardson. *The Diary of Virginia Woolf, Volume One: 1915–1919*, ed. Anne Olivier Bell (New York: Harcourt Brace Jovanovich, 1977), pp. 314–15. Bell citation from the *Biography*, vol. II, p. 42.

15. Winifred Holtby, an early critic of Woolf, interestingly emphasizes this

self-unification at the expense of the marriage plot: "a union not so much of a man with a woman, as of a man with himself, a woman with herself." *Virginia Woolf* (London: Wishart & Co., 1932), p. 93.

16. Avrom Fleishman has written about the book's abundant allusions to Shakespeare's festive and romantic comedies. His analysis of "comic vision and imaginative transformation . . . under the spell of love's illusions" is consistent with this argument. However, for him, love only, and not vocation, gives meaning. *Virginia Woolf: A Critical Reading* (Baltimore: The Johns Hopkins University Press, 1975), p. 28. Jane Marcus sees the work in the tradition of *The Magic Flute,* an "initiation into society, courtship, and marriage," as well as an initiation through quest. "Enchanted Organs, Magic Bells: *Night and Day* as Comic Opera," in *Virginia Woolf: Revaluation and Continuity,* ed. Ralph Freedman (Berkeley: University of California Press, 1980), p. 102.

17. Here as elsewhere my discussion of hierogamic marriage plots draws on Evelyn Hinz, "Hierogamy versus Wedlock: Types of Marriage Plots and Their Relationship to Genres of Prose Fiction," *PMLA* 91, 5 (October 1976): 900–913.

18. Margaret Comstock suggests that *Night and Day* rescripts the novel in a slightly different fashion, by giving it a double happy ending, marriage in one case, and successful political work in another, so that the single woman, Mary Datchet, has as happy an ending as the engaged couple. "'The current answers don't do': The Comic Form of *Night and Day,*" *Women's Studies* 4 (1977): 169.

19. "Personal relations, we recall, have limits," this passage in "Phases of Fiction" begins. And it ends, significantly for Woolf's project as a novelist, "Thus, it is possible to ask not that [Austen's] world shall be improved or altered (that our satisfaction forbids) but that another shall be struck off, whose constitution shall be different and shall allow of the other relations." *Granite and Rainbow,* pp. 117–18.

20. *"Jane Eyre* and *Wuthering Heights,"* in *The Common Reader,* p. 161.

21. "Modern Fiction," in *The Common Reader,* pp. 153–54. In a later chapter, I shall discuss the influence of Dorothy Richardson's project on this aspect of Woolf's.

22. Phyllis Rose discusses the essay as evidence of Woolf's own struggle— visible also in "Professions for Women"—between "a pre-existing (masculine) model of the well-made novel whose norms she has internalized and against whose authority she has begun to rebel." *Woman of Letters,* pp. 97–102.

23. "Women and Fiction," in *Granite and Rainbow,* p. 81.

24. *Moments of Being,* pp. 124–26, describes a typical scene between father and daughter. Woolf's intense rage and intense muteness constitute a crucial nexus in the formation of a female writer. See also Bell, *Biography,* vol. I, p. 63; my idea was inspired by Berenice A. Carroll, "'To Crush Him in Our Own Country': The Political Thought of Virginia Woolf," *Feminist Studies* 4, 1 (February 1978): 99–131.

25. Woolf, *A Writer's Diary* (June 1923), p. 57. The term "double" is also Woolf's, in her brief introduction to the novel, written in 1928, in *Virginia Woolf: A Collection of Criticism,* ed. Thomas S. W. Lewis (New York: McGraw-Hill Book Company, 1975), p. 36. This kind of structural idea had been dormant for years. A letter of 1903 to Violet Dickinson is extraordinarily suggestive of the tensions of *Mrs. Dalloway,* for in that letter Woolf plays with the idea of a couple that never forms, yet that remains the center of narrative attention. "I'm going to have a man and a woman—show them growing up—

never meeting—not knowing each other—but all the time you'll feel them come nearer and nearer. This will be the real exciting part (as you'll see)—but when they almost meet—only a door between—you see how they just miss—and go off at a tangent, and never come anywhere near again." Cited in Bell, *Biography,* vol. I, p. 125.

26. Phyllis Rose argues that the name Clarissa alludes to the Richardson heroine, who, after long resistance, suffers sexual violation, and that Clarissa's avoidance of intense sexuality and thralldom in love is a strategy to preserve her "sense of autonomy and selfhood." *Woman of Letters,* p. 144. Blanche Gelfant has discussed the way coercion and the desire to absorb and dominate are expressed in some of the love bonds in this novel. "Love and Conversion in *Mrs. Dalloway,*" *Criticism* VIII (Summer 1966): 229–45.

27. A number of studies point to the polarization of values by sex. Lee R. Edwards makes a subtle reading in which the feminine is seen as less implicated in the egotistical desire for power and dominance, and is offered not as a new absolute and inflexible standard, but as contributing to a society "in which the having of power is no longer paramount." "War and Roses: The Politics of *Mrs. Dalloway,*" in *The Authority of Experience: Essays in Feminist Criticism,* ed. Arlyn Diamond and Lee Edwards (Amherst: University of Massachusetts Press, 1977), p. 163. Jeremy Hawthorn sees that Woolf associates "atomism" and "division and compartmentalisation" with masculinity, authority, and the state, and unity and synthesis with the feminine, expressed in Clarissa's party. *Virginia Woolf's Mrs. Dalloway: A Study in Alienation* (Sussex: Sussex University Press, 1975), p. 88. With the feminine-masculine polarity, Woolf emphasizes the pernicious influence of dominant values and suggests that the marginal and powerless—among these, women and the mad—are the only social repository of countervailing values. This group can be activated, as Alex Zwerdling suggests, because of a historical crisis in the postwar period that finds a complacent governing class in decline, losing hegemony. "*Mrs. Dalloway* and the Social System," *PMLA* 92, 1 (January 1977): 69–81.

28. With a greater Stracheyan emphasis on the satiric reading of *Mrs. Dalloway,* Rachel Brownstein offers two observations that intersect with the argument here. First, the weakness, age, and partial complicity of Mrs. Dalloway in the false virtues of her society occur as Woolf's revisions of the ideal of the heroine. Second, the party at the novel's end is an exact substitute for the marriage of traditional courtship plots: "But unlike a marriage, it is a temporary union of a group, not a couple, sanctioned by no gods, and it changes nothing by occurring." *Becoming a Heroine: Reading About Women in Novels* (New York: The Viking Press, 1982), p. 269.

29. "Tunnelling process," from *A Writer's Diary,* pp. 59, 60. First, this is "how I dig out beautiful caves behind my characters: I think this gives exactly what I want; humanity, humour, depth. The idea is that the caves shall connect . . ."; it is elaborated as "my tunnelling process, by which I tell the past by installments, as I have need of it." J. Hillis Miller discusses this technique in "Virginia Woolf's All Souls' Day: The Omniscient Narrator in *Mrs. Dalloway,*" in *The Shaken Realist: Essays in Modern Literature in Honor of Frederck J. Hoffman,* ed. Melvin J. Friedman and John B. Vickery (Baton Rouge: Louisiana State University Press, 1970), pp. 100–27.

30. *To the Lighthouse* will be discussed at greater length in chapter 6, with other *Künstlerromane* by women writers.

31. The project was then called *Jessamy Brides* (*A Writer's Diary,* p. 104). It is

well established that the book was inspired by Woolf's relationship with Vita Sackville-West. Indeed, Vita Sackville-West teasingly responded to this work, suggesting that Woolf's creation was a rival for Woolf's love: "Also, you have invented a new form of Narcissism,—I confess,—I am in love with Orlando— this is a complication I had not foreseen." *The Letters of Virginia Woolf, Volume Three,* ed. Nigel Nicolson and Joanne Trautmann (New York: Harcourt Brace Jovanovich, 1977), p. 574. Much of the detail of the book is based on Vita's history of the Sackville family and on her personal life. Frank Baldanza, "*Orlando* and the Sackvilles," *PMLA* LXX (1955): 274–79. See also Joanne Trautmann, *The Jessamy Brides: The Friendship of Virginia Woolf and Vita Sackville-West* (University Park, Pa.: The Pennsylvania State University Press, 1973), pp. 41–48.

32. John Graham makes an elegant case for the biographical genre parodied ("The 'Caricature Value' of Parody and Fantasy in *Orlando,*" *University of Toronto Quarterly* XXX [July 1961]: 345–66). Fleishman sets this "parodic cultural history" in the context of the "encyclopedic" mode of modernism, also considering the work as a mock biography and a *Künstlerroman* (*Virginia Woolf,* pp. x, 139, 148). Trautmann offers a virtually exhaustive list of genres in *Jessamy Brides:* "a parody of biography, an essay in the exotic, a mock-heroic novel of ideas, an imaginative literary and social history of England, and a biography of Vita Sackville-West" (p. 40). J. J. Wilson makes a dashing case for *Orlando* as mainly an antinovel because it is a satire on literary convention (*New Feminist Essays on Virginia Woolf,* ed. Jane Marcus [Lincoln: University of Nebraska Press, 1981], p. 174). All are quite correct.

33. "Ambisexual" is Blanche Wiesen Cook's useful term in "'Women Alone Stir My Imagination': Lesbianism and the Cultural Tradition," *Signs* 4, 4 (Summer 1979): 723.

34. This analysis draws on Nancy Jay, "Gender and Dichotomy," *Feminist Studies* 7, 1 (Spring 1981): 38–56. In a context of argument similar to the general framework I have offered, Mary Jacobus, seeing a woman writer as both critic and inheritor, reads androgyny as "a Utopian vision of undivided consciousness," healing the split brought about by women's dual status. Mary Jacobus, "The Difference of View," in *Women Writing and Writing about Women,* ed. Mary Jacobus (London: Croom Helm, 1979), p. 20.

35. The utopian and critical hope presented in the idea of androgyny was eloquently presented by Carolyn G. Heilbrun in *Toward a Recognition of Androgyny* (New York: Harper and Row, Publishers, 1973).

36. Barbara Fassler has argued that the depiction and integration of masculine and feminine traits or any use of "opposite-sex character traits" would imply homosexuality. "Theories of Homosexuality as Sources of Bloomsbury's Androgyny," *Signs* 5, 2 (Winter 1979): 237–51.

37. The poem cited at the beginning of Woolf's Chapter 6 in the "contraband" section comes from Vita Sackville-West's work *The Land.* If one reads just a few lines beyond the four that Woolf cited, the tempting and exotic imagery alludes to lesbian desire. The foreign girl, "sulky, dark, and quaint" is "Dangerous too, as a girl might sidle up, / An Egyptian girl, with an ancient snaring spell, / Throwing a net, soft round the limbs and heart. . . ." The poem is found in Vita Sackville-West, *Collected Poems,* Vol. I (London: The Hogarth Press, 1933), p. 58. Sackville-West's ambivalent attitude toward the temptations corresponds to her sense of division. Barbara Fassler discusses this passage in the context of Sackville-West's lesbianism, linking it to the

allusions in popular and poetic myth to the Southern and Oriental "sotadic zones," where homosexuality is more dominant, according to theories popular since the 1890s. *Signs* 5, 2 (Winter 1979): 244–46.

38. H.D.'s companion Winifred Bryher wrote in *Two Selves* (Paris: Contact Editions, 1923) that she was really a "boy" unfortunately caged in the body of a girl.

39. Sigmund Freud, "The Psychogenesis of a Case of Homosexuality in a Woman" (1920), *Collected Papers*, Vol. II (London: The Hogarth Press, 1957).

40. Susan Gubar's tracing of culturally different "sapphistries" pointedly reminds us that the lesbian as a cultural and sexual identity has been constructed and utilized in various ways by writers. "Sapphistries," forthcoming, *Signs*.

5. Romantic Thralldom and "Subtle Genealogies" in H.D.

1. H.D., "Compassionate Friendship" (1955), Uncatalogued Typescript, Hilda Doolittle–Norman Holmes Pearson Collection, Collection of American Literature, the Beinecke Rare Book and Manuscript Library, Yale University, p. 30.

2. Ibid., p. 36. "Lord Howell" is H.D.'s name for Lord Hugh Dowding, Air Marshal during the Battle of Britain. In "Hilda in Egypt," Albert Gelpi has proposed a distinction between the soldier-"lover" and the occult-poetic types in H.D.'s ties to men. *The Southern Review* 18, 2 (Spring 1982): 233–50.

3. With Macpherson, among others. "Companionate women" is a phrase from Blanche Wiesen Cook, "The Historical Denial of Lesbianism," *Radical History Review* 20 (Spring/Summer 1979): 60. For biographical clarifications I have drawn on Susan Stanford Friedman, *Psyche Reborn: The Emergence of H.D.* (Bloomington: Indiana University Press, 1981), pp. 5, 303. From 1946 on, H.D. lived "alone most of the time" ("A Friendship Traced: H.D. Letters to Silvia Dobson," ed. Carol Tinker with notes by Silvia Dobson, *Conjunctions* 2 [Summer 1982]: 144).

4. This argument was first offered, in a different tonal and structural context, in my essay "Family, Sexes, Psyche: an essay on H.D. and the muse of the woman writer," *Montemora* 6 (1979): 136–56.

5. Some of the following analysis of H.D.'s novels, especially of *HERmione*, was developed independently, some in collaboration with Susan Friedman; we are sharing, for our scholarly work, the coauthored materials. Friedman and DuPlessis, "'I Had Two Loves Separate': The Sexualities of H.D.'s *Her*," *Montemora* 8 (1981): 7–30.

6. The reference to the "madrigal cycle" is in her memoir "Thorn Thicket" (1960), Uncatalogued Typescript, Beinecke Library. Information about her life and the composition of *Bid Me to Live (A Madrigal)* (New York: Grove Press, 1960; henceforth abbreviated as *BMTL*) comes largely from H.D.'s "Autobiographical Notes," p. 34, and her correspondence with Aldington and Bryher. Friedman suggests that H.D. may have begun the novel while in analysis with Freud in 1933 and 1934, because her letters to Bryher during this period refer to Freud's suggestion that she write of the World War I period to free herself of her writer's block.

7. This summary of events was developed jointly with Friedman. The sequence is as follows: H.D.'s love for and engagement to Ezra Pound (1906–1907); her parallel and competing love for Frances Josepha Gregg; the disin-

tegration of her engagement; her voyage to Europe with Gregg in 1911; Gregg's return to America and marriage to Louis Wilkinson; H.D.'s life as a woman in the European artistic milieu; her first publication (1913) in *Poetry* as "H.D., Imagiste," under Pound's aegis; her marriage to Richard Aldington later that year; her first pregnancy, ending traumatically with a stillborn child in 1914; the First World War and Aldington's service in the trenches; the dissolution of the imagist circle; Aldington's and H.D.'s affairs and the disintegration of their marriage during 1917–18; H.D.'s relationship with Bryher established during her second pregnancy in 1918; H.D.'s near fatal illness, the birth of her baby, and paternity questions in 1919; Bryher's role as physical and spiritual rescuer of the grimly depressed H.D.; their idyllic month in the Scilly Isles (May 1919), which created a bond to be maintained until H.D.'s death in 1961. See also Barbara Guest, *Herself Defined: The Poet H.D. and Her World* (New York: Doubleday & Co., Inc., 1984).

8. Entitled *Her* by H.D., the book was published as *HERmione* in order not to be confused with Lawrence Ferlinghetti's book of the same name on the New Directions list. This ingenious solution had the imprimatur of Perdita Schaffner. *HERmione* (1927; New York: New Directions, 1981; henceforth *H*).

9. The other novels of the cycle are *Paint It Today* (1921), *Asphodel* (in two parts, 1921–22), and *HERmione.* H.D. was quite conscious of her "cut" of this material, created by her choice to end *Bid Me to Live* before the date when Bryher entered this biographical sequence. She states in "Thorn Thicket": "Bryher came into the *Madrigal* cycle, July 17, 1918, but I do not bring her into the story. The story ends with the letter that Julia [H.D.] writes to Frederico or Lorenzo [Lawrence]. He had been dead 17 years," p. 28. In the *Montemora* study, Friedman and I speculate why H.D. saw fit to draw on only the "heterosexual" elements of this sequence for her published work.

10. Their relationship was what Perdita Schaffner calls an "*amitié amoreuse*" in "A Profound Animal," her important memoir of "the other Bloomsbury," which movingly discusses her mother and her discovery of her biological father. *Bid Me to Live* (Redding Ridge, Ct.: Black Swan Books, 1983), pp. 185, 186.

11. "Rico could write elaborately on the woman mood, describe women to their marrow in his writing; but if she turned round, wrote the Orpheus part of her Orpheus-Eurydice sequence, he snapped back, 'Stick to the woman-consciousness, it is the intuitive woman-mood that matters.' He was right about that, of course. But if he could enter, so diabolically, into the feelings of women, why should not she enter into the feelings of men?" (*BMTL,* 62).

12. First published in May 1917, "Eurydice," in H.D., *Collected Poems 1912–1944,* ed. Louis L. Martz (New York: New Directions, 1983; henceforth *CP*), pp. 51–55. A further elaboration of the questions this poem raises for the retelling of mythic narrative will be made in chapter 7. "Callypso Speaks" (a manuscript from the mid-1930s, newly published in full in the Martz edition) is another poem of female anger that retells and reverses a myth. The work represents a failed dialogue between the nymph and Odysseus; male and female speak different languages. See Friedman's analysis of this poem in *Psyche Reborn,* pp. 236–45.

13. From "Sea Rose": "Stunted, with small leaf, / you are flung on the sand"; from "Sea Lily": "Yet though the whole wind / slash at your bark, / you are lifted up"; from "Garden": "You are clear / O rose, cut in rock, / hard as the descent of hail" (*Collected Poems,* pp. 5, 14, 24). Georgia O'Keeffe's hard-

edged, sensuous flower paintings, roughly contemporaneous with H.D.'s poems, come to mind as a parallel appropriation of forms iconographically associated with the feminine, and their transformation into icons of female power. O'Keeffe's flower paintings are statements of grandeur, so massive that they preempt the whole field of vision, excluding everything that is not flower. In contrast, H.D. is acutely aware of the shaping, sculpting forces against which these flowers are poised.

14. For this aspect of the novel, underemphasized here, see the rich discussion of the maternal, semiotic register in H.D.'s language and texts in Deborah Kelly Kloepfer, "Flesh Made Word: Maternal Inscription in H.D.," *Sagetrieb* 3, 1 (Spring 1984): 27–48.

15. Fayne is a version of Frances Josepha Gregg, also mentioned in H.D.'s *End to Torment* (New York: New Directions, 1979) and *Tribute to Freud* (1956) (Boston: David Godine, 1974), who continued to appear at the fringes of H.D.'s circle for many years. A writer herself, she published in *The Egoist* and other little magazines. Hinting to Silvia Dobson that the relationship with Frances was a "'love terrible with banners,'" of the type that occurs only a few times in a life, H.D. goes on to say that Frances "took the 'wrong turning' toward prudery and convention and it didn't do anybody any good." This probably refers to her marriage. "A Friendship Traced," p. 117.

16. In "Paint It Today," the meeting of the H.D. figure with the Gregg figure is compared in its impact to the conversion of Paul of Tarsus, an illumination of paradigm-changing force. (Unpublished Typescript, Chapter I, 8). In "Asphodel," the following declaration is made:

> I, Hermione, tell you I love you Fayne Rabb. Men and women will come and say I love you. . . . Men will say I love you Hermione but will anyone ever say I love you Fayne as I say it? [. . .] I don't want to be (as they say crudely) a boy. Nor do I want you to so be. I don't feel a girl. What is all this trash of Sappho? None of that seems real, to (in any way) matter. I see you. I feel you. My pulse runs swiftly. My brain reaches some height of delirium [.] Do people say it's indecent? Maybe it is. I can't hear now see any more, people." (Unpublished Typscript, pp. 96–97)

In this passage the category "lesbian" as contemporaneously understood—the woman who is "really" a man—is rejected, while the emotions of love for a woman are embraced. In the same way the "Sapphic" is rejected, while H.D. recapitulates one of Sappho's famous love poems in her racing prose. Both typescripts, Beinecke Library, Yale University.

17. The poem quoted here and throughout *HERmione* is Algernon Swinburne's "Itylus," from his *Poems and Ballads, First Series* (London: Chatto & Windus, 1904), vol. I, pp. 54–55. Based on the Philomela myth, the poem explores the tabooed erotic attraction between women. H.D.'s decision to weave lines from Swinburne's poem throughout may well have been influenced by her friend Havelock Ellis's identification of Swinburne as one "among poets who have used the motive of homosexuality in women with more or less boldness." See Ellis, *Studies in the Psychology of Sex* (New York: Random House, 1905), vol. I, p. 200. The sister and swallow imagery, so prominent in "Itylus," was connected not only with Gregg but also with Bryher. In our *Montemora* article, Friedman has suggested that Fayne Rabb may well be a composite of both Gregg and Bryher. H.D.'s lyrical description of the

"sisters'" ecstatic moments evoked the month H.D. and Bryher spent in Corn-
wall in May 1919.

18. Catharine Stimpson, "Zero Degree Deviancy: The Lesbian Novel in
English," *Critical Inquiry* 8, 2 (Winter 1981): 366–67. "Does the kiss encode
transgression or permissibility? Singularity or repeatability? Impossibility or
possibility? . . . Does the kiss predict the beginning of the end, or the end of
the beginning, or a lesbian erotic enterprise? Or is it the event that literally
embraces contradictions?" asks Stimpson eloquently, in a discussion of kisses
exchanged in Stein's *Q.E.D.* and in two works by Virginia Woolf: "Slater's Pins
Have No Points" and *Mrs. Dalloway.*

19. By operations, abortions are meant.

20. A relevant passage begins with apology and ends with assertion:

> You might be angry with me. You might shrivel my hope. You might say I had
> no business writing of old shoes, ladies-bed-straw and the roots of the furze
> bushes you grubbed up and stacked under the stairs. There are still a few left.
>
> Perhaps you would say I was trespassing, couldn't see both sides, as you
> said of my Orpheus. I could be Eurydice in character, you said, but woman-is-
> woman and I couldn't be both. The *gloire* is both.
>
> *(BMTL,* 176)

21. *Notes on Thought and Vision* was recently published by City Lights Books,
but I am quoting the Unpublished Typescript in the Collection of American
Literature, Beinecke Rare Book and Manuscript Library, Yale University, p. 2.

22. Nancy Jay, "Gender and Dichotomy," *Feminist Studies* 7, 1 (Spring
1981): 38–56.

23. These transpositions were not only humble, but had a certain grandeur. Her claim to be a prophet—not unfamiliar to modernism, but one that,
made by a woman (rather than Pound, Lawrence, Yeats, Eliot), might seem
more garish than parallel claims by male poets—Freud taxed as
"megalomania." *Tribute to Freud,* p. 51. Susan Friedman and I discuss the way
Freud seems to have tried to defuse this claim in her analysis, and the ways
H.D. reasserts it in her poem to Freud, "The Master." "'Woman is Perfect':
H.D.'s Debate with Freud," *Feminist Studies* 7, 3 (Fall 1981): 417–30.

24. H.D., *End To Torment* (1958) (New York: New Directions, 1979), pp. 57–
58. H.D., *Helen in Egypt* (New York: New Directions, 1961; henceforth *H in E*).

25. Friedman reports that Dowding "had been relieved of his post as Chief
Air Marshal of the Royal Air Force shortly after his victory in the Battle of
Britain," because of his active advocacy of spiritualism. *Psyche Reborn,* p. 173.

26. Dowding's brush-off was a revelation that conventional sexual politics
operate in the spiritual realm, which H.D. had felt was exempt. See "The
Sword Went Out to Sea (Synthesis of a Dream)" [late 1940], pp. 173, 177, and
"Compassionate Friendship" (1955), pp. 78–79. Also see Friedman, pp. 174–
75.

27. Though Heydt was an analyst, he and H.D. did not have a doctor-
patient relationship. In the words of Perdita Schaffner, "They contracted a
great friendship" (personal communication, May 9, 1978).

28. She felt, in fact, that he had betrayed their "compassionate friendship."
"Erich did very well as my model for Paris, in the second part of my *Helen*
sequence. I only began writing the poems, as a continuation of the first Helen,
after he had gone away . . . leaving me with a quarrel or half-quarrel on my
hands," she wrote in 1953. "Compassionate Friendship," p. 78.

29. The phrase is from Ellen Moers, *Literary Women* (Garden City, N.Y.: Doubleday & Company, Inc., 1976), p. 123.

30. To indicate H.D.'s interest in a revisionary Helen, this note on a film is revealing: "they always make H. of T. [Helen of Troy] a cutie—is it the male conception? She was a Spartan, a goddess, etc. Well—I suppose mere-man can not swallow that." Letter to Norman Holmes Pearson, January 31, 1956, Beinecke Library, Yale University.

31. "[The woman writer] will find that she is perpetually wishing to alter the established values—to make serious what appears insignificant to a man, and trivial what to him is important." "Women and Fiction," in *Granite and Rainbow* (New York: Harcourt, Brace and Company, 1958), p. 81. The related passage in *A Room of One's Own* indicates that female sensibility ranged "among almost unknown or unrecorded things; it lighted on small things and showed that perhaps they were not small after all." *A Room of One's Own* (New York: Harcourt, Brace and World, 1929), p. 96.

32. The contrast between the hegemonic and the alternative is evoked by H.D.'s allusions to hieroglyphics and other forms of secret, encoded writing (zodiac in Part II, eidolon in Part III); hieroglyphics suggest an Egyptian mystery to balance and challenge the Greek authority of the text as we know it. As *picture* writing, furthermore, hieroglyphics may have seemed closer to the original strata of mind, a better epistemological source than the stages of narrative because closer to an intuitive flash. One recalls the prominence visualization plays in H.D.'s imaginative life, as in the "Corfu incident," recorded in *Tribute to Freud,* when H.D. saw visionary symbols projected on a wall, and her companion, Bryher, actually completed the vision when H.D. could see no more.

33. Susan Gubar offers an opposite interpretation of this line, while retaining the emphasis on woman as text. In the course of an argument that female protagonists mirror the status of the female author in culture—reified into an object, the creation, not the creator—Gubar identifies a series of female heroes and authors, including H.D.'s Helen, entrapped or "framed" into an unyielding story of womanhood, which links "female sexuality with textuality." My emphasis differs. Rather the line is optimistic and spoken in wonder; to become "writing" is to move beyond the thralldom of former plots that limit Helen to her sexuality and to the old story in which this was imbedded. Susan Gubar, "'The Blank Page' and the Issues of Female Creativity," *Critical Inquiry* 8, 2 (Winter 1981): 245, 254–55.

34. Susan Friedman has a parallel formulation: "H.D. centered her mythmaking in the 'rectification' of tradition itself." *Psyche Reborn*, pp. 243–44.

35. Although Achilles is based on Lord Dowding, it is also possible to associate him with the Aldington of the World War I era, viewing the character as a rescue operation performed on the memory of the terrible masculine husband who enjoyed returning to the front.

36. Thus the poem is not only about a woman slowly learning her story, but also about a man convinced of the correctness of the woman's story; like H.D.'s poem "The Master," it contains a muted fantasy or compensatory myth in which men take a totally different orientation to reality after the intervention of such a cogent female myth that males are converted. "The Master" was first published in *Feminist Studies* 7, 3 (Fall 1981): 407–16.

37. Norman Holmes Pearson makes the identification of Theseus with Freud in the interview conducted by L. S. Dembo, *Contemporary Literature* X, 4 (Autumn 1969): 443.

38. ". . . her wings are folded about her / and her wings only un-furl // at the cry of the New Mortal / or the child's pitiful call . . ." (*H in E*, 300).

39. Most often in H.D.'s poems, the child is male. Only in *Helen in Egypt* is the child both male and female, an additional complexity in the subtle genealogy that parallels Theseus's dual role as father and mother, and makes of Helen the absolute center of, and collection point for, the two sexes.

40. The fusion Helen-Hellas is analyzed by H.D. as an amalgam of a triple woman: "Helen is my mother's name + Hellas is Greece + Bryher, Perdita + I." *Hirslanden-Zurich Notebooks* (1957), Four Autograph Manuscripts, The Beinecke Library, Yale University, Notebook III, p. 27.

41. Norman Holmes Pearson, "Foreword" to H.D., *Hermetic Definition* (New York: New Directions, 1972), [p. viii]. "Winter Love" is the third poem in this book.

6. To "bear my mother's name"

1. There are two parallel discussions of the *Künstlerroman*. Grace Stewart discusses mother-daughter ties as "often central to the novel of the artist as heroine," but focuses on their negative character. *A New Mythos: The Novel of the Artist as Heroine, 1877–1977* (St. Alban's, Vt.: Eden Press Women's Publications, Inc., 1979), p. 41. In another consideration of this topic, Susan Gubar argues that two scripts felt to have been absolute alternatives—artistic production and biological reproduction—are joined in twentieth-century women's *Künstlerromane*, allowing female images of creativity to dominate the works. "The Birth of the Artist as Heroine: (Re)production, the *Künstlerroman* Tradition, and the Fiction of Katherine Mansfield," in *The Representation of Women in Fiction*, ed. Carolyn G. Heilbrun and Margaret R. Higonnet (Baltimore: The John Hopkins University Press, 1983): pp. 19–59.

2. A note on terminology. "Female artist" will refer only to the fictional figure; the person who invented the narrative is a woman writer. "Art work" will mean the imaginary text, painting, or performance described, the production of the female artist.

3. Janet Wolff, *The Social Production of Art* (London: Macmillan Press, Ltd., 1981), p. 27.

4. Elizabeth Barrett Browning, *Aurora Leigh and Other Poems*, introduced by Cora Kaplan (London: The Woman's Press, Ltd., 1978; henceforth *AL*).

5. Although, by its focus on closure, my interpretation emphasizes the relations of romance, this work, like *Jane Eyre*, has a powerful subtext of female love-hate relations among the women of all three social classes. Especially the tie between Marian Earle ("a monumental Madonna") and Aurora is discussed by Nina Auerbach, *Woman and the Demon: The Life of a Victorian Myth* (Cambridge: Harvard University Press, 1982), p. 151.

6. Cora Kaplan is admirable on this point, as on many others in her introduction.

7. In another reading, it is heterosexual romance that becomes a metaphor for creative identity. For Barbara Charlesworth Gelpi, Romney is first the interior, self-hating critic and then a "dramatic projection of . . . blind faith" in oneself. "*Aurora Leigh:* The Vocation of the Woman Poet," *Victorian Poetry* 19, 1 (Spring 1981): 48.

8. But this was also a shocking affirmation, for it violated "the social and public silence of women after puberty which was central to the construction of femininity in the nineteenth century." The Marxist Feminist Literature Col-

lective, "Women's Writing: Jane Eyre, Shirley, Villette, Aurora Leigh," in *1848: The Sociology of Literature,* ed. Francis Barker (Colchester: University of Essex, 1978), p. 202.

9. Elaine Showalter, *A Literature of Their Own: British Women Novelists from Brontë to Lessing* (Princeton, N.J.: Princeton University Press, 1977), p. 152.

10. Fanny Fern [Mrs. Sarah Payson (Willis) Parton], *Ruth Hall: A Domestic Tale of the Present Time* (New York: Mason Brothers, 1855), p. 333.

11. Rebecca Harding Davis, "The Wife's Story," *The Atlantic Monthly* XIV, 81 (July 1864): 1–19; abbreviated as "TWS."

12. Kate Chopin, *The Awakening* (New York: Capricorn Books, 1964).

13. Sarah Grand, *The Beth Book: Being a Study of the Life of Elizabeth Caldwell Maclure, A Woman of Genius,* with an introduction by Elaine Showalter (New York: The Dial Press, 1980). Abbreviated as *TBB.* Showalter also discusses this work in *A Literature of Their Own.*

14. Elizabeth Stuart Phelps Ward, *The Story of Avis* (Boston: James R. Osgood & Co., 1877), p. 126. Abbreviated as *SA.*

15. A contemporaneous, but unfinished work by Louisa May Alcott takes up the same question, and it is possible that Alcott knew Phelps Ward's work and was responding to it. *Diana and Persis* (1879) concerns two women friends, a sculptor and a painter, one opposed to marriage, the other sure that love could enrich her art. During a debate on whether one must make the either/or choice, Percy's husband says, "I believe a woman can and ought to have both if she has the power and courage to win them. A man expects them, achieves them, why is not a woman's life to be as full and free as his?" (*D&P,* 127). But the fragment is unfinished, and it is not possible to say whether Alcott would have produced the pessimistic "dusty paints" motif or whether she would have tried an allegory of success. Louisa May Alcott, *Diana and Persis* (New York: The Arno Press, 1978).

16. Indeed, in a notable conduct book, a sister writer deplores Phelps Ward's sympathetic depiction of Avis's dilemma, insisting that even an "emancipated schoolgirl" still needs practical knowledge of womanly, domestic tasks. With sharply selective citation, she makes Avis's complaints seem self-indulgent. Marion Harland, *Eve's Daughters, or Common Sense for Maid, Wife and Mother* (New York: J. R. Anderson and H. S. Allen, 1882), p. 326.

17. The same kind of ending is visible in Rebecca Harding Davis, *Earthen Pitchers* (1873–74), which offers similar motifs: the ruining of female talent, the insensitive but ill husband (here he is blind), the heritage in the child.

18. Phelps Ward was presenting a compensatory analysis of her own family. Her exacting and punctilious father had, in her view, stifled the ambitions and spirit of her talented mother, a writer, whose name the eight-year-old Elizabeth took in tribute after her mother's untimely death. The bond between Avis and her daughter takes on an extra dimension in the biographical context, in which the author, a daughter, did feel she was completing her mother's thwarted work. For the biographical information, see Christine Stansell, "Elizabeth Stuart Phelps: A Study in Female Rebellion," in *Women: an Issue,* ed. Lee Edwards, Mary Heath and Lisa Baskin (Boston: Little, Brown and Co., 1972): pp. 239–56. About this, Phelps Ward wrote, "Her last book and her last baby came together, and killed her. She lived one of those rich and piteous lives such as only gifted women know; torn by the civil war of the dual nature which can be given to women only." Cited from Phelps Ward, *Chapters from a Life,* 1897, in the Afterword by Mari Jo Buhle and Florence

Howe to *The Silent Partner* (1871) (Old Westbury: The Feminist Press, 1983), p. 362.

19. Because Avis cites *Aurora Leigh,* it is likely that the subject of her painting was inspired by these lines in Barrett Browning: "Or perhaps again, / In order to discover the Muse—the Sphinx, / the melancholy desert must sweep round, / Behind you as before" (*AL,* 70).

20. Charlotte Perkins Gilman, *The Yellow Wallpaper* (1899) (New York: The Feminist Press, 1973). Abbreviated as "YWP."

21. That powerful and loving doctor/lawgiver is a recurrent figure in women's writing, as in their lives, for he sums up the fascinated ambivalence of male culture toward the ambitious female as speaking subject: Freud and "Dora"; S. Weir Mitchell and Gilman; Otto Rank and Anaïs Nin; Freud and H. D. He recurs, transposed, in the Sir William Bradshaw–Septimus Smith tie in Woolf's *Mrs. Dalloway.*

22. "That one sex should have monopolized all human activities, called them 'man's work,' and managed them as such, is what is meant by the phrase 'Androcentric Culture.'" Referring to the difficulty of even naming "our androcentric culture" in a convincing way, Gilman remarks, "It is no easy matter to deny or reverse a universal assumption." *The Man-Made World, or, Our Androcentric Culture* (New York: Charlton Company, 1911), pp. 25, 21.

23. Raymond Williams, "Base and Superstructure in Marxist Cultural Theory," *New Left Review* 82 (November–December 1973): 9.

24. A veiled citation from ibid.

25. The gloss is Emily Dickinson, 435. "Much Madness is divinest Sense—/ To a discerning Eye—/ Much Sense—the starkest Madness—/ 'Tis the Majority / In this, as All, prevail— / Assent—and you are sane— / Demur—you're straightway dangerous—/ And handled with a Chain—" *The Complete Poems of Emily Dickinson,* ed. Thomas H. Johnson (Boston: Little, Brown and Company, 1960), p. 209.

26. As early motherhood and the strains of domesticity, added to a well-meaning but awkward marriage, overtaxed the ambitious Gilman and contributed to her breakdown, it was not more injunctions to domesticity and femininity that she needed. But this is what S. Weir Mitchell offered his female clients. Mitchell's treatment reflected nineteenth-century attitudes, inducing conformity with the duties of womanhood rather than exploring the conflict and anger within the individual. This point is made by Mary A. Hill, *Charlotte Perkins Gilman: The Making of a Radical Feminist, 1860–1896* (Philadelphia: Temple University Press, 1980), p. 149. In S. Weir Mitchell's home city there is, near 16th on Walnut Street, a plaque commemorating his accomplishments as "physician, physiologist, poet, man of letters" adding, "he taught us the use of rest for the nervous."

27. Gilman, *The Living of Charlotte Perkins Gilman: An Autobiography* (1935) (New York: Harper and Row, Publishers, 1975), pp. 96, 121.

28. After her own first marriage, she sank into a profound depression, which lifted almost the instant she separated from that husband, but whose effects lasted in what she perceived as a compromise of her abilities. Earlier, Gilman has seen her parents' marriage as "a long-drawn, triple tragedy," and said "mother's life was one of the most painfully thwarted I have ever known" *Living,* p. 8. Her mother was a pianist who sold the instrument to pay her bills; again the thwarted mother as artist motivates the achievements of the daughter. Gilman felt that it was possible to combine marriage, motherhood, and

vocation, but in her specific case, "it was not right." This may stem from the self-denial and deprivation to which she subjected herself.

29. Alice Walker, "In Search of Our Mothers' Gardens," in *In Search of Our Mothers' Gardens* (San Diego: Harcourt Brace Jovanovich, 1983), p. 241. Abbreviated as "SMG."

30. In Alice Walker's story "Everyday Use," the maternal heritage of quilts belongs to the down-home daughter, who will use them and who has the skills to replenish the stock, not to the urban chic daughter, who, discovering her rural roots, wants to hang the quilts on the wall and alienate them into quaintness. The story is a revisionary telling of the Jacob-Esau story, in which the matriarch works to equalize the "portion" of both sisters, when the more favored quick child has schemed to take part of that heritage although she does not honor it.

31. Where the writer is also concerned to show the artist completing the work of the thwarted father, the father will come from a historically marginalized, nondominant group. For example, in Doris Lessing's *The Golden Notebook*, the parental couple is transposed to Mother Sugar, Anna's analyst, and Charlie Themba, a (correctly) paranoid African leader. This use of parental figures often involves a distinct rewriting or an idealization, for example, using characters who are surrogate parents or grandparents, generationally displaced, or otherwise reassembled.

32. Virginia Woolf, *To the Lighthouse* (1927) (New York: Harcourt, Brace and World, Inc., 1955). Abbreviated as *TTL*.

33. Jane Lilienfeld forcefully sets the Ramsays in the historical and ideological context of Victorian prescriptive texts on marriage and concludes that Woolf hardly presents a celebration of this oft-debated union but rather a critique of it for its stasis. This presentation of Woolf as a critic of heterosexual institutions and arrangements, and as urging "new modes of human love and partnership" corroborates the position I have taken here. "Where the Spear Plants Grew: The Ramsays' Marriage in *To the Lighthouse*," in *New Feminist Essays on Virginia Woolf*, ed. Jane Marcus (Lincoln: University of Nebraska Press, 1981), pp. 162, 149.

34. It is striking how, in *Moments of Being*, the maternal and the visionary moments are both expressed in the image of a translucent dome of light: the "globular, semi-transparent" early ecstatic sensations, the "arch of glass" that domed Paddington Station, burning and glowing with light. *Moments of Being*, ed. Jeanne Schulkind (New York: Harcourt Brace Jovanovich, 1976), pp. 66, 93. So Mrs. Ramsey at that preoedipal moment of yearning (associated with both hieroglyphs and bees) ends as "the shape of a dome" (*TTL*, 80). This moment may be usefully compared to H.D.'s bell jar and jellyfish submergings into an under-consciousness—amniotic and filled with uneasy messages—as well as with Sylvia Plath's more negative and rejecting use of both the bell jar (as suffocating alienation, as objectification of self) and of the maternal jellyfish, aurelia, in her poem "Medusa." Gayatri C. Spivak's reading of *To the Lighthouse*, in showing how both main characters perceive Mrs. Ramsay, finds that "Woolf's emphasis falls . . . on the workshop of the womb that delivers the work." Thus Woolf's novel provides a (proto-Irigarian) critique of Freud and poses a mother-child dyad in which the child/artist produces the mother as "baby." "Unmaking and Making in *To the Lighthouse*," in *Women and Language in Literature and Society*, ed. Sally McConnell-Ginet, Ruth Borker and Nelly Furman (New York: Praeger Publishers, 1980), p. 324.

35. Virginia Woolf, *A Writer's Diary*, ed. Leonard Woolf (New York: Harcourt, Brace and Company, 1954), pp. 102, 105.

36. How to achieve this ending was the subject of Woolf's entry on 5 September 1926, which interestingly reveals that in the original conception, Lily and her picture were secondary, and "summing up [Mr.] R's character" seemed to be primary. The shift from a patrifocal narrative to one focused on balance between the generations and on the daughter's vision of the mother serves as further evidence of the thesis of this chapter. *Writer's Diary*, p. 98.

37. The fact that naming these feelings made Woolf nervous can be surmised from the critical word that she repeatedly fears will be applied to this novel. The word is "sentimental." Virginia Woolf, *A Writer's Diary*, pp. 98, 100; *The Letters of Virginia Woolf, Volume Two, 1912–1922*, ed. Nigel Nicolson and Joanne Trautmann (New York: Harcourt Brace Jovanovich, 1976), pp. 374, 379.

38. Maurice Beebe, *Ivory Towers and Sacred Founts: The Artist as Hero in Fiction from Goethe to Joyce* (New York: New York University Press, 1964), p. 308. According to Beebe, the hero becomes an artist "only after he has sloughed off the domestic, social, and religious demands imposed upon him by his environment. Narrative development in the typical artist-novel requires that the hero test and reject the claims of love and life, of God, home and country, until nothing is left but his true self and his consecration as an artist," p. 6.

39. Vita Sackville-West, *All Passion Spent* (Garden City, New York: Doubleday, Doran and Company, Inc., 1933), p. 143. Abbreviated as *APS*. Direct influence as well as intricate ties of love and mutual inspiration linked Woolf and Sackville-West during their most productive years. *All Passion Spent*, Louise A. DeSalvo argues, is a fictional treatment of the analysis in *A Room of One's Own;* its key scene draws on *To the Lighthouse*. "Lighting the Cave: The Relationship Between Vita Sackville-West and Virginia Woolf," *Signs* 8, 2 (Winter 1982): 195–214.

40. Margaret Atwood, *Surfacing* (Ontario: Paperjacks, 1973).

41. Christina Stead, *The Man Who Loved Children* (New York: Avon Books, 1966), p. 491. The book contains an imbedded art work—Louie's play, in an invented language, which depicts to her father a distinct, bitter message about the tie between Snake Man and his daughter: "You are killing me" (*MWLC*, 378).

42. See Jane Flax, "The Conflict Between Nurturance and Autonomy in Mother-Daughter Relationships and Within Feminism," and Judith Kegan Gardiner, "A Wake for Mother: The Maternal Deathbed in Women's Fiction," which discusses how "mothers in death embody the negative aspects of female personality and role," both in *Feminist Studies* 4, 2 (June 1978): 171–89; 146–65.

43. Tillie Olsen, "Tell Me a Riddle," in *Tell Me a Riddle* (New York: Dell Publishing Company, 1960), p. 86. Abbreviated as "TMR."

44. The term *Sprechstimme* (literally "speech voice") is a distinctive form of writing for the voice in twentieth-century music. Grove's *Dictionary of Music and Musicians* defines it as a "kind of vocal declamation which partakes of the characteristics of both song and speech."

45. The same multiple populist inspiration, double artist figures, mother-daughter and father-daughter ties, and proliferating works of art occur in Margaret Laurence's *The Diviners* (1974) (New York: Alfred Knopf, 1974). By

stories, ballads, and novels, the politically outcast Canadian strains—Celtic, French, and Indian—are synthesized and become oppositional to the powerful British minority.

46. Tillie Olsen, *Silences* (New York: Delta, 1979), is a book of essays and collaged citations, dedicated jointly to the silenced, whose life is "consumed in the hard, everyday essential work of maintaining human life," and "their kin and descendents," who, in being able to speak, can bear witness "to what was (and still is) being lost, silenced." Quotation in my text from p. 6.

47. Doris Lessing, *The Golden Notebook* (New York: Ballantine Books, 1968).

48. Doris Lessing, *A Small Personal Voice* (New York: Alfred A. Knopf, 1974), pp. 15, 81, 33.

49. Ibid., p. 32.

50. Ibid., p. 81.

51. Ibid., pp. 35, 36.

52. This is cited by John L. Carey from the dust jacket of the British edition of *The Golden Notebook;* "Art and Reality in *The Golden Notebook*," *Contemporary Literature* XIV, 4 (September 1973): 437.

53. In her analysis of artist novels, Gubar calls this "revisionary domestic mythology." *The Representation of Women in Fiction,* p. 39.

54. The particularly privileged mother-daughter connection for creative women was verified in Bell Gale Chevigny's "Daughters Writing: Toward a Theory of Women's Biography," *Feminist Studies* 9, 1 (Spring 1983): 79–102.

55. Judith Kegan Gardiner corroborates this connection between art and life, tracing it to fluid ego boundaries in women's psychological identity. "On Female Identity and Writing by Women," *Critical Inquiry* 8, 2 (Winter 1981): 347–61. In considering stances plausible for a feminist poetics, Lawrence Lipking discusses several issues that this study has also put forth: the pressure on women of an injunction to silence, the personal, rather than objective, stake women have in analyses made of them, and therefore the lack of aesthetic distance and the attempt to build a poetics and a criticism based on affiliation, not authority. "Aristotle's Sister: A Poetics of Abandonment," *Critical Inquiry* 10, 1 (September 1983): 61–81.

56. Herbert Marcuse, "The Affirmative Character of Culture," *Negations: Essays in Critical Theory* (Boston: Beacon Press, 1968), pp. 95–96. One might fruitfully compare the black aesthetic, as enunciated by Gwendolyn Brooks in her introduction to *Jump Bad,* an anthology of black poetry from Chicago. "These black writers do not care if you call their product Art or Peanuts. Artistic survival, appointment to Glory, appointment to Glory among the anointed elders, is neither their crevice [*sic*] nor creed. They give to the ghetto gut. Ghetto gut receives. Ghetto giver's gone." *Report from Part One* (Detroit: Broadside Press, 1972), p. 195.

57. Theodor W. Adorno, "Cultural Criticism and Society," *Prisms* (London: Neville Spearman, 1967), p. 26.

58. William Morris, "The Lesser Arts" (also given under the title "The Decorative Arts," 1877), in *The Political Writings of William Morris,* ed. A. L. Morton (London: Lawrence and Wishart, 1973), p. 32.

7. "Perceiving the other-side of everything"

1. Roland Barthes, *Mythologies,* trans. Annette Lavers (New York: Hill and Wang, 1972), p. 110.

2. Ibid., p. 129. Also, "myth is constituted by the loss of the historical

quality of things; in it things lose the memory that they once were made,"
p. 142.

3. The fact that myth is a culturally and historically formed narrative is
always brought home to me when I consider that Vishnu is blue, but, despite
knowing this, I have not the faintest response to it (except that he's pretty that
way), because the meaning of that code is not part of my cultural apparatus.

4. Josephine Donovan, "The Silence is Broken" citing Walter J. Ong, *The
Presence of the Word:* until the nineteenth century, Latin was a "sex-linked
language, a kind of badge of masculine identity." *Women and Language in
Literature and Society,* ed. Sally McConnell-Ginet, Ruth Borker, Nelly Furman
(New York: Praeger Publishers, 1980), p. 206.

5. H.D.'s earliest poems were modeled on Theocritus: Norman Holmes
Pearson Interview conducted by L. S. Dembo, *Contemporary Literature* X, 4
(Autumn 1969): 437; the impact of Greek culture was often noted and acknowledged by H.D., as in the poem "Epitaph": "so you may say, / 'Greek
flower; Greek ecstasy / reclaims forever // one who dies / following / intricate
song's lost measure,'" H.D. *Collected Poems 1912–1944,* ed. Louis L. Martz
(New York: New Directions, 1983), pp. 299–300. Subsequent references to
this edition, abbreviated *CP.* H.D.'s "contemporary collaboration" with Sappho—she wrote five original poems starting with Sappho's fragments—is
traced in Susan Gubar's study of the influence of Sappho on modern women
writers. Gubar poses a major tactic of cultural confrontation: by such strategies of collaboration, women writers could invent a poetic heritage of their
own to avoid the inflection of masculine views and to free them from the
"anxiety of authorship" whose impact Gilbert and Gubar had traced throughout the nineteenth century. "Sapphistries," forthcoming, *Signs.*

6. Sandra Gilbert and Susan Gubar, *The Madwoman in the Attic: The Woman
Writer and the Nineteenth-Century Literary Imagination* (New Haven: Yale University Press, 1979), passim.

7. Alicia Ostriker, "The Thieves of Language: Women Poets and Re-
visionist Mythmaking," *Signs* 8, 1 (1982): 72. This chapter and Ostriker's
article are like sisters: conceived separately, growing independently, yet from
the same family.

8. Geoffrey Kirk, *Myth: Its Meaning and Functions in Ancient and Other
Cultures* (Cambridge: Cambridge University Press, 1970), p. 253.

9. Adrienne Rich, "When We Dead Awaken: Writing as Re-vision," in *On
Lies, Secrets, and Silence: Selected Prose 1966–1978* (New York: W. W. Norton
and Company, 1979), p. 35.

10. Formulated independently, the terms displacement and delegitimation
may be compared to a similar pairing of terms by Gayatri Chakravorty Spivak
in "Explanation and Culture: Marginalia," *Humanities in Society* 2, 3 (Summer
1979). Her term *reversal* brings us to the other side of narrative, and her term
displace is parallel to the rupture of narrative sequence in my term *delegitimate.*
Stephen Heath makes a similar distinction: "The humanist gesture is to appeal to an unknown 'look of the woman' to be given expression, the political—
as in filmmaker [Laura] Mulvey—is to analyse the fact of 'look' and 'woman' in
the structure of its definition and to appeal to the necessity to work to end that
structure and the location of man/woman it operates." "Difference," *Screen*
19, 3 (1978): 99.

11. Virginia Woolf, "Romance and the Heart," in *Contemporary Writers*
(New York: Harcourt Brace Jovanovich, 1965), p. 125. The subject of this

review, Dorothy Richardson, will be discussed in chapter 9. "The other-side of everything" is a citation from the H.D. poem "The Moon In Your Hands," *CP,* 413. In her germinal work of feminist criticism, Ellen Moers proposed reversal as one of the central features of literary heroinism; for example, nineteenth-century female poets had "the conscious intention to reverse the ancient tradition of love poems all by men." *Literary Women* (New York: Doubleday and Co., Inc., 1976), p. 165.

12. In *No More Masks!* ed. Florence Howe and Ellen Bass (New York: Doubleday Anchor Books, 1973), p. 68. Similarly the contemporary poet and critic Alicia Ostriker, speaking about her own poems of mythopoesis, notes, "What I remember about composing these poems is my conviction that I was telling what actually occurred, the way it must have been, what Homer and Aeschylus left out. . . ." *Writing Like a Woman* (Ann Arbor: University of Michigan Press, 1983), p. 135.

13. Robin Morgan, *Monster* (New York: Vintage Books, 1972), p. 86.

14. Louise Bogan, "Medusa," in *The Blue Estuaries, Poems 1923–1968* (New York: The Ecco Press, 1977), p. 4. On Bogan's blockage, see Gloria Bowles, "To Be (or Not to Be?) Woman Poet," *Women's Studies* 5, 2 (1977): 131–36, and Louise Bogan, *Journey Round My Room: The Autobiography of Louise Bogan,* ed. Ruth Limmer (New York: Penguin Books, 1980).

15. May Sarton, "The Muse as Medusa," in *Selected Poems of May Sarton,* ed. Serena Sue Hilsinger and Lois Byrnes (New York: W. W. Norton and Company, Inc., 1978), p. 160. The poem contains the critical query, "How to believe the legends I am told?" which itself conceals, in its tone, an oscillation between assent (making oneself believe) and doubt.

16. Sylvia Plath, "Medusa," in *Ariel* (New York: Harper & Row, Publishers, 1965), pp. 39–40.

17. This is, after all, the premise of Woolf's *Flush.*

18. This paraphrases Gerda Lerner, "Autobiographical Notes, by way of Introduction," in *The Majority Finds Its Past: Placing Women in History* (Oxford: Oxford University Press, 1979), p. xxxi.

19. One can point to other poems that use the underworld as an image of the otherness, a displacement to the other side: Muriel Rukeyser's "In the Underworld" and Adrienne Rich's "I Dream I'm the Death of Orpheus," whose reversal is perfectly compensatory. Orpheus, experiencing the helplessness of the Eurydice figure, is "learning to walk backwards against the wind / on the wrong side of the mirror," while a woman successfully appropriates the moment of orphic discipline and will: "a woman feeling the fullness of her powers / at the precise moment she must not use them." Rich, *Poems Selected and New, 1950–1974* (W. W. Norton and Company, Inc., 1975), p. 152; Rukeyser, *The Collected Poems of Muriel Rukeyser* (New York: McGraw-Hill Book Company, 1978), pp. 519–23.

20. Margaret Atwood, *You Are Happy* (New York: Harper & Row, Publishers, 1974); pp. 46–70.

21. Margaret Atwood, *Survival: A Thematic Guide to Canadian Literature* (Toronto: House of Anansi Press, 1972), p. 36. Abbreviated as *S.* I would rather substitute the word "colonized" for "victimized." Most specifically, she means Canadian literature and the materialist argument about culture, as George Woodcock summarizes it: "that our literature is still scarred and distorted by the mental condition that emerges from a colonial past." "Bashful but Bold: Notes on Margaret Atwood as Critic," in *The Art of Margaret Atwood: Essays in*

Criticism, ed. Arnold E. Davidson and Cathy N. Davidson (Toronto: House of Anansi Press, 1981), p. 237. But the arguments she makes about the particular force of cultural marginality are equally applicable to women. Barbara Charlesworth Gelpi has also noted Atwood's typology in the analysis of contemporary women's poetry; "A Common Language: The American Woman Poet," in *Shakespeare's Sisters,* ed. Sandra Gilbert and Susan Gubar (Bloomington: Indiana University Press, 1979): pp. 269–79. See also Albert Memmi, *The Colonizer and the Colonized* (Boston: Beacon Press, 1967).

22. Margaret Atwood, *Second Words: Selected Critical Prose* (Toronto: House of Anansi Press, 1982), p. 360.

23. From Gwendolyn Brooks, *The Bean Eaters* (1960); the poem will be cited from Brooks, *Selected Poems* (New York: Harper and Row Publishers, 1963), pp. 75–81. Abbreviated as *SP.* "Bronzeville" is the black ghetto in Chicago.

24. Till was a fourteen-year-old Chicagoan visiting Money, Mississippi, in 1955. Alleged to have made "advances" to a white woman, he was lynched.

25. Angelina Weld Grimké (1880–1958): "There is a tree, by day, / That, at night, / Has a shadow, / A hand huge and black, / With fingers long and black, / All through the dark, / Against the white man's house, / In the little wind, / The black hand plucks and plucks / At the bricks. / The bricks are the color of blood and very small. / It is a black hand, / Or is it a shadow?" From *The Poetry of the American Negro, 1746–1970,* ed. Langston Hughes and Arna Bontemps (New York: Doubleday and Co., Inc., 1970), p. 58. Wind as well as color is a motif in both poems.

26. The *Contemporary Literature* interview is cited from Gwendolyn Brooks, *Report from Part One,* prefaces by Don L. Lee and George Kent (Detroit, Mich.: Broadside Press, 1972), pp. 165–66.

27. Unpublished letter, H.D. to Bryher, November 24, 1934. Beinecke Library, Yale University. I am indebted to Susan Friedman for this reference.

28. H.D., *Trilogy,* in *Collected Poems,* with the separate sections as follows: *The Walls Do Not Fall (WDNF),* 1944; *Tribute to the Angels (TA),* 1945; *The Flowering of the Rod (FR),* 1946. This work is marked by other kinds of dissenting traditions, including the alchemical, as Adalaide Morris strikingly points out in a major reading of H.D.'s oeuvre accomplished through various meanings of the concept *projection.* "Projected Pictures: H.D.'s Visionary Moments," typescript.

29. There are any number of citations from the Gospel of John and from the Book of Revelations in *Trilogy,* as Norman Holmes Pearson pointed out in his introduction to the New Directions edition, using H.D.'s letters to him.

30. In the words of the novelist Dorothy Richardson, ". . . and why not say: man, it is not very graceful to say it, is the male of woman? If women had been the recorders of things from the beginning it would all have been the other way round . . . Mary. Mary, the Jewess, write something about Mary the Jewess." *The Tunnel* (1919), in *Pilgrimage* (New York: Popular Library, 1976), p. 251.

31. The source in Revelations is discussed by both Susan Gubar and Susan Friedman. Gubar, "The Echoing Spell of H.D.'s *Trilogy,*" in *Shakespeare's Sisters,* ed. Sandra M. Gilbert and Susan Gubar (Bloomington: Indiana University Press, 1979), pp. 200–18; Friedman, *Psyche Reborn,* p. 246.

32. As Gubar says, H.D. questions John's vision in order to offer "her own revision," adding that "she seems to be arguing with John directly because his vision seems warped," "The Echoing Spell," p. 209.

33. The passages occur in Matthew, 26:6–13; Mark, 14:3–8; and John, 11:2–12:3. The detail about the hair is peculiar to John. Friedman notes that H.D. combines two biblical Marys: Martha's sister, who did not want to house-keep and serve if she could listen to Christ, and the prostitute Mary Magdalene. *Psyche Reborn*, p. 78.

34. Elaine Pagels, "What Became of God the Mother? Conflicting Images of God in Early Christianity," in *Womanspirit Rising: A Feminist Reader in Religion*, ed. Carol P. Christ and Judith Plaskow (San Francisco: Harper and Row Publishers, 1979), pp. 107–19.

35. H.D., *The Gift* (New York: New Directions, 1982). Abbreviated as *G*.

36. This is one of the several notable passages excised from the New Directions version of *The Gift*. For the chapters entitled "Dark Room" and "The Dream," the following versions respectively are more reliable than the published book: *Montemora* 8 (1981): 57–76, and *Contemporary Literature* X, 4 (Autumn 1969): 605–26. For the remaining chapters, the reader is well advised to consult the typescript held at the Beinecke Rare Book and Manuscript Library, Yale University. This citation comes from chapter VII, p. 27.

8. The Critique of Consciousness and Myth in Levertov, Rich, and Rukeyser

1. "Professions for Women," *Collected Essays*, II (New York: Harcourt, Brace and World, 1967), p. 44.

2. Denise Levertov, *O Taste and See* (New York: New Directions, 1964), p. 70.

3. Muriel Rukeyser, *The Collected Poems of Muriel Rukeyser* (New York: McGraw-Hill Book Company, 1978), p. 492. Abbreviated as *CP*.

4. The poem appears in Rich, *Poems Selected and New, 1950–1974* (New York: W. W. Norton and Company, Inc., 1975), pp. 47–51. Abbreviated as *PSN*. The citation is from Rich, "When We Dead Awaken: Writing As Re-Vision," in *On Lies, Secrets, and Silence, Selected Prose, 1966–1978* (New York: W. W. Norton and Company, Inc., 1979), p. 44.

5. Rich's recounting of her own mother's history offers not only background and context for the portrait in the first section of "Snapshots," but confirmation, as well, of the pattern that was discussed in chapter 6: the role played by observation of the thwarted career of a maternal artist in the forming of the daughter's artistic ambition. "Once married, she gave up the possibility of a concert career, though for some years she went on composing, and she is still a skilled and dedicated pianist." *Of Woman Born: Motherhood as Experience and Institution* (New York: W. W. Norton and Company, Inc., 1976), p. 221.

6. Two versions of the poem exist, each with different lines from Dickinson. "This is the gnat that mangles men" emphasizes the sapping of energy by diffusion; "My life had stood—a loaded gun . . ." suggests explosive, possibly disciplined power. In "Vesuvius at Home: The Power of Emily Dickinson," Rich examines in 1975, years later than the poem, the canny strategies by which Dickinson accomplished her work. Domesticity and withdrawal to her family's house are viewed differently in "Snapshots" and in the essay.

7. As Rich stated in a 1972 interview with *The Saturday Review*, "The whole convention of lyric poetry is written in a sense as a misleading script for women." April 22, 1972, pp. 56–59.

8. "When We Dead Awaken," in *On Lies, Secrets, and Silence,* p. 35.

9. *CP,* 527–35.

10. Denise Levertov, *To Stay Alive* (New York: New Directions, 1971), p. 29.

11. They shared more than that as well. During this period, as Levertov later recalled, Rukeyser was an exemplary personal figure. The poets went to Hanoi together in 1972 as activists in the anti-war movement, and several of Levertov's poems are dedicated to Rukeyser—"The Unknown" and "Joy" in *The Sorrow Dance* and "In Thai Binh (Peace) Province" in *The Freeing of the Dust.* Their relationship—"as colleagues who became friends—fellow votaries of Poetry who were also mothers and political allies"—had a further dimension. "After my mother died in 1977, when I told Muriel forlornly that I felt myself to be a middle-aged orphan, she said, 'Oh, I'll adopt you. You'll be my Adopted Something.' She meant that and I felt it, felt warmed and strengthened." "On Muriel Rukeyser," in *Light Up the Cave* (New York: New Directions, 1981), p. 194.

12. The poem is in Rich, *Poems Selected and New,* pp. 198–202. In 1973, Rich wrote: "The bombings, for example, if they have anything to teach us, must be understood in the light of something closer to home, both more private and painful, and more general and endemic, than the institutions, class, racial oppression, the hubris of the Pentagon, or the ruthlessness of a right-wing administration: the bombings are so wholly sadistic, gratuitous and demonic that they can finally be seen, if we care to see them, for what they are: acts of concrete sexual violence, an expression of the congruence of violence and sex in the masculine psyche." *On Lies, Secrets and Silence,* p. 109.

13. From *The Speed of Darkness, CP,* 435. Elly Bulkin reads this and other opening poems in this book as coming-out poems; Rukeyser participated in the 1978 lesbian poetry reading at the Modern Language Association. "'A Whole New Poetry Beginning Here': Teaching Lesbian Poetry," *College English* 40, 8 (April 1979): 884–85.

14. "Orpheus," *CP,* 291–300.

15. Muriel Rukeyser, *The Life of Poetry* (New York: Current Books, Inc., 1949), discusses the composition of "Orpheus."

16. *CP,* 278–80, 498.

17. Denise Levertov, *Relearning the Alphabet* (New York: New Directions, 1970), pp. 110–21. Abbreviated as *RA.* The poem is dated 1968–69.

18. From *Diving into the Wreck, Poems 1971–72,* reprinted in *Poems Selected and New,* pp. 196–98.

19. There are some uncanny resemblances between the imagery of Margaret Atwood's *Surfacing* and that of Rich's "Diving into the Wreck," which suggest either that Rich assimilated the novel within her poem (which was written in 1971, the year that Atwood was published in Canada), or, more likely, that the act of critique in which both writers were engaged led them to similar patterns of visualization. These include, in Atwood: the drowned brother's face; the father's camera; the album of pictographs and drawings that become instruction; the "forgetting the reason" for coming to the woods; and the drowned father/fetus/self who is confronted. In Rich: the "drowned face with open eyes"; the camera as part of the equipment; the "book of myths," which, read differently, become "maps"; the forgetting "what one is here for"; the dead body inside the wreck that must be investigated.

20. Erich Neumann, *The Origins and History of Consciousness,* Bollingen Series 42 (Princeton, N.J.: Princeton University Press, 1954), p. 199.

21. This moment of fusion ("I am she: I am he") is, in a later poem, transposed and rearticulated, without heterosexuality. *"I am the lover and the loved, / home and wanderer, she who splits / firewood and she who knocks, a stranger / in the storm."* "Transcendental Etude," in *The Dream of a Common Language, Poems 1974–77* (New York, W. W. Norton and Company, Inc., 1978), p. 76. Abbreviated as *DCL.*

22. *On Lies, Secrets, and Silence,* p. 183.

23. *The American Heritage Dictionary,* S.V. "ideal."

24. This process was publicly completed by 1975, when Rich published poems in the anthology *Amazon Poetry,* ed. Joan Larkin and Elly Bulkin (New York: Out and Out Books, 1975). This point is made by Judith McDaniel in *Reconstituting the World: The Poetry and Vision of Adrienne Rich* (New York: Spinsters, Ink, 1978).

25. See, for example, Charlotte Bunch: *"Lesbian-feminist theory,* as a critique of male supremacy and heterosexism, is a perspective, analysis and commitment that can be embraced by anyone, gay or straight, female or male—just as socialism or Pan-Africanism are theories that can be adopted by anyone regardless of race, sex or class." "Lesbian-Feminist Theory" (c. 1978), in *Women and the Politics of Culture,* ed. Michele Wender Zak and Patricia A. Moots (New York: Longman, 1983), pp. 417–18.

26. Rich, "Compulsory Heterosexuality and Lesbian Existence," *Signs* 5, 4 (Summer 1980): 631–60. Rich's position is consistent with that held by Blanche Weisen Cook, "'Women Alone Stir My Imagination': Lesbianism and the Cultural Tradition," *Signs* 4, 4 (Summer 1979): 718–39. See especially Cook's definition of lesbian: "Women who love women, who choose women to nurture and support and to create a living environment in which to work creatively and independently," p. 738. In the debate occasioned by Rich's essay, in *Signs* 7, 1, Ann Ferguson, criticizing as romanticized the overarching cross-cultural, cross-historical approach positing a "lesbian continuum," points out that if this perspective were applied too literally, women who had any nurturing or mutually interested connections with men—women like Virginia Woolf or H.D.—would be definitionally excluded from the category lesbian, which, given everything, would not see them whole. "Patriarchy, Sexual Identity, and the Sexual Revolution," *Signs* 7, 1 (Autumn 1981): 158–72.

27. In "One is not Born but Made a 'Woman,'" (Paper delivered at the Simone de Beauvoir Conference, The Second Sex—Thirty Years After: A Commemorative Conference on Feminist Theory, New York, September 1979), Monique Wittig similarly insisted that "woman" is the name given to a female being who has been socially constructed and historically sculpted by patriarchal relations. What does one call the new woman who has formulated herself in a critical resistance to patriarchy? Wittig too answers *lesbian.* The point is similarly polemical and lexical, offering a new name with old connotations, and using the force of the taboo to declare one's rupture from the dominant. The implication that lesbianism is the highest stage of critique occurs in passing.

28. *The Dream of a Common Language,* pp. 60–67. Other moments of reassessment, which I do not have the space to discuss here, can be traced in Rich's writing on Emily Dickinson throughout her career. When she writes the poem "I Am in Danger—Sir—" (1964), she characterizes Dickinson as "you, a woman, masculine in single-mindedness"; when she writes "The Spirit of Place," with its section on Dickinson, she corrects the attribution of single-

mindedness to a "masculine" sensibility by giving firm attention to the poet's maternal lineage and her defining love for Sue Gilbert. *Poems Selected and New,* p. 84, and *A Wild Patience Has Taken Me This Far* (New York: W. W. Norton and Company, Inc., 1981), pp. 40–45 (abbreviated as *AWP*). Furthermore, she vows to reject any future discussion of Dickinson, condemning these exercises as self-centered acts of appropriation, insensitive to Dickinson's desire for privacy.

29. The word *androgyne* also occurs in "The Stranger," written in 1972, the same year as "Diving into the Wreck"; the line "I am the androgyne" refers to a new fused person. This poem does not appear in Rich's *Poems Selected and New,* because, as Rich has commented, androgyny now seems to be a "liberal" solution to the woman question, one that cares more about liberating men than women. See Elly Bulkin, "An Interview with Adrienne Rich (October 1976)," *Conditions One* (1977): 61–62. Susan Friedman has discovered a parallel kind of self-critical change undertaken to deemphasize interest in male transformation or situation. The version of "When We Dead Awaken: Writing as Revision" in *On Lies, Secrets, and Silence* removes a section that had once evinced a welcoming interest in male change. "H.D. and Adrienne Rich: an Intertextual Study," *Signs* 9, 2 (Winter 1983): 228–45.

30. The degree to which this represents a shift can be measured by Rich's comment (1972) about mythic narrative (e.g., in *Wuthering Heights*), which offers an "archetypal bond between the split fragments of the psyche, the masculine and feminine elements ripped apart and longing for reunion," *On Lies, Secrets, and Silence,* p. 90. This remark provides a context for "Diving into the Wreck"; at that point, Rich considered that the hierogamic version of a heterosexual love plot could extend into the romantic quest for soul-making. Marriage could be a "continuation of her self-creation," in *Jane Eyre*. At the same time, this essay ("Jane Eyre: The Temptations of a Motherless Woman") was the first to discuss maternal-sororal ties as a major source of soul-making in that novel.

31. Janet Wolff, *The Social Production of Art* (London: The Macmillan Press Ltd., 1981), p. 130.

32. Donna J. Haraway, "In the Beginning was the Word: The Genesis of Biological Theory," *Signs* 6, 3 (Spring 1981): 479.

33. Already referred to, these are *The Dream of a Common Language* (1978), *A Wild Patience Has Taken Me This Far* (1981), and *Sources* (Woodside, Calif.: The Heyeck Press, 1983), a poem in twenty-three parts, dated August 1981–August 1982 (abbreviated as *S*). This may be a good time to remark that with Rich, as with several other authors discussed in this book (Lessing, Walker, Brooks, Atwood, Piercy, Russ, and Morrison among them), we are, at this date in 1983, talking about living writers, whose capacity for change, modulation, reiteration, externally directed debate, and internally produced self-criticism should not be underestimated.

34. Adrienne Rich, *Of Woman Born,* p. 255.

35. Joanne Feit Diehl discusses this desire and Rich's distrust of language in "'Cartographies of Silence': Rich's *Common Language* and the Woman Poet," *Feminist Studies* 6, 3 (Fall 1980): 539–44.

36. Margaret Homans, *Women Writers and Poetic Identity: Dorothy Wordsworth, Emily Brontë, and Emily Dickinson* (Princeton, N.J.: Princeton University Press, 1980), p. 223.

37. I have argued this in an early version of this chapter, in *Shakespeare's*

Sisters, ed. Sandra Gilbert and Susan Gubar (Bloomington: Indiana University Press, 1979): pp. 280–300.

38. Indeed, Homans's book suggests an essential project for feminist poetics: "Hierarchy in language must be undone in other ways than by denying otherness," p. 40.

39. These critical questions about de Beauvoir were elegantly posed by Mary Lowenthal Felstiner, in "Seeing *The Second Sex* through the Second Wave," *Feminist Studies* 6, 2 (Summer 1980): 267–71.

9. "Beyond the hard visible horizon"

1. Often the quest plot is strongly marked by death, but it is not the death of the main character but of a surrogate sufferer: Tea Cake in Hurston, Camera in Alice Walker, the suicidal mother in Dorothy Richardson.

2. *Pilgrimage* was written over a period of forty years; it is more than 2000 pages long and is divided into four volumes, each containing several "chapters" (novel-length sections). The sequence is as follows, along with the abbreviations I shall use to designate individual chapters: Volume I: *Pointed Roofs* (1915, *PR*), *Backwater* (1916, *B*) *Honeycomb* (1917, *H*); Volume II: *The Tunnel* (1919, *Tun*), *Interim* (1919, *In*); Volume III: *Deadlock* (1921, *D*), *Revolving Lights* (1923, *RL*), *The Trap* (1925, *Tr*); Volume IV: *Oberland* (1927, *O*), *Dawn's Left Hand* (1931, *DLH*), *Clear Horizon* (1935, *CH*), *Dimple Hill* (1938, *DH*), and the posthumously published, unfinished *March Moonlight* (1967, *MM*). I will designate citations by chapter abbreviation, volume, and page. This citation comes from *MM,* IV, 630—that is, *March Moonlight* in Volume IV (New York: Popular Library, 1976; reprint of the 1967 Alfred A. Knopf edition), p. 630.

3. Richardson, Foreword to Volume I, p. 9. The alternative is "following one of her regiments," an allusion to Lyndall's summary of options for women in Schreiner.

4. Similarly, Richardson says about herself and marriage that "on more than one occasion I withdrew a provisional pledge." "Data for Spanish Publisher," ed. Joseph Prescott, *London Magazine* 6, 6 (June 1959): 19.

5. Or, they appear lesbian to a contemporary reader. In correspondence with Rose Odle, Alan Odle's sister-in-law, Veronica Grad, the "original" of Amabel, reported of Mag and Jan that "their relationship was much like D's [Richardson's] and mine only less so" [1957]. By this Veronica Grad apparently meant that the two were deeply in love but sexually platonic. For Dorothy and Veronica "were twins—no two halves"; the context makes clear that Grad means complementary halves—one person an egotist, the other selfless. The publication of this correspondence, offering very important documentation about Richardson, is one of several critical and archival contributions made by Gillian E. Hanscombe, *The Art of Life: Dorothy Richardson and the Development of Feminist Consciousness* (London: Peter Owen, 1982), pp. 180, 184.

6. The interplay between life and work is traced in great detail in Gloria G. Fromm's *Dorothy Richardson: A Biography* (Urbana: University of Illinois Press, 1977). During the late twenties and thirties, after a moment of efflorescence marked by a trip to Paris in 1924, Richardson's inner dynamic of stubbornness and personal encapsulation, and the *solitude à deux* of her marriage slowly crimped her. She marginalized herself, and financial exigencies contributed to that isolation. Her book kept being written, but the project

had been set inflexibly. By 1938, the prospect of a shaping completion became quite difficult for her to face (as difficult as was Schreiner's for *From Man to Man*). It took fifteen years for Richardson to not quite finish a rather turgid *March Moonlight*, the final chapter.

7. Richardson letter to Bryher, September 1923. Norman Holmes Pearson Bequest, Beinecke Rare Book and Manuscript Library, Yale University. The letter begins, "it is just now my problem how to get my books done with even the minimum of high intensity in them." The rest of the letter is devoted to "him."

8. Fromm, *Richardson*, p. 99. Fromm suggests an alternative view, that Richardson's self-appointed role as a "guardian" to Odle—more like a mother than a wife—resolves the conflict or "deadlock" between maleness and femaleness with a third way—maternity, p. 137. Odle did not die until 1948, at the age of sixty. Dorothy Richardson was then seventy-five.

9. In a manuscript from 1957, "Some Memories of Dorothy M. Richardson and Alan Odle," Rose Odle confirms the permanent trauma that her mother's suicide caused for the author. Dorothy Richardson Collection, Beinecke Library, Yale University.

10. As Hanscombe says, "Richardson endorses Miriam's claim here that the fruit of the union of her friends is her own fruit, created by her initiative and will and returning to her a sense of fulfillment," *The Art of Life*, p. 159. A curious revisionary Madonna.

11. "I must make a monstrous confession. I was feeling that everything that man had written to date was somehow irrelevant." Louise Morgan, "Dorothy Richardson" [a pamphlet], reprinted from *Everyman*, October 22, 1931, p. 7. A parallel formulation concerning the inception of her writing career occurs in a letter to Henry Savage, January 6, 1950: "Monstrously, when I began [writing], I felt only that all masculine novels to date, despite their various fascinations, were somehow irrelevant. . . ." Cited in Horace Gregory, *Dorothy Richardson: An Adventure in Self-Discovery* (New York: Holt, Rinehart and Winston, 1967), p. 12.

12. "All the conceptual space," from Dale Spender, "Theorising about Theorising," in *Theories of Women's Studies* II, ed. Gloria Bowles and Renate Duelli-Klein (Berkeley: Women's Studies, University of California, 1981), p. 121.

13. In *Oberland*, IV, 92–93.

> "They seem incapable of unthinking the suggestions coming to them from centuries of masculine attempts to represent women only in relation to the world as known to men."
> It was then he was angry.
> "How else shall they be represented?"
> "They *can't* be represented by men. Because by every word they use men and women mean different things."

14. This is part of Sydney Janet Kaplan's thesis. The feminist context, she argues, gave an impetus to early twentieth-century experimental writing by women beyond the purely aesthetic. Their shared project was the exploration and registering of the minds of women in a way that broke both stereotypes about women and narrative conventions of depiction. Kaplan devotes one

important chapter to Dorothy Richardson. *Feminine Consciousness in the Modern British Novel* (Urbana: University of Illinois Press, 1975), pp. 1–2.

15. Gillian Hanscombe also identifies the erotic bond to women, putting a good deal of weight on the second such moment, with Jean, in *March Moonlight*, as a "symbolic" bond that gives Miriam a "clue to the nature of reality." Thus Hanscombe argues that the feminine principle that Dorothy Richardson sought and the examination of female reality are consciously "generated and developed" by Richardson's depiction of Miriam's affectual ties to women. *The Art of Life*, p. 129.

16. Richardson, "Leadership in Marriage," *New Adelphi* 2 (June–August 1929): 347. Notice the following allusion to George Fox, which links women to the Society of Friends.

> The characteristic . . . of being all over the place and in all camps at once, accounts both for her famous inability "to make up her mind," her unashamed inconsistency and her ability as a peacemaker. It explains her capacity for "living in the present" and at the same time her uncanny apprehension of what is yet to be. This apprehension, "the spirit of prophecy in the daughters" which George Fox bade men respect when he was trouncing them for claiming authority over their wives, is the informing substance of her life.

17. The definition of liminality is based on Victor Turner, *Dramas, Fields, and Metaphors: Symbolic Action in Human Society* (Ithaca: Cornell University Press, 1974).

18. "Data for Spanish Publisher," p. 19. To gloss the use of the term *horizontally*, one might look at Richardson's "Adventure for Readers," *Life and Letters To-Day* (July 1939): 51. There she exhorts readers to release their consciousness "from literary preoccupations and prejudices, from the self-imposed task of searching for superficial sequences in stretches of statement regarded horizontally. . . ." Thus the term is a synonym for narrative sequence, chronology, causation. She is reviewing Joyce's *Finnegans Wake*.

19. Richardson, "Literary Essays, Memory of 1909," autograph manuscript, The Dorothy Richardson Collection, Beinecke Library, Yale University, p. 2.

20. The citations are first from Richardson, "Adventure for Readers," p. 47, then from "Literary Essays 1908: Began Writing Middles for *The Saturday Review*," autograph manuscript, Beinecke Library, p. 1.

21. Thanking Winifred Bryher for the volumes of Proust she had sent as a gift, Richardson mentions her procedures for reading: "I cut all those 5 vols. piecemeal, leaving them all over the room, and read them in the same way, taking up the first handy vol. and opening at random. At last the whole hung and hangs, a tapestry all round me." Autograph Letter to Bryher, Norman Holmes Pearson Bequest, Beinecke Library, Letter from 1925, p. 2 of two. Bryher and H.D. were friends of Richardson's; Bryher was characteristically generous with very necessary loans, Christmas baskets, and gifts of books.

22. Richardson, "Novels," *Life and Letters* 56 (March 1948): 192.

23. Richardson, Letter to Henry Savage, January 6, 1950, cited in Gregory, *Dorothy Richardson*, p. 12. There are some good descriptions, notably in *Backwater*, of Miriam's addiction to such ladies' fiction as Gothics and romances (*B*, I, 283–86).

24. May Sinclair, "The Novels of Dorothy Richardson," *The Egoist* V (April 1918): 57–58. The patent convenience and at least partial accuracy of that term made it useful; it is a label that Richardson resentfully worried for the rest of her life. In "A Last Meeting with Dorothy Richardson," *London Magazine* 6 (June 1959), Vincent Brome records her statement: "stream of consciousness is a muddle-headed phrase. It's not a stream, it is a pool, a sea, an ocean. It has depth and greater depth and when you think you have reached its bottom there is nothing there, and when you give yourself up to one current you are suddenly possessed by another," p. 29. The antilinear bias could not be clearer. However, its resulting statement and backtrack, so that virtually everything in the book is doubled or neutralized, and the sequences pooling into epiphanal circles can produce an understandable frustration. Readers of Richardson thus have tended to be polarized between uncritical admiration and unadmiring criticism. Caesar Blake and Elaine Showalter are two eloquent examples; respectively *Dorothy M. Richardson* (Ann Arbor: University of Michigan Press, 1960), and *A Literature of Their Own* (Princeton: Princeton University Press, 1977), pp. 248–62.

25. The citation is from *The Tunnel*, 118. Virginia Woolf, "The Tunnel" and "Romance and the Heart," in *Contemporary Writers: Essays on Twentieth Century Books and Authors* (New York: Harcourt Brace Jovanovich, 1965), pp. 120–22, 123–25. Woolf began "Modern Fiction" a few months after finishing the 1919 review. Gloria G. Fromm briefly traces Richardson's later response to Woolf, which was generally hostile to her class and stylistic magnificence, *Richardson*, pp. 318–19. Richardson called Woolf "a diluted male, wobbly and irrelevant," a poignant missing of the target. Letter to Henry Savage, January 1950, cited in Gregory, *Dorothy Richardson*, p. 12.

26. *Contemporary Writers*, p. 122.

27. Ibid., p. 120.

28. Ibid., p. 125.

29. For example, Woolf says that by claiming a female perspective, Richardson "adds an element to her view of things which has not been noticed before, or, if noticed, has been guiltily suppressed," *Contemporary Writers*, p. 125. Diane F. Gillespie has also discussed the importance of the Woolf-Richardson conjuncture in "Political Aesthetics: Virginia Woolf and Dorothy Richardson," in *Virginia Woolf: A Feminist Slant*, ed. Jane Marcus (Lincoln: University of Nebraska Press, 1983), pp. 132–51. It is clear that Woolf was acutely aware of the pitfalls of Richardson's approach, the "damned egotistical self" that "ruins Joyce and Richardson to my mind," for she posed the question whether there is "in the helter-skelter of flying fragments some unity, significance, or design." Respectively, Woolf, *A Writer's Diary*, ed. Leonard Woolf (New York: Harcourt, Brace and Company, 1954), p. 23 (from 1920), and *Contemporary Writers*, p. 121. Indeed, much later, Richardson acknowledged the justice of that latter criticism.

> To take a single second, subject it to microscopic inquisition, and peer at the wonderful organisms undetected by the normal eye, was to see the nuance, the tendril, the amoeba, the very stuff of creative life, but life had movement, and an appalling confusion of speeds were intrinsically part of the moment itself. Striking the perfect balance between movement and minutiae was impossible. Sub-aqueous depths could become too fascinating. One remained too long probing in the hope that one day, some inner pattern of psychic significance would at last fuse in the imagination.

In short, it did not cohere. Vincent Brome, "A Last Meeting with Dorothy Richardson," p. 30.

30. Dorothy Richardson, "The Reality of Feminism," *The Ploughshare* n.s. 2 (September 1917): 245:

> But the fact of woman remains the fact that she is relatively to man, synthetic. Relatively to man she sees life whole and harmonious. Men tend to fix life, to fix aspects. . . . Woman is metaphysical, religious, an artist and scientist in life. Let anyone who questions the synthetic quality of woman ask himself why it is that she can move, as it were in all directions at once, why, with a man-astonishing ease, she can "stake up" everything by turns, while she "originates" nothing? . . . Why she can solve and reconcile, revealing the points of unity between a number of conflicting males—a number of embodied theories furiously raging together. . . .

31. "Data for Spanish Publisher," p. 17.
32. Ibid., p. 18.
33. Ibid.
34. Dorothy Richardson, *The Quakers, Past and Present* (London: Constable, 1914), p. 22. The same year, Richardson published *Gleanings from the Works of George Fox.* Avrom Fleishman's study of *Pilgrimage* emphasizes the Quaker influence and the organization around the spiritual motifs of autobiography: "Edenic childhood and its loss, aimless wandering and hellish torment, vision and conversion." In Richardson, these are not distinct stages in pilgrimage but "repetitive patterns of living." *Figures of Autobiography: The Language of Self-Writing in Victorian and Modern England* (Berkeley: University of California Press, 1983), p. 430.
35. The reference also clarifies what the one final flare of romance also reveals. Despite the eagerness of the Quaker farmer Richard Roscorla, Miriam again avoids marriage as closure, avoids the "home," which she continues to view as a "prison" (*DH*, IV, 533).
36. "[Man] has hated and loved and feared [woman] as mother nature, feared and adored her as the unattainable, the Queen of Heaven; and now, at last, nearing the solution of the problem, he turns to her as companion and fellow pilgrim, suspecting in her relatively undivided harmonious nature an intuitive solution of the quest that has agonised him from the dawn of things." Richardson, "The Reality of Feminism," p. 246.
37. In Richardson's view, "women had never been subject and never would be. The 'disabilities, imposed by law, [were] a stupid insult to women, but [had] never touched them as individuals.'" Fromm, *Richardson,* 287–88. The citations are drawn from letters of 1935.
38. "Alice Walker," in *Interviews with Black Writers,* ed. John O'Brien (New York: Liveright, 1973), p. 192.
39. Zora Neale Hurston, *Their Eyes Were Watching God* (Urbana: University of Illinois Press, 1978), p. 284. Abbreviated as *TEWWG.*
40. *I Love Myself When I Am Laughing . . . And Then Again When I Am Mean and Impressive: A Zora Neale Hurston Reader,* ed. Alice Walker (Old Westbury, New York: The Feminist Press, 1979), pp. 75, 77, 78. The citations are taken from *Dust Tracks on a Road* (1942), Hurston's autobiography.
41. Robert E. Hemenway, *Zora Neale Hurston: A Literary Biography* (Urbana: University of Illinois Press, 1977), p. 231.

42. Both Mary Helen Washington and Robert Hemenway make this point as well. Hemenway, *Hurston,* p. 239, and Mary Helen Washington, "The Black Woman's Search for Identity: Zora Neale Hurston's Work," *Black World* 21, 10 (August 1972): 74–75.

43. Walker has published several essays on Hurston. In a Foreword (1976) to Robert Hemenway's biography, entitled "Zora Neale Hurston: A Cautionary Tale and a Partisan View," Walker praises Hurston's "racial health—a sense of black people as complete, complex, undiminished human beings," Hemenway, *Hurston,* p. xii. A second, extraordinary Walker essay is a pilgrimage to and through Hurston, discussing her life and counterpointing this with a search for her unmarked grave, on which Walker placed a long-belated commemorative stone. "In Search of Zora Neale Hurston," *Ms.* 3 (March 1975): 74–76, 78–79, 85–89; also published in The Feminist Press's *Zora Neale Hurston Reader,* along with Walker's "Dedication: On Refusing to Be Humbled by Second Place in a Contest You Did Not Design; A Tradition by Now."

44. *I Love Myself. . . . ,* p. 51.

45. Ibid., p. 68. The centrality of Hurston's anthropologist's vision to her novels has also been noted by Barbara Christian, *Black Women Novelists; The Development of a Tradition, 1892–1976* (Westport, Ct.: Greenwood Press, 1980), p. 57, and by Ellease Southerland, "Zora Neale Hurston: The Novelist/Anthropologist's Life/Works," *Black World* 23, 10 (August 1974): 20–30. For a complex and elegant dissenting statement, see Hortense J. Spillers, "A Hateful Passion, A Lost Love," *Feminist Studies* 9, 2 (Summer 1983): 293–323. Spillers argues that within Afro-American literature by women a cultural typology has emerged, with a maternal black woman as one pole, and a single, singular subject, one with "hateful or somewhat nihilistic passion" (p. 317) who "departs dramatically from the iconography of virtue and endurance" (p. 297), at the other pole. Hurston's Janie is therefore seen in a diametrically opposite way; I see her as a multiple individual, with the anthropological element making a critique of romance; Spillers sees her tending toward individualism, and takes to task "the anthropological strategy" for "all but ruin[ing] this study of a female soul," p. 308.

46. The political and spiritual elements are combined. "The white women writers that I admire: Chopin, the Brontës, Simone de Beauvoir, and Doris Lessing, are well aware of their own oppression and search incessantly for a kind of salvation. Their characters can always envision a solution, an evolution to higher consciousness on the part of society, even when society itself cannot." So too, Walker's tribute to Hurston focuses on *Their Eyes Were Watching God* as a juncture of politics and spiritual understanding. Interview with Alice Walker, in O'Brien, pp. 193, 205.

47. In a 1973 interview with Washington, Walker speaks of this assimilationist strategy and the effects of exceptionalism on the one selected. Washington brilliantly applies the analysis to Walker's poem "For My Sister Molly Who in the Fifties," from *Revolutionary Petunias and Other Poems* (1973), a poem that details the slow change of the sister who, alienated from her family and her social origins, finally "frowned away / Our sloppishness" and "Left us." The degree to which being the antonym of this sister defines Walker's poetic career is becoming clearer. Mary Helen Washington, "An Essay on Alice Walker," in *Sturdy Black Bridges: Visions of Black Women in Literature,* ed. Roseann P. Bell, Bettye J. Parker, Beverly Guy-Shaftall (New York: Anchor Press, 1979), pp. 143–45.

48. The situational, narrative use of the Movement as a rupture with feminocentric plots (as well as with the damages of black life) appears at the end of Walker's first novel, *The Third Life of Grange Copeland*. Black militancy and the black-white coworkers of the Civil Rights Movement will offer Ruth the way out of a three-generation family morass that involves madness, murder, poverty, and bitter hatred, the fruits of racism played out over the almost helpless bodies and souls of all the characters.

49. Alice Walker, *Meridian* (New York: Pocket Books, 1977), p. 19. Abbreviated as *M.* The wounded and "seely" main character of Walker's most recent novel, *The Color Purple* (1982), is healed from the damages caused by the rigid application of these women's roles by the gradual invention of a caring community of an extended family. The growth of Celie is tied not to dissociated individualism or to the possessive heterosexual couple, but to women-loving bonds and to the multiple individual: "us can spend the day celebrating each other," *The Color Purple* (New York: Harcourt Brace Jovanovich, 1982), p. 243.

50. The novel is "'about' the civil rights movement, feminism, socialism, the shakiness of revolutionaries, and the radicalization of saints." Alice Walker, "*One* Child of One's Own: An Essay on Creativity," *Ms.* VIII, 2 (August 1979): 74. Walker wants to make certain that readers understand that the final refusal of martyrdom is positive. In an interview with Brenda Payton, *Oakland Tribune*, Sunday, May 18, 1980, E-1 and E-16, Walker states, "Meridian chooses not to be a martyr. The book sets her up in a way as being a martyr in order to explore the possibilities of declining that honor."

10. "'I' rejected; 'We' substituted"

1. Adrienne Rich, "Snapshots of a Daughter-in-Law," *Poems: Selected and New, 1950–1974* (New York: W. W. Norton and Company, Inc., 1975), p. 49.

2. Woolf, "Women and Fiction," in *Granite and Rainbow* (New York: Harcourt, Brace and Company, 1958), p. 83. In an astonishing sentence, she predicts that "the novel will cease to be the dumping-ground for the personal emotions," p. 84. The essay dates from 1929.

3. Ibid., p. 83. As *Three Guineas* will later suggest, Woolf was more sanguine in the late twenties than in the late thirties about a natural propensity to critique.

4. Read as a prefiguration of *Between the Acts*, the passage is especially compelling: the new novel "will be written in prose, but in prose which has many of the characteristics of poetry. It will have something of the exaltation of poetry, but much of the ordinariness of prose. It will be dramatic, and yet not a play. It will be read, not acted." "The Narrow Bridge of Art," in *Granite and Rainbow*, pp. 18–19.

5. Indeed, in an essay (on Turgenev) written in 1933, after the completion of *The Waves* and during the inception of *The Years*, Woolf reflects that for a novel combining fact and vision, the poetic and the commonplace, poetry and realism—that is, the novel she excitedly contemplated as *The Years*—character as it is known in English novels must be sacrificed. Characters "dominate" and "destroy" the balance she sought. "The Novels of Turgenev," in *The Captain's Death Bed and Other Essays* (New York: Harcourt Brace Jovanovich, 1950), p. 57. For reasons of space, this chapter cannot consider *The Waves*.

6. Joanna Lipking, "Looking at Monuments: Woolf's Satiric Eye," *Bulletin*

of the New York Public Library 80, 2 (Winter 1977), also sees the utopian character of the novel, which, in her phrase, "runs *ahead* of history," p. 142.

7. Raymond Williams, *Marxism and Literature* (Oxford: Oxford University
Press, 1977), p. 175.

8. Evidence for the rejected working titles is found in *A Writer's Diary,* ed.
Leonard Woolf (New York: Harcourt, Brace and Company, 1954), pp. 228,
229.

9. Virginia Woolf, *Between the Acts* (New York: Harcourt Brace
Jovanovich, 1969), p. 70. Abbreviated as *BA.* Originally published in 1941.
Woolf's death prevented the final revisions of her text.

10. *A Writer's Diary,* p. 279, planning for *Between the Acts.* This interestingly
ungrammatical entry of April 26, 1938, is also the source of the citation that I
have used to title this chapter.

11. Ibid., p. 310 (December 18, 1939). "Freud on Groups" is a reference to
Sigmund Freud, "Group Psychology and the Analysis of the Ego," in *A General Selection from the Works of Sigmund Freud,* ed. John Rickman (Garden City,
N.Y.: Doubleday and Company, Inc., 1957), pp. 169–209. In her analysis of
Woolf's connection to this essay, Maria di Battista also notes that Woolf's
group was not based on the Freudian drama of "rebellion, usurpation, and
ritual murder in which the 'king must die' in order for the creative individual
to emerge. . . ." *Virginia Woolf's Major Novels: The Fables of Anon* (New Haven:
Yale University Press, 1980), pp. 228–29.

12. Woolf, *The Years* (New York: Harcourt, Brace and World, Inc., 1937),
p. 44. Abbreviated as *Y.* One might well apply to *The Years* Woolf's description
of the "private house" in *Three Guineas:* "its cruelty [as Martin to Rose]; its
poverty [girls' resources as opposed to boys']; its hypocrisy [Delia's sham grief
at her mother's death]; its immorality [Abel's mistress]; its inanity [watching
the kettle boil]." *Three Guineas* (New York: Harcourt, Brace and World, Inc.,
1938), p. 39. Abbreviated as *TG.*

13. This is a revision from *The Pargiters,* which made Delia a feminist (not,
as in *The Years,* a Parnellite) and a violinist. The linking of "politics" to fantasies of thralldom, and the erasure of any interests in the two girls makes
them more colorless characters, but more dramatic embodiments of the
patriarchal system.

14. Here, as throughout the novel, Woolf was interested in the political
implications of "point of view" as a narrative tactic, a way of showing that one
sees differently from different social, gender, class, and age perspectives.

15. The link between the communal protagonist and female identity is
made more plausible when we find that one of Woolf's earliest structural
plans for the novel centered on paired women: Eleanor, more prosaic and
stolid, and Elvira [Sara], more febrile and visionary; this female bonded couple, reminding us of the variant couples in her first phase, soon expands to
the choral protagonist. The history of the composition of *The Years* and some
of the material cut from the novel at the galley-proof stage are very effectively
presented in Grace Radin, *Virginia Woolf's "The Years": The Evolution of a Novel*
(Knoxville: The University of Tennessee Press, 1981), p. 148.

16. As James Naremore has reminded us. "Nature and History in *The
Years,*" in *Virginia Woolf: Revaluation and Continuity,* ed. Ralph Freedman
(Berkeley: University of California Press, 1980), p. 242.

17. For this critique of the separate spheres, I draw on Michele Z. Rosaldo,
"The Use and Abuse of Anthropology: Reflections on Feminism and Cross-
cultural Understanding," *Signs* 5, 3 (Spring 1980): 404.

18. *Three Guineas* is a gloss on Rose's limitations. In its climactic passage, Woolf creates an oath for the disfranchised, an oath designed to hold them on the cusp between the mainstream of public life in professional and economic terms and alternative values in ethical and ideological terms: "freedom from unreal loyalties." "You must rid yourself of pride of nationality in the first place; also of religious pride, college pride, school pride, family pride, sex pride and those unreal loyalties that spring from them," p. 80.

19. As the term *androgyny* does not appear in *Orlando* but is the explanatory concept Woolf worked out in her critical prose, so *Society of Outsiders*, a term appearing in *Three Guineas*, can guide a reading of *The Years*. *Three Guineas*, a work about women, fascism, and British society, was so related to the project of the novel that Woolf "lump[ed them] together as one book—as indeed they are," *A Writer's Diary*, p. 284, entry from June 3, 1938.

20. *A Writer's Diary*, p. 214, August 7, 1934. My opinion of the way the communal protagonist functions as a critique both of narrative and of social ideologies was formed without specific reference to Jane Marcus's and Margaret Comstock's studies of the novel, which confirm my interpretation. Marcus sees the political message of the uniting of outsiders and the way the form is an "opera for the oppressed." Jane Marcus, "*The Years* as Greek Drama, Domestic Novel and Götterdämmerung," *Bulletin of the New York Public Library* 80, 2 (Winter 1977): 293. Comstock lucidly shows how the novel's "metaphors and its structures imply the need for a collaborative effort," and suggests that, through the form, Woolf was making a specifically anti-Fascist statement. Margaret Comstock, "The Loudspeaker and the Human Voice: Politics and the Form of *The Years*," *Bulletin of the New York Public Library* 80, 2 (Winter 1977): 274.

21. In *The Years/Pargiters:* Nicholas and Rose, who is identified as a lesbian only in the Pargiter material (Radin, *Virginia Woolf's "The Years,"* pp. 54–56, 119). In *Between the Acts*, William Dodge and Miss La Trobe.

22. After naming her tie to Leonard, her "plunges" into London, and her sense of the limitations of male homosexuality in apprehending her view of the world she wants, Woolf says, "Where people mistake, as I think, is in perpetually narrowing and naming these immensely composite and wide flung passions—driving stakes through them, herding them between screens. But how do you define 'Perversity'? What is the line between friendship and perversion?" *The Letters of Virginia Woolf, Volume Four, 1929–1931*, ed. Nigel Nicolson and Joanne Trautmann (New York: Harcourt Brace Jovanovich, 1978), p. 200 (August 15, 1930).

23. In a number of ways, *The Four-Gated City* seems to draw on *The Years*, both in details—like the similarity between Sara and Lynda, the confrontation with anti-Semitism in the main character, the visionary "here and now"—and in its large design. Lessing, as we shall see in the final chapter, also uses the communal protagonist to break with the lacerating boredom of social replication.

24. In line with this massive yet tentative revisionary glance at Christianity goes H.D.'s almost contemporaneous critique of patriarchal values and her approach to the same religion in *Trilogy*, whose final book sets itself the task of adding to the New Testament.

25. See Woolf, "Anon" [an unfinished essay from 1940]; and Brenda Silver, "'Anon' and 'The Reader': Virginia Woolf's Last Essays," *Twentieth Century Literature* 25, 3/4 (Fall/Winter 1979): 382, 383; and 356–68.

26. The first volume and most of the second (of 7¼ volumes of holograph)

are available as *"The Pargiters": The Novel-Essay Portion of "The Years,"* ed. Mitchell A. Leaska (New York: Harcourt Brace Jovanovich, 1977). Abbreviated as *P.*

27. The phrase is Gillian Beer's, from "Beyond Determinism: George Eliot and Virginia Woolf," in *Women Writing and Writing about Women,* ed. Mary Jacobus (London: Croom Helm, 1979), pp. 90, 91, 94: "the means by which, as writers who are women, they bring that dominant order into question," through "the reorganization of experience," changing the relations of writer to text, and rejecting plot, especially "origins, sequence, consequences, discovery, exclusion, and closure." This aspect of Beer's argument parallels mine.

28. At one of the moments when her conception of the work was changing (between January and February 1933), Woolf noted, "I'm afraid of the didactic," ad by February, she was choosing to leave out the essays. *A Writer's Diary,* p. 188. In early 1935, she read Aldous Huxley's *Point Counterpoint,* finding that the "interest in ideas" could "make people into ideas." Ibid., p. 230. She is haunted by that, fearing that her own "fiction [*The Years*] is dangerously near propaganda." Ibid., p. 236.

29. Her changes extended even to the title. The original title means *whitewashers* (as Jane Marcus and Mitchell Leaska have shown). The title was changed between the essay-novel and the novel to deemphasize this evasive quality of bourgeois life, not because "pargetting" did not remain one of Woolf's major subjects in *The Years,* but because she wanted to register a greater degree of sympathy with its causes. Jane Marcus, in the *Bulletin of the New York Public Library;* Mitchell Leaska, *The Novels of Virginia Woolf: From Beginning to End* (New York: John Jay Press, 1977).

30. *A Writer's Diary,* p. 191, April 25, 1933.

31. Radin, *Virginia Woolf's "The Years,"* p. 148. It is possible that Woolf felt these scenes privileged one character—Eleanor—at the expense of the collectivity.

32. Susan Squier, in her book in progress, *The Politics of City Space: Virginia Woolf and London,* with a chapter "Achieving an Authentic Voice: Virginia Woolf's Feminist Struggle Revealed in her London Essays."

33. "Professions for Women," in *The Death of the Moth and Other Essays* (New York: Harcourt Brace Jovanovich, 1970), p. 153. The essay dates from 1931.

34. *A Writer's Diary,* p. 345; she also calls it a "medley," p. 298.

35. Nora Eisenberg, "Virginia Woolf's Last Words on Words: Between the Acts and 'Anon,'" in *New Feminist Essays on Virginia Woolf,* ed. Jane Marcus (Lincoln: University of Nebraska Press, 1981), pp. 253–66; Eisenberg also discusses how the "little language . . . fosters our common life," p. 254.

11. "Kin with each other"

1. In the article on which this chapter is based, I call this group of works "feminist apologues," because an apologue is "a work organized as a fictional example [using fictional means, like character and plot] of the truth of a formulable statement." Sheldon Sacks, *Fiction and the Shape of Belief: A Study of Henry Fielding, With Glances at Swift, Johnson and Richardson* (Berkeley: University of California Press, 1964), p. 26. "The Feminist Apologues of Lessing, Piercy, and Russ," *Frontiers* IV, 1 (Spring 1979): 1–8. Because they break with the rules of the world, these fictions may propose specific changes in values and institutions, in, say, parent-child bonds, or in the way work is organized. Carol Pearson catalogues alternative values and institutions quite usefully: "Women's Fantasies and Feminist Utopias," *Frontiers* II, 3 (Fall 1977): 50–61.

2. The term "assertive discourse" is from Paul Hernadi, *Beyond Genre: New Directions in Literary Classification* (Ithaca, N.Y.: Cornell University Press, 1972), p. 166.

3. Darko Suvin, *Metamorphoses of Science Fiction: On the Poetics and History of a Literary Genre* (New Haven: Yale University Press, 1979), pp. 6–8. All the speculative fictions to be discussed in this chapter fit to a certain degree into the generic category of SF ("science fiction"), which Suvin has elegantly defined. But if these works are science fictions in some senses, they fall suspiciously away from Suvin's definition in one important particular: the completed definition he offers talks of "*cognitive* estrangement." "SF is, then, a literary genre whose necessary and sufficient conditions are the presence and interaction of estrangement and cognition, and whose main formal device is an imaginative framework alternative to the author's empirical environment." In basing the definition on cognition, he excludes the mythic, the supernatural, and any unhistorical attitude that sees the one-time achievement of a static, permanent good: he also absolutely excludes fantasy, fairy tale, and myth, as examples, rather, of noncognitive estrangement.

4. Charlotte Perkins Gilman, *Herland, Forerunner* 6 (1915), and *With Her in Ourland, Forerunner* 7 (1916) (New York: Greenwood Reprint Corporation, 1968). Abbreviated as *H* and *WHO* respectively. *Herland* was reprinted with an introduction by Ann J. Lane (New York: Pantheon Books, 1979), but citations will be to the periodical version.

5. Sara Ruddick, "Maternal Thinking," *Feminist Studies* 6, 2 (Summer 1980): 342–67.

6. "Racial motherhood" is an alternative to physical motherhood that extends nurturing into the public sphere in reform projects and in careers in health and social administration. Jeffrey Weeks, *Sex, Politics and Society: The Regulation of Sexuality since 1800* (London: Longman, 1981), p. 128.

7. Charlotte Perkins Gilman, *The Man-Made World; Or, Our Androcentric Culture* (New York: Charleton Company, 1911), p. 102. Incidentally, "Gilman insisted she was not a feminist; rather the world was 'masculinist,'" and she was righting the balance. Ann J. Lane, "The Fictional World of Gilman," in *The Charlotte Perkins Gilman Reader* (New York: Pantheon Books, 1980), p. xiv.

8. *The Man-Made World*, p. 105. The objection of a woman asked to give up her career ("her humanness") for marriage, the discontent of the middle-aged woman who wants not more love but more business in life, the ties between women, and the interaction between mother and child, including painful and disappointing aspects, are some of the other new plots Gilman proposed.

9. Weeks, *Sex, Politics, and Society*, pp. 127–28.

10. Joanna Russ, "What Can a Heroine Do? or Why Women Can't Write," in *Images of Women in Fiction*, ed. Susan Koppelman Cornillon (Bowling Green, Ohio: Bowling Green University Popular Press, 1972): pp. 3–20. I cannot trace the date of this essay, but would venture 1969–72. Articulate commentary on Russ can be found in Marilyn Hacker, "Science Fiction and Feminism; The Work of Joanna Russ," *Chrysalis* 4 (1977): 67–79.

11. Russ, "What Can a Heroine Do?" pp. 4, 5.

12. Ibid., p. 18.

13. Joanna Russ, *The Female Man* (New York: Bantam Books, 1975). Abbreviated as *FM*.

14. Russ has commented that "the women in it (except for Laur) are really parts of one woman. . . . It's an attempt to get my head together—literally, in

the novel, where there are at least four women with one head apiece, none of whom is a whole woman until they finally do get together . . . for Thanksgiving dinner." "Reflections on Science Fiction: An Interview with Joanna Russ," *Quest: A Feminist Quarterly* II, 1 (Summer 1975): 42, 43.

15. Mary Daly, *Beyond God the Father: Toward a Philosophy of Women's Liberation* (Boston: Beacon Press, 1973), pp. 40–43.

16. Marge Piercy, *Woman on the Edge of Time* (Greenwich, Conn.: Fawcett Publications, Inc., 1976). Piercy remarks on her aim: "In *Woman on the Edge of Time,* I wanted very strongly to create a society not at all fantastic but one we can have if we fight for it, one almost attainable now, in which feminist values are the prevailing values. I wanted to imagine the people of a non-sexist society, one which socialized people to be cooperative, gentle, open, respectful of other live beings, in touch with their own various layers of mind and feeling." *Frontiers: A Journal of Women Studies* II, 3 (Fall 1977): 64.

17. Catharine A. MacKinnon has argued that consciousness raising constitutes a "feminist method," rejecting the subject/object distinctions of knower and known, fusing common sense and criticism, "proceeding connotatively and analytically at the same time," being, in sum, "the collective critical reconstitution of the meaning of women's social experience, as women live through it." "Feminism, Marxism, Method, and the State: An Agenda for Theory," *Signs* 7, 3 (Spring 1982): 535–36, 543.

18. In general, the novel is conceived as an answer to the fifties; Piercy has catalogued what was lacking in that era: "a sense of possibilities, of alternate universes of social discourse, of other assumptions about what was good or primary, of other viable ways of making a living, making love, having and raising children, being together, living, and dying." "Through The Cracks" [A Symposium On the Fifties], *Partisan Review* XLI, 2 (1974): 208.

19. For Lessing, feminism, although correct, is "small and quaint" in light of "the cataclysms we are living through," which shake the world "into a new pattern." Lessing, "Preface to *The Golden Notebook*," in *A Small Personal Voice: Essays, Reviews, Interviews,* ed. Paul Schlueter (New York: Alfred A. Knopf, 1974), p. 25. The cataclysm to which Lessing refers is shaped by the atomic era. "I feel as if the Bomb has gone off inside myself, and in people around me. That's what I mean by the cracking up. It's as if the structure of the mind is being battered from inside. . . . Maybe out of destruction there will be born some new creature. I don't mean physically. What interests me more than anything is how our minds are changing. . . ." Doris Lessing at Stony Brook: An Interview by Jonah Raskin," in *A Small Personal Voice,* pp. 65–66.

20. The five volumes are as follows, with their original publication dates: I. *Martha Quest* (1952); II. *A Proper Marriage* (1954); III. *A Ripple from the Storm* (1958); IV. *Landlocked* (1965); V. *The Four-Gated City* (1969). (New York: New American Library, 1976). As elsewhere, initials will be used for in-text citation of these titles. The intervening publication of *The Golden Notebook,* in 1962, explains why the "Preface to *The Golden Notebook*" contains useful critical clues about *The Children of Violence.*

Lessing's new work-in-progress, *Canopus in Argos: Archives,* is also a multivolume experiment in representing the future, in opening individual consciousness, and in giving fiction a didactic role. For reasons of space and balance in this chapter, I have had regretfully to exclude consideration of this work.

21. "Afterword to *The Story of An African Farm,*" in *A Small Personal Voice,*

pp. 98, 99, 100. Lessing and Schreiner are both women novelists of Africa, and Schreiner has functioned as a "touchstone" for Lessing, as the creator of quest allegories and of a work in which spiritual and political yearnings are melded. See Claire Sprague, "Olive Schreiner: Touchstone for Lessing," *Doris Lessing Newsletter* (Winter 1976): 4–5, 9–10.

22. *A Small Personal Voice*, p. 14.

23. This summary, no longer entirely apt, was forged in the Cold War Era (c. 1957). The oscillation is even expressed, in curiously symbolic terms, in the two men she married, each for four years: Frank Wisdom (her husband from 1939 to 1943), who eventually became a Master of the High Court in the Ministry of Justice, Rhodesia, and Gottfried Lessing (her husband from 1945 to 1949), a Communist who later settled in East Germany and became the Commissar of Trade. Biographical information is from Dee Seligman, "The Four-Faced Novelist," *Modern Fiction Studies* 26, 1 (Spring 1980): 8–9, 13.

24. Lessing calls the work a *Bildungsroman* in her "Author's Note" on the last page of the last volume, *Four-Gated City*.

25. *A Small Personal Voice*, p. 33.

26. Nancy Bazin makes a related point in noting a difference in the function of epiphany in Lawrence and Joyce as compared with Lessing: theirs occurs to define the protagonist as a striving, ecstatic individual; hers is shown to be necessary for "human survival." That Lessing asks epiphany to function didactically and collectively is consistent with the project of speculative fiction. Nancy Topping Bazin, "The Moment of Revelation in *Martha Quest* and Comparable Moments by Two Modernists," *Modern Fiction Studies* 26, 1 (Spring 1980): 98.

27. Claire Sprague, also noting these doublings, finds that the A/M initials are a "projection of the self . . . [and] multiply from the parent couple. . . . These A/M repetitions signal Martha's great fear that we are fated to become like our parents." " 'Without Contraries is No Progression': Lessing's *The Four-Gated City*," *Modern Fiction Studies* 26, 1 (Spring 1980): 100.

28. Lessing, "What Looks Like an Egg and is an Egg?" *The New York Times Book Review*, May 7, 1972, p. 42.

29. An illuminating account of Lessing during the postwar years, her transition from Africa to London, and her situation on the Left is found in Jenny Taylor, "Introduction; situating reading," in *Notebooks/ memoirs/ archives: Reading and Rereading Doris Lessing,* ed. Jenny Taylor (Boston: Routledge & Kegan Paul, 1982): pp. 1–42.

30. Seeing the existence of some kind of collective protagonist in this work is not original to this study. Dagmar Barnouw identified the three characters as the protagonist in "Disorderly Company: From *The Golden Notebook* to *The Four-Gated City*," in *Doris Lessing,* ed. Annis Pratt and L. S. Dembo (Madison: University of Wisconsin Press, 1974), p. 90. For Claire Sprague, the "collaborating triad" is a center of Lessing's concern, " 'Without Contraries.' " What is original here is the identification of the group protagonist as a strategy common to several female modernists, and the linking of this tactic to the critiques of ideology and narrative on the issues of gender.

31. Faris, a pun, perhaps, on Pharos or lighthouse, beacon (Lessing's version, then, of *To the Lighthouse*?), may also be the place beyond the ferris wheel of replication and thus a solution to the thematic and narrative problem posed in the first books.

32. This reading is corroborated by Mary Ann Singleton's view of the

ending in *The City and the Veld: The Fiction of Doris Lessing* (Lewisburg, Pa.: Bucknell University Press, 1977), p. 210.

33. Elizabeth Abel is eloquent on the structure and functions of female ties of friendship in recent literature; indeed, the Lynda/Martha tie is one of her examples. The "collaborative construction of meaning," the intimacy and the interchangeable roles of the friends, are traced to the continued articulation of the preoedipal tie. "(E)Merging Identities: The Dynamics of Female Friendship in Contemporary Fiction by Women," *Signs* 6, 3 (1981); 418–21.

34. In a Laingian phase, Lessing noted, "People who are called mentally ill are often those who say to the society, 'I'm not going to live according to your rules. I'm not going to conform.' Madness can be a form of rebellion." *A Small Personal Voice*, p. 69.

35. Lessing, "A Revolution," *The New York Times*, August 22, 1975, p. 31; cited in Roberta Rubenstein, *The Novelistic Vision of Doris Lessing: Breaking the Forms of Consciousness* (Urbana: University of Illinois Press, 1979). Betsy Draine usefully discusses Lessing's postulation that these massive changes will occur as part of a natural process of human evolution. *Substance Under Pressure: Artistic Coherence and Evolving Form in the Novels of Doris Lessing* (Madison: University of Wisconsin Press, 1983), pp. 60–65.

36. *Iron Heel* alludes to Jack London's political apologue. *A Small Personal Voice*, p. 70.

37. Woolf, "Thoughts on Peace in an Air Raid," in *The Death of the Moth and Other Essays* (New York: Harcourt Brace Jovanovich, 1942), p. 246.

INDEX

247

RACHEL BLAU DuPLESSIS, Associate Professor of English and Director of the Women's Studies Program (1982–85) at Temple University, is a published poet and author of articles in *Feminist Studies, The Massachusetts Review,* and *Montemora.*